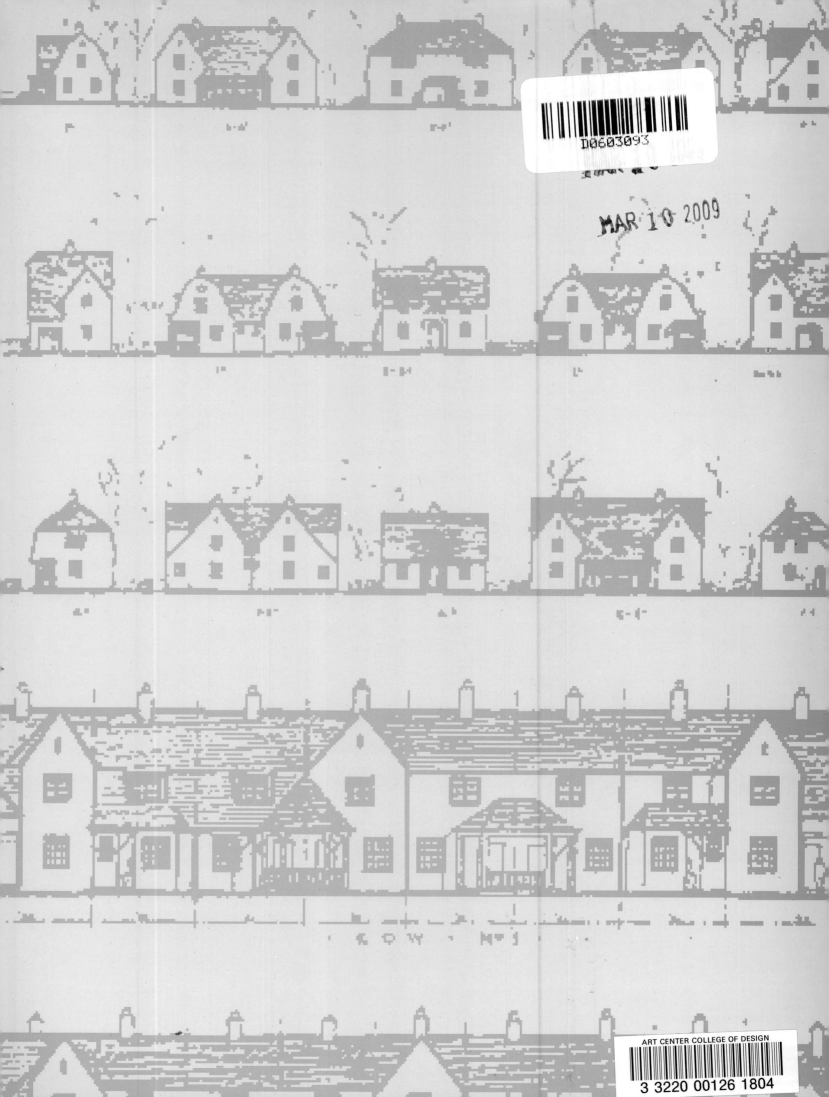

THE IDEAL HOME

1 9 0 0 — 1 9 2 0

THE IDEAL HOME
1900 — 1920

THE HISTORY OF TWENTIETH-CENTURY AMERICAN CRAFT

JANET KARDON, *Editor*

JANET KARDON, JOHN PERREAULT, NINA STRITZLER, *Curators*

WITH ESSAYS BY

EILEEN BORIS

BEVERLY K. BRANDT

W. SCOTT BRAZNELL

EDWARD S. COOKE, JR.

JANET KARDON

JAMES D. KORNWOLF

ELAINE LEVIN

LINDA M. PAPANICOLAOU

JOHN PERREAULT

GEORGE E. THOMAS

CHRISTA C. MAYER THURMAN

Harry N. Abrams, Inc., Publishers,
in association with the American Craft Museum

This book is published on the occasion of the exhibition
The Ideal Home: 1900–1920
American Craft Museum, New York
October 21, 1993–February 15, 1994

The History of Twentieth-Century American Craft: A Centenary Project
Janet Kardon, Project Director
Robert Hornsby, Project Coordinator

For Harry N. Abrams, Inc.:
Editor: Ruth Peltason
Designer: Carol Robson

For American Craft Museum:
Editor: Gerald Zeigerman

Captions for pages 1–6:
Page 1: Louis Comfort Tiffany. *Window (Parrots and Magnolias).*
c. 1900–20. Designed for Tiffany Studios. Leaded Favrile glass, 26 × 17³/₄″.
Collection The Metropolitan Museum of Art, New York

Page 2: Frederick Carder. *Cintra Bowl.* c. 1916–17.
Designed for Steuben Glass Works. Glass, 8³/₄ × 10 × 10″.
Collection Stephen Milne

Page 5: Anna Frances Simpson. *Table Runner.* c. 1909–29.
Produced at Newcomb College. Linen, silk, 5′3¹/₂″ × 16″.
Collection Museum of Art, Rhode Island School of Design, Providence.
Gift of Mrs. Eliot A. Carver

Page 6: Fulper Pottery. *Vase.* 1914. Glazed stoneware, 12¹/₈ × 10 × 10″.
Collection The Newark Museum, New Jersey

"The History of Twentieth-Century Craft in America: A Centenary Project" is a decadelong program of symposia, exhibitions, and catalogues organized by the American Craft Museum to write the history of twentieth-century American craft by the year 2000. "The Ideal Home: 1900–1920" is the first in a series of eight exhibitions on the history of twentieth-century American craft.

"The History of Twentieth-Century Craft in America: A Centenary Project," beginning with "The Ideal Home: 1900–1920," is made possible by a major grant from the Lila Wallace–Reader's Digest Fund.

Additional generous support has been given by the National Endowment for the Arts, the Rockefeller Foundation, the Norman and Rosita Winston Foundation, Inc., and the Cowles Charitable Trust.

The catalogue *The Ideal Home: 1900–1920* is made possible by a generous grant from the J. M. Kaplan Fund.

Library of Congress Cataloging-in-Publication Data
The Ideal home 1900–1920 : the history of twentieth-century craft in
America / general editor, Janet Kardon.
p.   cm.
Includes index.
ISBN 0–8109–3467–1
1. Arts and crafts movement—United States.   2. Decorative arts—
United States—History—20th century.   3. Interior decoration—
United States—History—20th century.   I. Kardon, Janet.
NK1411.I33   1993
745′.0973′09041—dc20   93–3121
CIP

CONTENTS

Contributors 16
Lenders to the Exhibition 17
American Craft Museum Board of Governors 18

Acknowledgments by Janet Kardon 19

A CENTENARY PROJECT: STAGE ONE—THE HOME AS IDEOLOGICAL PLATFORM *by Janet Kardon 22*
STARTING FROM HOME: TWENTIETH-CENTURY AMERICAN CRAFT IN PERSPECTIVE *by John Perreault 29*

Crossing Boundaries:
The Gendered Meaning of the
Arts and Crafts
by Eileen Boris
32

The Critic and the
Evolution of Early Twentieth-
Century American Craft
by Beverly K. Brandt
46

Metalsmithing
and Jewelrymaking,
1900–1920
by W. Scott Braznell
55

Arts and Crafts Furniture:
Process or Product?
by Edward S. Cooke, Jr.
64

Ceramics:
Seeking a Personal Style
by Elaine Levin
77

Colored Light: Glass,
1900–1920
by Linda M. Papanicolaou
92

Textiles:
As Documented by
The Craftsman
by Christa C. Mayer Thurman
100

The Arts and Crafts in
American Houses
and Gardens
by James D. Kornwolf
111

William Price's
Arts and Crafts Colony at
Rose Valley, Pennsylvania
by George E. Thomas
125

CATALOGUE OF THE EXHIBITION 136

RESOURCE LIST 236
ARTISTS' BIOGRAPHIES 237   COMMUNITIES 253   EXHIBITIONS 254   GUILDS AND SOCIETIES 256   PERIODICALS 259
PRODUCTION CENTERS: Ceramics 261   Glass 266   Metals 267   Textiles 269   Wood 269   General 271
SCHOOLS 271   SETTLEMENT HOUSES 274   SMALL PRESSES 275

Notes 277
Selected Bibliography 287
Checklist of the Catalogue 291
Index 296
Photograph Credits 304

Charles Fergus Binns. *Vase*. 1909
Stoneware, 8³/8 × 4⁷/8 × 4⁷/8″
Collection Museum of Ceramic Art at Alfred, Alfred University,
Alfred, New York

William B. Mundie. *Vase.* c. 1906
Designed for Teco Pottery/Gates Potteries
Ceramic, 13 × 10 × 10″
Collection Stephen Gray

Jane Carson Barron and Frances Barnum Smith
Cross. c. 1904
Silver, amethyst, enamel, 16 × 3^1/$_2$ × 2^1/$_2$″
Courtesy ARK Antiques, New Haven, Connecticut

Frank Gardner Hale. *Brooch*. c. 1920
Gold, zircons, diamonds, Montana sapphires, tourmalines,
peridot, $2^{1}/_{2} \times 1^{1}/_{2}$"
Private collection

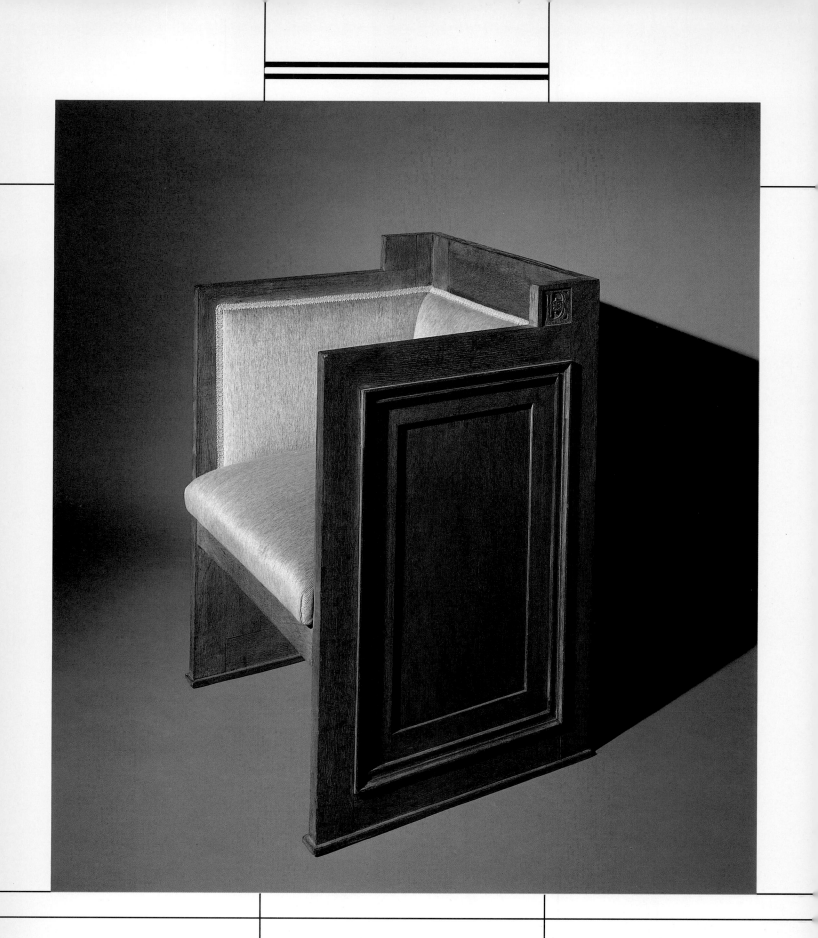

George Grant Elmslie. *Box Chair.* 1912
Designed for Babson House
Oak, 37 × 25 × 23^{1}/$_{8}$″
Collection Dr. David Gebhard

Frank Lloyd Wright. *Armchair*. 1904
Wood, 32 × 23 × 23"
Collection Albright-Knox Art Gallery, Buffalo.
Gift of Darwin R. Martin, 1968

Louis Comfort Tiffany
Vase (Opaque & Iridescent). 1900–1910
Designed for Tiffany Furnaces
Favrile glass, 11 × 5 × 5″
Collection The Brooklyn Museum. Gift of Charles W. Gould
(14.739.16)

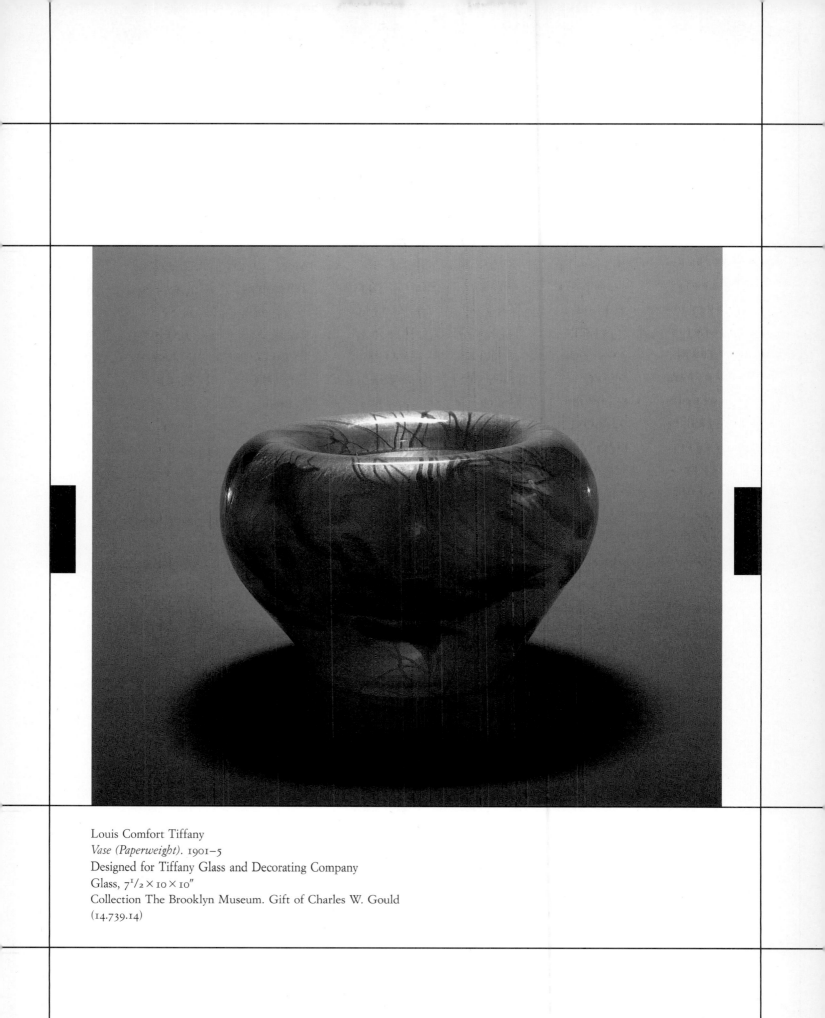

Louis Comfort Tiffany
Vase (Paperweight). 1901–5
Designed for Tiffany Glass and Decorating Company
Glass, 7¹/₂ × 10 × 10″
Collection The Brooklyn Museum. Gift of Charles W. Gould
(14.739.14)

Contributors

Eileen Boris, Associate Professor of History at Howard University, is the author of *Art and Labor: Ruskin, Morris, and the Craftsman Ideal in America* (Temple University Press, 1986), the co-editor of *Homework: Historical and Contemporary Perspectives of Paid Labor at Home* (Illinois University Press, 1989), *Major Problems in the History of American Workers* (D.C. Heath, 1991), and the forthcoming book from Cambridge University Press *In Defense of Motherhood: The Politics of Industrial Homework in the United States*. She was consultant to the Museum of Fine Arts, Boston, exhibit, " 'The Art That Is Life': The Arts & Crafts Movement in America, 1875–1920."

Beverly K. Brandt is the Director of the Herberger Center for Design Excellence and an Associate Professor of Design at Arizona State University. Publications include articles in *Tiller, Journal of the Archives of American Art, American Craft*, and *Designers West* and chapters in *The Encyclopaedia of Arts & Crafts* (Dutton 1989) and *The Substance of Style: New Perspectives on the American Arts and Crafts Movement* (1990 Winterthur Conference Report, forthcoming).

W. Scott Braznell has been engaged in full-time research of twentieth-century design since 1978. A contributing author to museum exhibitions, notably Boston's Museum of Fine Arts, "The Art That Is Life," he has written and lectured widely about metalwork and jewelry. From 1988 to 1992, he was the curator of the American Silver Museum project in Meriden, Connecticut.

Edward S. Cooke, Jr. is the Charles F. Montgomery Associate Professor in the History of Art at Yale University. Formerly, he was the Associate Curator of American Decorative Arts and Sculpture at the Museum of Fine Arts, Boston, where he curated "New American Furniture," and also held an appointment as an Adjunct Associate Professor in American Studies and Art History at Boston University. He has published extensively on both historical and contemporary furniture.

James D. Kornwolf is Professor of Fine Arts at the College of William and Mary. He has lectured widely and published articles and reviews on British and American architecture. He has authored, edited, or co-edited seven books including *M. H. Baillie-Scott and the Arts and Crafts Movement* (Johns Hopkins Press, 1972), and *In Pursuit of Beauty: Americans and the Aesthetic Movement*. His forthcoming book, *Architecture and Town Planning in Colonial North America: 1562–1792,* will be published by Cambridge University Press.

Elaine Levin is an art historian, specializing in ceramics, and lecturer at the University of California, Los Angeles and at Otis/Parsons School of Design. Her book, *The History of American Ceramics*, was published by Harry N. Abrams, Inc., in 1988. She has written over eighty articles, reviews, and catalogue essays and curated five exhibitions.

Linda M. Papanicolaou has a Ph.D. in art history from the Institute of Fine Arts, New York University. She is regional director for New Jersey in the Census of Stained Glass Windows in America. Her research on John Gordon Guthrie is funded in part by a grant from the National Endowment for the Humanities.

George E. Thomas is a Lecturer in the Historic Preservation Department of the University of Pennsylvania. He has written on Frank Furness, Philadelphia architectural patronage, and early twentieth-century American architectural theory, and is presently preparing a monograph on William L. Price.

Christa C. Mayer Thurman is the Christa C. Mayer Thurman Curator of Textiles, The Art Institute of Chicago. In her twenty-five years at the Art Institute, she has built a comprehensive historic collection covering twenty centuries. She is the author of *Claire Zeisler: A Retrospective* (1979); *Aqua Lapis: Embroidered Wall Sculptures by Nancy Hemenway—1925–1950*, and a contributing author to *Modern Design: 1935–1960.*

Lenders to the Exhibition

Adirondack Museum, Blue Mountain Lake, New York

Albright-Knox Art Gallery, Buffalo, New York

The Art Institute of Chicago, Illinois

Andrew Bergman, Mountain Lakes, New Jersey

The Brooklyn Museum, New York

John Bryan, Chicago

Buffalo and Erie County Historical Society, Buffalo

Beth Cathers, Tenafly, New Jersey

The Cleveland Museum of Art, Ohio

Cranbrook Academy of Art Museum, Bloomfield Hills, Michigan

Cooper-Hewitt National Museum of Design, New York

Elaine Dillof, Croton Falls, New York

Bill Drucker, Brooklyn

Everson Museum of Art, Syracuse, New York

Susan Fetterolf and Jeffrey Gorrin, New York City

Dr. Thomas C. Folk, Bernardsville, New Jersey

Henry and Barbara Fuldner, Milwaukee, Wisconsin

The Gamble House, Pasadena, California

Dr. David Gebhard, Santa Barbara, California

Glencairn Museum, Bryn Athyn, Pennsylvania

Stephen Gray, Philmont, New York

Raymond Groll, New York City

Mary and Oliver Hamill, Cambridge, Massachusetts

The Henry Francis du Pont Winterthur Museum, Winterthur, Delaware

Historical Design Collection, Inc., New York City

Mr. and Mrs. Robert Hut, New York City

Joyce Jonas, New York City

Sydney and Frances Lewis, Richmond

Donald Magner, Brooklyn

Don Marek, Grand Rapids, Michigan

John Markus, New York City

The Metropolitan Museum of Art, New York

Marilee Boyd Meyer, Cambridge, Massachusetts

Stephen Milne, New York City

Mr. and Mrs. Hyman Myers, Merion Station, Pennsylvania

Milwaukee Art Museum, Wisconsin

The Minneapolis Institute of Arts, Minnesota

Museum of Ceramic Art at Alfred, Alfred University, Alfred, New York

Museum of Fine Arts, Boston

National Museum of American History, the Smithsonian Institution, Washington, D.C.

The Newark Museum, New Jersey

Tazio Nuvolari

Norwest Corporation, Minneapolis

The Oakland Museum, California

Pewabic Pottery, Detroit

Pocumtuck Valley Memorial Association, Memorial Hall Museum, Deerfield, Massachusetts

David Rago, Lambertsville, New Jersey

Struve Gallery, Chicago

Barbara Taff and Alan Sachs, Washington, D.C.

Nicole Teweles, Milwaukee

Victorian Chicago Arts and Crafts Antique Gallery, Chicago

Virginia Museum of Fine Arts, Richmond

The Wolfsonian Foundation, Miami, Florida, and Genoa, Italy

Yale University Art Gallery, New Haven

Yellin Metalworkers, Philadelphia

Kurland-Zabar, New York City

American Craft Museum Board of Governors

Charles D. Peebler, Jr.
HONORARY CHAIRMAN

Jerome A. Chazen
CHAIRMAN

Walter A. Forbes
TREASURER

Nancy Marks
SECRETARY

Ann Rooke-Ley Berman
Edna Sloan Beron
Judy Bloomfield
Arlene Caplan
Carol Edelman
Gwen Feder
Seymour Finkelstein
Judie Ganek
Seth Glickenhaus
Jane Korman
Lewis Kruger
Jack Lenor Larsen
Nancy Rabstejnek Nichols
Christie C. Salomon
The Reverend Alfred R. Shands III
Benjamin Strauss
Barbara Tober
Ann Ziff

Janet Kardon
DIRECTOR

The Board of Governors of the American Craft Museum wishes to extend profound gratitude to the Lila Wallace-Reader's Digest Fund for its major grant for "The History of Twentieth-Century Craft in America: A Centenary Project," a decadelong program of symposia, exhibitions, and catalogues organized by the American Craft Museum to write the history of twentieth-century American craft by the year 2000.

Acknowledgments

"The History of Twentieth-Century American Craft: A Centenary Project," conceived to document, analyze, and exhibit the best of American craft of this century, will culminate with a multivolume history by the year 2000. The project is made possible by a major grant from the Lila Wallace–Reader's Digest Fund. Additional generous support has been given by the National Endowment for the Arts, the Rockefeller Foundation, the Norman and Rosita Winston Foundation, Inc., and the Cowles Charitable Trust. The first catalogue, *The Ideal Home: 1900–1920*, is made possible by a generous grant from the J. M. Kaplan Fund.

A project of the magnitude of "The Ideal Home: 1900–1920," the first in a series of eight exhibitions, was accomplished through the dedicated and expert participation of many individuals, foundations, and public agencies over a period of four years. A simple outline, drawn in the spring of 1989, has been developed, refined, and enriched by the energy and commitment of more than two hundred individuals. Participants in the public symposium and first planning session ably introduced the project: Gary E. Baker, curator, glass, the Chrysler Museum; Eileen Boris, associate professor, history, Howard University; Leslie Greene Bowman, curator, decorative arts, Los Angeles County Museum of Art; W. Scott Braznell, curator, American Silver Museum; Martin Eidelberg, professor, art history, Rutgers University; Elizabeth Milroy, assistant professor, art history, Wesleyan University; Christa C. Mayer Thurman, curator, textiles, The Art Institute of Chicago; and Kenneth R. Trapp, curator, crafts and decorative arts, The Oakland Museum. Jonathan Fairbanks, the Katherine Lane Weems curator of American decorative arts and sculpture at the Museum of Fine Arts, Boston, acted as our indispensable project advisor. We relied on his wisdom at critical moments.

Exhibitions, by definition, have a limited life span. This publication, conceived as the first book in a comprehensive multivolume history of twentieth-century craft in the United States, is assured of longevity. It is conceived as a vehicle to bring the contributions of artists working in craft media into the larger cultural mainstream. Experts throughout the country have been encouraged to participate in this project, and this book is a result of their dedicated scholarship. Writers have addressed their areas of expertise within the museum's parameter: These two decades are to be viewed as the breeding ground of the American craft movement.

As Centenary project director, I have attempted to provide the overview of this decadelong project as well as the thesis for the inaugural exhibition. The contributors to this publication have written illuminating essays that offer an overview of the first two decades of the century. John Perreault, reporting on the current status of craft as art, supplies an enlightened definition of craft that differentiates between craft and other forms of contemporary art. He also examines the process of writing a history of craft that reflects sociological and political value systems.

Several of our writers have provided a contextual background for the objects created during the period. Eileen Boris presents a social, political, and economic overview of the period, a useful backdrop for viewing the actual objects produced. Her discussion illuminates the effect of gender upon the creation, use, and interpretation of craft objects. Beverly K. Brandt describes the role of critics in championing craft through lectures, articles, and books, and the manner in which critics strived to elevate standards of discourse while offering practical instruction on methods to improve craft. George E. Thomas considers the dynamic of the characteristic craft Utopia, using Rose Valley, near Philadelphia, as a paradigm of an American Arts and Crafts community. Containing both houses and workshops, Rose Valley attempted to produce museum-quality pieces as well as more modest ones, but, like many of its counterparts, could not survive the persistent economic realities. W. Scott Braznell tracks the schools, museums, and manufacturers that provided formal training in metal; the publications, societies, exhibitions, and sources of patronage that advanced knowledge of working with metal; and the presence of metalsmiths in every geographic center of the country, as well as the diverse metals they employed. Edward S. Cooke, Jr., notes a bifurcation between the moral virtue attributed to the craft process and consumerism, social ambition, and economics. Cooke calls attention to the contradiction between actual practice and the marketing of products that reveals the period's ambivalent attitudes toward the machine. Elaine Levin traces the evolution of ceramics of the Arts and Crafts movement in the early part of the twentieth century. She discusses stylistic, philosophic, and technical changes in clay production and notes the relationship of craft and industry during World War I. Linda M. Papanicolaou discusses the important contributions of John La Farge and Louis Comfort Tiffany to opalescent glass and its influence upon the American glass studio. The role of the Arts and Crafts movement in the patterning of glass windows is also described. Christa C. Mayer Thurman examines textiles, utilizing, as a running commentary, excerpts from articles that appeared in Gustav Stickley's seminal publication *The Craftsman*. She cites, too, the Shaker influence as well as important techniques and centers for textile training. In discussing American Arts and Crafts architecture, James D. Kornwolf acknowledges Frank Lloyd Wright as its most original designer. He identifies the primary roles of ethics, craftsmanship, and vernacular and indigenous aesthetics that characterized the movement in America. He astutely observes that the Arts and Crafts movement in America was born of democratic instincts.

The American Craft Museum is grateful for the vital assistance it has received from each of these writers.

I am delighted to acknowledge my cocurators at the American Craft Museum—John Perreault, senior curator, who curated the ceramics and glass sections, and Nina Stritzler, curator of exhibitions, Bard College Graduate Center, New York City, who curated sections on books, metals, and textiles. John Perreault has also been a welcome partner in the formulation of the Centenary project.

Linda Craighead, our first Centenary project coordinator, and her successor, Robert Hornsby, have overseen the execution of the many aspects of this complicated project with expertise and patience. Other members of the American Craft Museum staff have made vital contributions to the project. We are indebted to Virginia Strull, former chief development officer; Darcy Gilpin, chief development officer; Elizabeth Massey, senior development officer; Joan McDonald, public relations officer; April Kingsley, curator; Ursula Newman, associate curator; Doris Stowens, registrar; Olga Valle, curatorial assistant; and Scott VanderHamm, collections manager. Research assistants Anita Dickhuth, Gordon Frey, Marc Rabun, Anne-Marie Schaff, Tara Tappert, and Polly Ullrich have made invaluable contributions to this publication, as have volunteers Eun-Ju Bae, Kathleen Fitzpatrick, Pat Gabay, Andrea Grayson, and Colleen Weis.

Gerald Zeigerman has served as our impeccable and conscientious editor. The suggestions of Wendy Kaplan, editor of *"The Art That is Life,"* who acted as reader, proved very constructive. Eva Heyd and Sheldon Comfort Collins were responsible for many of the excellent photographs. It has been a great pleasure to collaborate with the publishing house of Harry N. Abrams, Inc., and its representatives—in particular, Ruth Peltason, senior editor, and Carol Robson, who created the fine design for this book.

The board of governors of the American Craft Museum, led with vision at the inception of the project by Charles D. Peebler, Jr., and followed by the enlightened commitment of Jerome Chazen, chairman, has steadfastly and generously offered enthusiasm and support to the project.

Among the countless individuals who have been helpful, I must mention Edith Alpers, Rosalie Beberian, Beth Cathers, Jessica Chao, Edward S. Cooke, Jr., Jonathan Fairbanks, Jeannine Falino, James Findlay, Selwyn Garraway, Stephen Gray, Patricia Kane, Jovin Lombardo, Daniel Mack, Ray Peterson, Lisa Phillips, Nancy Pressley, David Ryan, Eleanor Thompson, Kenneth R. Trapp, Tran Turner, Dawn von Wiegand, Clare Yellin, and John Zimmerman.

Museums across the country have been very generous in extending loans from their collections. Other lenders to the exhibition have parted with splendid objects from their own homes. They all have our heartfelt gratitude.

Our ultimate appreciation must go to the pioneers of the American craft movement—the men and women who were responsible for the creation of the objects as well as those who generated and preserved the history by providing education, safe repositories, and written observations.

JANET KARDON
DIRECTOR

A Centenary Project: Stage One— The Home as Ideological Platform

by Janet Kardon

As we approach the new century, the environment is permeated by computer technology and dominated by electronic media. Still, there is a centurylong alternative voice, a leitmotiv, a quiet but powerful counterpoint to be found in craft, the art form that pays particular homage to the hand, to material, to process. Craft has its own historical continuum, imperatives, and leading artists, as well as its own masterpieces. Throughout the century, it has responded to its own moment, reflecting societal, political, and economic events, and often sharing many of the aesthetic issues of painting and sculpture; but as a visual art, craft diverges from painting and sculpture when it is created to serve a function.

When I became director of the American Craft Museum, in 1989, I found it amazing that a single, comprehensive overview of the contribution of artists working in craft media in the United States did not exist. A gap of such major proportions was allowed to persist despite the existence of regional pockets of information, fragmented histories of a particular discipline, and isolated critical studies. Because I felt compelled to address this vacuum in our cultural history, the American Craft Museum organized a symposium in January 1990: "Twentieth-Century American Craft: A Neglected History." During the proceedings—which convened scholars in anthropology, the decorative arts, art history, and craft—it became evident that the field was still seeking its parameters, even forging its definitions. The consensus was that adequate recognition of craft activity had been stifled by the imperatives of a cultural hierarchy that, in marginalizing this important aspect of the history of art and material culture, had suppressed a significant voice in contemporary expression.

Part of the responsibility may reside within craft itself—a field that is fervent about its ideals while it suffers from lethargic attitudes toward its own history and from internal divisions that have established media barriers that do not encourage analytic crossovers. We lack not only a comprehensive overview of postwar American craft but a scholarly documentation of its early twentieth-century antecedents as well. Without a true sense of parentage, craft struggles to establish its legitimacy without ever having attained, or perhaps even sought, the proper credentials. It has become evident that the individuals and institutions most committed to the achievements of American craft must assume responsibility for recording this history before craft can enter the larger cultural mainstream. Having identified the problem, the American Craft Museum has accepted this enormous challenge.

In 1990, after several months of intensive planning, the museum initiated "The History of Twentieth-Century American Craft: A Centenary Project," a decadelong undertaking to write this significant chapter of our cultural history. To accomplish this vast mission, the century has been divided into sequential time periods.[1]

Formal research on each period begins with an all-day symposium featuring leading experts in craft, art history, the decorative arts, material culture, and social and political history. After this public presentation, smaller working conferences—attended by the assembled scholars, invited guests, and the museum's curatorial staff—begin to formulate the structure and guidelines for an exhibition on the period.

Concurrently, the contents, possible curators, and potential writers of the exhibition catalogue are discussed. These publications might contain essays by specialists in a particular subject, by scholars in each of the craft disciplines—clay, fiber, glass, metal, and wood—as well as by contextual experts on material culture; art, social, and political history; and the decorative arts. Thus far, almost one hundred scholars from this country and abroad have enthusiastically agreed to participate in the Centenary project. In addition, emerging scholars have assisted in compiling biographical and bibliographical information on artists, societies, exhibitions, collections, and schools. This indispensable data, found in the end section of the book, will also be an integral part of the succeeding volumes.

The series of annual exhibitions, each on a specific period and accompanied by a scholarly catalogue, begins in 1993 with "The Ideal Home: 1900–1920." As the 1990s progress, annual exhibitions will report on sequential periods of the century. The last exhibition on craft of the nineties will be presented concurrently with the publication, in the year 2000, of the final volume on the history of twentieth-century American craft.

THE FIRST EXHIBITION

The first Centenary symposium, "The Foundation of the American Craft Movement, 1900–1918," was held at the museum in November 1990 to prepare for this exhibition. The participants represented a range of academic disciplines and craft media. My overview, "The History of Twentieth-Century Craft: A Centenary Project," introduced the session. The invited speakers and their topics were Gary E. Baker, "American Art and Luxury Glass from the Aesthetic Movement to 1918"; Eileen Boris, "The Craft Revival: Social Context"; Leslie Greene Bowman, "American Arts and Crafts Furniture"; W. Scott Braznell, "Silver, Other Metalwares, and Jewelry of the Arts and Crafts Movement, 1900–1918"; Martin Eidelberg, "Art Pottery and the Studio Movement"; Elizabeth Milroy, "Reaching the Public: Arts and Crafts and the National Salon"; Christa C. Mayer Thurman, "The Field of Textiles in America, 1900–1918"; and Kenneth R. Trapp, "Some Thoughts on the Arts and Crafts Movement."[2] Participants delivered public lectures on November 17, 1990, and convened the following day to discuss the future exhibition and identify issues and appropriate areas of investigation for the American Craft Museum. In conducting the proceedings, the goals were to identify the critical issues and the respected scholars as well as other important leaders of the period— in particular, the artists. It was also expedient to avoid redundant research; much useful and reliable information already exists.

Three previous exhibitions have been devoted to the Arts and Crafts movement in the United States;[3] nevertheless, it was agreed that a useful vantage point and appropriate issues remained for the American Craft Museum's exhibition. Our studies would be enhanced by the intensive research that has focused on the Arts and Crafts movement during the past several years. Past shows had viewed the objects of this time as American offspring of the English Arts and Crafts movement, which indeed some are. As works created at the waning of a movement, however, the objects often were perceived as diluted descendants of earlier expressions that had reflected a more erudite philosophy. The premise of this exhibition is that the origins of the American craft movement can be traced within the period, and this was our perspective when selecting and interpreting works produced during these

The figure of Astronomy. Detail from
Liberal Arts Window. 1913

decades.[4] The writers responded to our interest in identifying particular American characteristics of the period. Some important differences that have been noted are the diverse vernacular sources that influenced American objects, the advocacy of making objects for the home as an appropriate leisure-time activity, the equitable inclusion of women, and the more widespread acceptance of the machine. Our research has been directed toward identifying prescient signals of a century's activity, for, in our context, these important first two decades provide an aesthetic lens for the rest of the century.

"The Ideal Home: 1900–1920" bears an exceptional burden. As the first exhibition of the series, it is charged with identifying the leading themes and issues that may recur, if intermittently, throughout the century. There is also the possibility that a model may be formulated for interpreting each of the succeeding periods and that guidelines may be established to interpret future decades. A more precise critical language and a useful methodology should emerge from the vast amount of information and interpretation that has been amassed. Readers may note that our scholars do not always agree, and can assume that this represents differences of opinion or reflects certain unresolved issues. In selecting the objects for the exhibition, our particular focus led us to find objects that seemed to express an American sensibility, straightforward use of materials, and an inventive spirit that often permeated Modernist forms, and what Edward S. Cooke, Jr., has referred to as "the inherent benefits of well-designed, highly regulated workmanship." We sought to identify examples that are paradigms, not only of their moment, but also signifiers of the inception of a centurylong movement that is still evolving.

TOWARD A DEFINITION OF CRAFT

Our premise must begin with a definition of craft.[5] Is it different from other visual expressions, and if so, what are the differences? What is unique to craft, and how is it similar to other art forms? Where does it converge or diverge from the history of painting, sculpture, architecture, design, and the decorative arts? Who are its leading figures? What are the seminal works? What have been the critical issues? What are its primary documents? In mobilizing this inquiry into what has been an undervalued but significant area of artistic endeavor, these appropriate questions will receive thoughtful responses by the most informed and dedicated scholars we can identify.

A respect, a reverence for materials is inherent in craft. Traditionally, many artists demonstrate a commitment to one of the five craft materials, or disciplines, that have delineated the field—clay, fiber, glass, metal, or wood. Material has been so strong a determinant that each medium has attracted its own artists, writers, societies, publications, schools, collectors, exhibitions, and even museums. In fact, the permanent collection of the American Craft Museum is catalogued according to the five disciplines. These media barriers, although useful, unfortunately have often precluded discourse across media.

Technique, the handmaiden of material, was learned in the late nineteenth century and these early decades of the twentieth century through an apprentice system, membership in a society or club, in a program in a settlement house or other neighborhood facility, or at pioneering schools, such as Newcomb College and Alfred University. Later in the century, colleges and universities provided training, effecting a significant shift toward the professionally trained artist. There would always be the untrained homemaker engaged in beautifying the home as well as the unskilled worker earning a living by performing prescribed tasks in a factory or workshop, but over time these have become distinguished more and more from the professionally trained, creative artist-designer. Technique has occasionally galvanized artists, societies, schools, galleries, and collectors to concentrate upon a single method, such as wood turning. Innovative processes gained increasing importance and visibility with the passing decades. Because training has been such an enduring requirement, this volume contains important information on communities, societies, and schools of the period.

Ancient craft was functional—Egyptian wood furniture, Greek clay pots, Roman glass vessels, Etruscan gold jewelry, Mesopotamian textiles. Objects emerged from necessity as well as the impulse for adornment and status symbols, while they also conveyed messages about the society that bred them. Craft objects were first segregated from mainstream art history in the Renaissance, but in the nineteenth century their utility relegated them to the decorative or minor arts and nurtured the perception that they lacked the moral intent required of high art. Countering this designation later in the century, John Ruskin and William Morris, the leading theorists of the English Arts and Crafts movement, initiated what was to become a persistent debate to assign craft equal status with painting and sculpture. Nonetheless, function, whether considered an asset or a disclaimer, was the primary progenitor of twentieth-century craft objects until well after World War II, and it still remains an enduring voice in craft production. Even today, most objects are either functional or deliberately deny or parody function.

While the scale of painting and sculpture has fluctuated throughout history and in different cultures, its intermittent largeness often has signified importance. The scale of most craft objects traditionally has been ruled by function and, therefore, the scale of the human form, thus imparting to craft a significant human quotient. Although some recent craft objects have attained monumental scale,[6] prevailing modest scale relegated craft to the domain of the merely decorative. This is despite the fact that many craft objects are repositories for spiritual, political, or societal attitudes most clearly observed in the artists' affinity to the actual materials or to the process as well as to the final product. The act of making a craft object often resonates with a spiritual aura that can bestow a vestige of spirituality upon the object itself.

Textile patterning, glass etching, wood carvings, metalwork figuration, and ceramic glazes often draw on the aesthetic traditions of painting. But, like architecture, historically a good craft piece has to serve a particular function. In addition, craft must exist in space as a satisfying three-dimensional work, or as sculpture. The expectations are rigorous; the artwork created in craft media must possess aesthetic distinction, cultural significance, intellectual content, evidence of innovation, and often fulfill a functional requirement. The most critical assignment for the curator or collector is identifying objects that emit the highest aesthetic quality and relevant social references, differentiating them from their more mundane counterparts.

The sense of touch, the tactile, a presence ubiquitous in craft objects, creates an unfortunate paradox in their presentation in an exhibition. These objects were often created to invite the caress of usage. Now, the proprieties of the museum and the status that the passage of time and increased economic value have bestowed make these objects, ironically, untouchable for visitors.

Some artists repeat a few forms or processes throughout their entire career. Increasingly in this century, however, innovation in process, technique, material, or form has been a critical attribute of craft, distinguishing craft from folk art, which relies upon the utilization of traditional forms. In Asian American, Native American, African American, and Hispanic cultures, the artist often consciously creates such traditional configurations. Because the Centenary project is dedicated to entering the voices of diverse cultures into the history, we have the added challenge of identifying objects that meet our particular criteria for craft. This requires thoughtful definition and careful differentiation of craft works from folk art. Training is often a valid indicator. The craft artist is generally a technical master who has received formal training through schools, workshops, or apprenticeships.

GENESIS OF THE AMERICAN CRAFT MOVEMENT

The Arts and Crafts movement emerged in England as a response to the Industrial Revolution—its primary imperative being the delegation of aesthetic and intellectual control to the individual artist. That there is not a division of labor, that the artist is also the maker, has remained a most important signifier of craft in this country. Preindustrial skills are valued—casting the machine as an anomaly, as a necessary if clandestine partner. Respect for materials and a tradition of technical excellence characterize European and Asian as well as American craft. But objects in this country were generally produced for the middle or upper-middle class; we lack a nobility. Twentieth-century American craft is an offspring of a democratic society, despite such prominent exceptions as Louis Comfort Tiffany or the Greene brothers.

In constructing the climate of each period, multicultural, regional, national, ethnic, and spiritual contributions must be acknowledged. The development of the craft movement also can be better perceived against a backdrop of social and political reforms, of changing attitudes, and even laws regarding gender. In the beginning of the century, women played an increasingly visible role, particularly in craft, achieving greater stature and recognition. Finally, in 1920, they even received the right to vote.

From its inception, twentieth-century American craft intersected vigorously with industrial design. It challenged, and was challenged by, practices in the division of labor. There were also radical changes in the workplace, in economic developments, in the prominence of international expositions and world's fairs, and in the perception that the production of craft objects might be a viable means of providing income for the disadvantaged or therapy for the ill. During this period, the nation became a consumer society; new systems evolved for the distribution of goods. Society was irreparably changed by mechanization, immigration, and urbanization as well as the rise of the unions, the large corporation, and a new middle class of professionals and managers who shifted class divisions. Such sociological, political, and economic changes in the first two decades provided a fertile context for craft, whether in the individual studio, the craft community, the school, or the factory.

THE DOMESTIC ENVIRONMENT

The domestic environment is the theme of "The Ideal Home"; many of the icons of these years were created to serve a domestic purpose. This not only demonstrates a primary distinction between the origins of craft in function and the history of painting and sculpture, it underscores the usefulness of this theme for our particular focus.

Objects created for the home were often vehicles for ideology. The nexus for the ideals of the time, the home, became a propagandistic device to dispense proper attitudes and activities. It was a barometer of changing attitudes toward gender as well as other economic, political, and social trends. The age's commitment to reform, to change, could be easily observed in the home's contents. Sentiments first formulated within the home—our earliest training ground for human relationships—indelibly mark our lives. The communal spirit that is often part of the craft ethos has a counterpart, if not a

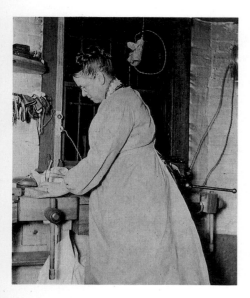

Frances McBeth (Mrs. John J.) Glessner in the basement of her home at 1800 S. Prairie, Chicago. She is probably metalsmithing.

model, in the domestic experience. The home, therefore, as the focus for this exhibition, offers a cohesive rubric to generate a useful, appropriate, and possibly even more accurate aesthetic portrait of the period. The title "The Ideal Home" reflects the role of the home as an avatar for the social, political, and aesthetic ideologies of the period.

Despite the egalitarian aspirations of the period, the home remained a barometer of economic hierarchies. Dwellings ranged the spectrum from the less costly, spare repository for factory-made, mail-order products of the Stickley or Roycroft genre to a sumptuous Greene and Greene environment, in which every detail of the architecture and furnishings was not only exquisitely handcrafted but harmoniously integrated. For both ends of the economic spectrum, furniture and accessories were devised to cohabit with the architecture in a unified statement. This affinity between craft and architecture resulted from mutual pursuits—a shared desire for a coalescent total environment.

The model home of the period contained clay vessels, embroidered textiles, stained-glass windows, metal lamps, and wood furniture—objects representing all of the five craft media, or disciplines, and new craft categories as they emerged. The floors and walls, each piece of furniture, and every accessory provided opportunities to promote aesthetic and moral ideals. Prototypical room settings, as seen in photographs and perceived from descriptive material, often included kindred objects made by or influenced by Native American, Asian American, African American, and Mexican-American artists.

As a platform for contemporary ethics, the home could be a model for the good life, "good" exemplified by a simple and direct use of indigenous natural materials, dedicated craftsmanship, a minimum of superfluous decoration, and forthright structure. Morality was even signified by straightforward craftsmanship, as evidenced by the directness of exposed mortise-and-tenon joinery. A relationship between outdoors and indoors was encouraged even as the most advanced interior spaces flowed more freely within the house. The outdoors was referenced by organic motifs and palette, or actual visual access. The vacation or suburban bungalow was the most distilled model of simplified, direct forms and an affinity with nature.

It was also an esteemed attribute if the inhabitants were hands-on homemakers involved in the embroidering of textiles or the crafting of furniture and accessories. Leisure time offered productive moments to make or embellish domestic furnishings. The designation of each room and the content and decoration of the home demarcated gender territories. The bedroom, considered the feminine domain, might contain painted furniture; natural oak was thought to be more suited to the man's den, and the earlier, formal reception room assumed the aura of a masculine retreat. The drive for efficiency, appropriated from the factory, was shared by both genders.[7]

Arts and Crafts communities fulfilled important roles as forums for ideas and the production of objects. If the single-family home was the microcosm, the craft community—of dwellings, workshops, and, often, salesrooms—was the macrocosm. The community, which occasionally included living quarters, provided an expanded platform for the ideals of the time. The community was also the backdrop for playing out the dichotomy between the hand and the machine, the finely crafted and the rustic, the untrained and the highly skilled craftsperson. Often, an attempt was made to commingle economic imperatives with aesthetic ambitions—an effort that was not uniformly successful; however, there is no doubt that prevalent use of the machine and the demands of commerce tinged the purity of the handmade object in the Stickley and Roycroft communities, for example.[8] A number of these communities produced some of the most beautiful domestic items of the era, as well as important publications intended to instruct on life-styles and to enable anyone to learn how to appreciate, create, or acquire noble and beneficial works of art.

PARAMETERS FOR "THE IDEAL HOME"

Objects have been selected, first, for their aesthetic value, even as the search focused upon examples that could be considered prescient introductions to the American craft movement. Within each discipline, an attempt was made to identify objects that were created originally for the domestic environment. It was unavoidable, because of the practices of the time, that certain objects, particularly furniture, were "manufactured." They are included as well, along with many unique and limited-production pieces that visibly confirm the involvement of the hand. A straightforward presentation of natural material, even a profound respect for material, is evident in most of the objects. Space limitations required that the most characteristic aspects of the period be represented; therefore, this exhibition was not intended, nor could the appropriate research be undertaken within our time stricture, to include the work of little-known artists. Many of these figures, though, are listed in the resource section of this book, awaiting future scholarly pursuit.

How do we begin to measure the success of this monumental Centenary project? A single exhibition and book, even a cluster of such projects, can only attempt to survey the rich territory of twentieth-century American craft. Gaps may remain, but if the Centenary project serves to illuminate them, it will have achieved one measure of success. There is no simple remedy for a centurylong void in the cultural continuum, nor is there a readily available solution for decades of curatorial, critical, and economic marginalization. The categories established by our museums and our universities—our centers for research in the visual arts—are in part responsible for displacing craft from the mainstream. Because university and museum departments are defined by time periods, media, or nationality, for the young scholar there is no easy entry into specializing in craft, nor is there a role model or mentor. Most of our museums do not have craft departments, or craft curators, to encourage either the acquisition of craft objects for a museum's collection or the presentation of craft exhibitions. Periodicals and newspapers lack staff critics specializing in craft. If the Centenary project entices aspiring critics, curators, and other scholars, it will be a second, and considerable, measure of success.

The Centenary project, culminating in a pioneering overview, will place craft history books on the shelves of university, museum, and public libraries, making knowledge of this centurylong noble endowment available to scholars and representatives of many disciplines. If the Centenary project thereby nurtures the process of entering the contribution of craft artists into the cultural mainstream, this will be a signal measure of our success.

JANET KARDON
DIRECTOR
AMERICAN CRAFT MUSEUM

Starting from Home: Twentieth-Century American Craft in Perspective

by John Perreault

Significant developments in craft in this country from the end of World War II to the present indicate that a change in degree has become a change in kind. From 1945 to the present, innovation in craft has taken place at such a rate that, if we are to agree with one ethnological definition of art as any chronological series of objects that exhibits a rapid succession of technologically unwarranted stylistic changes, it is clear that craft is now art. Yet, conformity to this practical definition is not the only sign of a change of status. In the United States, contemporary craft is finally being treated as art; as during the Arts and Crafts movement, it is being produced and purchased as art, but now it is being written about and studied as art. And it is also being preserved as art. I am referring to what might be called the high end of the craft continuum, for handmade objects may range from the strictly therapeutic to the sublime. Furthermore, not all art-world participants have been enlightened about craft. In some quarters, craft is anathema; nevertheless, aesthetic achievement is overcoming prejudice and vested interest. Craft is art, and craft is here to stay. Whether the phenomenon is called the American craft movement or the artworks are labeled contemporary craft or new craft, something of international significance has happened.

Today, craft in the United States is accepted as an art form equal to but different from painting and sculpture. The Centenary project, through eight exhibitions and related publications, will attempt to determine why. We are beginning with our national manifestation of the Arts and Crafts movement. This will be followed by an investigation of craft revivals and survivals between the two world wars. And then the roots of contemporary American craft will be established decade by decade, not only through objects and artists but through cultural contexts and ideologies. Although the beginnings of contemporary craft are to be found in preindustrial utilitarian and decorative forms and traditions, craft is now a distinct area of aesthetic production that is differentiated from design, folk art, and the decorative arts. Insofar as it is usable art or refers to or employs the forms of use—vessels, furniture, among others—it is distinct from traditional sculpture but not sculpture that proposes or parodies use, such as the furniture art of Richard Artschwager or Scott Burton.

The Industrial Revolution largely eliminated the need for hand production of everyday, useful objects. Craft, then, was free to become the content and the form of a new art. This new art was linked to traditional craft by the use of preferred materials, such as clay, wood, fiber, metal, and, eventually, glass, and the employment of customary techniques of creation that did not require the division of labor or the elaborate machinery of factory production. Contemporary craft is, most often, art for use or about use, and like most art, it is also used as decoration, but it is intended to be more visible and meaningful than the traditional decorative arts. Large, omnibus museums still include contemporary craft in decorative rather than fine arts departments, an unfortunate convenience since much contemporary craft requires the interpretive and scholarly skills now deemed essential for painting and sculpture. On the other hand, as students of the decorative arts move to the subject area now referred to as material culture, they can apply sociological and ethnological methodologies to craft that even would enhance our understanding of painting and sculpture.

Craft tends to be body-centered in scale and imagery; hence, its appeal to those uncomfortable with more public forms of art or more nonreferential abstraction. It is this relationship to the body and to use, however, that causes some to deny—puritanically, I think—art status to craft. The association of the tactile to the optical in craft is also too unusual for some to deal with. The tactile and the optical are in balance. Craft, today, is also more widely distributed than painting and sculpture, and appears to have a broader market. Both of these factors may be related to the social idealism that lingers in and around craft production. One of the many paradoxes of contemporary craft is that as it succeeds as fine art, it becomes less and less accessible to the general public. Craft attempts to be an art for people rather than princes, for the home rather than the palace.

The craftsperson tends to privilege material, process, and utilitarian, or previously utilitarian, form. Although self-expression and social statement are permitted, historically they have not been foregrounded as in painting and sculpture. Instead, the hand transmits the body's way of thinking. Idealism is expressed through the notion of making art for the use and appreciation of ordinary persons. Although there is a tradition of tour de force, decorative furnishings and even of ceremonial objects, in this country the democratic tradition is much stronger. As craft began the process of finally becoming accepted as art—and grew more costly—the democratic ideology became threatened.

Contemporary craft is a complex phenomenon. It contains echoes of and references to the past in shifting combinations, according to each craftsperson's understanding, need for expression, cultural background, and educational experience. The Centenary project identifies the sources of those echoes and references—the traditions and ideologies that have created craft today. Beginning with the Arts and Crafts movement, the political and the aesthetic were united in craft objects. And this unity persists.

What is now required is a historical overview that will provide a context for understanding contemporary craft and that will stimulate further historical and critical investigation. To do this will require the construction of a narrative. Although facts are the basis for speculation and interpretation, no mere compendium of dates and objects will suffice. The tendency to imitate simplified, linear, univocal modes—until recently, the customary formats of generalized histories of painting and sculpture—will be resisted. In order to correspond with reality, the story of craft in the United States, which has never before been attempted, will be as multivoiced and multileveled as craft itself.

How do you write history? You engage more than one hundred carefully selected scholars. This does not mean that you end up with more than one hundred conflicting histories. Scholars tend to specialize, and we capitalize on that. To avoid duplication and repetition, we commissioned each writer to address a specific topic or area. Where there is overlap and correspondence, we have points of evidence. We must bear in mind that history is no longer equal to a story in the sense of a grand narrative, such as the rise and fall of the Roman Empire or even the triumph of American painting.

History is only a story if we expand the meaning of story beyond that of a linear narrative with a beginning, middle, and ending—a fable with a moral at the conclusion. Instead, we should be thinking of Modernist or, some may say, Postmodernist narrative. For our world, history is a text composed of many smaller texts written in many voices, some of them contradictory. Think of

Joyce's *Ulysses*; think of *Rashomon*. History is a hypertext. We are constructing an encyclopedia rather than composing a novel, or perhaps it is a novel in the form of an encyclopedia that may be entered at several points and that is composed of many cross-references, sidebars, windows, overlaps, layers, directions, and interlocking themes. One may follow this story in the endnotes, by isolating themes in the index, through the stories of craftspersons' lives, through great social events. In yet another sense, we are writing the history of how we see the past today. All history is present tense.

We are writing history with objects. Objects live. The objects chosen by curators tell stories. Most tell more than one story. We determine a narrative by the objects we choose—and the artists we select. It is clear that during the two decades that begin our survey, design and craft categories were not as distinct as they are now. In writing this history from a contemporary perspective, we have favored the selection of artists who created most of their work themselves rather than designers who created objects for production and had little or no hands-on relationship with the objects produced.

The dangers inherent in writing a history are obvious. History has been deconstructed; histories have been exposed as ethnocentric, self-serving, class-biased propaganda. If it is art history, the suspicion is that stories are determined by art-market participants who, directly or indirectly, subsidize the research and speculation that portray current taste as inevitable and irrevocable. On the other hand, compendia of materials, measurements, and dates are not enough—nor are iconographic explorations, appreciations, technical formulas, or biographical tales. Eyewitness accounts, confessions, and contexts are required, but so is explanation. Explanation is causality and causality is narrative.

Although research is still required, the basic events and objects are known, if not completely understood. This is not to say that there cannot be another George Ohr—who, having made barely a mark in his lifetime, was rediscovered in the 1970s and is now acclaimed as a great artist. Among women metalsmiths, there may be comparable discoveries. Downgrading can also take place. But these are matters of achievement and taste, to be worked out and then worked out all over again. What is crucial is an overview.

As writers, curators, critics, historians, artists, collectors, and connoisseurs of contemporary American craft, we are stuck in time. Something vital has come to pass: Craft is art again. Composing a story that makes sense will not only ease some misgivings, it will make a case for others. If these efforts are truthful, the narrative will have been fashioned from several intertwined stories, for it is clear that craft is, and has been, many things to many people. A single voice or a single methodology cannot suffice. If it is possible to create such a history without suppressing contradictions and divergence, then profit will have been gained from the mistakes of other historians.

An effective, truthful narrative must be contrapuntal, examining important craft themes through time as they are worked out under different social circumstances. Such themes include: craft in relation to painting and sculpture, industry, folk art; women in craft and gender issues in craft, in general; cultural diversity in craft; craft education and craft ideology; craft distribution, marketing, collecting, and critical reception; the tension between entrepreneurism and idealism; and, last but not least, craft as social reform and social critique.

JOHN PERREAULT
SENIOR CURATOR
AMERICAN CRAFT MUSEUM

Crossing Boundaries: The Gendered Meaning of the Arts and Crafts

by Eileen Boris

The Arts and Crafts movement in the United States marks the modern recognition of the artistic worth of the crafts. Inspired by the example of John Ruskin, the art critic, and William Morris, the poet, decorative artist, and Socialist, the movement developed in the late nineteenth century as a protest against the transformation of work and the degradation of beauty under industrial capitalism. It responded to urbanization, immigration, and intense economic change: division of labor and mechanization in the workplace; the growth of the corporation; the rise of a new middle class of professionals and managers; uneven regional development; and growing class divisions.[1]

Historians call this period the Progressive Era, a time of optimistic reform when the new middle class sought to alleviate the ills generated by industry. These managers and professionals were to rationalize business and government, stymieing class conflict in the process. Some from their class sought to mitigate the excesses of the age through social-welfare programs that would aid the poor while uplifting them. The working class was growing more militant, while middle- and upper-class women were demanding political equality, especially the vote. At the same time, Americans experienced legalized segregation and a rising tide of racism toward both African Americans and new immigrants. Social reform, which would improve daily life, and social control, which would remake "the other" in the image of the middle class, merged into each other.[2]

Gender ideology—cultural notions of masculinity and femininity—provided a lens through which participants were able to understand these turbulent years. Women and men of the prosperous classes crossed boundaries—women into the world of work, men into the world of the home. Despite such behavior, they brought with them their concepts of manhood and womanhood. The Arts and Crafts movement incorporated dominant understandings of womanhood and manhood even as some of its major figures challenged them. Although this movement reflected a class response to social change, it facilitated the crossing of boundaries. Women's busywork became elevated to art, providing educated women an opportunity to become professionals. Manly furniture entered the home, no longer a feminized space. The crafts movement provided a material culture counterpart to the "masculine domesticity" that historian Margaret Marsh found resulted from the joining of the suburban ideal with the cult of domesticity. Men returned to the home, aided in its maintenance, and supervised children, but on their own terms of recognized superiority. Although craft practice was divided along sexual lines, the home itself became a place of suburban togetherness.[3]

Late nineteenth-century Victorian Americans inherited an ideal of domesticity that associated women with the home and assigned nurturing, intimacy, care, piety, and morality to the female sex. In this belief system, social life dichotomized into male and female, work and home. Men were to be breadwinners, and women, bread-givers. Politics were for men; church and family for women. Men would tame nature and remake the world through production; women would clean up the resulting environmental and social dislocation through philanthropy. Both men and women accepted notions of

An image of family togetherness showing gender roles, on the cover of *The Bungalow Magazine* (October 1909)

female difference: Women, because they were "the mothers of the race," differed in physical and intellectual ways from men. If women were biologically weaker, though, they were stronger morally. Men were to be manly, tough-minded but responsible, while women were to be tender.[4]

Such a division of social life and space, however, was too simple. The home was the site of women's work of cleaning, cooking, and child care; the science of home economics developed in recognition of this reality. The homes of the immigrant poor served as workshops, where garments, foodstuffs, and industrial processes entered the place reserved for child nurture. Men maintained their legal and social status as heads of the household. They claimed the home as a place of rest. For recently emancipated slaves in the South and the poor, no matter their region, the home and family were not places separate from the world but open to intrusion by courts, charity workers, and other agents of the state. We must understand private and public, home and work, as shifting terms, dependent on whether class and race could shelter a woman from moving beyond the confines of domesticity.[5]

The actual lives of women and men were undergoing changes that would complicate these ideas about gender. Daughters from all classes and races were entering the paid labor force. In 1890, women over sixteen constituted 19 percent of the labor force; 68 percent of them had never married. The number working as domestics declined sharply as new arenas opened up to native-born white women, especially clerical and sales work in offices and department stores. But African-American women continued as servants and agricultural laborers throughout this period. Their labor-force participation was double that of white women, with a quarter of married black women earning wages as opposed to only 3 percent of native-born and immigrant whites. Much of the paid labor of mothers remained unrecorded, however, because it occurred at home, through the taking in of boarders or industrial homework. White immigrants concentrated on service and industrial work, especially laundry and the needle trades.[6] Meanwhile, increasing numbers of middle-class white women entered higher education and the professions. Women comprised nearly 37 percent of college students in 1900 and 47.3 percent twenty years later. Despite their access to training, professionals, like other laboring women, crowded into a limited number of occupations. In 1910, for example, only 1 percent of lawyers and 6 percent of doctors were women, but women represented 52 percent of social workers and 79 percent of librarians. The great majority of college graduates became teachers.[7]

Women's public activity soothed the ravages of the industrial system; they created, according to historian Sara Evans, a "maternal commonwealth that fused public and private concerns, domesticity and politics." Through voluntary associations—women's clubs, temperance societies, settlement houses, and consumers' leagues—women redefined the political to include municipal housekeeping: pure milk, cleaner streets, maternal and infant health, better housing. They created social services, from playgrounds to welfare, that later became public programs. Women were to bring the values of the home into the public realm, making the world more homelike. As the president of the Chicago Woman's Club explained, in 1910, "The home is the center of life, and if we can take art into the homes and then through the homes into the neighborhood, and then from one neighborhood into another, we shall soon make our whole city beautiful." Not only would they beautify the environment, they would extend their housekeeping to the inner workings of sewers and marketplaces. Such municipal housekeeping, they argued, justified suffrage. In the process of cleaning the city, they reaffirmed their ties of sisterhood. That premier social-housekeeping institution, the settlement house—where privileged women (and a few men) went to live among the poor to improve urban life—re-created the sororal experience of the women's colleges.[8]

Meanwhile, middle-class men were seeking a new fraternalism, ways of being that challenged the role of competitor fostered by capitalist social relations. Nearly one-third of all adult men in 1897 were members of a fraternal order, such as the Red Men, Odd Fellows, or Freemasons; according to one study, millions more belonged to other orders with secret rituals, from the Grand Army of the Republic to the Grange, which brought together farmers and other rural residents. Men sought to re-create the family through benevolent father figures amid brotherhood. In their leisure, they could reach a higher form of cooperation. But, as historian Mark C. Carnes has concluded, "Even as the emerging middle classes were embracing capitalism and bourgeois sensibilities, they were simultaneously creating rituals whose message was largely antithetical to those relationships and values. . . . By providing solace from the psychic pressures of these new social and institutional relationships, they ensured [their] survival."[9]

Men were facing a new world of work. The artisan found himself in a minority, and while many industries combined crafts and skilled manual labor with mechanized and unskilled work, the rise of both the corporation and the factory seemed to dwarf the actual persistence of craft in industry. By

1900, industrial wage earners nearly equaled the number of people laboring on the farm. Not only did planning separate from making but making became de-skilled. By the turn of the century, pottery, for example, had expanded from fifteen job enumerations to about forty-five different tasks, excluding decoration. Glassmaking, printing and bookbinding, textiles and clothing—all of these crafts witnessed a devolution of skill.[10]

Garmentmaking became the most degraded of crafts, even though the industry was not very mechanized. That sewing seems to be woman's normal occupation appeared a truism in nineteenth-century America, which justified low wages in the developing ready-made clothing industry, where women finished garments and embellished them, often as sweated workers in their own homes. Prior to the late nineteenth century, women sewed most of their family's clothes. By 1890, however, more than 60 percent of menswear was ready- as opposed to custom-made. The transformation of tailoring from an artisanal craft to a divided trade came from the arrival of cheap and less skilled workers, and also from increased competition among manufacturers based on this expanding consumer market. The contract system developed, in which the inside shop, run by a merchant tailor, brought cloth to be prepared and cut out for bundles to be distributed to numerous contractors. Clothing was actually assembled in the outside shop of the contractor, "an organizer and employer of immigrant labor." The contractor might subcontract the work to those with shops and to tenement homeworkers. After 1900, especially with less fashion-conscious menswear, larger garment factories grew. It was against this industrial profile, where Italian mothers and daughters cut lace and embroidered at home for pennies, that the artistic revival of the textile crafts was to occur, redefining women's fancywork as art.[11]

This era also witnessed the middle class of nonmanual proprietors and salaried professionals and managers separating from the growing working class of manual laborers and machine tenders to form a white-collar social grouping. Such white-collar workers were three times greater in 1900 than 1860. The number of store clerks and clerical office workers, a half-million in 1880, had tripled twenty years later. Corporations created levels of management as they instituted new accounting procedures and product lines. Professionals found themselves hired by institutions, the university as well as the corporation. The federal bureaucracy expanded. Even architectural offices ceased to be one-man operations and became the employers of college-trained men. "The middle class is becoming a salaried class, and rapidly losing the economic and moral independence of former days," declared *Independent* magazine in 1903.[12]

Class position certainly shaped work experience. Some professionals sharply distinguished between their labor and that of the working class. As the Wellesley College professor Vida Scudder, a Christian Socialist follower of John Ruskin, explained: "In the days of handicraft, work was its own reward; it is so no longer. The professional classes possibly work as hard as manual laborers. But their work is life . . . they employ, cultivate, delight the higher faculties. But to iron two thousand linen collars a day . . . to carry on any one of the minute occupations introduced by the division of labor, leaves people where it found them, only a little more stupefied."[13] Certainly, the separation of art and labor, play and work, creativity and drudgery had occurred for many manual laborers. But white-collar male workers also discovered themselves as team players, part of a bureaucratic chain of command and no longer independent professionals.

The crafts revival transformed this anxiety over loss of control by celebrating the autonomy and independence of the past. For intellectuals and other salaried white-collar workers cut off from manual labor, the return to

35

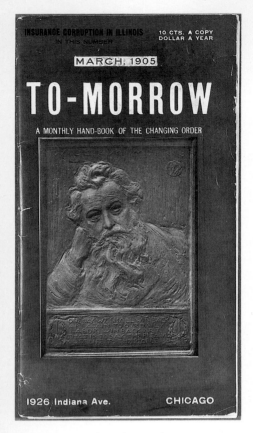

William Morris by Julia Bracken.
Reprinted as the cover of *To-Morrow:
A Monthly Hand-Book of the Changing
Order* (March 1905)

handicraft promised to end their own alienation at work and restore, for men, their sense of manliness. For men who no longer made things with their hands, the crafts movement offered an avocation through which they could become real men again, in control of their lives. California aficionado and preserver of Native American cultures Charles F. Lummis best summarized this sentiment: "Any fool can write a book but it takes a man to dovetail a door." University of Chicago professor and crafts publicist Oscar Lovell Triggs similarly linked masculinity with the goals of the crafts revival when he identified, in 1902, "industrial liberty" with "the return of manhood to common work."[14]

At a time when art was still associated with effeteness, William Morris had proved that manly men could be artists. An extremely appealing figure, he embodied many of the longings of the new middle class. Writing in the popular, genteel magazine *Scribner's*, his British associate Walter Crane described Morris as having "the robust figure of the craftsman . . . in his blue shirt-sleeves, his hands stained blue from the vat where he had been at work." With his seafarer's bluffness, leonine looks, blue shirt, cape coat, and slouch hat, Morris contained all the energy, vitality, and passion lost in the routine world of the office and factory. He was "the most strenuous man of genius whom our age has produced," declared one writer upon his death, in 1896. Morris was a red-blooded man's man, "the laureate of sweating men," able to fight "a good fight and [quit] oneself like a man." His virile strength contrasted with the Byronesque collars and affectations of the stylized poet. "Though a man of genius he was a man," proclaimed Horace Traubel, the biographer of Walt Whitman. "He produced major effects by the free virility of his affirmations."[15]

Manliness assumed heroic proportions when Morris became identified with the Norse warriors of his saga translations and the medieval knights of his prose romances. He appeared as one of nature's noblemen. For a generation of native-born intellectuals, who associated childhood with the folk and who thought spontaneity and naturalness were missing from their own lives, Morris stood as a reincarnation of the world's simpler, childlike, and less artificial past. At the same time, late nineteenth-century Victorian Americans admired Morris for his "shrewd head" and "uniform success." Although widely recognized as the poet of dream and escape, Morris aimed "to prove that the day was not idle and that idlers were no more than lumberers of the ground." He understood that beauty was "a practicable, realizable dream," and possessed the keen business sense necessary to make art-manufacturing profitable. For a public that celebrated the businessman as the modern equivalent of the knight, no contradiction existed between Morris's business activities and his championship of the Middle Ages. For those equally aware of the sins of commercialism, the Englishman proved that "there is no necessary antagonism between the genuinely ideal and the truly practical."[16] Arts and Crafts, the work ethic, and anticommercialism could form an organic whole.

Men longed for fellowship, a brotherhood of art that provided them with a masculine equivalent to the homosocial community constructed by educated white women in their schools and settlement houses.[17] They formed craft societies, such as Rose Valley, in Pennsylvania, and the New Clairvaux, in Montague, Massachusetts, out of this belief. In Chicago, a number of organizations emerged to meet a growing interest among university people and other professionals in the work of William Morris and the arts and crafts. Dedicated to "the dignifying of labor—the magnifying of its possibilities— the inspiring and educating of the man who personifies it," the Industrial Art League from 1899 to 1905 promoted "the new industrialism," wherein workshop, school, and studio combined to end the stultifying hierarchy of modern production. The South Park Association consisted of University of Chicago faculty, students, and their families; it provided classes in bookbinding and woodworking and discussions of the life and work of William Morris. It hired a Scandinavian cabinetmaker to execute orders and train amateurs, professional men looking for a leisure-time outlet. These and other groups, such as the Morris Society, contained "polemical friends of the producer" but few craftsmen.[18]

Artists, architects, and artworkers had initiated local Arts and Crafts societies, but those that grew after 1896 drew more members from amateurs and dues-paying patrons than from professionals. In Boston, Detroit, Providence, and several New England villages, wealthy women joined with male connoisseurs and male architects to dominate the movement. Some societies had their roots in women's clubs. But even where women predominated among the membership of urban organizations, men often held more leadership posts, as with the Boston Society of Arts and Crafts.[19]

Poster for Will Price's play *The Artsman*, in Rose Valley, Pennsylvania, 1917

Craft practice divided along gender lines. Men were architects; they took up printing, metalwork, and carpentry. Women chose china painting, textiles, and jewelry, although there were a number of prominent female metalworkers, such as Janet Payne Bowles and Clara Barck Welles, who combined jewelry with art metalwork. Gender could determine the division of labor within a craft: Women designed but men hammered metal; men shaped but women decorated pottery. Art bookbinding promised careers for women because it required "little heavy manual labor and great patience, with dexterity and neatness raised to the level of a fine art."[20]

Embroidery, basketry, weaving, and rugmaking had become women's crafts, as sophisticated urbanites associated these arts with the work of preindustrial and Native American women. They celebrated "the first Indian woman who, to meet the needs of her family, invented baskets and pottery, twine, and wove fabrics; and, not content with bare utility, set to work to adorn her handicraft with decorative forms learned from no school but that of Nature." They identified with their colonial foremothers, "who patiently, industriously, sat at the wheel and the loom, weaving yard upon yard for the comfort and warmth of the family." They discovered Arts and Crafts' success stories in Appalachia and immigrant districts, where women retained knowledge of traditional crafts.[21]

A woman's relation to the craft revival varied with her class position. While immigrant and poor rural women became the targets of improvement through craft industries, middle-class suburban housewives and upper-class urban matrons formed decorative-arts societies. Candace Wheeler linked together both activities. In 1877, she organized the New York Society of Decorative Art, "to encourage profitable industries among women who possess artistic talent, and to furnish a standard of excellence and a market for their work." A separate women's exchange aided the needy in selling their homemade wares. In midlife, this wife of a successful stockbroker forged a career in home decoration and the textile arts through the Associated Artists—first, as a partnership with Louis Comfort Tiffany and then as her own firm. She hired art-school graduates to form a "unique little band of accomplished American gentlewomen" who translated the preparatory drawings, or cartoon, into actual textiles. Wheeler also established a rugmaking industry near her Catskill summer home that uplifted local women through the crafts. While providing opportunity for other women, she retained control of the artistic content of the work, separating design from execution and thus belying the movement's claim to reunite them.[22]

Middle- and upper-class mothers and their daughters attended the new art institutes. The Cincinnati women who were to play a major role in the Queen City's art revival, who were crucial to the production of art pottery, began with wood-carving and drawing at the city's school of design. Both Ellen Miller and Margaret Whiting, founders of the Deerfield Society of Blue and White Needlework, had studied at the National Academy of Design, in New York, and summered at an artists' colony in Keene, New Hampshire. Others sought a livelihood through art education. Both the Massachusetts Normal School of Art and the Rhode Island School of Design trained women to teach art in the public schools and to design for industry. Newcomb Pottery, at Sophie Newcomb Memorial College, in New Orleans, organized to "provide a livelihood for that large number of women who have artistic tastes, and who do not find the schoolroom or the stenographer's desk or the counter altogether congenial." It offered a model of art manufacturing for the New South through its professional training for women, but attendees of the college were overwhelmingly from the white elite of New Orleans and the lower South. They could afford to go to school and afterward decorate for

A Zuni blanket weaver at her loom,
San Juan, New Mexico, 1900

THE DESIGNING-ROOM.

Not satisfied, however, with producing stuffs to exchange for the plentiful shekels of American plutocracy, the artists have wisely carried their experiments into the region of cheap materials. One result is a fabric of raw silk, serving to utilize the waste of costlier webs, and dyed in the skein, in varied tints of the same color, giving it when woven all the effect of the Eastern hand-dyed, hand-woven stuffs so much admired. This is sold at a very moderate price. Chintzes and cottons receive as much care in the design as their expensive brocades, and Kentucky jean or denim has been known to take upon itself the semblance of Oriental drapery for wall or door. A sort of dado of this homely dark blue design is studied with reference to use. A woven stuff designed by Miss Ida Clark for the hangings of a palace car has for

The design room of Candace Wheeler's Associated Artists. From *Harper's New Monthly Magazine* (August 1884)

the pottery, or make their own ware as part of the Newcomb Guild.[23]

The Cincinnati Women's Pottery Club, under Mary Louise McLaughlin, brought together women of "culture, taste, and refinement" from prominent families. It served as a prototype for clubs in other cities around the country. In 1880, one of their number, Maria Longworth Nichols, built her own pottery, Rookwood. Rookwood evolved into a major art manufactory that employed women art students as decorators of its slipware. Some of these went on to found or direct other potteries: Laura Fry taught industrial art at Purdue University and Mary G. Sheerer supervised the Newcomb Pottery. Other women art-school graduates found themselves hired to curb the power of skilled craftsmen. Louis Comfort Tiffany, for one, redefined his categories of labor to undermine the glassmakers' rules on apprentices by having young women prepare working drawings and match glass to the artist's cartoon.[24]

While some women brought the crafts to the poor, others sought to learn the crafts from them. Designer Helen R. Albee formed the Abnakee Rug Industry, near her summer home in Pequaket, New Hampshire, in 1897, to elevate the hooked rug from a drab patchwork made of cast-off clothing to a work of art. She hired the rural poor. Mrs. Arnold Talbot, of the Providence Handicraft Club, employed Portuguese immigrant women to weave her designs. Berea College defined mountain homespun as art and set about improving the quality of coverlets and quilts through "homespun" fairs and its own "fireside" industry. One Tuskegee teacher, a leader in the National Association of Colored Women's Clubs, formulated a rugmaking program for rural black Alabamians that exemplified the goals of other rural craft efforts: to end idleness, use normally discarded material, and provide useful items for the home. The Paul Revere Pottery, in Boston's North End, offered "a happy, healthful, wage-earning occupation" for immigrant daughters and useful work for two middle-class professional women—Edith Guerrier and Edith Brown. Also in Boston, Florence Weber established a lacemaking venture that taught Irish working girls to tat lace. She had attended sessions at the School of the Museum of Fine Arts to learn this craft, but only upon finding an old Italian woman who could show her the work was she able to re-create the art of torchon. Chicago art patron Frances Glessner took lessons from an immigrant jeweler connected with Hull-House; while living in Boston, Janet Payne Bowles discovered a Russian immigrant metalworker to aid her in perfecting her craft.[25]

Settlement-house workers stood in a more complicated relationship to their immigrant neighbors. They promoted "immigrant gifts," the skills and aesthetics of traditional southern and Eastern European cultures. The Hull-House Labor Museum, opened in 1900, demonstrated the old craft processes in textiles, metals, wood, grain, and books. Its living-history exhibits attempted to bridge the culture and work experiences of Chicago's immigrant population. Women showed how they spun and wove in their homelands: A Sicilian twisted a stick that had two discs; a Syrian, one with a small wooden disc at the top; a Russian ran a flax frame; an Irishwoman, a spinning wheel. Boston's Denison House formed an Italian Arts and Crafts exhibit when the concept of cultural pluralism was a radical idea and Americanization programs dominated the public schools and other aspects of settlement work. The Scuola d'Industrie Italiane, at Richmond Hill House, sought to bring to New York the revival of traditional crafts taking place in Italy. Countess Amari came to instruct her immigrant compatriots, and prominent social

Young women at Paul Revere Pottery. From *The Craftsman* (November 1912)

reformers organized the venture as a means to provide women with an alternative to both factory and tenement labor, encouraging craft in the process.[26]

Some settlement-house craft projects inappropriately addressed the concerns of working people. Ellen Gates Starr established the Hull-House Bookbindery in 1899, after apprenticing herself to the English Arts and Crafts leader and idealist-socialist T. J. Cobden-Sanderson. In the 1890s, a number of society women followed New York's Emily Hunter Nordhoff into this craft. But working women found themselves binding for the trade, not engaging in the art, and even then very few worked in the job or art binderies. Most performed preparatory processes, such as wire-stitching, rather than tooling designs into leather. Not surprisingly, over the years Starr had few pupils for a craft that used expensive materials and produced "articles of luxury," as she later characterized her work. Yet, Starr was among the best art bookbinders, although her delicately tooled designs too often repeated Cobden-Sanderson's conventionalized flowers.[27]

Ellen Gates Starr also served as a pungent critic for the movement from within. A Christian Socialist and labor militant, she integrated the workshop and studio, "working 'in the spirit of the future.'" But, she warned, "A pottering lack of thoroughness and workmanlike quality, often crying for mercy under the cover of 'Woman's Work,' while at the same time confronting you with the assurance of a new fad, does not make for regeneration." Those who took up handicraft, either as another fashionable diversion or to make a profit from people's real need for beauty, she condemned. But even these "false motives," Starr argued, pointed to "the existence of a genuine craving."[28]

Her Deerfield, Massachusetts, cousins, Mary and Frances Allen, shared such sentiments. Deafness forced these teachers into a new profession, art photography. They were among the leaders of the Deerfield Society of Arts and Crafts. All of the leaders were unmarried women in their thirties whose family obligations kept them at home. Deerfield was more than a sewing circle. While its founders remained within woman's sphere, channeling their art training into objects and activities judged appropriate for women and

An Irishwoman at a spinning wheel in the Hull-House Textile Room, c. 1910

reviving "the feminine handicrafts," they expanded the meaning of "woman's sphere." Appearing as female counterparts to the medieval craftsman, they claimed the right to "joy in labor." They converted women's culture—especially the blue-and-white needlework of their colonial foremothers—into a source of cash, expanding moneymaking opportunities for many and professional options for a few.[29]

Arts and Crafts, as well as suffrage, appealed to individual freedom. The Deerfield women's club, run by the needlework leaders, functioned as the local women's suffrage society. Other prominent crafters, such as Ellen Gates Starr and Mary Ware Dennett, of Boston, were suffragists; Ware Dennett was a prominent proponent of birth control as well. Indeed, craft's ties with women's reform were close. Chicago's Julia Bracken, a member of the Bohemia Guild of Arts and Crafts, who did bas-reliefs of Ruskin and Morris that hung in the offices of the Industrial Art League, designed the emblem of the National Women's Trade Union League. The social settlement houses and suffrage parlors were decorated with craftsman furniture, as if to express their solidarity with the new age of sturdy simplicity that would lessen housework and provide women with more time for public life.[30]

A sisterhood of art, perhaps, was the most significant gain for these middle- and upper-class women. Like other talented women of the day, they found support and understanding in lifelong female friendships, forging a sense of community that developed through networks of friends and common activity. A San Francisco woman summarized the vision best when she imagined "an annual pilgrimage" of women potters to Cincinnati: "It would be so delightful to go to the center of the great sisterhood of states, as delegates, to see and admire the handy-works of our sister women." She signed her letter, "Truly yours for women's progress."[31]

Women's progress meant that some craftswomen entered a bohemian world of the time that questioned bourgeois life-styles along with capitalist social relations. Dressed in an embroidered smock, with matching clothes for her children, such women lived "the simple life," close to nature. Alice Hubbard, the wife of crafts promoter Elbert Hubbard, summarized the attitude toward dress reform when she declared, "Woman is so great when she is honestly herself that she need not attempt to be anyone else. . . . Her clothing will be so adapted to the needs of the body in its work that the subject will be only a small item in her mind and leave time and energy for things of more benefit to herself." Janet Payne Bowles wrote on "Artistic Dress for Children," and attired her own children in healthful cotton clothes. With her printer husband, Bowles lived in a number of artists' colonies, the most interesting of which was Helicon Hall. Socialist writer Upton Sinclair set up this utopian colony in the New Jersey countryside, where artists and radicals could practice cooperative housekeeping and communal child care. Other craft colonies were more conventional in their household arrangements, but the craftsman home promised simplified housekeeping with its dust-free built-ins, simple lines, and functional kitchens that evoked "old-time comfort and convenience." Still, its kitchen was a workplace for the housewife, even as its spaces had opened up to serve as a family room for all.[32]

In her 1908 book *Woman's Work*, Alice Hubbard envisioned equality between the sexes, with men and women shouldering the burdens of the "world's work." But she feared that "men have successfully invaded the home and taken away not only most of the drudgery but also the work that involved action of head, hand and heart—the vital quality . . . of the housewife has

British author Arnold Bennett (at left) and Chicago writer Hamlin Garland relaxing in the Cliff Dwellers Club, a Chicago literary and artistic society, November 1911. Collection the Cliff Dwellers Club of Chicago

Interior No. 14. Advertisement for wall treatments by M. H. Birge & Sons Company, New York, 1904

gone." The architecture of the Arts and Crafts movement, particularly the bungalow and craftsman home, reflected the entrance of suburban men into the life of their families in a manner that promised a new togetherness but could lead to male dominance in yet another realm of social life. In the home itself, there was a crossing of boundaries that, at first, maintained male spaces and then, as critic Cheryl Robertson has pointed out, elevated "masculine" design as appropriate for the home as a material culture expression of family life. Gender segregation would end, but gender difference would remain.[33]

From the 1880s, Morris-inspired forms provided the style for the man's room, the den or library, and for men's clubs. There even was a "Smoker's Morris." Rustic and sturdy, oaken furniture evoked the outdoors and male pursuits of hunting and fishing. So did Native American artifacts, symbols of "savage" communion with nature. Indeed, later on, resorts decorated in rustic Mission, fraternities furnished rooms with craftsman, and individuals chose the styles for their summer homes. *House and Garden* assured readers that women would "value" such furniture developed to promote "masculine comfort."[34]

Gustav Stickley's craftsman home—with its low roof lines and overhanging eaves, straight lines hugging the ground, native materials, and economical use of space—was a cultural equivalent to the politics of Theodore Roosevelt. In his *Craftsman* magazine, furniture manufacturer Stickley extolled Roosevelt for the politician's sincerity, honesty, energy, industry, self-sacrifice, and enthusiasm—virtues central to the craftsman ideal. One *Craftsman* writer explicitly linked Roosevelt's Square Deal to the "natural" material and "honest" structure of Stickley's designs.[35]

Stickley addressed his architectural and decorative prescriptions to the male heads of households. Warning them to match styles with their station in life and family needs, Stickley offered his own home as an example—with its disciplined geometry, generous proportions, rationality, and sturdiness. It presented the personality of a man in contrast to "the majority of modern houses . . . built to meet the ideas of women, whose tendency is still to emphasize emotion—to minimize reason." Made of oak—"a robust, manly sort of wood"—craftsman furniture further promised stability and permanence. As *The Ideal House* claimed, in 1906, "Mission is a 'masculine' style." It was also "a home style." Indeed, it would transform the living room into a masculine preserve. This room opened up the first-floor space of the bungalow into a continuous flow, one that broke down the separate domains of individual family members to provide them with a common place. As Stickley described the living room, "It is the place to which a man comes home when his day's work is done and where he expects to find himself comfortable and at ease in surroundings that are in harmony with his daily life, thought, and pursuits."[36]

Sears, Roebuck, Montgomery Ward, and the Aladdin Company, along with numerous bungalow books, spread this message beyond the business and professional classes that could afford to hire architects like Frank Lloyd Wright to design such a home. Even workers at Henry Ford's Highland Park plant could afford a prefabricated version of a Craftsman bungalow, while Big Bill Haywood, of the syndicalist International Workers of the World, promised to provide strikers with morris chairs in the factory itself.[37] Consumers agreed with promoters: The crafts brought men relief from the disorderly world of work. But, while men were resting at home, women were following the crafts into the world, learning the joy—along with the sorrow—of labor.

The Arts and Crafts movement reflected, even as it facilitated, a move in gender ideology that extended the proper arena for both womanhood and manhood. Rather than denying gender difference, it brought the sexes together through a common focus on the home and its decoration. At a time when the white middle and upper classes were reforging their cultural hegemony over the rest of society, the Arts and Crafts movement promised refuge and relief from the world of work. Those who no longer labored with their hands, those whose lives belied simplicity, those who had left the countryside for the city or the suburb, such women and men could find a new wholeness through crafts production, consumption, and display. By creating artistic environments, they could seal themselves off from the ugliness of industrialized America. They could return home to nature, where men were manly and women truly women again, and still be prepared to meet the challenges of the modern world. Crossing boundaries maintained distinctions for the many while opening up possibilities of creative expression for the few.

The Critic and the Evolution of Early Twentieth-Century American Craft

by Beverly K. Brandt

At the beginning of the twentieth century, American artists working in craft media sought to distinguish their work from products manufactured in quantity by machine. They insisted that crafts possessed a quality that machine-made products did not—a "power of expression" transcending utility and beauty. That expressive capability, they explained, enabled a handmade object to convey the thoughts, feelings, and beliefs of the maker while arousing an intellectual, emotional, and spiritual response in the user. The resulting symbiosis, they argued, differentiated the handmade from the machine-made, while suggesting that the expression of the handmade was both an extension of the maker's character and a reflection of that of its user.[1]

Critics associated with the Arts and Crafts movement—an Anglo-American campaign for reform that lasted from 1860 to 1920—were among the first to acknowledge the expressive capabilities of the crafts. They based their arguments upon the philosophy of aesthetics, a discipline that had contemplated the "power of expression" for centuries—but only as it applied to the so-called fine arts, that is, architecture, painting and sculpture, literature, poetry, and music. By suggesting that the so-called applied arts, or crafts, aroused a similar intellectual, emotional, and spiritual response in the user, critics claimed they were thus equal to the fine arts. As such, they elevated the discussion of craft to the level of scholarly debate, one requiring a practical knowledge of materials and techniques combined with a thorough understanding of history and theory.[2]

The generators of the Arts and Crafts movement—Henry Cole, organizer of the Great Exhibition of 1851, John Ruskin, and William Morris—established a need for critical contemplation of the crafts as early as the 1840s. Within fifty years, such criticism appeared regularly in treatises published in England and abroad as it became an established part of the creative process. This occurred casually, when master and apprentice discussed a proposed solution in the workshop or studio, as well as formally, when distinguished members of juries of review debated the relative merits of crafts displayed at international expositions. Such contemplation and the discourse that it provoked were important components of the reform movement. Improvement of the crafts required evaluating conceptual, aesthetic, and technical shortcomings, and then proposing alternatives that might ensure greater success. Both tasks were among the many assigned to the critic, whose participation in the creative process came to be regarded—by craftspersons and consumers alike—as essential.[3]

Improving the state of American craft and ameliorating the conditions under which craftspersons labored were two goals uniting critics in the early twentieth century. But despite their shared interests, critics comprised an eclectic group whose collective background was as diverse as that of the audience it addressed. Many were practitioners—familiar firsthand with wood, metal, glass, clay, fiber, and related media—but others were amateurs who lacked hands-on experience. Some were journalists, connoisseurs, or educators, and a few were historians of ornament, philosophers, or theorists. Architects comprised an important—and very vocal—group, whose concern for the quality of the crafts arose, in part, from self-interest: They recognized that their own success depended upon that of craftspersons with whom they collaborated on interior fittings and furnishings. Viewing criticism as a vital part of their own newly emerging profession, they were eager to explore its implications for the crafts and trades.[4]

Critics such as these addressed their comments to everyone involved in any way with the production, distribution, and utilization of the crafts. Some focused upon makers, hoping to strengthen craftspersons' qualifications or improve their working conditions; others concentrated upon users, seeking to educate consumers about their societal responsibilities for the state of art, craft, and design. All wished to make discussions of the crafts more intellectual and contemplative and to enforce increasingly higher standards governing appearance and execution. In addition, critics struggled to heighten public sensitivity to the significance of craft within American culture and to dispel the notion that the making of crafts was less prestigious than other artistic occupations.[5]

They disseminated their ideas primarily through lecturing and writing, suiting their tone to match the sophistication of their audiences. Some wrote books, intended for practitioners, on specialized subjects—the historical, theoretical, or practical aspects of a particular craft, aesthetics or art appreciation, educational reform or manual training—while others contributed evaluative essays to exhibition catalogues aimed at consumers. A select few—such as Frederick W. Coburn, Sylvester Baxter, and William Howe Downes[6]—wrote columns and reviews for local newspapers on a regular basis. But most critics published their work in magazines having a national or international readership. These ranged in scope from general interest publications—addressing current affairs, literature, science, or education—to women's magazines, such as *House Beautiful* (1896), *Woman's Home Companion* (1873), and *The Ladies' Home Journal* (1883). Some of the most famous critics of the crafts—Gustav Stickley, Irene Sargent, and Mariana Griswold van Rensselaer—wrote for specialty publications dedicated to reform of the arts and crafts, including *The Craftsman* (1901), *Handicraft* (1902), *Brush and Pencil* (1897), *Keramic Studio* (1899), and *The International Studio* (1897).

Among the most relevant criticism was that written *by* craftspersons *for* craftspersons. The English émigré ceramist Charles Fergus Binns, for example, wrote his book *The Potter's Craft* (1910) for the benefit of other "artist critics" sharing his expertise in ceramics along with his "enthusiasm, skill, discrimination and infinite patience" as a worker. In addition to documenting techniques that he had perfected during his career, Binns offered a critique of the craft to which he owed his livelihood, proposing numerous ways to improve it. He urged his colleagues to join with him in demonstrating the "courage to destroy that which is below standard" and the "self-denial to resist the temptation to sell an unworthy product." Treating his readers as equals, Binns offered to them his "counsel as a fellow craftsman," hoping that they might be "stimulated, guided, helped and encouraged" by his insight and his example.[7]

Artist critics such as Binns clearly offered one another good advice. But amateurs questioned the critical ability of such practitioners, arguing that they lacked the objectivity that an outsider might provide. "The worker in any branch of the arts, as well as in anything that man's hand or brain can be occupied with," stated one, in defense of her calling, "is surely not the best person to write or talk on that particular subject. As Benvenuto Cellini so truly put it," she concluded, in a questionable assertion, "'they of the craft are for the most part better at work than at talk.'" While artist critics and amateurs argued the relative merits of practical experience, others dismissed such discussions as irrelevant: "The question to be asked about the critic,"

BIGELOW,
KENNARD
& CO.

From
Monday March 25
until Saturday April
6 *will be shown at
our store* the entire
collection of Grueby
Pottery selected for
the Pan-American
Exposition ⚹ *All
interested in this
splendid faience
are cordially invited*
511 WASHINGTON ST.

Ceramics such as these, featured in this advertisement for Bigelow, Kennard & Co., were designed by Addison Le Boutillier in collaboration with William H. Grueby, two of Ernest Batchelder's colleagues and fellow members of the Society of Arts and Crafts, Boston. As published in Ernest A. Batchelder, *The Principles of Design* (Chicago: Inland Printer Company, 1904)

asserted the writer A. Clutton-Brock, "is not whether he is an amateur as an artist, but whether he is an amateur as a critic." What these differing opinions suggest is that critics' qualifications were as much a topic of concern as were their criteria and recommendations.[8]

Critics were eager to demonstrate that their judgments were neither arbitrary nor subject to personal whim. Thus, they turned to theories—founded upon strict principles—for justification. They referred to these principles variously: as rules or laws, conventions or canons, precedents or standards, conditions, or even "recipes." Their nomenclature differed but their attitudes were similar, as all regarded principles as fundamental, universal, timeless—and inviolate. They insisted that principles must dictate every decision a craftsperson made during the creative process and must inform every opinion a critic rendered regarding a finished product. By acknowledging the importance of such principles, critics linked their opinions to established philosophies of aesthetics as well as to newly emerging theories of "pure Design." Their interest in linking theory with practice arose out of a strongly felt desire to articulate and to systematize what formerly had been an intuitive part of the creative decision-making process.[9]

Critics believed that the application of theory founded upon principles might ensure a uniform standard of excellence among the crafts while eliminating the "artistic anarchy" caused by apostasy. Using terms that were ubiquitous throughout the literature of criticism—although definitions of them seemed to vary from one critic to the next—they agreed that every handmade object must be graceful and elegant, harmonious and orderly, well proportioned and balanced regardless of medium. They insisted that ornamentation must "seem to be inseparable" from the form that it embellished. And they argued that every work must reveal the nature and capacities of the material from which it was made, while demonstrating clearly the tools and processes used in its execution. Nevertheless, they were wary of enforcing "rigid rules as of cast iron" indiscriminately, knowing that novices might benefit from them but suspecting that experienced masters could willfully violate them with great success. Therefore, critics advised their constituents to keep principles in mind and yet remain open to fortuitous "accidents" that might lead to unexpectedly innovative results.[10]

Armed with a particular theory as justification, critics sought ways to strengthen the character of American craft. In doing so, they seemed more comfortable addressing conceptual or technical issues than those of an aesthetic nature, and they resisted promoting a specific style. They did not hesitate to say exactly how an individual might construct or finish an object of a certain material—finish was an almost obsessive preoccupation—but they avoided dictating how that object should look. On the rare occasions when they did discuss appearance, they tended toward vagueness, often defining one abstraction with another. Statements such as that offered by the American ceramist, educator, and theorist Ernest Batchelder—"We might define 'style' as direct, straightforward simplicity"—must have been infuriating to craftspersons hoping for advice that was specific and easy to implement.[11]

Regardless of their diverse theoretical positions, critics shared similar views on the pitfalls that craftspersons should avoid. Most decried "novelty for novelty's sake," questioning examples that seemed fashionable or short-lived in appeal. They denounced elements that were, in their words, inconsistent or incongruous, startling to the mind, or confounding to the senses. They condemned any aspect of a work that seemed false or ingenuous, or that might be construed, according to their criteria, as cunning or smug. Above all, they preferred crafts having an expression that was, in the words of the American critic and educator Denman W. Ross, "simple, clear, reasonable, consistent

BIGELOW, KENNARD & CO.

GOLDSMITHS, SILVERSMITHS AND
IMPORTERS · DESIGNERS & MAKERS
OF FINE HALL & MANTEL CLOCKS

MARCH 25 · TO · APRIL 6ᵀᴴ
the Easter Exhibit of ↝
Grueby Pottery including
the entire collection selected
for the Buffalo Exposition·
1 9 0 1

511 WASHINGTON STREET BOSTON

An example of the graphic design style
that Batchelder espoused in *The Principles
of Design*, featuring ceramics from the
Grueby Faience Company of Boston.
From the *Masters in Art Series* (April 1901)

and true." As this statement suggests, critics often described the expression of exemplary crafts in the same terms used to discuss the qualifications of outstanding craftspersons. Viewing the handmade object as a mirror of its creator, critics vowed that the principles shaping the former dictated a way of life for the latter.[12]

Critics believed that American craft failed to measure up to an ideal, in part, because of a disregard for fundamental principles. In addition, they felt that crafts—especially those that mimicked European examples—betrayed a dependency upon models that were, in their eyes, inappropriate. They set about identifying suitable sources to which craftspersons might turn for inspiration, while suggesting a methodology by which they might adapt or transform such sources into works that were both conceptually meaningful and culturally relevant.[13]

In the manner of their nineteenth-century counterparts, critics promoted two conceptual paradigms—history and nature. They believed that the craftsmanship of the past provided invaluable lessons for the present. And they regarded nature as a constantly regenerating font of freshness and originality. The challenge for craftspersons, critics warned, was not to copy history or nature literally but, instead, to abstract from and to interpret each in a way that was personal and appropriate to the modern age. But the popularity of such books as Lewis F. Day's *Nature in Ornament* (1892) and Walter Crane's *The Bases of Design* (1898)—both of which continued to appear on recommended reading lists decades after their date of publication— attests to the difficulties craftspersons encountered in replicating the spirit of such models without resorting to line-for-line duplication.[14]

The key to success, critics indicated, was conventionalization. As a concept, it was so important that it appeared in most turn-of-the-century treatises on the crafts; as a methodology, however, it seems to have been universally misunderstood. This may explain why it figured prominently in the literature of criticism and why prolific artist critics such as Day devoted part of every book to the subject. "To conventionalize," he wrote in *Nature in Ornament*, "is to simplify," a recommendation that craftspersons evidently found difficult to assimilate, for twelve years later, in *Ornament & Its Application*, Day still elaborated upon the same theme: "Conventionality in ornament," he stressed, "is the natural consequence of reticence or self-restraint, of doing not all that the artist could have done, but just what is called for by the occasion." Such advice cleared the way for twentieth-century Modernism and its minimalist approach, but it must have seemed perplexing to craftspersons surrounded by the historicist and revivalist vestiges of the late nineteenth century—a time when "conspicuous consumption" was the rule rather than the exception.[15]

Critics never defined it as such, but they suggested that language might serve as another model to craftspersons seeking inspiration. Drawing parallels between expression in word and expression in craft, they identified the latter as a form of communication. They advised their constituents against producing objects "having nothing meaningful to say," or that made statements that might be denounced as elaborate, affected, pretentious, artificial, or strained. They often defined abstract concepts that were difficult to comprehend by means of a linguistic metaphor: "Fit treatment," wrote Day, addressing a chief concern of the reform movement, "is, in fact, the translation of natural or other form, not merely into the language of art, but into the dialect of some particular handicraft. We detect in it," he continued, "the homely accent of sincere workmanship. . . . It is because we find in it no turn of native or vernacular expression," he concluded, "that modern manufacture is so dull."[16] Although such linguistic metaphors littered their writing, critics failed to identify language per se as a conceptual or procedural model. One exception, however, was Owen Jones—a member of Henry Cole's circle in the mid-1800s, and an important first-generation reformer of the applied arts—who called attention to the parallel between language and craft in the title of his influential book *The Grammar of Ornament* (1856).

As Day's comments suggest, critics who employed a linguistic model rejected high-toned rhetoric in favor of simple, everyday speech. Similarly, when they advised their constituents to turn to history for inspiration, they recommended that they overlook foreign, academic, high-style examples in favor of those that were domestic, unstudied, and vernacular. These included folk motifs based upon local flora and fauna, forms produced by self-trained, anonymous craftspersons of the past, works executed in indigenous materials, and those using traditional construction techniques developed within a particular geographic region. The vernacular thus served as a model, whether one sought inspiration from history or from language. It informed both the concrete and the abstract—influencing form, ornament, materials, and technique along with the overall expression to which such elements contributed.[17]

This obsession with language extended to critics' judgment of their own work. They sought to render opinions that were constructive and comprehensible, but admitted that discrepancies in language jeopardized their statements' effectiveness: "People will judge and decide, without any doubt of their own competency," wrote the Scottish critic W. Proudfoot Begg, in 1887, "on the comparative merits of plants and animals and dresses, of paintings and poets and furniture; and the awards of qualified critics and judges at exhibitions," he continued, "are usually held to be rationally given, and to have truth at the root of them. But," he lamented, "that still leaves the question to be settled as to what their standard of judgment is, and whether it is the true one. And the difficulty has not been lessened, but very much increased," he concluded, "by the vague and indefinite language which has been used [regarding] a standard." Fifty years later, British silversmith Bernard Cuzner corroborated that point of view, suggesting that criticism still showed room for improvement: "Beware of catch words and phrases," he warned his readers. "To say a thing is 'fit for its purpose' is far better than the newer 'functional.' Each generation," he continued, "will use different terms, just as each generation sees things from a different point of view. What matters," he

Batchelder's alter ego was the rabbit. He often incorporated a rabbit holding a carrot with his initials on letterhead and ceramic tiles. As illustrated in *The Principles of Design*, 1904

concluded, "is that terms really mean something and that the views are broad and true." Evidently, critics sought within their own discipline the same refinement of expression that they hoped to instill within the crafts. And their wish to be frank and direct in their pronouncements was as protomodernistic as the aesthetic of simplicity that they promoted. Their concern for language and meaning has continued to inform the approach of their successors today who apply linguistics, semantics and semiotics, structuralism and deconstruction, among other theoretical frameworks, to discussions of contemporary craft.[18]

The relative newness of their discipline compromised the effectiveness of critics undertaking reform of the crafts during the first decades of the twentieth century. They struggled to define their own discipline—

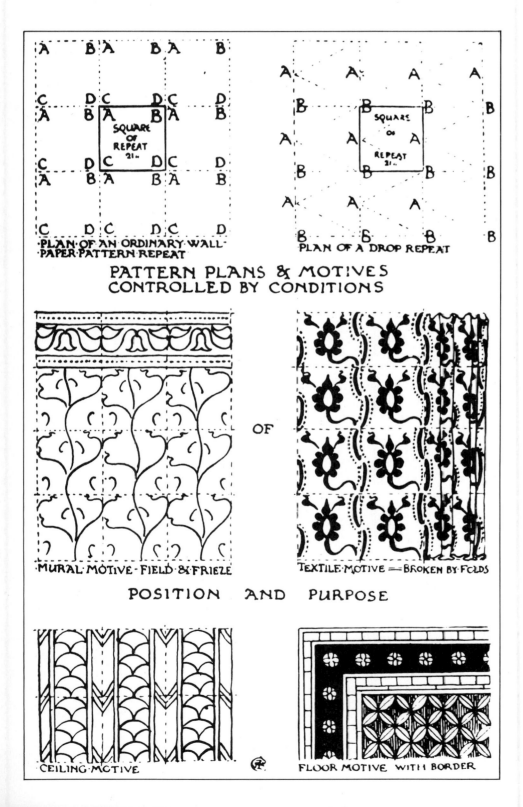

Repeat patterns and their application as wall murals, draperies, or floor and ceiling embellishments, in Walter Crane's *The Bases of Design* (London: George Bell and Sons, 1898)

Considering drapery designs and their applications, Frank G. Jackson concluded that "patterns having . . . horizontal and oblique striping are more distinctly suitable. . . . Again, the scale of the ornament used is an important matter. The patterns should be designed for and adjusted to the size of the folds into which the material naturally falls." Plate v from Jackson, *Theory and Practice of Design, An Advanced Textbook on Decorative Art* (London: Chapman and Hall; Philadelphia: J. P. Lippincott Co., 1894)

Lewis Day wrote, "Ornament is constructed . . . patiently built up on lines inevitable to its consistency—lines so simple, that to the expert it is not difficult to lay bare its very skeleton . . ." An illustration by Day in *The Anatomy of Pattern* (London: B. T. Batsford, 1887)

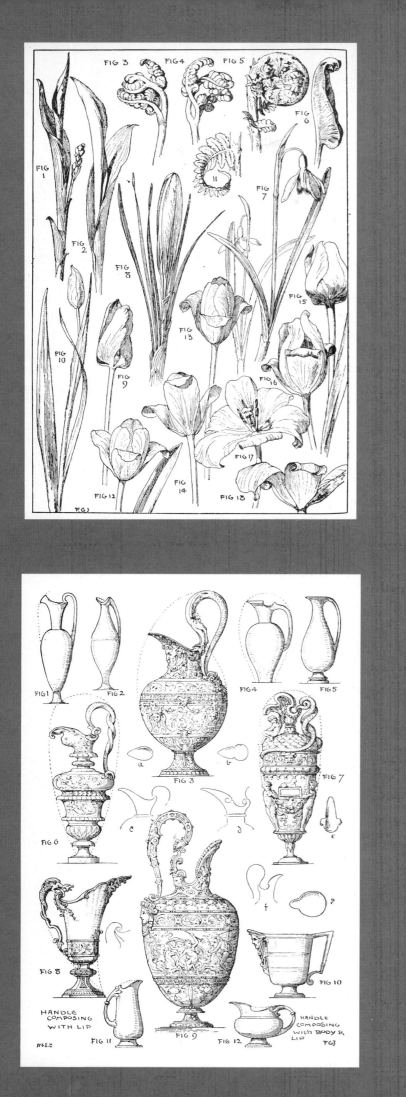

Like most turn-of-the-century theorists, Frank Jackson advocated conventionalization: "In all naturalistic treatments, the direction of stems and their general composition should be closely studied for the ornamental lines that may be abstracted from them for decorative purposes." An illustration of "Vegetable Elements" from Jackson's *Theory and Practice of Design*, 1894

In his "Evolution of Industrial Objects," Jackson considers "the proper relation of [handles to] the lips and spouts [of pouring vessels], so that the weight of the vessel and its contents may not be against the action of the pouring." From Jackson, *Theory and Practice of Design*, 1894

determining its objectives, methods, and merits—even as they sought to apply it to the professions or avocations of others. In the process, they came to realize that criticism faced some of the same challenges as craft: "Criticism has value for mankind and not merely for artists or critics," explained Clutton-Brock. "But the value of it does not lie in the judgment of the critic any more than the value of art lies in the judgment, taste, or preference of the artist. The value in both cases lies in the power of expression; and by that art and criticism are to be judged." Critics, therefore, could not begin strengthening the "power of expression" of the crafts without first enhancing the expressive capabilities of the criticism that they offered.[19]

Critics were as realistic in recognizing their own limitations as they were idealistic in setting their goals. They intended to "stimulate, guide, help and encourage." But when craftspersons failed to respond—as often occurred—they conceded that "it is not possible to force a reform . . . upon an unwilling people." Ultimately, critics concluded, the impetus to improve the crafts must arise from within the individual and not be imposed by an outsider. "In all probability," Lewis F. Day explained, in words equally applicable to craftsperson or consumer, "neither the cautious man nor the adventurous man will be influenced materially by anything that is said or written on the subject. . . . All that words can well do," he concluded, with a degree of resignation, "is to strengthen him in his resolve, or to awaken in him a suspicion that others too may be right from their point of view." Like Day, many reformers looked forward to a time when everyone involved in any way with the creative process might function as critics in their own right. Yet, they recognized, with some regret, the irony of that situation: As the critical thinking of others improved, the need for an outside opinion diminished—and the job of the professional critic became obsolete.[20]

In the United States, the craft of metal and the related crafts of jewelry and enamels were late to respond to the reform principles of the English Arts and Crafts movement. In the late 1890s, Americans began to pursue the design and creation of metalwork and jewelry as a reform movement activity. Julian Yale, who was self-taught, and his sister, Madeline Yale Wynne, who learned from him, exhibited metalwork and jewelry in the 1897 Easter art exhibition at Hull-House, the Chicago settlement house that Jane Addams and Ellen Gates Starr were inspired to found, in 1889, after visiting C. R. Ashbee's Guild and School of Handicraft at London's Toynbee Hall.[1] Metalwork was taught at Hull-House by 1899.[2] At the inaugural exhibition of the Chicago Arts and Crafts Society, in 1898, Yale, Wynne, and other amateur metalsmiths, working in protest against machine-made commercial work and valuing the earnestness of their purpose more than the outcome of their efforts, exhibited work that drew praise and comment on its barbaric quality.[3] In 1897, George P. Kendrick showed silver and copper metalwork in an exhibition, organized by arts and education leaders in Boston, that led to the founding of that city's Society of Arts and Crafts the same year.[4] Amateurs as well as manufacturers participated in the inaugural exhibition of New York's National Arts Club in 1899, an exhibition of articles in gold and silver.[5]

Nevertheless, prior to 1900, the opportunities to learn silversmithing in all its branches were rare. The Society of Arts and Crafts, Boston, was unsuccessful in its efforts to organize workshops and classes after its founding, in 1897.[6] Training in silversmithing in America took place in factories, where the focus was on specialized steps in manufacturing. In order to undertake its ambitious art-silver line, which came to be called Martelé, the Gorham Manufacturing Company even found it necessary to establish a special school within its factory, in 1896, to perfect manual skills for forming and ornamenting silver.

Between 1901 and 1907, academic institutions and museum schools began offering formal instruction in "art metal" and jewelry, often in close cooperation with manufacturers. The first formal academic classes commenced in early 1901 at Brooklyn's Pratt Institute and Providence's Rhode Island School of Design; the latter advertised that its classes offered "art training with practical professional metalworking."[7] European-trained Joseph Aranyi, who was also employed at Tiffany & Company, taught the first metalwork classes at Pratt Institute, and in 1904, Carl F. Hamann expanded and continued instruction to include modeling, design, jewelry, and enameling.[8] At Rhode Island, American Laurin H. Martin, who had recently trained in England at the Birmingham School of Arts and Crafts and with enamelist Alexander Fisher, taught the practical side of metalsmithing.[9] Under an advisory committee, Manufacturing Jewelry and Designers, which included the Gorham Manufacturing Company's well-known chief designer William C. Codman, a new jewelry department was established at the Rhode Island School of Design, with evening classes that began in November 1903. Charles E. Hansen directed it while maintaining his position as foreman jeweler at Gorham. The school's metalwork classes were also held in the evening,

The "Chasing Room" at the Gorham Manufacturing Company, 1892. As reproduced in *Views, Exterior and Interior of the Gorham Manufacturing Company Silversmiths* (Providence: Gorham Manufacturing Company, 1892)

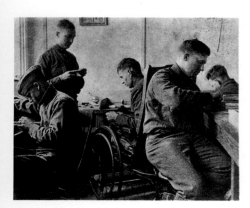

Handicapped men working on jewelry at the Department of Occupational Therapy, Reconstruction Division, Walter Reed Hospital, Washington, D.C., 1919. From *The Jewelers' Circular* (April 9, 1919)

"intended for artists and artisans connected with the different industries."[10] In 1903, the Pennsylvania Museum School of Industrial Art, in Philadelphia, offered metalwork classes with Karl G. Nacke, and the Art Institute of Chicago introduced a metalwork course taught by W. T. Meyer.[11] By 1910, additional art schools offered metalwork classes.[12]

American publications also provided instruction for metalsmithing and jewelrymaking. Periodicals led the way; they presented amateur projects submitted by metalworkers, jewelers, and enamelers, and published responses to readers' questions on technical problems.[13] Periodicals devoted to art and the home, as well as trade journals, illustrated the work of native and foreign craftsmen and reported on traveling exhibitions, awards, school activities, and summer classes.[14] Augustus F. Rose's *Copper Work*, of 1906 (which was in its eighth printing by 1931), was the most influential American text on art metal, jewelry, and enamels. Important among later works was Arthur F. Payne's *Art Metalwork with Inexpensive Equipment* (1914).[15]

Summer schools provided opportunities for specialized training and the instruction of elementary-school teachers interested in establishing art-metal classes. Precedents for elementary-school metalsmithing classes go back to the 1880s with the manual-training movement led by Charles G. Leland, whose crusade to ally arts teaching with manual training included basic hammering and repoussé techniques that were actually taught to Philadelphia schoolchildren in the 1880s.[16] The first Arts and Crafts summer schools, established about 1903 in New York State, included art-metal classes.[17] As the decade progressed, others followed in the East and Midwest, so that by 1911, alternative summer instruction in metals and jewelry was available through-out the country.[18] By about 1915, grade schools across the nation had teachers trained and equipped to teach a generation primary metalwork techniques. Much of the unsigned metalwork that survives from the period was probably made in these classes. The promotion of metalwork and jewelrymaking as beneficial occupational therapy for handicapped veterans of World War I also heightened amateur interest in these crafts.[19]

Leading artists working in metal, jewelry, and enamel routinely took on apprentices and offered private instruction in their studios. In 1904, Chicago socialite Frances McBeth Glessner began lessons with Madeline Yale Wynne. The same year, Laurin H. Martin began teaching enameling; his pupils eventually included such distinguished achievers in the field as Elizabeth E. Copeland, Douglas Donaldson, and Mildred G. Watkins. From 1905, an important group associated with Boston's Society of Arts and Crafts taught and practiced various phases of metalwork and enameling in a cooperative arrangement at 79 Chestnut Street.[20] Grace Hazen offered instruction in jewelry from her studio at the National Arts Club, in New York, and at East Gloucester, Massachusetts, by 1909, as well as at the Detroit Society of Arts and Crafts. George C. Gebelein taught silversmithing to Mildred G. Watkins, Sybil Foster, and Katherine Pratt; the latter two had completed studies in design at the School of the Museum of Fine Arts, Boston, and became his pupils under scholarships from the Women's Educational Industrial Union of Boston.[21]

By the middle of the first decade of the twentieth century, Arts and Crafts societies had been organized from coast to coast and played a crucial role in supporting metalcrafts. Some, such as the Society of Arts and Crafts, Boston, maintained comprehensive libraries for craftsmen to consult.[22] Craft organizations helped set quality standards by utilizing jury systems. *International Studio* reported that entries for an Arts and Crafts exhibition, held in

Examples of hammered copper work by
students at Pratt Institute, 1910.
From *The Jewelers' Circular* (December 21, 1910)

1902 by the St. Louis Wednesday Club, were "passed upon by a severe jury," and noted that "one of the most important of the exhibits and by far the most popular was that of the jewelry and metalwork."[23] The Society of Arts and Crafts, Boston, which emerged as the leading crafts organization following the Louisiana Purchase International Exposition, in 1904, in St. Louis—where its members took more than half the prizes—had a rigorous process of jury review that scrutinized the work metalsmiths and jewelers submitted for exhibition and consignment. Some individuals thought that the society's jury was too restrictive, such as art critic Frederick W. Coburn, who wrote, "To accept and readapt is safe and sane. . . . Serious work passes the jury. Of exuberance and jollity of design and execution, very little."[24] The society also had a ranking system in which its members advanced to master craftsman from craftsman only after meeting certain standards.

Craft organizations also established awards to recognize skill and achievement. In 1913, the Society of Arts and Crafts, Boston, instituted its Medalist award, given annually to no more than three craftsmen. Of the twenty craftsmen so honored through 1920, fourteen were metalworkers or jewelers.[25] In 1916, the National Arts Club awarded Grace Hazen a life membership for proficiency in jewelry.[26] Craft organizations also facilitated the cooperative interaction of designers, craftsmen, and patrons. The Society of Arts and Crafts, Boston, sought commissions for trophies and commemorative pieces from its noncraftsmen associate members and others, and provided designs, usually from member architects, to be executed by member silversmiths.[27]

Perhaps the most important function of these organizations was the promotion and marketing of work through exhibition and display. From 1900, annual exhibitions of the Architectural League of New York included some Arts and Crafts metalwork, especially in iron and bronze.[28] The National Arts

Metalwork in the 13th Annual Arts and Crafts Exhibition, The Art Institute of Chicago, October 1–23, 1913

Club organized a large exhibition of old and new jewelry in 1903. Its affiliate organization, the National Society of Craftsmen, founded in 1906, stated that one of its purposes was "to promote the creation and sale of products of the arts and crafts."[29] The society's annual exhibitions, the second of which, in 1907, included a particularly comprehensive display of metalwork and jewelry, were held at the club and represented work ranging from well-known professional craftsmen to Native Americans of the Southwest and students from Pratt Institute and the New York Evening School.[30] The Society of Arts and Crafts, Boston, opened its salesroom in 1901, and sale of work by the society's silversmiths and jewelers from 1907 into the Depression typically comprised over half of its receipts.[31] The Minneapolis Handicraft Guild was among those organizations in which amateur metalwork done in classes was available in a salesroom. By the second decade, exhibitions were even originating from the West Coast, notably the 1916 "California Exhibition of Applied Arts," of the Los Angeles Society of Arts and Crafts Club, which traveled to the Society of Arts and Crafts, Boston, and the National Arts Club.[32] Within the largest craft organizations, guilds were formed for specific aspects of metalsmithing and they routinely organized metalwork and jewelry exhibitions.[33]

In addition to craft organizations, international expositions and museums also supported the display of Arts and Crafts metalwork, jewelry, and enamels. A noteworthy display of work at the 1901 Pan-American Exposition was followed by an important early showing of artistic handwrought metalware, jewelry, and enamels at the 1904 Louisiana Purchase International Exposition, where many prizes went to Americans. The earliest museum exhibition of Arts and Crafts metalwork was in 1900, when the Chicago Arts and Crafts Society held its third exhibition, at the Art Institute of Chicago. The Art Institute began its own annual Arts and Crafts exhibitions two years later, and was followed by the Detroit Museum of Art in 1904.[34] Later, the Museum of Fine Arts, Boston, the Newark Museum, and the National Museum, Washington, D.C., held Arts and Crafts exhibitions.[35] By 1917, however, when the Metropolitan Museum of Art, in New York, implemented a policy to educate designers, craftsmen, and manufacturers with annual exhibitions, the first such, "Exhibition of Work by Manufacturers and Designers," with its shift in emphasis from studio makers of metalware and jewelry to manufacturers of metalware and jewelry, signaled that a new generation of arts leaders was more interested in the challenge of bringing art to industrial production than in labor reform and the promotion of preindustrial craft practices.

Museums also played an important role by displaying metalware from the preindustrial past, especially early-American silver, that provided models for contemporary Arts and Crafts metalsmiths.[36] Arts organizations also routinely showed historical metalwork—for example, the National Society of Craftsmen, whose exhibitions were comparative, "by placing in juxtaposition with modern work loan exhibits of medieval and foreign handicraft."[37] The Rhode Island School of Design's metalwork loan exhibition, in 1901, held in conjunction with its first art-metal classes, included old and exotic metalware borrowed from the notable collector Alexander W. Drake.[38]

Most skilled makers of handwrought art metalware worked in silver and, to a small extent, copper. Because of its high cost, gold rarely was used, other than for jewelry or occasional ecclesiastical and presentation commissions. Factory-trained silversmiths—many of whom were immigrants—established some of the first shops. They sought spiritual rewards in an environment in which they were responsible for the product through every stage of its development, as opposed to the dehumanizing factory or piecework system. The English émigré silversmith Arthur J. Stone, who ended his association with the manufacturing world of silver at fifty-four, established one of the first silversmithing shops of the craft revival, in Gardner, Massachusetts, in 1901. Boston's Handicraft Shop, established the same year, was managed by veterans of the silver factories. They produced modest, utilitarian forms in a cooperative teaching and working arrangement wherein the skills of male silversmiths were allied with the academic designer training of Mary C. Knight. In February 1908, Frederick W. Coburn, in reference to metalworkers, reported that "Tiffany and the Gorham [Manufacturing Company] have yielded to the arts and crafts movement a small but influential contingent of skilled designers who know the modern and ancient practices of their craft, and who are outside the big commercial establishments solely because they prefer to produce under individualistic conditions which do not exist there."[39]

Ohio had a significant number of artists who worked in silver and other metals, jewelry, and enamels in the very first years of the twentieth century. Work by Dayton financier Brainerd B. Thresher was influenced by international Art Nouveau artist Edward Colonna and, from 1902, it received wide acclaim. Best known of the Cleveland group was Horace E. Potter, a teacher of design, from 1900, at the Cleveland School of Art. In 1908, he returned from training in London at C. R. Ashbee's Guild and School of Handicraft to found the Potter Studio. Other Cleveland artisans working in the first years of the twentieth century included Jane Carson Barron, Frances Barnum Smith, Mildred G. Watkins, Wilhelmina P. Stephan, and the Rokesley Shop, founded by Carolyn Hadlow Vinson, Mary Blakeslee, and Ruth Smedley.

Chicago, along with Boston and Cleveland, was a major center of metalsmithing activity and drew a number of émigré silversmiths, especially of Scandinavian heritage. From about 1905, the Kalo Shop, founded by Clara Barck Welles, in 1900, made art metalware, and it continued to thrive as the city's leading silverware producer for more than three generations. Robert R. Jarvie, who began his metalsmithing career as a recreation from his job as a clerk in Chicago's city government, established his shop in 1904, and from about 1910 he produced major trophies and presentation commissions.

Beginning in the last years of the first decade of the century, new silversmiths' shops were established. Some were founded by craftsmen who had lost their factory jobs in the financial panic of 1907. Clemens Friedell, who was among the many silversmiths laid off at the Gorham Manufacturing Company in 1908, moved to California the next year and established a workshop, in Pasadena, where wealthy midwestern and eastern families seeking a winter retreat gave him years of patronage. Other shops opened as spin-offs of the earliest ones. George C. Gebelein, with the financial support of his pupil David M. Little, left the Handicraft Shop in 1909 to open his own business. Boston silversmith James T. Woolley opened his shop in 1908, having been associated for a time in 1907 with George J. Hunt, whose shop opened in 1905. In 1909, George Porter Blanchard left the establishment of Arthur Stone, and with his children, Porter, Richard, and Ida—all silversmiths—founded the Blanchards.[40] In Chicago, enterprises founded by former Kalo Shop employees included the TC Shop, of Emery W. Todd (and associate Clemencia Cosio); the Randahl Shop, of Swedish émigré Julius O. Randahl; the shop of Russian-born Falick Novick; and the Volund Shop, of Norwegian émigré Kristopher Haga and Grant Wood. From the Jarvie Shop came yet another Norwegian émigré, silversmith John P. Petterson, who opened a business in 1912.

Directories and exhibition catalogues from the period readily identify silversmiths located elsewhere across the nation, mostly in cities but occasionally in small towns. More work from these artists, especially those in New York, Philadelphia, and Minneapolis, eventually will come to light. Baltimore,

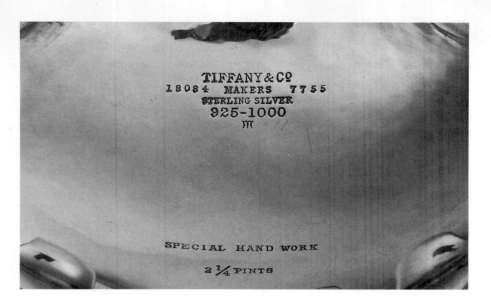

"Special Hand Work," Tiffany & Company mark, c. 1915

an early center for silversmithing, was the location of some notable activity because of the work of Carl Schon, who fashioned marine life into electroplated silverware and jewelry, as well as Theodore H. Pond, who taught and made silver there, in his Pond Applied Art Studios, from 1911 to 1914, while creating and heading a department of applied design at the Maryland Institute.[41] On the West Coast at the turn of the century, Shreve and Company, of San Francisco, began producing a line of silverware that suggested hand-wrought and preindustrial metalwork through applied ornamentation evoking medieval hardware. Important silverware was also made in Los Angeles by Douglas Donaldson, who, from 1919, taught metalwork, jewelry, enameling, and decorative design at the Otis Art Institute.

After 1910, art metalware began to appeal to a greater patronage, and the demand for silver evidencing handwork captured the competitive interest of large manufacturers. Most responded by treating stock, machine-produced designs with a hammer-faceted texture. In about 1914, Tiffany & Company began limited production of a high-quality line of silverware, marked "Special Hand Work," that shared the substantial weight and shimmering surface of work by studio silversmiths. In a mixture of pride of craftsmanship, exclusivity, and defense against less expensive imitations, many makers of art silver—particularly in Chicago—marked their work "Hand Wrought."

Jewelry was among the most popular pursuits of the Arts and Crafts movement. Most jewelers took the lead of C. R. Ashbee, who, deploring the use of jewelry to display wealth, sought to revitalize it as an art. Faceted stones were eschewed for cabochons. Color became of paramount importance, with pearls and shell favored for their iridescence and opals prized for their intrinsic fire. Glass and even pebbles were used. The texture and color of these materials were played off against the muted finishes of the metal settings—typically, oxidized silver, but also gold, copper, and brass, sometimes in combination with enamel—the whole often arranged to convey a narrative. Some jewelers, such as Madeline Yale Wynne and Grace Hazen, followed the fine-arts practice of naming their creations. These women, along with Brainerd B. Thresher, Florence D. Koehler, Elinor E. (Mrs. William H.) Klapp, and Ednah S. Girvan (Mrs. Augustus B. Higginson), were among the pioneer jewelry practitioners. Boston claimed the most distinguished corps of studio jewelers, including Josephine Hartwell Shaw, Frank Gardner Hale, Margaret Rogers, Edward E. Oakes, and Florence A. Richmond.[42] Based in Chicago, James H. Winn taught widely around the country and, in 1913, received unusual recognition when jewelry by him and by Louis Comfort

Tiffany was voted best in the United States.[43] Other leading jewelers were Ida Pell Conklin, Lila Whitcomb Davis, husband and wife Eda Lord Dixon and Lawrence B. Dixon, Jessie Ames Dunbar, Millicent Strange Edson, Herbert Kelly, and the Elverhoj Colony, led by A. H. Anderson.

The use of enameling to decorate small tableware, especially boxes, sometimes in conjunction with semiprecious stones, was an important artistic contribution of the Arts and Crafts movement. Before 1900, Louis Comfort Tiffany employed a group of women, supervised by Julia Munson Sherman, to produce enameled metalware; their work was shown at the Paris Exposition of 1900.[44] Elizabeth E. Copeland and Douglas Donaldson achieved high artistic success in enameling. Other important enamelists included Jane Carson Barron, Frank Gardner Hale, Mabel Wilcox Luther, Frank J. Marshall, Horace E. Potter, Wilhelmina P. Stephan, and Mildred G. Watkins, in addition to Laurin H. Martin and Edmund B. Rolfe, influential instructors in this craft.[45]

Most art metalware was made of nonprecious metals, principally copper and brass. Copper, the first choice of amateurs and professional metalworkers, combined superior working properties for patination and enameling with low cost. The Busck Studio, of New York City, was among the earliest producers of distinctive art copperware.[46] Commercial shops, such as the Art Crafts Shop, in Buffalo (succeeded by the Heintz Art Metal Shop), the Forest Craft Guild, in Grand Rapids, and Frost Art Metal Shops, in Dayton, produced a large output of readily affordable wares in copper and brass. Electrified light fixtures were of special interest to metal artists of the period as vehicles for the combined effects of color and iridescence, and patination. Outstanding examples are those by Leonide Cecilia Lavaron, of Chicago, and Elizabeth Eaton Burton, of Santa Barbara, who both used translucent shells over the light source, and Dirk Van Erp, of San Francisco, who used mica. In the following decade, Marie Zimmermann, of New York, received publicity for her patinated metalware inspired by Far Eastern and other historic examples. Large-scale production of base metalware began about 1905 with the Craftsman Workshops of Gustav Stickley, followed by the Roycrofters, in a shop led by Karl Kipp, in 1909.

In the craft revival, bronze, iron, pewter, and occasionally lead were seen. Among early art metalware were those in cast bronze. Examples by Louis Comfort Tiffany, of New York, are well known, but the work of Charles H. Barr, of East Greenwich, Rhode Island, was also widely exhibited and published in the period.[47] Tiffany influenced Robert R. Jarvie's early, noteworthy candlestick designs, many of which were in bronze. Jessie Preston was another Chicagoan who made candlesticks and other ware in bronze. Artwork in lead from the period is seldom seen; however, Janet Payne Bowles, of Indianapolis, made a lead box, probably the box that won her a medal in 1915 at the Panama-Pacific International Exposition. Pewter became popular with the Colonial revival prior to 1920, and fine examples based on early-American work were made by Lester Vaughan, of Taunton, Massachusetts. A number of ironworkers who made small-scale portable works received attention, such as Thomas F. Googerty, of Pontiac, Illinois, and Cyril Colnik, of Milwaukee, but distinguished achievement in forged iron, particularly for architectural commissions, was led by Frederick Krasser and Frank L. Koralewsky, of Boston, and Samuel Yellin, of Philadelphia.[48]

The work of studio metalsmiths and jewelers would not have been possible without affluent patrons committed to the support of Arts and Crafts movement ideals.[49] Some provided financial backing for shops, such as Arthur A. Carey and his support of Boston's Handicraft Shop.[50] Patrons sometimes aided individual craftsmen, such as Sarah Choate Sears, the patron of Elizabeth E. Copeland, and David M. Little, the financial backer of George

C. Gebelein. Silversmiths regularly received commissions for births, marriages, and wedding anniversaries, as well as prestigious commemorative commissions for achievement and service awarded by private clubs, academic institutions, and businesses. Some silversmiths specialized in ecclesiastical commissions, among them, Helen Keeling Mills and George E. Germer.[51] Important patrons of studio silversmiths included Julia Marlowe Sothern, George G. Booth, and Francis P. Garvan.[52] Nevertheless, the most productive and successful years for pioneer metal and jewelry craftsmen who opened shops at the turn of the century came with the boom economy of the late 1920s.

At the beginning of the century, few people were both designing and fabricating metalware, enamels, or jewelry, but within the short span of a decade, individuals across the nation unified these skills in a renaissance of preindustrial craft activity. This phenomenon resulted from the impact of English reform ideas in design and labor practices upon a diverse range of society—from affluent members who took up art-metal crafts as protest against the vulgarity of manufactured goods to immigrant master silversmiths who eschewed the factory labor system to open shops of their own, to teachers inspired to avail children and impoverished immigrants of the spiritual and regenerative rewards found in art metalwork. Their work is typically valued now, as it was then, for its human, as opposed to machine, imprint. Women as well as men pursued art metalwork, and they comprised the majority of the new breed of studio jewelers and enamelists. In the movement to ally artist with artisan, a generation not only practiced these crafts but promoted their dissemination and ensured their perpetuation. Training, as developed for apprentices in small shops, conducted in school classes, and advanced through exhibitions of Arts and Crafts societies and museums, laid the foundation for formal educational programs on the craft of metal and the related crafts of jewelry and enamels as they continue today.

Arts and Crafts Furniture: Process or Product?

by Edward S. Cooke, Jr.

In the past decade, Arts and Crafts furniture has attracted considerable popular and scholarly attention. Spurred on by the path-breaking 1972 exhibition at the Princeton University Art Museum, "The Arts and Crafts Movement in America, 1876–1916," scholars have sought to examine the output and influence of various firms; dealers and auction houses have sought to develop a strong market; and collectors have passionately purchased "simple, honest" work. The thrust of this synergy has been a preoccupation with the identification of makers and a hierarchical ranking of these makers. The understanding of furniture produced between 1900 and 1920 seems to be based upon two assumptions: an obsession with moral aesthetics, such as honest craftsmanship, regional vernacular style, or international reform styles, as well as a belief that, during the period, there was a declension from pure high-minded philosophy to crass commercialism. Even recent writings have tended simply to increase the number of styles under the Arts and Crafts umbrella, to identify additional examples of regional work, or to chart the specific demise of the ideal. Such an emphasis has been derived from an uncritical use of the voluminous writings of the period.[1]

The literature of the American Arts and Crafts movement emphasizes that there was a single, politically correct sort of artistic production, one that was described as "handcrafted." In the early twentieth century, the meaning of this word combined intent—new design, sensitive use of local materials according to local vernacular traditions—and performance—those noble, honest construction practices thought to have been followed in preindustrial craft shops. Such a linking tended to blur distinctions between various steps of design and workmanship and precluded a popular understanding of the vast, complex choices faced by furnituremakers of all sizes and foci. This blending ensured the ultimate desired result: the unity of design and workmanship and the joy of workmanship. The inclusiveness of the term *handcrafted* has continued to affect popular perceptions about Arts and Crafts furniture. Current writers continue to focus only on the virtues of crafted objects. To date, there has been no attempt to step outside the period rhetoric and analyze furniture design and fabrication more closely, with particular attention to design, workmanship, and context.[2]

Essential to a new approach is a reconsideration of the term handcrafted. It is not so much a technical term that describes an unchanging, specific set of materials, tools, methods of work, and construction conventions but, rather, a malleable social and technical term that had a time-specific meaning. As such, it reveals more about the values of the time period in which it was used than about the actions on the shop floor. Furnituremakers first used the term in the 1880s. Smaller, custom shops in the older East Coast cities, such as Baltimore or Boston, employed the term in their advertising to distinguish themselves from larger manufactories. Even though these small firms used the latest appropriate machinery, particularly in the preparation of materials and joints, they emphasized their technical ties to older, traditional sorts of work. Stylistically, these small shops tended to favor revival forms and decoration.[3] In their appropriation of "handcrafted," these furnituremakers were responding to a new consumerism that arose in the third quarter of the nineteenth century. Larger firms churned out great quantities of furniture in a variety of styles, thereby forging a new, widespread consumerism that placed more value on quantities of goods with densely packed meanings than on coherent taste. Handcrafted furniture, which tended to be relatively expensive, was intended for an emerging group of consumers who sought to distinguish themselves and their social identity through superior aesthetic vision. Preindustrial techniques and styles were one means of establishing an artistic balance to the banalities of excess.[4]

The philosophy of the Arts and Crafts movement merely provided a broader context in which the existing notion of handcraftsmanship could flourish. It could be used not only in an exclusive manner to distinguish a class with taste but also in an inclusive sense to socialize and elevate the greater population. During a period of intense interest in various aspects of reform, handcraftsmanship became an integral tool to justify the dignified pursuit of domestic goods.[5] Although used in a homogeneous fashion to evoke a whole range of interconnected qualities, the term was appropriated in a variety of ways that affected both production and purchasing. Some furnituremakers focused upon the technical aspects of the term, some on the design implications, and some on the marketing power. In essence, the term was given new meaning by the aesthetic philosophers and academicians of the period, and then overlaid onto the existing capitalist modes of production.

Examination of the furniture made in the first two decades of this century leads not so much to a discussion of handmade versus machine-made but, rather, to issues regarding control of design and workmanship. During this time, there was a range of different responses to joy in labor and design unity. At one end of the spectrum were those who placed the greatest emphasis on the process of integrated design and work. The ability of an individual to conceive and execute a piece of furniture gave that person a significant sense of accomplishment and purpose while bestowing on the finished product both moral and aesthetic integrity. It was the making of an object rather than the design or the final product that was important. At the other end were those who stressed the final product and maintained absolute control over those who did the work. In this case, the designer believed that his or her ideas would bring joy to the maker and consumer who lacked sophisticated aesthetic knowledge. For these designers, it was the overall scheme, the unified look of the product, that was essential.

The moral importance of the craft process, first stressed by John Ruskin, was embraced predominantly by intellectuals and academics who had little actual experience on the shop floor. Through writings, Arts and Crafts organizations and clubs, and lectures, such activists as Oscar Lovell Triggs, Charles Eliot Norton, Benn Pitman, Irene Sargent, and Louis Millet inspired many to take an interest in the applied arts and to undertake their own craft work. Craft work proved particularly alluring to women, well-educated elites, and the increasing number of white-collar workers.[6]

During the Aesthetic movement of the 1870s and 1880s, designers and academics recognized and exploited the aesthetic talents of women as carvers, china painters, and binders. At this time, however, few women actually prepared the wood and joined the furniture; their task was to decorate the pieces made by male craftsmen. Under the aegis of the Arts and Crafts movement, women such as Madeline Yale Wynne undertook complete control of their products, from design to fabrication, to decoration, to marketing. Heir to the Yale Lock fortune, and a painter who had studied in Boston and New York, Wynne had the wealth, the time, the exposure to aesthetic concerns, and the inclination to experiment in a number of media, including jewelry, leatherwork, needlework, and furniture. In the 1870s, she purchased a summer home in Deerfield, Massachusetts, where she set up a metal and painting studio. She also engaged in other antiquarian and craft pursuits, helping to establish the Deerfield Society of Blue and White Needlework and the Deerfield Society of Arts and Crafts. In 1893, Wynne established a winter residence in Chicago, where she opened a studio in 1896 and became a founding member of the Chicago Arts and Crafts Society in 1897.

In the early twentieth century, Wynne made several bridal chests, inspired by a Hadley chest she had seen in Deerfield. Her chest for Bertha Bullock, who married William R. Folson, in 1900, exemplifies the work of visionaries who followed the philosophy of Ruskin. Drawing inspiration from an American vernacular form, Wynne retained the visible mortise-and-tenon construction, updated the decoration with abstract motifs on the front and side panels, left consciously evident gouge marks in the carved areas and hammer marks on the ironwork, and painted a beautiful landscape on the inside of the lid. The tactile quality of the carved wood and forged iron and the rich blues and greens of the painted decoration bespeak the personal joy and artistic success possible when a single craftsperson undertakes the complete task. Like many other women, though, Wynne only dabbled in furnituremaking for a short time. In Chicago, women made furniture in the period between 1895 and 1903; after that, they turned to smaller, often costly goods, such as jewelry, needlework, and leatherwork.[7]

Well-to-do individuals who had been exposed to the intellectuals' calls for a simple life, in which making objects provided personal satisfaction, moral uplift, and community betterment, also devoted themselves to an obsession with craftsmanship. Harvard-educated Charles Lummis settled in Pasadena, California, where he studied, lectured about, and lived the simple life of the Southwest frontier. For his own thirteen-room home, inspired by the vernacular Mission style, Lummis relied on the labor of young Native American boys from New Mexico, general visitors, and artist friends such as Maynard Dixon. This organic approach to building resulted in more than twenty years of construction. While he furnished some of the house with factory-made Mission furniture, Lummis produced much of the woodwork himself on-site. The cupboard in the dining room features doors with lightninglike splats, purported to have been made by an eighteenth-century New Mexican *carpintero* for an *alacena*, or wall cabinet. Lummis incorporated these elements in a built-in door-and-drawer unit that featured "hand-wrought" surfaces typified by visible adz and gouge marks, lines that were not quite straight, and personal or abstracted decoration based upon historical examples.[8]

Other prominent figures sought to establish utopian communities in which noble craftwork played a part. Raymond Pitcairn, son of the founder of the Pittsburgh Plate Glass Company, was a well-known, knowledgeable collector of medieval art and architectural elements. When planning the new Swedenborgian community of Bryn Athyn, Pennsylvania, Pitcairn drew upon his knowledge of medieval craft and the advice of such scholars as William Goodyear, Ralph Adams Cram, and Arthur Kingsley Porter to set up craft guilds. These guilds of skilled craftsmen ensured that the central cathedral and other important buildings evolved organically on-site, the basic plan constantly subjected to revision and changes according to the eye of the participating craftsmen. Frank Jeck, a Czechoslovakian woodworker who worked on part of the cathedral, also made furniture for the Pitcairn family. Instead of sawing or riving out and then planing the framing members of the family crib, Jeck consciously shaped the parts with an adz, a historically inappropriate technology that satisfied the contemporary interest in surface and formal variation. Jeck was a skilled craftsman who adjusted his skills to produce a desired aesthetic that had its rationale in the writings of the academic medievalists of the period. The craftsmanship worked in conjunction with the design process and the motifs to elevate the lives of the maker, the Pitcairns, and the rest of the Swedenborgian community.[9]

Ralph Radcliffe Whitehead, heir of a British industrialist, was a student and friend of Ruskin who established the Arts and Crafts community of Byrdcliffe Colony, in Woodstock, New York, in 1902. In determining the artistic rationale and the physical plan, Whitehead relied on the advice of academics such as Bolton Brown, Hervey White, and Denman Ross. Recruiting a variety of designers and craftsmen, he set up a woodworking shop intended to provide essential satisfaction to members of the community and a marketable commodity to support the colony. Although Whitehead had apprenticed to a woodworker in Berlin, it is unclear how much actual cabinetmaking he did at Byrdcliffe; rather, it appears that he and Dawson Watson, a Canadian woodworker, provided most of the designs. Zulma Steele and Edna Walker, two graduates of Pratt Institute, also provided designs, derived from studies of nature, for decorative panels and framing members. Much of the construction work, however, was supervised by Fordyce Herrick, a local carpenter. Giovanni Trocholli, a professional carver and member of the Boston Society of Arts and Crafts, also performed some work in the Byrdcliffe shop. The intricate, time-consuming decoration and staining of the work, and the difficulty of getting the heavy, over-engineered forms to market, doomed the financial feasibility of the Byrdcliffe work. For example, a Byrdcliffe cabinet sold for $160, while the most expensive piece of furniture made by L. and J. G. Stickley had a price of $62. Like much of the other work made at Byrdcliffe, the furniture was conceived and executed with great passion and aesthetic care, but, ultimately, it was supported solely by Whitehead's fortune and elevated the lives of the members of the immediate community. The fertilization of high-minded artistic ideas was paramount, while the actual production, pricing, and marketing was deemed less important. As a result, the woodworking shop operated for a mere two years, the great majority of its products unsold.[10]

The Philadelphia architect Will Price was another individual who

Will Price. Pair of Side chairs. 1901–6. Made by the Rose Valley Shops. Oak, 36$^1/_2$ × 13 × 18″. Collection Museum of Fine Arts, Boston. Frank B. Bemis Fund

Joseph McHugh. Side chair. 1894–
c. 1920. Oak with rush seat,
36 × 17 × 17³/4″. Collection Robert
Edwards

sought to establish an experimental Arts and Crafts community based upon the period notion of craftsmanship. At Rose Valley, Price set up a small shop with no more than five cabinetmakers, who made one-of-a-kind pieces of furniture designed by Price. The architect strictly adhered to the philosophy of constructional reformers; he favored heavy, medieval forms of oak with elaborate carving. In spite of his plans to market the work in nearby Philadelphia, Price's uncompromising commitment to handcraftsmanship proved fatal to the shop, which was open only from 1901 to 1906: His insistence on handwork made the final products prohibitively expensive; it proved difficult to recruit skilled craftsmen, even immigrants, to perform the work according to his designs; and the time necessary to design and oversee one-of-a-kind furniture allowed less time for his architectural practice.[11]

While much of the true, philosophically guided furnituremaking had failed by 1906, intellectual and academic interest in the importance of craftsmanship did lead to its integral role in design schools as well as manual-arts programs. Schools such as the Pennsylvania Museum School of Industrial Art and the California College of Arts and Crafts exposed their students to the principles of two- and three-dimensional design, the historical styles, the importance of drawing ideas from nature, and the need for a thorough understanding of materials and processes. The placement, however, of craft education within the academy rather than in apprenticeship had a greater effect on design than on production. The schools were intended primarily to provide a more knowledgeable group of designers for industry and teachers of industrial arts. The training of talented craftspeople was a secondary goal. Nevertheless, some talented craftspeople did learn their craft in this manner. Opportunities for women were formalized, even though few became full-time professionals. Marjory Wheelock, for example, was a talented student at the California College of Arts and Crafts who made a set of furniture for exhibition at the Panama-Pacific International Exposition, in 1915. Her work manifests an understanding of the appropriate use of materials and decoration, yet she did not remain a furnituremaker. Instead, she married her classmate, the metalworker Harry St. John Dixon, and worked for him.[12]

The emphasis on process also appealed to the white-collar class, who sought to balance the mental activity of office work with the physical activity of manual labor in its leisure time. This segment of the population provided a number of eager amateurs who believed that making their own furniture would restore a feeling of wholeness. With the wider availability of woodworking tools and domestic-scale power tools and the growing do-it-yourself literature, hobbyists could benefit from both making the furniture and using it in a modern, moralistic home. For them, it was not inconsistent with Arts and Crafts philosophy to work according to readily available designs; their main interest lay in the process of using tools to make something useful.[13]

The intellectual leaders and the devoted amateurs criticized many of the products made and distributed by furnituremaking firms. Among the shortcomings that Will Price addressed were the indiscriminate use of inferior wood or excessively dimensioned stock; the use of improper construction techniques, such as doweled joints, applied wedged-through tenons, butterfly splines, unnecessary laminations, and mixed construction; and the deliberate avoidance of carving and shaping. Although faulted for their misappropriation of the reform philosophy, many firms embraced the new English and European designs as an ideal opportunity. The style was avant-garde, yet could be adapted easily to the existing cost-efficient processes and machinery.[14]

For many furnituremakers in the United States, the Arts and Crafts line was less a personal, moral stance than an attempt to set or lead trends in an increasingly competitive market. Eschewing some machinery, such as the lathe and carving machines, they used table saws, band saws, planers, mortising or doweling machines, shapers, and rotary dovetail cutters in combination with handworked detailing and finish so that they could offer well-made, affordable work in the latest style. The furniture trade proudly pointed out that the "vast American factory, with its elaborate sub-division of labor, its specialization of skill, the substitution of mechanical for hand labor wherever possible, and the great output, not only materially cheapens the cost of fine furniture, but also lends itself to a superior style of internal as well as external finish in the medium and better grades. In design, material, construction and finish it excels the so-called hand-made furniture."[15]

In short, the professionals were not romantic technological determinists. They recognized the inherent benefits of well-designed, highly regulated workmanship and were not taken by the emotional attraction of rough workmanship for its own sake.[16] They argued that a high degree of perfection was possible in the finest factory-made furniture, and therefore disagreed with the "professional decorators and dilettante writers" who deplored the lack of "true artistic merit and workmanship" found in machine-made furniture.[17] These critics notwithstanding, the trade did achieve considerable success, as a 1901 review in *The International Studio* points out: "From a purely craftsman point of view, the Mission furniture has an excellent quality which is the outcome of good workmanship. The joints and dovetailing are excellently finished, the material treated *as if* the worker took a delight in handling it, and the articles look *as if* they begged to be used for the several purposes for which they were intended [emphasis added]."[18]

Joseph P. McHugh, head of the firm that apparently offered the first Mission line of furniture, was initially an interior decorator whose Popular Shop began to import Liberty of London furnishings in 1882. Soon thereafter, he set up his own furniture manufactory and produced his first slat-back, rush-seated Mission chairs, for the Swedenborgian Church of the New Jerusalem, in San Francisco. Through his imports, annual buying trips, or periodicals, McHugh had become familiar with English Arts and Crafts designers, particularly M. H. Baillie-Scott and C.F.A. Voysey, and had developed a whole line of Mission furniture, ranging from golf clubs or log holders to bureaus and china cabinets. McHugh already produced a number of these forms in several other styles, but missionized them by adding cross braces, keyed tenons, and swelled spade feet. After a successful exhibition of this line at the 1901 Pan-American Exposition, in Buffalo, the company concentrated on the style for the next three years. Nevertheless, the severe rectilinear was simply one style among many in the McHugh repertoire.[19]

Gustav Stickley, a furnituremaker with considerable experience in the industry, was another craftsman greatly inspired by a trip to England in the late 1890s. Influenced by the English designers, as well as such American designers as McHugh and George Clingman, of the Tobey Furniture Company, in Chicago, Stickley developed a Mission line of furniture for the 1900 Grand Rapids Furniture Exposition. Stickley was not interested in handwork for its own sake but, rather, in producing furniture in the latest style and marketing it aggressively within the existing channels. His Syracuse, New York, firm used readily available oak, doweling or mortising machines for carcass construction, rotary-cutting dovetailing machines for drawer dovetails, and hammered sheet or cast hardware. The finished product featured machine construction with detailing and hand-finishing designed to evoke craftsmanship. To reach an upper-class market, Stickley even employed the architect Harvey Ellis to design several pieces of furniture with elaborate inlaid decoration. Although these inlay examples were never produced in

Stickley Brothers Company. Hall chair. c. 1905–10. Oak, walnut, tulipwood, and beech, 44 1/8 × 13 1/4 × 16″. Collection Los Angeles County Museum of Art. Gift of Max Palevsky and Jodie Evans

quantity, some of Ellis's efforts to lighten the lines of the structural members became a part of the standard Stickley production. Stickley even sought to enlarge the market by the publication of a monthly, *The Craftsman*, and the addition of metalworking, leatherworking, and building businesses. Stickley's company thus became a classic, horizontally integrated American company of the early twentieth century, although he overextended in 1915 and eventually went bankrupt.[20]

Stickley's brothers demonstrated a similar commitment to integrating the reform aesthetics into existing trade practices. Stickley Brothers, a firm in Grand Rapids headed by Albert Stickley, offered work distinguished by sophisticated progressive designs similar to English work and by inlay derived from Austrian Secessionist designs and Japanese woodblocks. The English-trained designers Arthur E. Teal and D. Robertson Smith and the inlay and marquetry specialist Timothy A. Conti allowed the firm to take a leading role in the American furniture field. Stickley Brothers produced both common and quality examples of the reform styles, yet throughout made use of the latest techniques and processes: doweled joints, peeled veneers in noncrucial or nonvisible areas, and plywood drawer bottoms.[21]

The Limbert Company, based in nearby Holland, Michigan, employed similar technology with attention to detail and finish, but favored a more Viennese style, possibly because of the influence of the designer William S. Gohlke. Charles Limbert, like Gustav Stickley and other reform furniture-makers, also recognized the interrelationship of rustic furniture with the "quaint" or "new American style"; the sophisticated merging of design and material provided a household with personality, sincerity, and morality. In the late nineteenth century, Limbert served as a sales representative for the Old Hickory Company, in Martinsville, Indiana. In spite of a rough, folklike appearance, the Old Hickory chair was produced in a modern factory: The posts were boiled and bent on patented metal frames; a machine cut the splint from hickory bark; women and children bottomed the seats; and the final products were sold throughout the nation.[22]

Firms at the high end of the furniture industry also adapted aesthetic principles of the reform style to the highly decorative "art furniture." As was the case in the middle range of producers, designers worked closely with specific craftsmen to develop distinctive responses. In San Francisco, the French-trained artist Arthur Mathews and his wife, Lucia, provided designs and supervised the painting and carving of suites of furniture and small accessories in a firm called the Furniture Shop. The Mathewses combined an academic interest in historical styles with a painterly decorative style that blended the tonality of Postimpressionism, the composition principles of Japanese woodcuts, and the light, colors, and vegetation of the Bay Area. The resulting mix was referred to as the California decorative style. The Mathewses and the skilled cabinetmakers who comprised the Furniture Shop produced a range of labor-intensive works for a wealthy area clientele. The products featured solid wood, extensive handwork in assembly, and intricate decoration. Unlike the Byrdcliffe work, the Furniture Shop's products could be marketed as custom, high-end furniture. Their decorative quality and apparent workmanship justified their price.[23]

In Pasadena, California, the architects Charles and Henry Greene relied on a mill-work firm, the Hall Manufacturing Company, to execute their designs. While the Greenes developed their own aesthetic sense, based upon local California materials and motifs, Asian imagery and details, and a fondness for the structural forms of Mission furnishings, they merely provided the overall design and truly collaborated on the final product with the Hall brothers. The Halls interpreted the designers' ideas in mahogany or teak,

Old Hickory Furniture Company. Chair. c. 1902–22. Bentwood.

Ernest Stowe. Sideboard. c. 1904.
Applied white birchbark and yellow birch
with watercolor scene, $78^3/_4 \times 52^3/_4 \times 26^3/_4''$.
Collection The Adirondack Museum

within a Scandinavian woodworking convention that relied on table-sawn joints of various sorts, preshaped parts that did not require later paring of joints, and slotted screw fastening to permit the expansion and contraction of the material. The furniture featured elaborate decoration, such as carving and inlay. When providing furniture and fittings for an entire house of their design, the Greenes used specific motifs or combinations to link the suite of furniture and its specific room context. The master-bedroom chiffonier from the Gamble House, of 1908, exemplifies this approach: The case is constructed with several table-saw joinery techniques, such as finger joints for the drawers; the softly modeled, stepped drawer pulls are derived from Chinese furniture; and the sword-guard appliqué and asymmetrical inlay are inspired by Japanese work. The latter details provided the visual link between the various forms of the room, including the dresser, writing desk, bedside table, beds, and chairs. Like the Furniture Shop, the collaboration between the Greenes and the Halls demonstrates a rich use of vernacular images and materials and an appeal to the reform language of craftsmanship to maintain an exclusive level of production, a different goal than that embraced by many other firms.[24]

Another designer of art furniture who employed some of the aesthetics and rhetoric of the Arts and Crafts movement was Charles Rohlfs, of Buffalo, New York. A former actor who turned to furnituremaking by 1890, Rohlfs headed a small shop of up to eight craftsmen that produced one-of-a-kind pieces as well as a few limited-production works. Rohlfs not only catered to wealthy clients but also aggressively showed his work at the 1901 Pan-American Exposition, in Buffalo, the 1902 International Exhibition of Modern Decorative Arts, in Turin, and the 1904 Louisiana Purchase International Exposition, in St. Louis. He evoked the structural style in his designs, but, in truth, the construction was simple. Boards for boxes and small chests were often held together with iron corner plates, while the boards on other case furniture were often simply butted and screwed together with protruding plugs decorating the surface. Although the joinery is straightforward but dressed up to look honest, the products of the Rohlfs shop demonstrate an emphasis on graphic design achieved through the effect of sawn profiles and carved ornament. Drawing inspiration from Art Nouveau, Moorish, Chinese, Norwegian, and a variety of other sources, Rohlfs believed that he demonstrated his "profound regard for a beautiful thing in nature" through embellishment consisting of "line, proportion, and carving." The results were a flamboyant use of simple oak construction.[25]

Yet another regional response at the high end of the spectrum is revealed in the work of Ernest Stowe, of Saranac Lake, New York. Stowe, a skilled woodworker with a knowledge of traditional furniture, responded to an upper-class demand for morally charged rustic furniture in the early twentieth century. Unlike the Old Hickory Company, which marketed the appearance of rustic style, Stowe worked by himself for a local clientele. Using local Adirondack materials in new ways to construct and decorate a variety of forms, including a sideboard, he internalized the rustic philosophy of the architects and designers active at that time in the Adirondacks.[26]

While the Greenes and the Mathewses employed designs that were derived from a synergy of two-dimensional design and principles of workmanship, other architects and designers imposed their ideas on the making of the work. Possessing little respect for the process, these professionals were more interested in controlling and justifying their ideas so that their vision of unity would be preserved. For these architects, furniture was but one piece in a larger scheme. As the Chicago architect Elmer Gray wrote, in 1907: "The architect must be at the head in all attempts to bring his work and that of craftsmen closer together. All such attempts should begin on the working basis of the cooperation of an architect's office with a practical (but not with a visionary) craftsman's shop."[27]

The ultimate importance of design control, and the resultant preference for pliant, efficient manufactories, is best seen in the work of the Prairie School, in Chicago. The little regard for structural or functional integrity, the ability to contract out work to a variety of firms, and the published justifications all point out the emphasis placed on the product rather than on the process. A chair with a V-shaped splat, designed by George Grant Elmslie and made by the Jean B. Hassewer Company, documents the architect's total concern with the graphic effect of the form. Poorly executed tenons along the rear stile and an inadequate miter joint on the front corner of the seat demonstrate that the strength of the joinery was compromised to achieve the desired effect of the horizontals and massing. Other Prairie School designs compromised notions of comfort and function with their unusual proportions and angular shapes and moldings. As Frank Lloyd Wright said, "I found it difficult . . . to make some of the furniture in the 'abstract.' That is, to design it as architecture and make it 'human' at the same time—fit for human use."[28]

Frank Lloyd Wright. Tall Slat-back chair.
c. 1903. One of three chairs for the
Dana House Dining Room. Oak,
original upholstery foundation, new
leather cover, $51 \times 17^7/8 \times 18^1/2''$.
Collection Dana House Museum,
Springfield, Illinois

George Grant Elmslie. Side chair. 1910–12.
Produced by Jean B. Hassewer
Company; from the Harold C. Bradley
House, Madison, Wisconsin.
Oak, $50 \times 20^3/8 \times 21^1/4''$.
Collection Sigma Phi Society, Alpha, Wisconsin

George Washington Maher. Rocking chair. c. 1912. Designed for *Rockledge,* Homer, Minnesota. Oak, leather, 37 × 27¹/₂ × 33¹/₂″. Collection Museum of Fine Arts, Boston. William E. Nickerson Fund

The drawing-based orientation is also borne out by the ability of architects to turn to various manufacturers. Wright, for example, had at least four different companies make the tall, slat-back chairs with slightly kicked rear feet and flared ears. In early examples, such as those for the Willits House (1902) or the Dana House (1903), he had the John W. Ayers Company, of Chicago, make them. The Matthews Brothers Furniture Company, of Milwaukee, made the chairs for the Darwin D. Martin House (1905), while the F. H. Bresler Company, of Milwaukee, made those for the Evans House (about 1908). For the Allen House (1917), Wright contracted out the work to Niedecken-Walbridge, of Milwaukee. Although much of the work was skillfully executed, the variety of firms suggests that Wright merely shopped around and did not necessarily depend upon a specific, trusted manufacturer. What was important was that the firm produce his designs on time and within budget.[29]

Many of the Chicago architects wrote about the need for their primary role in the desired product. Wright argued against the whim of freestanding furniture, seeking to design built-in furniture, massive furniture, or furniture inextricably linked to the architectural elements and, therefore, impossible to remove. George Washington Maher referred to such an integrated design plan as the "motif rhythm theory." To unify the exterior and interior, he focused upon the visible decorative details: "There must be evolved certain leading forms that will influence the detail of the design; these forms crystallize during the progress of planning and become the motifs that bind the design together. These motifs are susceptible to repetition, varying in proportion and ornateness as the various situations arise." Maher's early work of the late 1890s and early 1900s featured natural, organic motifs, resulting in elaborately carved furniture. After seeing the German and Austrian exhibitions at the 1904 Louisiana Purchase International Exposition, in St. Louis, he turned to a lighter, more geometrically based philosophy. For the E. L. King residence, *Rockledge* (1912), Maher designed furniture that fit the specific space: The greenish-brown stain mirrored the colors of the cliff behind the house and the surrounding foliage; the segmental arch, canted buttresses, and trapezoidal guttae were to be found throughout the exterior and interior of the house and on many of the custom-designed furnishings within. Like Wright, Elmslie, and his other colleagues in the Prairie School, Maher found that a geometrically derived, graphically oriented style was well suited to the implementation of this design philosophy.[30]

Looking at the furniture of the first two decades of the twentieth century, it is clear that a pure philosophy did not trickle down to a mass-produced style. From the late nineteenth century on, there was a range of simultaneous responses to and uses of Arts and Crafts ideas and rhetoric. The recognizable styles of the Arts and Crafts movement may have changed with fashion and been replaced by Colonial revival, Beaux-Arts, and moderne styles, but the legacy of the movement in American furniture was fourfold.

First, the language of craftsmanship became a new means of marketing furniture. Through the various writings on both intellectual and popular levels, "craftsmanship" became a signifier recognized by both consumer and producer. In merchandising their works in a more competitive fashion, firms sought to educate their clientele about quality through broad general advertising and instructive booklets. Mere pictures of products and prices were not sufficient. The new advertisements and publications emphasized the importance of construction and the integrity of the process and maker. For example, the Limbert Company described its workers as being "in sympathy with our ideals of furniture making—men of quick perception and skill, who take an interest in their work and enter into it with enthusiasm—men who derive pleasure and satisfaction in producing articles of superior modeling and construction."[31] In the 1920s, the importance of craftsmanship fueled the interest in colonial cabinetmakers and contributed to the widened popularity of American preindustrial furniture, or antiques, which possessed the important qualities of high technical accomplishment by hardworking, honest men. Even as recently as the early 1980s, craftsmanship remained a primary measure of quality. A catalogue from 1981 explained: "Essential to the success of any piece is the quality of its execution—command of technique through discipline is the sine qua non for any object."[32]

Second, the groundswell of home workshops preserved some basic technical traditions and laid the foundation for a resurgence of handcrafted furniture in the 1950s. During the prosperity after World War II, many college graduates turned their avocation into a career. But the hobbyist emphasis of much of the century actually led to technical atrophy in the custom part of the industry. No base for training existed, and it became harder to recruit qualified woodworkers. Lost was the cumulative intensity of a continuous tradition.

Third, the aesthetic nature of the reform debate, occurring at a time when marketing and advertising began to exert great influence upon production and consumption decisions, spurred the beginning of academic interest in furniture design and construction. Initially, this could be seen in the design programs or schools set up by the firms, or in the art schools associated with museums. The former tended to foster the professionalization of in-house furniture designers, and the latter tended to produce interior designers or informed consumers. Although the new academic training focused closer attention on the style of furniture, making design the key signifier in the late 1920s and 1930s, it did not produce a new generation of school-trained craftsmen to replace the dwindling supply of apprentices or immigrant craftsmen. Only after the GI Bill, the expansion of craft curricula in the 1950s, and the growth of woodworking programs in the 1960s and 1970s was there a sufficient critical mass of skilled furnituremakers trained in the university system. The training of skilled craftspeople lagged behind that of designers.[33]

Last, the production and writings of architects who favored a graphic, two-dimensional approach to furniture became the philosophical legacy for the notions of pure design favored by the next generation.[34] Architects' interest in furniture, and their self-conscious writings about their furniture, introduced many to the notions of ahistorical design based upon the principles of harmony, balance, rhythm, symmetry, and other graphic abstractions. This activity also provided the precedent for the anointment of architects, such as Michael Graves and Robert Venturi, as "design stars" in the 1970s and 1980s. These architects provided designs for furniture, coffee services, jewelry, and even doghouses.[35] In these ways, the Arts and Crafts movement in furniture design and construction had far-reaching effects that continue to color the making and buying of furniture today.

Ceramics: Seeking a Personal Style

by Elaine Levin

"It is most desirable that American artists should cultivate a style of their own."[1] Charles Binns stated a theme in 1899 that would be the thrust and, at times, the despair of critics and potters as the new century commenced. As the director, in 1900, of the newly established New York School of Clayworking and Ceramics at Alfred University, in New York State, Binns was at the right place at the right moment to influence profoundly the direction of American ceramics. He did so on a number of levels and, in the process, served as a linchpin for many ceramists who needed encouragement as they progressed toward an individual style as studio potters.

The traditional European concept of studio pottery denoted a workshop in which apprentices learned the processes, assisting the director who oversaw each operation. The apprentice was qualified to open his own workshop only after passing rigorous tests of his ability. American potters never adopted the European system of apprenticeship. Instead, the art pottery movement, as part of the Arts and Crafts movement, fostered a much looser situation. In the twenty years before 1900, the ground for what was to become the American studio pottery movement had been plowed by a number of creative potters. George Ohr, who opened the Biloxi Art Pottery in 1880, in Mississippi, and was considered an eccentric in his day, produced a profusion of hand-thrown vessels remarkable for their thin construction, tentacular handles, and unusual glazed surfaces. Ohr brought out the plastic quality of clay by altering the thrown forms through twisting, wringing, crushing, and indenting the still-wet, very thin clay walls. In contrast to the vast numbers of art potteries using molds and other production methods, Ohr and his contemporary Theophilus Brouwer, Jr., who opened the Middle Lane Pottery, on Long Island, New York, in 1894, did all the throwing and were responsible for each step of the process.[2] Brouwer's unorthodox method of firing resulted in a glazed surface he called "fire painting." Long before his contemporaries, he achieved iridescent surfaces and used gold-leaf inlay between layers of glaze.

An important pioneer in bringing the art pottery movement to the West Coast was Alexander Robertson, who left Massachusetts for California, arriving in 1884. His younger brother, Hugh, remained in charge of the Chelsea Keramic Art Works, which Alexander had founded, in Massachusetts, in 1872. Alexander arrived in San Francisco, certain he could locate the necessary minerals and clay for pottery production. There he was joined by Linna Irelan, a china painter and the wife of a mineralogist, whose knowledge of the state's clay resources aided in their determination to open an art pottery. In 1898, after several disappointing ventures, the Roblin Art Pottery began production. Robertson handled all the processes while Irelan did some of the decorating. Much of the work resembled the ware of the Chelsea pottery, modified by bas-reliefs of mushrooms and lizards modeled by Irelan. Although Robertson preferred simple shapes, often unglazed to show the fine quality of the clay, all the decorative techniques developed for art pottery production during the previous twenty years were employed.[3]

Meanwhile, at Chelsea Keramic, Hugh Robertson had embarked on a quest, inspired by the exhibit of Chinese monochrome glazes at the Philadel-

Alexander Robertson. *Vase*. 1914.
Produced by Alberhill Pottery.
Ceramic, 5$^1/_4$ × 5$^1/_4$ × 5$^1/_4$″. Collection
The Oakland Museum

George Ohr. *Lidded Teapot*. c.1885–
1900. George Ohr Pottery, Biloxi,
Mississippi. Ceramic with pink and
gray volcanic glaze, 6$^1/_4$ × 8$^1/_2$ × 8$^1/_2$″.
Collection Dillenberg-Espinar

phia Centennial International Exposition of 1876. After four years of research, during which time the pottery's commercial production languished, Hugh developed a palette of rich glazes—apple green, sea green, mustard yellow, turquoise, and crackle. By 1888, he had also perfected an oxblood red, his crowning achievement. In recognition of the difficulties he had perfecting this glaze, he named the best examples Robertson's Blood. He probably did not realize the appropriateness of this label until he went into bankruptcy, in 1889. Fortunately, his talent did not go unnoticed. With the backing of several wealthy Bostonians, Hugh moved to Dedham and established the Dedham Pottery, in 1895, for the production of dinnerware, which was distinguished by the crackle glaze he had discovered earlier.

Ohr, Brouwer, and Hugh Robertson were more adventuresome and original in their approach than Alexander Robertson, but what they all had in common was the attitude of a studio potter toward their respective work. Ohr and Brouwer had assistants who helped in minor ways. The concept of the studio potter as being solely responsible for each object, which Ohr, Brouwer, and the Robertsons embraced in a natural way, was not a possibility for the china painters working in the early years of the art pottery movement. The women—Mary Louise McLaughlin, Maria Nichols, Laura Fry, and their followers—were decorators with no knowledge of pottery processes other than surface embellishment, which was just one aspect of production. Curiously, in spite of that limitation, some of the women who engaged in decoration used that background to educate themselves on all aspects of pottery, becoming recognized in later years for developing their own identifiable style. The man who encouraged these women and advanced their education in ceramics was Charles Fergus Binns.

CHARLES BINNS: EDUCATOR AND POTTER

Charles Fergus Binns was an Englishman, brought up in the shadow of the Royal Porcelain Works, in Worcester, England, where his father served as director. Binns began working there at fourteen. He learned the operations of the company and traveled to promote trade with Europe and America. He boldly changed the direction of his career in 1897 when, at forty, he became the principal of the Trenton Technical School of Science and Art, in New Jersey, and superintendent of its sponsor, the Ceramic Art Company—later renamed the Lenox China Company. A prolific writer of books and articles before moving to America, Binns continued in that vein and also became one of the founding members of the American Ceramic Society, in 1898. The society's intention was to serve as a forum for an exchange of information and to encourage education in order to improve the products of the ceramics industry.

In 1900, Binns came to the attention of the president of Alfred University, at the moment when this college, like many state schools, was opening a department for ceramic technology. A number of state legislatures had concluded that in order to increase state revenues, education in the technology of such resources as clay was imperative. The New York School of Clayworking and Ceramics opened in 1900, with Binns as its first director.

Unlike most of the other state-financed schools, where the emphasis was on ceramic engineering, the New York School, under Binns's direction, wedded the aesthetics of clay to the technology. The first class, held in the summer of 1901, enrolled fifty-seven artists from seven states. One member wrote that the students "learned how American shales and clays might become artistic pottery and fine porcelain."[4] The summer classes were open to teachers from high schools, vocational and private schools, settlement

houses, and summer camps. Binns was particularly encouraging to the women
who entered his classes. It was in these classes that the china painters moved
beyond painting on porcelain blanks to a greater involvement with clay.
During the regular school year, classes were formulated to prepare men for
ceramic-factory management as part of the legislature's mandate. But Binns's
vision was to merge chemistry and art; as his graduates found factory and
teaching jobs around the country, that vision was to prevail and ultimately
educate the generation that became studio potters.[5]

In spite of his knowledge of clay processes, Charles Binns did not learn to
use the potter's wheel until he became the director of the Alfred University
school. He progressed rapidly and, like Hugh Robertson, took inspiration for
form and glazes from the Chinese as well as from ware he had observed in
European museums during his travels for the Royal Porcelain Works. Stoneware clays and the beauty of a lustrous, monochrome glaze on a simple form
became his trademarks. In formulating a glaze, he approached the problem
scientifically rather than intuitively, unlike most potters of his time. He and
his students learned what each item in a glaze formula contributed to the
whole, a concept vitally important to the advancement of the technology and
the art of clay.

PORCELAIN: THE PATH TO STUDIO POTTERY

Many of the women attracted to Charles Binns's classes had entered the
field of ceramics by way of china painting. Painting metallic oxides on once-
fired porcelain dishes combined art with ware for the home. The woman
responsible for making china painting a household word by the mid-1870s was
Cincinnati native Mary Louise McLaughlin. The sister of a prominent architect, McLaughlin pursued her interest in art at the Cincinnati School of Art,
taking classes in wood-carving and painting until she discovered china and
underglaze painting. Her books, detailing both techniques, and her establishment of the Cincinnati Pottery Club, in 1879, converted women across the
country to the art of decorating pots. For various reasons, McLaughlin moved
to other forms of art about 1885, returning ten years later to work once again
with clay. McLaughlin seemed always to seek a challenge, so it is understand-
able that after ten years, she turned to porcelain.

Undaunted by the scarcity of information, although she did acquire
direction and locate some formulas in books on the composition of porcelain

clay bodies, McLaughlin began to experiment, ultimately producing a translucent, cream-colored porcelain. As she wrote in an article for *Keramic Studio*, "It was found that the very thing pronounced impossible by even experienced potters proved to be entirely feasible."[6] She named the ware Losanti, after Losantiville, the original name for Cincinnati. An invention that encouraged her return to clay was the Revelation kiln, in a portable model developed by Horace Caulkins, in 1892, and promoted by Mary Chase Perry, the founder of Pewabic Pottery. Instead of being dependent upon commercial pottery companies to throw and fire ware, as were the china painters of the 1880s, McLaughlin now had more control over her work. A small kiln was installed in her garden, where, in spite of some complaints from neighbors about obnoxious smoke, she persevered, hiring a thrower to make the shapes she required. As one critic noted, "It may be that her very lack of experience contributed to her success in that she was not bound by any rule or precedent."[7]

McLaughlin's experience with wood-carving probably led her to the carved, raised surfaces of Losanti ware. Losanti ware is an example of the American adaptation of the Art Nouveau style, which began before the turn of the century in France. There, the emphasis on a curvilinear line that suggested movement and growth began to dominate all areas of the crafts. McLaughlin, like others in American art, took a conservative approach to the more exaggerated and flowing lines in French ware. Following her own advice to others to emulate the Art Nouveau style with caution, she carved flowers, stems, and leaves on her vessel surfaces to complement the simple shapes and to conform to the "structural naturalism" of American Art Nouveau.[8] McLaughlin exhibited Losanti ware at the Cincinnati Art Museum and, in 1901, at the Pan-American Exposition, in Buffalo, where the work was awarded a bronze medal.

By 1906, having achieved her goals for producing porcelain, McLaughlin left to explore other forms of art. But the beauty of porcelain was destined to advance in other capable hands, namely those of Adelaide Alsop Robineau. In 1899, Robineau, with her husband, Samuel, founded, edited, and published *Keramic Studio*. Although a few earlier magazines had addressed china painters, *Keramic Studio* brought to its pages a wide range of articles on both technical and aesthetic matters, written by some of the foremost potters, educators, art historians, and critics. Yet, at the very moment when china painting was attracting more and more women, the judges at the Paris Exposition of 1900 declared china-painted ware unacceptable for judging as an art form, since the decorator was not responsible for the total object. Robineau, a bright woman who earlier had earned her living as a teacher of china painting, considered this decision prophetic. If one had to be responsible for the total object, she concluded, she would need to learn all the processes for producing clay vessels. With characteristic determination, Robineau decided to master the potter's wheel, thereby becoming the first American woman to enter what had been considered the domain of men.

Perhaps it was Charles Binns who encouraged Robineau to disregard convention when he wrote, "A potter without a wheel seems like a man without a wife — incomplete."[9] Charles Volkmar, an established potter who had written an article for *Keramic Studio*, consented to give Robineau lessons on the potter's wheel. While mastering this essential tool, Robineau began to inquire about clay bodies and glazes, attending Charles Binns's classes at Alfred University. McLaughlin's article in *Keramic Studio* on her experiments with porcelain, and an article about Taxile Doat, the director of Sèvres, the French national porcelain factory, started Robineau on the path toward pursuing porcelain. Doat's book *Grand Feu Ceramics*, published in France, discussed porcelain techniques and the achievement of crystalline glazes.

What would not have interested her as a china painter now offered to open the way to a new art form. Samuel Robineau, a French émigré, provided the translation, while Charles Binns helped convert French materials and formulas into their American equivalents. Like McLaughlin, Robineau turned to the Revelation kiln. Situated in the basement of the Robineau home, the kiln provided the final tool in effecting her transition to independent studio potter.

At first, Robineau decided to establish a production pottery, using molds to form small household objects—tiles, doorknobs, garden pottery, and other decorative accessories. Difficulties with glazes and the boredom of repetitive shapes caused Robineau to reconsider her goals and return to throwing individual pieces on the potter's wheel. By 1904, working with Taxile Doat's formulas, Robineau developed a palette of crystalline glazes, which she exhibited at the Louisiana Purchase International Exposition, in St. Louis, that year. Like McLaughlin, Robineau, by pursuing crystalline glazes that were difficult to achieve, accepted a most challenging direction for her work. Even though she was able to produce large, crystal clusters, overlapping crystals, and pansy and snowflake shapes, losses, because of the flowing nature of the glaze during the firing, were often as high as thirty percent.

Robineau received high praise from Taxile Doat[10] and Charles Binns for her exceptional glazes, but the high percentage of loss probably persuaded her once again to seek a new direction. In Binns's classes at Alfred University, Robineau, along with other students, translated the geometric designs of Native American pottery on ware. Although she produced a number of vessels supporting these designs, the historical forms and designs Robineau most admired were those of the Orient. The first of Robineau's new work to show this influence appeared in 1905 with the *Viking Ship Vase*, named for the tiny sailing ship carved into the shoulder and repeated on the delicate stand that steadied the tapering form.

Viking Ship Vase was Robineau's entry into the carved vessel. She moved quickly from carving a small area to an entire surface and to more complex patterns, emulating Oriental objects of ebony and ivory. In the process, her work became much more rigid, restricted within circles and borders and following a strict vertical axis, as in *Lantern Vase* (1908). The high point for Robineau's new ware occurred in 1910 when she accepted a teaching position at the People's University, an establishment funded by the American Women's League, close to St. Louis.

CERAMIC EDUCATION IN THE PRIVATE SECTOR

Edward J. Lewis founded the American Women's League, in 1907, an extension of his interests in education and publishing. The university offered correspondence courses in a variety of subjects, but the University City Pottery was the area that flourished, if only briefly. Lewis had read Samuel Robineau's translation of Taxile Doat's *Grand Feu Ceramics*, and was himself an amateur potter. He hired a distinguished ceramics department faculty—Doat, the Robineaus, Kathryn Cherry, a specialist in china painting, and Frederick H. Rhead, an accomplished potter—to handle correspondence and in-residence courses. The department fired its first kiln in 1910. Close to three hundred correspondence students studied china painting, while twenty to thirty worked with the faculty on the campus. Lewis's goals were rather lofty, according to a statement in the school's brochure: "to cultivate a widespread appreciation of art and to make possible production of artistic work but also to discover and develop genius."[11]

In his establishment of the University City Pottery, Lewis was responding, somewhat belatedly, to a need that earlier saw the growth of schools and courses for women seeking a career in art. Sophie Newcomb Memorial College for Women at Tulane University, in New Orleans, created a pottery in 1895 as part of the school's curriculum to train women to earn a livelihood. The wisdom of this approach was not lost on private art and museum schools. The Art Institute of Chicago notified *Keramic Studio* that a class had been formed to teach handbuilding in clay but not casting, which was considered a factory process and inappropriate for beginning potters. In 1902, Pratt Institute, in Brooklyn, added a ceramics class taught by Charles Volkmar. The Pennsylvania Museum School of Industrial Art in Philadelphia, hired Leon Volkmar, Charles's son, to teach its pottery class. Settlement houses, beginning with Chicago's Hull-House, which was founded in the 1890s, viewed classes in decorating pottery as a path to some financial independence for immigrant women. Henry Street Settlement House and Greenwich House, both of New York City, established similar classes in the early 1900s.

In part because the People's University was such a latecomer to this scene, its life span was destined to be limited. Before it expired, in 1914, however, Lewis published *Palette and Brush*, a new magazine, which the Robineaus edited. Adelaide Alsop Robineau and Taxile Doat pursued their own projects. That they learned from each other is evident in Robineau's *Poppy Vase*, which supports a design created by inlaid, colored slips, a technique perfected earlier by Rhead.

Robineau was destined to bring fame, if not fortune, to this enterprise with her vase *The Apotheosis of the Toiler*, a masterpiece of intricate carving in porcelain. Working with a crochet needle for a thousand hours, she used the scarab, a beetle, as her primary allover design element. This ginger jar, along with several other of her porcelains, was awarded the grand prize in 1911 at the International Exposition of Decorative Arts, in Turin, Italy. She was the first woman and the first American to be so honored. Unfortunately, this recognition did not save Lewis from serious financial problems. In 1912, the Robineaus returned to their home in Syracuse, to their magazine, and to Adelaide Alsop Robineau's pursuit of studio pottery.

A PARALLEL MOVEMENT—THE SMALL-SCALE POTTERY

As noted earlier, the Arts and Crafts movement inspired a return to handcrafted ware that initially encouraged the embryonic studio-pottery direction for George Ohr, Theophilus Brouwer, Jr., and the Robertson brothers. Other potteries began small-scale production as a result of some of the economic and social changes affecting American society. That some women had the time to study art, to organize art schools and museums, was due in part to the affluence of the post–Civil War period. In 1880, Cincinnati matron Maria Nichols's wealthy father, Joseph Longworth, supported her desire to open a pottery. Rookwood Pottery, for the first three years of its operation, produced the work of Nichols and her china-painting friends, including Mary Louise McLaughlin and members of the Cincinnati Pottery Club. When William Watts Taylor was hired as business manager, in 1883, the nature of the operation gradually changed to large-scale production. Rookwood, however, remained the model for other potteries—the Newcomb Pottery of Sophie Newcomb Memorial College (1895), Artus Van Briggle's Colorado pottery (1901), Mary Chase Perry's Pewabic Pottery (1903), and for numerous small art potteries that blossomed in the early 1900s.

At its inception, Newcomb Pottery hired Cincinnati china painter Mary Sheerer and, in 1896, a thrower, Joseph Meyer. Labeled the southern Rookwood, Newcomb Pottery developed into a regular staff of five women, graduates of the college, who decorated the vases, tiles, lamp bases, bowls, and coffee sets. In 1910, Paul Cox, a graduate of Charles Binns's classes at Alfred University, was hired to improve the clay body and add a matte glaze to the decorative treatment. During the pottery's early years, Charles Binns was consulted regularly for technical advice and for personnel, as the pottery changed to keep up with the shifts in styles.[12]

Artus Van Briggle was hired by Rookwood in 1887, and soon became a talented member of the decorating staff. Unfortunately, a lingering case of tuberculosis forced him to leave. He moved to the drier climate of Colorado, where, by 1901, he felt well enough to establish a pottery. Within a year, he had a staff of fourteen. Van Briggle made the models from which molds were produced. The palette of matte glazes applied by an atomizer and the floral or plant forms uniting shape and decoration firmly placed the ware as being part of the American expression of the Art Nouveau style. When Van Briggle died, in 1904, his wife, Anne Gregory Van Briggle, continued production, using the extensive number of molds and glazes her husband had originated.

Before opening her own pottery, Mary Chase Perry had been a china painter and a member of the National League of Mineral Painters, which had been founded, in 1892, by china painter Susan Frackelton. Perry had studied in Cincinnati, and in 1901 and 1902, she attended glaze chemistry classes with Charles Binns at Alfred University. Inspired by Maria Nichols, Perry began Pewabic Pottery, in Detroit, in 1903, in partnership with Horace Caulkins, the inventor of the Revelation kiln. Perry's early work emulated popular ware—matte glazes and modeled leaf forms. Even after 1907, when tile commissions began to dominate production, Perry continued producing functional ware. Still, she kept the staff and technical equipment to a minimum. In 1909, her first example of an iridescent glaze emerged from the kiln, inspiring her to pursue such other exotics as crystalline, luster, and Egyptian blue on a high-fired clay body. She and Adelaide Alsop Robineau corresponded about techni-

Pewabic Pottery. *Jar.* c. 1910–12.
Ceramic, 18³/₄ × 12³/₄ × 12³/₄".
Collection Founders Society, Detroit
Institute of Art. Gift of Charles L. Freer

cal problems and equipment. Perry had learned to use the potter's wheel but, unlike Robineau, she hired a thrower to free herself for extensive glaze research.

Pewabic, a Chippewa word meaning clay with a copper color, was Perry's tribute to her upper-Michigan origins. W. A. Long, founder of Clifton Art Pottery, of Newark, New Jersey, acknowledged the influence of Native Americans in another manner by introducing Clifton Indian ware in 1906. No longer a threat to settlers in the West, the Native American, by the 1900s, was viewed as an exotic, a noble savage whose stern portrait in feathered headdress graced vases by Rookwood and other art potteries. The Clifton Art Pottery went a step further, appropriating the geometric designs and buff color of native pottery for one of its art lines. Jugs, vases, candlesticks, and umbrella stands— forms unrelated to Native American originals—acquired Indian-influenced designs. As noted earlier, students in Charles Binns's classes in 1902 looked to Indian ware for designs. During its six-year existence, the dozen or so employees at the Clifton Art Pottery also produced ware featuring semi-crystalline and matte glazes.

The four sisters who opened the Overbeck Pottery, in 1911, in Cambridge City, Indiana, each had some art-school education. Two years earlier, Elizabeth Overbeck had taken a ceramics course with Charles Binns at Alfred University, bringing to the group a technical background in glaze formulas and clay bodies and experience on the potter's wheel. Mary Frances, Margaret, and Hannah had published china-painting designs in *Keramic Studio*. Hannah served as the principal designer. Their portable Revelation kiln, in a building at the rear of the family home, fired the first matte glazes, in subdued colors, on bowls, vases, tea sets, and tiles. Wheel and handbuilt ware distinguished the output of the pottery, with many of the designs inspired by forms in nature. The women added to their income by teaching pottery classes in Cambridge and nearby Richmond. Margaret died the year the pottery opened, but since her sisters were capable of performing all the necessary tasks, the pottery continued until 1955, when Mary Frances, the sole survivor, died.

A late addition to small pottery operations was Cornelius Brauckman's Grand Feu Pottery, which opened in 1912, in Los Angeles. Although there is no conclusive evidence that Brauckman was familiar with Taxile Doat's book *Grand Feu Ceramics*, the name of the pottery suggests that he had read the translated material published in *Keramic Studio*. Indeed, Brauckman's pottery displayed a wide range of high-fired glazes on classically simple forms, similar to the spectrum of Doat's ornamental glazes. Little information has come to light about the pottery's operation, except that the ware produced during its brief, six-year existence was of a very high quality.

SMALL POTTERIES WITH A SOCIAL CONSCIENCE

The social impulse that initiated settlement houses to integrate immigrants into American culture also recognized the therapeutic possibilities of working with clay. That the Arts and Crafts movement's emphasis on hand-crafted ware could serve the needs of patients recovering from mental illness occurred first to Dr. Herbert J. Hall, who, in 1904, opened a sanatorium in Marblehead, Massachusetts. Shortly after the pottery operation began, with patients performing simple, manual tasks, Hall realized he needed guidance. Arthur Baggs, a student of Charles Binns's, arrived with professional ideas that soon phased out the amateur assistance of patients. By 1909, Marblehead Pottery's small staff—five, besides Baggs—had established a reputation for muted matte glazes and conventionalized patterns of seaweed, fish, gulls, and

sailing ships, a reflection of the town's fishing village origins. The pottery remained small, even after 1915 when Baggs purchased the operation and divided his time between teaching and Marblehead's artistic direction.

Women with tuberculosis were able to regain their health and learn a skill at Arequipa Pottery, in northern California. In 1911, Dr. Philip King Brown, following Dr. Hall's lead, hired Frederick H. Rhead, who had left the University City Pottery, to integrate occupational therapy with pottery production. The steadily changing decorating staff made this a marriage destined for failure. In 1913, Rhead left. Two other distinguished potters, Albert L. Solon and Fred H. Wilde, also tried to place the pottery on a more professional level, to improve glazes and expand the markets for the ware, but to no avail. The marginal operation finally closed as World War I approached.

Halcyon, a community concerned with physical therapy treatment, also had utopian social goals. Incorporated in 1903, near the California town of Pismo Beach, the colony hired Alexander Robertson, in 1910, to open a pottery and an art school to help support the membership of this cooperative venture. As he did during his association with the Roblin Art Pottery, Robertson used local clays and minerals. He also encouraged students of the art school to apply modeled, natural forms of plants and animals similar to those on his earlier ware. When the association that supported Halcyon dissolved in 1913, Robertson left, and the pottery closed.

The Saturday Evening Girls' Club was a Boston club for young women who met on that day of the week for cultural activities. The group's sponsor, Mrs. James Storrow, purchased a kiln in 1906 and engaged an English ceramist, Thomas Nickerson, to teach glazing and firing. Two years later, when the group moved to a house near the Old North Church, famous for Paul Revere's ride, the pottery operation took his name. About fourteen workers, including ten decorators, handled all the work in the period before World War I. Charles Binns wrote that Paul Revere Pottery had a distinctive character in design and technique, and he praised director-designer Edith Brown for this achievement.[13] What Binns did not mention was that the cost of production constantly exceeded income, even when the pottery moved to a new building in 1915 and expanded its equipment and staff. Remarkably, Mrs. Storrow's subsidies kept the marginal operation functioning through the Depression and other economic difficulties, until it closed in 1942.

THE ARTS AND CRAFTS MOVEMENT'S LEGACY

Many of the small potteries operated for no more than five or ten years. Rookwood understood that in order to maintain its lead in the art pottery field, it was necessary to incorporate more and more factory procedures. Some potteries, like Marblehead, did not resort to molds, sustained instead by the loyalty of the original workers familiar with its operation. But many pressures for change were at work. By the second decade of the twentieth century, the china painting movement, which had laid the foundation for the rise of art potteries, was on the wane; the style had outlived its popularity. Indeed, china painting as an art form had become the territory of hobbyists, as Adelaide Alsop Robineau had anticipated.

The decorative style that replaced painting on the vessel's surface was the ornamental glaze in the tradition of Chinese monochrome glazes. The matte glazes that were produced—including those by William Grueby and Artus Van Briggle, Adelaide Robineau's crystalline glazes, George Ohr's and Tiffany's Favrile mottled glazes—all contributed to expanding the allover glaze vocabulary. Commercial potteries, such as Fulper, with its introduction of Vasekraft in 1909, and Jacques Sicard's metallic luster glazes produced for Samuel Weller's art line, beginning in 1903, joined the march away from the painted surface toward an alluring, glazed surface. Then, too, the ornamental glaze flattered simple shapes, which did not compete with the beauty in color and texture of this surface. The appendages that were part of the Art Nouveau style were now no longer viable. The clean lines of simple, classical shapes also fit a philosophy that tried to reconcile the handcrafted with industrial products. By the end of the new century's first decade, many potteries had already accepted the inevitability of incorporating some mass-production procedures while trying to retain a handcrafted appearance. Using molds, as did Van Briggle, was just the first step.

The Arts and Crafts movement retained its viability through those individual potters who continued with variations on the ornamental glaze— Charles Binns, Adelaide Alsop Robineau, Mary Chase Perry. The movement also lived on through a steadily rising interest in the use of tile for homes and public and private buildings. American pottery companies, inspired by a display of British tile at the Philadelphia Centennial International Exposition of 1876, entered the industry just as the decorative uses for art tile were expanding. Practical, moderately priced, and artistic, tiles for fireplaces, garden planters, and fountains added accents of color and texture to home and garden. One of the first companies to produce art tiles was Low Art Tile Works, which opened in 1878. John G. Low had apprenticed with James Robertson at Chelsea Keramic Art Works, learning press molding, impressing, and bas-relief, which the Robertson family had practiced before emigrating from England. Low, in turn, taught the process to William Grueby, who began his own tile operation shortly after his ten-year apprenticeship.

In 1894, the Grueby Faience Company began producing glazed bricks, tile, and terra-cotta. Grueby worked with architects who commissioned tiles generally in historical styles and glossy glazes. This changed when he began experimenting with matte glazes in earth tones. Addison B. Le Boutillier designed tiles for Grueby with conventional landscapes, flowers, and animals, patterns reflecting the influence of Japanese art. Grueby's tiles were press molded, the designs outlined by slightly raised ridges that also served to retain flowing glazes. In 1897, William Grueby introduced a line of art pottery that later was discontinued because of financial problems.

About the same time, Mary Chase Perry was gearing up for tile production. In 1907, she received her first residential commission from her partner, Horace Caulkins, and soon added financier Charles Freer's home, as well as hotels, churches, and libraries. Each commission was treated individually. The Griswald House Hotel tile featured signs of the zodiac, while Freer's house was decorated with tiles of an iridescent glaze. Among the many special requirements fulfilled by Pewabic Pottery were the tiles for the children's section of the Detroit Public Library, which featured depictions of well-known characters from children's literature. The Ford Motor Company was expanding to other cities in 1916, and it ordered varying amounts of tile for exterior decoration on service buildings around the country. Oberlin College art gallery and a theater in Louisville kept Mary Chase Perry and her staff busy developing special glazes for each of these projects during the war years.

A Harvard graduate and University of Pennsylvania law student, Henry Chapman Mercer was more interested in archaeology and history. When he failed to learn the skill of throwing, he turned to tile making. The Moravian Pottery and Tile Works began in 1898, in Doylestown, Pennsylvania, with Mercer making tiles by hand in designs inspired by the molded decorations on early cast-iron stoves. He made impressions of early English floor tiles and ancient tiles he found while visiting decaying English abbeys.[14] In later work, Mercer turned to American flora and fauna and scenes of life on the frontier.

On the other side of the country, in southern California, Ernest Batchelder left the teaching of design theory to produce tiles in his backyard. As the Batchelder Tile Company, he began, in 1909, by handpressing tiles in designs that reflected the then rural atmosphere of Pasadena. Bas-reliefs of rabbits, fish, vines, local flowers, and live oak trees were among the many subjects that were to border fireplaces and adorn garden planters and fountains in southern California bungalows built from 1910 through the 1920s. As styles changed and the business moved to an industrial site in 1912, the pressure of commissions caused Batchelder to introduce industrial methods, even though he attempted to maintain a craftsman approach. Designs became flatter and simpler, and the shades of brown reflecting the California hills gave way to lighter colors that corresponded to the Mediterranean architectural styles of homes during the 1920s.

William Grueby. Beaver tile. 1904. Ceramic, 6 × 6″. Installed at Astor Place subway station, New York City.

One of the many benefits of the Arts and Crafts movement was the focus on a better home environment through handcrafted ware. But the movement's rejection of the machine could not withstand the pressure of forces at work on the decorative arts since the beginning of the century. Like Rookwood and Batchelder, pottery and tile companies, large and small, bowed to industrial practices in order to survive financially.

As early as 1901, architect Frank Lloyd Wright proposed broadening William Morris's ideas by adapting design to the machine. His lecture on this subject, delivered in Chicago, was ridiculed and scorned. Between 1911 and 1916, several museums and national expositions featured exhibits of the decorative arts as a cooperative effort between designers and manufacturers.

Clean, uncluttered lines marked the new designs. The ornamental glaze, introduced in the early 1900s, fit the new standards, but without the extra trimmings associated with the Art Nouveau style. In fact, the popular matte glazes were about to meet serious competition. In 1915, Rookwood introduced a high-gloss glaze on porcelain vases as its transition from the Arts and Crafts matte glazes to the modern style.[15] Others looked to historical ceramics for inspiration. Adelaide Alsop Robineau, true to her taste for the carved surface, selected the more intricate patterns of Mayan and Incan pottery. The Panama-Pacific International Exposition of 1915 recognized her unique craftsmanship with a grand prize for a group of her porcelains. While Robineau maintained her individuality, the featured exhibit at this San Francisco fair was twelve rooms whose furnishings conformed to a single motif.

Ceramics in the 13th Annual Arts and Crafts Exhibition, The Art Institute of Chicago, October 1–23, 1913

William Bragdon. Mission design tile.
c. 1916. Produced at California
Faience. Ceramic, $4^1/_2 \times 4^1/_2 \times {}^3/_4''$.
Collection James and Janeen Marrin

Ceramics, as part of the decorative arts, felt the pressure of integrating with manufactured products for the home.

Part of the impetus for creating a climate for good design in industry was World War I, which was in progress, in Europe. American manufacturers were concerned that at the war's end a race to capture world trade would follow. Only the country with well-designed products could meet the competition. Yet several familiar voices were raised, warning of this rush to join a factory rather than continue as a studio artist. Frederick H. Rhead was critical of the business mind, which he believed focused on the profit motive and would work to the detriment of using an individual's skills and resources.[16] Charles Binns wrote that the poor quality of pottery manufacturing was attributable to employing a modeler with inadequate training. While stressing the need for a well-educated designer, Binns suggested that cultivating a critical sense through the study of past historical styles also offered a path to the development of an individual direction.[17]

The challenge to continue studio pottery was met by William Bragdon, who had graduated from Charles Binns's program at Alfred University in 1908. After a career of teaching, Bragdon and a partner, Chauncey R. Thomas, launched a new pottery in 1916, in Berkeley, California. The firm changed names several times, finally settling, by 1924, for California Faience. Even though the small operation opened very late for the art pottery era, the monochrome matte and high-gloss glazes on simple forms found a market, especially for florist ware. Tiles were also produced using press molds and matte glazes.

By the time America entered the war, in 1917, the disruptive effects of what began in 1914 were now more evident. Except for tile production, the war hastened the demise of the Arts and Crafts movement. Samuel Robineau wrote to Mary Chase Perry that the war had substantially decreased interest in china painting, causing a loss of subscriptions and advertisers for *Keramic Studio*.[18] Since publishing generally was in trouble, Frederick H. Rhead rather unwisely chose 1917 to launch his monthly magazine, *The Potter*. This ambitious undertaking survived for only three issues, even though the magazine balanced pertinent articles on historical ceramics with practical technical information.

Another pottery entrepreneur and former Binns student at Alfred University had a better appreciation of the temper of the times. R. Guy Cowan, with the encouragement of the Cleveland Chamber of Commerce, opened a pottery in that city in 1912. Five years later, when the pottery was recognized with a first prize at the International Show at the Art Institute of Chicago, Cowan joined the army and closed the operation. He returned in 1919 to revamp the facilities, move to a new location, and begin producing molded ware and small figurines. Cowan was riding that wave of energy, released by the end of the war, that now accepted with enthusiasm the meshing of art and industry. Some of the optimism generated by the end of the war was directed to creating a better world through design. This concept, whose development had been delayed by the war years, evolved along with the growth of the European workshop movement, reaching a new stage with the opening of the Bauhaus, in Germany, in 1919. The Bauhaus philosophy tied good design to the machine for the mass production of affordable products. Cowan understood how to unite these elements in decorative and functional ceramics for the home. Like his influential teacher Charles Binns, Guy Cowan and the Cowan Pottery were to be, in the coming decade, the seminal force for Modernism in ceramics. Wearing the Binns mantle, Cowan made the commercial environment a training ground for the next generation of ceramists. As sculptors of popular figurines, produced by Cowan Pottery in limited editions, this group retained its individuality and later, when the times permitted, developed a personal style as studio potters.

The Arts and Crafts movement abetted the emergence of American ceramics from industrial production toward the individualistic aspirations of the studio potter. By the close of the second decade of the twentieth century, both trends began to merge. Like the patterns in a kaleidoscope, each direction defined during this period would continually shift in relation, one to another.

Colored Light: Glass, 1900–1920

by Linda M. Papanicolaou

Stained glass, wrote John La Farge, "is the art of painting in air with a material carrying colored light."[1] What he meant can best be understood by a visit to the cathedral of Notre-Dame de Chartres, in France, whose magnificent ensemble of twelfth- and thirteenth-century glass he knew well. To the medieval mind, glass was a precious, miraculous material, often likened to rubies and sapphires, with its property of translucence signifying the incarnation of Christ or the light of the Gospel illuminating the world.[2]

America at the turn of the century, the age of John La Farge and Louis Comfort Tiffany, possessed a far better scientific and technical understanding of this venerable art than had the Middle Ages, but it was, in its own way, just as enthralled with colored light. The defining features of the new American glass were multifold: the use of a semitranslucent, or opalescent, glass, which gave the movement its name; the achievement of painterly effects through plating together multiple layers of glass; and the use of vitreous paint, only where absolutely necessary, to depict the faces, hands, and feet of human figures. These techniques made it possible to render light, shadow, color, and atmospheric perspective according to the painting style of the late nineteenth century, but in glass and light rather than in oil paint on canvas.

The years of the nineteenth century leading up to La Farge and Tiffany's period of activity had seen a great resurgence of interest in both the study of medieval stained glass and the problems of creating a viable modern equivalent to this magnificent art. Whether it was La Farge or Tiffany who invented the American opalescent stained-glass window is an argument that began with the artists themselves. The ultimate consensus is that the original impulse was La Farge's, although its success as an art movement must be credited to Tiffany.

La Farge and Tiffany professed that it was an encounter with medieval stained glass that induced them to take up the craft. Each began in the early 1870s, and they described their initial years of experimentation as being continually frustrated by the glass available on the market, which did not equal the twelfth- and thirteenth-century glass they had seen in Europe, as well as by the impossibility of finding craftsmen who could translate their ideas into glass and lead.

The problem was not that the craft was "lost," as some have claimed; contemporary methods of stained-glass windowmaking were more or less what they had been in the Middle Ages. Pot metal, a bubbly, transparent blown glass, was used for windows. To execute a panel from an artist's sketch, a scale cartoon was drawn in which lines were indicated for cutting individual shapes, such as a head or a hand, from glass of the desired color. Facial features and drapery folds were painted with a vitreous enamel that was then fired in a kiln, and the pieces were assembled with cames of lead.[3] What La Farge and Tiffany wanted, though, was not traditional stained glass, but the equivalent of contemporary painting, reflecting contemporary theories and concerns about light and color.[4]

Opalescent glass, which was opacified by the addition of an agent such as bone ash, was not blown but poured. The originator of its use in windows was

La Farge. One day, while lying ill in bed, he noticed the sunlight shining through a toothpowder jar made of a cheap, opaline glass. He realized that this streaky white, which possessed the mysterious ability to express a range of tonal values and depth within a single piece of glass, was what he sought in his windows. He first used it in glass in 1878, as an accent color in a painted, pot-metal window for the Watts Sherman House, in Newport, Rhode Island.[5] Tiffany first used opalescent glass in the same year.[6]

Many studios were making windows of opalescent glass. In 1888, when the mural painter Will H. Low wrote an article on the new American glass, he mentioned a number of prominent artists who had designed windows, among them F. D. Millet, E. H. Blashfield, Elihu Vedder, Kenyon Cox, as well as Low himself.[7] Wealthy Americans commissioned windows for their houses, churches, mausoleums, theaters, clubhouses, banks, and railway stations, while those of more modest means received mail-order stained glass for their dining rooms, stairwells, or storefronts.[8] The result, as Thomas Hoving noted, is that there is more stained glass in New York today than ever existed in any medieval city.[9]

THE OPALESCENT MOVEMENT

By 1900, every American studio was working in opalescent glass. Windows were essentially renditions of Renaissance-revival scenes of ancient architecture, with classically garbed females and acanthus ornament, that appeared in other painting media. Among artists active in the New York area alone were Charles Rollinson Lamb and his brother, Frederick Stymetz Lamb, of J. & R. Lamb; Francis Lathrop, a former student of Burne-Jones; David Maitland Armstrong and Mary Tillinghast, protégés of La Farge; and J. A. Holtzer, head of the mosaic department at Tiffany.[10]

By the start of the new century, La Farge and Tiffany had diverged. Tiffany became more deeply involved in glass as a material, while La Farge developed a working method in which gradations of tone and texture were built up like brushstrokes, with single, small pieces of glass and leading.[11]

The Tiffany Studio was a production line, each window passing from designer to cartoonist to color selector, cutter, painter, and glazier. In the social hierarchy of the studio, the designers, who were the educated artists, were the elite. Tiffany visited periodically. Windows awaiting his approval would be set up and a chair produced for him, while the workers gathered to await his verdict. An anecdote related by a young designer named Gordon Guthrie, who worked briefly for Tiffany around 1902, concerned a window

Otto Heinigke. *Test Panel with Evangelist Symbol.* c. 1915. Stained glass. The Metropolitan Museum of Art. Gift of Mrs. Otto Heinigke, 1916

Duffner and Kimberly. *The Lawyers'
Club Window.* 1912. Stained glass.
Designed by J. Gordon Guthrie

that had been hastily leaded and set up because the patron, a prominent New York dowager, was arriving with Mr. Tiffany to approve it. In the process, a piece of blue glass destined for the sky was chipped, revealing a small gash of white. They glazed it in anyway, assuming that the window was large enough that no one would notice.

The client seemed pleased, but she gazed for a time at the sky and eventually asked Mr. Tiffany what the little speck of white was. Tiffany did not miss a beat. "That, Madame," he declared authoritatively, "is a feather dropped from the wing of a passing angel."[12]

ART GLASS

Throughout history, the manufacture of glass and the making of windows existed separately, but La Farge and Tiffany were the exceptions in the field. As early as the 1870s, they were experimenting with glassmaking. La Farge was, perhaps, the greatest innovator in the history of modern stained glass, but well before 1900 he had stopped glass experiments, finding the varieties available on the market sufficient for the direction his art was taking.

Tiffany persisted in experimentation. In 1892, he hired a glass technologist, Arthur J. Nash, from Stourbridge, England, and founded a glass house at Corona, Long Island, giving his stained-glass studio unprecedented access to its own supply of custom-made window glass. He also entered the highly competitive nineteenth-century field of art glass by including a glassblowing shop.[13]

Closely involved with glass- and windowmaking in his early years, Tiffany had learned how to work with blown glass. In the nineteenth century, glassmaking was an industrial art rather than a product of individual creativity. Tiffany's was typical of art-glass houses of that century, in which designing was the province of the artist and blowing the work of the artisan. Glass was made by a team of workers called a "shop," composed of a gaffer, or master craftsman, and his various assistants, to whom were assigned precise roles in the ritual of glassmaking: mixer, server, blower, and decorator. The entire operation was directed by a glass technologist, a factory manager who had the requisite knowledge of glass chemistry and production and, for art glass, a flair for design.

Information on Arthur Nash is fragmentary, and a full picture of the creative collaboration that produced Favrile glass cannot be drawn.[14] Fortunately, Frederick Carder, founder of the Steuben Glass Works, is much better known. Like Nash, Carder was originally from Stourbridge. He emigrated to the United States and founded Steuben, in Corning, New York, in 1903. He was easily the most accomplished glass technologist in the American art-glass industry. Like Nash, he did not blow glass, but at Steuben he performed the functions that Tiffany and Nash shared at Corona. He designed, developed all the glass formulas, and managed sales and marketing as well.[15]

Steuben represented the most serious challenge to Tiffany, but there were firms that as yet have not been adequately studied. The most important was the Quezal Art Glass and Decorating Company, a venture begun on Long Island, in 1902, by a disgruntled Tiffany employee, Martin Bache, who had been the mixer in the first Favrile shop and therefore knew the Tiffany glass formulas. Others were the Union Glass Company, in Somerville, Massachusetts, and the Alton Manufacturing Company, in Sandwich, Massachusetts, both of which also produced imitations of Favrile with the aid of former Tiffany blowers.[16]

Art glass did not survive. Steuben, classified a nonessential industry during World War I, subsequently was bought by the Corning Glass Works. In 1919, both Tiffany and Nash retired from active involvement in their enterprises. Quezal closed in 1924, although its last blowing shop, which was an especially skillful one, moved to the Durand Art Glass Company, in Vineland, New Jersey, and continued to produce art glass until 1930.[17]

ALTERNATIVES TO THE OPALESCENT PICTURE WINDOW

The opalescent-school picture window of La Farge, Tiffany, and their colleagues represents high art of the period 1900 to 1920, but there were artists who turned its techniques to the creation of a simpler style, consistent with the tenets of the American Arts and Crafts movement. The new glass, as advocated by Otto Heinigke and Harry Eldredge Goodhue, avoided the elaborate illusionism of the high opalescent style, relying instead on the graphic design of its leads to create a simple image. A former Tiffany employee, Emil Lange, who made glass for the architects Greene and Greene, of California, created spectacular windows in this style. The Tiffany Studio itself occasionally produced panels in an Arts and Crafts style.[18]

Not a variant but a reaction to opalescent stained glass was the Prairie School, whose chief designers of glass were Frank Lloyd Wright and George Grant Elmslie. By the 1900s, Wright had developed an abstract style that combined ordinary, clear window glass with color chips of opaline in rectilinear patterns that articulated their architectural context. Wright's draw-

Otto Heinigke. Untitled window. c. 1900. Opalescent glass, pot metal. 15′ × 8′6″. Plymouth Church of the Pilgrims, Brooklyn Heights, New York

Nicola D'Ascenzo. Stained-glass window for the Tabard Inn Food Co. c. 1905. From Harry Goodhue, "Stained Glass in Private Houses," *Architectural Record* 18 (1905)

Henry Wynd Young. *Te Deum
Window*. 1919. Stained glass. Emanuel
Episcopal Church, Newport, Rhode
Island. Designed by J. Gordon Guthrie

ings for windows survive, but one should remember that he—and Elmslie,
too—gave over the production to professional glass studios, and some of those
began to imitate his style in ready-made panels that could be ordered through
catalogues.[19]

To modern eyes, the Prairie School may seem the most advanced of the
early twentieth-century stained-glass styles, but it was a style without immediate issue. Wright began using plate glass in his windows and discontinued
stained glass after the 1920s. The near future belonged to another, alternative
style, which, at first glance, seems the most retrogressive of the possibilities
open to an American artist of that time: the Neo-Gothic.

Neo-Gothic stained glass was an attempt to return to the time-honored
stained-glass techniques of pot-metal glass and painting. Even by 1900, as
opalescent stained glass was achieving hegemony on the American market, a
reaction was developing among artists seeking an architectural art who had
become dissatisfied with pictorialism and with the deadening quality of
opalescent light.

The leading polemicist of the movement was Ralph Adams Cram, Amer-

William and Ann Lee Willet. *Liberal Arts Window*. 1913. Stained glass. Proctor Hall, Princeton University, New Jersey

ica's most prominent church architect. To Cram, the Middle Ages represented an ideal, a harmonious time when man lived in secure social groups—family, community, guild, monastery, chivalric order—and workmen took honest pride in their craft. To cure the ills of modern society required re-creating medieval society—and creating a contemporary church architecture based upon medieval principles was a major part of his plan.

By 1915, there were several studios whose windows met with Cram's approval. Among them were those of Otto Heinigke, a close friend of La Farge's, and William Willet, a onetime director of La Farge's studio, who now had a studio in Philadelphia. Heinigke had become interested in medieval glass on a trip to Europe, and by 1900, he was including accents of pot metal in his opalescent windows. A pot-metal medallion window, made in 1905 for the First Presbyterian Church, in Pittsburgh, brought Willet to Cram's attention and gained him a commission, in 1910, for a chapel at West Point.[20]

It may not have been realized at the time but La Farge's death, in 1910, was the turning point for American stained glass. Not long before, Tiffany had provoked Cram's rage by inducing Mrs. Russell Sage to put a magnificent opalescent landscape window in the church that Cram had built for her at Far Rockaway, Long Island. In 1911, Cram obtained an appointment to complete

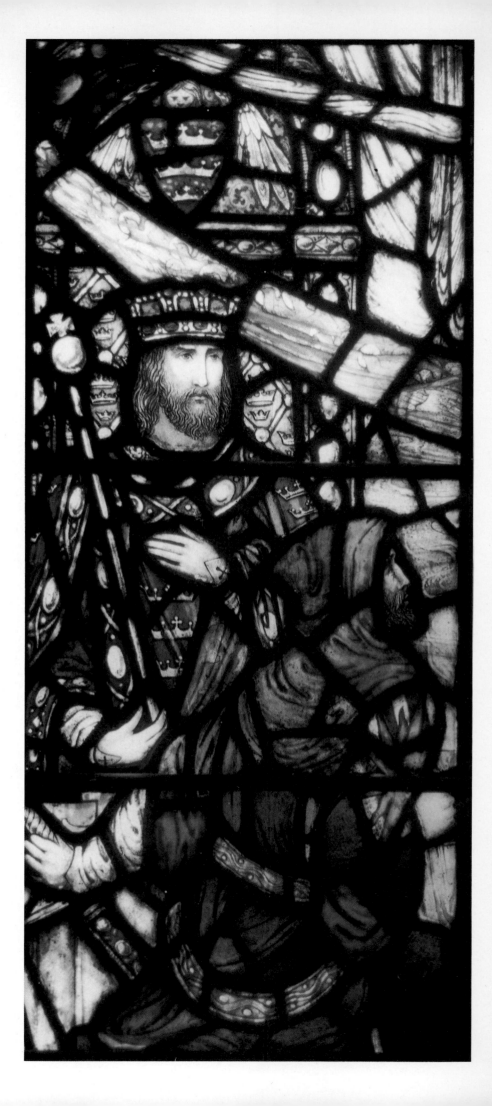

Charles J. Connick. *Holy Grail Window*
(detail). 1919. Proctor Hall, Princeton
University, New Jersey

the Cathedral of St. John the Divine, in New York, in the Gothic style. He promptly sealed off the Tiffany chapel from the 1893 Chicago World's Columbian Exposition, which, having been donated to the cathedral, had been in use.[21] Tiffany Studios tried making medieval-style windows in opalescent glass, and in pot metal as well, but they were not among the studio's better efforts.[22] By 1919, when Louis Tiffany retired, the younger American studios were all working in pot metal, and opalescent glass was no longer a vital artistic movement.

The opalescent aesthetic created by John La Farge and Louis Comfort Tiffany was a truly original American contribution to the history of glass. The origins of the opalescent movement lie in the boom years of the last quarter of the nineteenth century. The writings of artists and critics reflect a period that saw itself unabashedly casting aside the restraints of tradition in the pursuit of creating something newer and better—something American.

The sheer size of his studio, the thousands of windows it produced, and the number of his workers who eventually established studios of their own make Tiffany important to the history of American glass. Because the focus has been on La Farge as an artist, with glass but one aspect of his art, his place in the rise of American glass as a craft tradition is more complex. He was clearly the better artist. Although he lacked Tiffany's resources and his studio was much smaller, it produced a number of artists, such as Mary Tillinghast, David Maitland Armstrong, and Joseph Lauber, who themselves made contributions to the opalescent school.

La Farge's influence on the subsequent generation who found opalescent glass exhausted and were drawn instead to the potential of pot metal, has scarcely been investigated. La Farge was, without qualification, the only American artist of the opalescent school who truly understood stained glass. He understood that the darks of the lead lines were not an unfortunate distraction necessitated by the limitations of technique—something that Tiffany never quite learned—but a vital part of the window's color. And he had absorbed the lessons of his visits to Chartres—that the art of painting with colored light was not simply the making of luminous paintings but the creation of a light-controlled interior.

It is significant that the American Craft Museum has included glass in its discussion of the development of craft in America during the opening years of the twentieth century. The term *glass* actually includes two distinct crafts— art glass, or hot glass, and stained glass—and it has been a rare artist who practices both. It was no accident that John La Farge and Louis Comfort Tiffany were among these rare few, as both began working in stained glass as an outgrowth of their respective interest in problems of depicting light in opaque media. Among the craft media, stained glass occupies a unique position, since it is also an architectural and a representational art.

The period from 1900 to 1920 was pivotal for American glass. Artists began to develop a self-conscious identification with stained glass as an art with a unique craft tradition. A major development was the reaction against the elaborate illusionism of the picture window developed by La Farge and Tiffany, and eventually the total repudiation of the opalescent glass that the previous century had hailed as La Farge's and Tiffany's greatest invention.

This development established the direction that American stained glass was to take until well into the century. The elite artist-designer of the opalescent school disappeared. The new ideal was a guildlike workshop organized on the Arts and Crafts principles. An understanding of the workshop organization is particularly important for understanding stained glass and the highly technical craft of art glass as well, for historically glass has been a collaborative rather than an individual art.

Textiles: As Documented by

The Craftsman

by Christa C. Mayer Thurman

The home was the focus of artistic endeavor in the field of textiles in the first two decades of the twentieth century. The affluent interior was furnished with products or artifacts from far-distant places. Those who could afford English Arts and Crafts, despite stiff import tariffs in existence since 1890, continued to buy them. For the middle class, a national taste was fostered through magazines as well as companies that issued catalogues or advertised their products through kits. Creative design emanated from professionally trained architects and interior designers; very few names of textile artists or craftsmen have come down to us.

The concept of beautifying one's home triggered the populace, especially women, to contribute to this effort. Even women who were unable to attend the societies, or the few colleges and schools that began teaching weaving and needlework, wanted to participate, and the industry was quick to respond by providing kits that could be purchased from art supply or department stores or through the mail. Today, these companies are long forgotten, and only through an occasional surviving catalogue can their existence be documented. A similar fate applies to actual designs that, if not completed or only partially executed, may still carry the name of the company. Like *The Craftsman*, with its pillows, runners, and curtains, commercial companies, such as the H. E. Varren Company, Richardson Silk Company, Brainerd and Armstrong Company, and M. Heminway & Sons Silk Company, distributed their patterns throughout the United States.[1] The kits were good advertising for some. The Carlson Currier Company, for instance, produced silk threads for embroidering, sewing, and knitting; to enable the purchaser to try out its threads, a stamped design on linen or cotton fabric was sent along.[2]

A recent, fortuitous find of several extant pieces clearly shows how such designs were planned and laid out. The stenciled motif was presented in specific colors and supplied with matching threads. Once the pattern was executed, over-embroidering would have made it look like the pillow sham from the Richardson Silk Company, and the company's name would have been either cut off or worked into a seam at the time of completion. A page from the 1911–12 catalogue of the Valley Supply Company is most enlightening. The ad for this St. Louis company featured Royal Society Package Goods, and boasted that the packages "contain Royal Society embroidery floss to finish the article and instructions and materials as listed." Royal Society was the trademark of H. E. Varren, one of the largest wholesale companies of needlework kits, who sold to the Valley Supply Company, who, in turn, issued the catalogue and filled mail orders. One of these kits, for example, was a handbag described as "tinted on dark linen," and sold for fifty cents, plus seven cents postage.[3] The Pacific Embroidery Company, in existence from 1909 to 1929, in San Francisco, likewise carried out special commissions and issued kits.[4]

The techniques that came into wide use between 1900 and 1920 were needlework, appliqué, and stenciling, with the emphasis on quick execution. Unfortunately, inexpensive, even cheap, fabrics, for the most part, were used, and the works were unsigned or unmarked, except for stamped designs issued by companies. On the rare occasions when a textile from this period has survived, it is difficult to assign a designer, maker, or a precise location or date. The work is not of the highest caliber, but given the fact that the kit business was so extensive and that stamped patterns were the normal route, individual perfection and top quality were less important overall. As long as the object was functional, inexpensive, and tied in with an allover design concept for a room or house, the solution had been found.

Contrary to the American Arts and Crafts tendency to utilize machine production, the few extant embroidered and stenciled textiles were done by hand and within the home. The machine did play a role in domestic endeavors, particularly in large, pile woven carpets and mass-produced woven yardage, echoing past and present European styles and designs.

It is generally accepted that America adopted England as a prototype in advocating its own Arts and Crafts movement. Yet there was another source of inspiration, on American soil, and it was found in the Shaker communities throughout New York State.

In 1774, eight Shakers, with their leader, Mother Ann Lee, emigrated from Manchester, England. After Lee's death, in 1784, the communities continued under the leadership of Joseph Meacham. These settlements were governed by beliefs that not only stood for equality among the sexes but a uniform life-style based upon the group's moral, philosophical, and political outlook, adhering to such criteria as "utility, simplicity and perfection" in furnishings and objects.[5] The axioms established standards that, decades later, were to find echoes in the American Arts and Crafts movement. The movement differed from its English counterpart in that it adapted hand-crafted concepts, applied them to standardized styles, and utilized machines to execute the various products.

In 1898, Gustav Stickley founded his own company at Onondaga, three miles from Syracuse, New York. This came after a trip to England, where he had been introduced to the work of the architects and designers C.F.A. Voysey and C. R. Ashbee, and had met Samuel Bing, the dealer and entrepreneur.

In United Crafts, which later became the Craftsman Workshops, Gustav Stickley strove "to promote and to extend the principles established by Morris, in both the artistic and the socialistic sense . . . to substitute the luxury of taste for the luxury of costliness; to teach that beauty does not imply elaboration or ornament; to employ only those forms and materials which make for simplicity, individuality and dignity of effect."[6] Four years later, he stated: "We are influenced by our surroundings more than we imagine."[7] The materials used at United Crafts were American oak, leather, and metal, and the necessary textiles and fabrics were provided as well. One of Stickley's major critical contributions was the establishment of the monthly publication *The Craftsman*, whose premier issue appeared in October 1901. In its pages, he discussed vital issues or invited others to present concerns close to their hearts. In addition, the monthly became a vehicle for advertisements, such as the textile and carpet ads that documented the taste of the time and, for scholars, have become an important source in reconstructing the period under discussion. Better, perhaps, than any other record, the magazine mirrors American textile involvement in those years. In 1916, however, *The Craftsman* ceased publication, a year after Stickley had declared bankruptcy.

The first textile ads appeared in September 1903 with the introduction of "the Craftsman fabrics which comprise the following Craftsman canvases. These are offered in two weights: the firmer and less expensive for wall hangings; the finer and lighter for portieres, curtains, cushions, pillows, counterpanes, scarves, etc. They are obtainable in an extended gamut of color with delicate subdivisions of shades—the soft, dull effects now so desirable

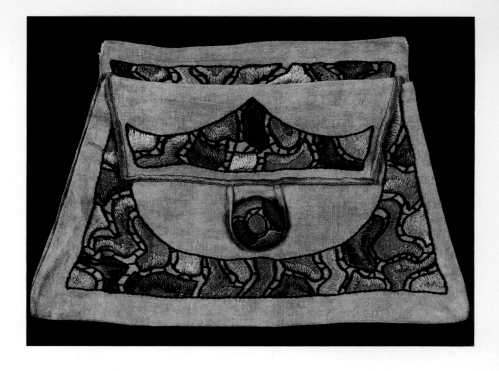

Handbag. c. 1910–15. Made from kit
produced by H. E. Varren Company.
Linen embroidered with silk, 8¼ × 12½".
Collection The Art Institute of Chicago

being obtained through qualities of texture." The advertisement next listed
Craftsman linens: "These are designed for use in wall hangings, tapestries,
friezes, portieres, curtains, counterpanes, table covers, etc. These colors and
shades, constituting a full palette . . . to be employed in tapestries (linen upon
linen, or linen upon canvas), done in appliqué and stenciling." The third
category listed was Craftsman taffetas: "They are particularly effective in
shades of green and olive, and in certain tones of red peculiar to the old
Venetian masters. They present inequalities of texture which produce beautiful 'accidents' of light and shade."

Further listings referred to Craftsman weaves. This heading included
certain distinctive fabrics for use in household decoration that otherwise
could not be classified. "They are effective, refined and unusual." And, finally,
there were Craftsman goathair fabrics, "characterized by soft coloring, by
fineness and pliability of texture and by durable qualities which warrant their
price." The advertisement concluded: "The Craftsman Workshops will furnish designs, finished embroideries and tapestries . . . fabrics in any desired
quantity, embroidery materials, and all requisite information as to measurements and processes." In the same issue, a separate listing advertised leatherwork: "The skins being subjected to processes which preserve and enhance
all natural qualities: wall hangings, screens, cushions, and pillows." A listing
for textiles and rugs addressed, specifically, "Silk, linen and cotton fabrics for
wall hangings, portieres, curtains, screens, covers and scarves. Tapestries and
embroideries executed; designs, measurements and processes furnished
upon request."[8]

The December 1903 issue carried an advertisement for fabrics from the
Craftsman Workshops. It listed Craftsman canvases "for hangings and cushions. Strong, even fabrics in a variety of soft, dull tones, for use in simple
schemes of furnishings and decoration. Finely adapted texture and weight to
cross-stitch and hemstitch. Samples of principal colors and shades mailed to
any address in the United States upon receipt of a two-cent stamp." In the
listing for Craftsman linens for covers, screens, wall hangings and appliqué
upon Craftsman canvas, plain, heavy weaves and pleasing colors were recommended. A new listing for bloom linen and linen of natural color completed
the ad. Bloom linen was "woven like changeable silk, to show an undercolor;
especially adapted for embroidering with linen floss." Linen of natural color

was intended "for window curtains. Even weave and loose mesh falling in graceful folds."[9] But *The Craftsman* offered further options to its public. Specific designs, for table scarves, squares, curtains, pillows, luncheon sets, and portieres, could all be ordered from the Craftsman Workshops. In the July 1905 issue, *The Craftsman* ran its ad as "A Suggestion": "What better way to spend the leisure hours of vacation time than with some of the Craftsman needlework. It is not tedious and is just the thing to take with you to the country or the seaside. It may be there is need for a pillow in your window seat; a pair of portieres for the winter home; a luncheon set as a Christmas gift. Any of these we will be glad to send you stamped, with all materials, ready for working. Our fabrics—including Craftsman canvas, for portieres and pillow covers; plain and bloom linens in almost any shade desired, together with the unbleached homespun—form a pleasing selection from which to choose. Samples upon request."[10] Stickley also issued an illustrated catalogue for only ten cents.[11]

In November 1903, *The Craftsman* announced the establishment of "The Craftsman Homebuilders Club" and the opportunity to receive, free of charge, "secure complete plans and specifications for a home." These ads complemented the series "A Craftsman House." The series on houses began in January 1904 and continued through May 1907. The ad utilized an illustration of a dining room that had been described, floor plan and all, in the July 1903 issue. "*The Craftsman* is a magazine devoted to the new domestic art. Each issue for 1904 will present complete designs for a house in which every architectural detail will serve a well-defined constructive use. The decorative features will result largely from the introduction of proper colors in the materials. These plans for homes will vary in cost from two thousand to fifteen thousand dollars. They will be supplemented with complete details from our architectural department free of cost."[12] A unifying, geometric, meandering pattern was chosen for table scarves and the outer border of the carpet; echoes of related designs were to be found in window curtains and inlaid glass, augmented by the use of wooden wall paneling and straight, angular pieces of Stickley furniture.

In August 1905, Craftsman needlework was featured in the section "Our Home Department." Precise instructions were given for table scarves and luncheon sets. Fabrics were described, as were the stitches and yarns to be used, and patterns such as Checkerberry, Jewel, and Cornflower were illustrated in fully executed table scarves.[13] In the same issue, another key object in home decoration was introduced: the portiere. A heavy curtain, used for door openings, it could be embellished with designs and, often, unify an interior. In the August 1903 *Craftsman*, eight alternate designs were described as "designs for handiwork which may be easily executed by needlewomen with no special training." Materials for the panel itself and for the patterning appliqué were available in an array of colors and shadings, "so that the worker may use these fabrics in color schemes much as a painter composes upon his palette."[14] The eight patterns shared an organic design source; they were intended to cover the entire panel and not just the lower segment of the curtain. The main accent, however, occurred either on the top or bottom section of the portiere, connected frequently by thin, linear elements or a powdered field with a small, patterning device. The motifs were stamped onto the fabric and, thereafter, embroidered or worked in appliqué. The fabrics were Craftsman canvas, figured linen, bloom linen, or homespun linen, and the designs were appliquéd in linen.[15] The portiere was fully sewn, but sold with floss for carrying out the needlework.

A far less expensive way of patterning portieres was by block printing the design on canvas, a treatment suggested for bungalows or country houses.

They were advertised as being nine feet long, for the special price of twelve dollars a pair.[16]

Stickley was not alone in identifying Native American blankets and rugs as suitable decoration for the home. While Stickley was forming his workshops and introducing reforms, another American, Elbert G. Hubbard, founded the Roycrofters, in 1895, at East Aurora, New York, near Buffalo, after visiting William Morris, in 1892, at Hammersmith, England, where he saw the Kelmscott Press. The Roycrofters' foremost concerns were printing, bookbinding, and furnituremaking. The furniture was simple and straightforward, rectilinear in appearance, and decorated only with functional ornament, such as hinges and knobs for doors and handles to open drawers.[17] Of particular importance to textiles is an illustration that appeared in *The Book of the Roycrofters*, published in 1907, showing medium-size, Native American carpets on the floor of a room appointed with Roycrofters furniture. This coincides with an ad in *The Craftsman* that identifies the Francis E. Lester Company, in Mesilla Park, New Mexico, as an importer of "genuine Indian blankets, direct from the Indian weaver to the customer, for the past 15 years. . . . The blankets I sell are entirely handwoven by the best Navajo and Pueblo Indian weavers of their tribes, from pure native wool, handclipped by the Indians from their own sheep, and entirely handspun. . . . It is woven under my personal supervision and every strand of it is pure native handspun wool. . . . The design is an original Indian figure in lightning and ceremonial cross pattern. I can send you the rug in any of three shades, the design in black and white, with the ground color in either a deep rich red, a dark olive green, or a deep Indian blue. The weave is close and heavy, just right for floor use, and the rug will literally last a life time."[18]

Other suppliers of fine Navajo blankets and rugs were John B. Moore, a United States–licensed Indian trader, in New Mexico, who published catalogues between 1903 and 1911[19]; C. N. Cotton, who sold his blankets through mail-order catalogues between 1896 and 1919[20]; and the Pendleton Woolen Mills, in Pendleton, Oregon, which sold "Indian design" bed blankets, robes, steamer rugs, bathrobes, couch covers, tapestries, and shawls.[21] The initial Pendleton catalogue was dated 1915, although the company was founded in 1895.

In the October 1903 *Craftsman*, an article appeared on "Three Craftsman Canvas Pillows" with Native American designs. The illustrations showed embroidered motifs inspired and taken from pottery and basketry of the Pueblos. Designs used were a "pine-tree motif," a "deer motif," and a "bear motif." The pillows were described as having greater durability and strength.[22] Another article presented "Nursery Wall Coverings in Indian Designs." Five designs were not only suggested, described, and illustrated but presented for "educational and artistic purposes," and a parallel was drawn between these Native American designs and "Briton and Celtic systems which are now in active, enthusiastic revival in England."[23] Pictographs were described as "one of the most fruitful primary sources of historic knowledge, and those originating among the sierras and on the mesas of the New World, are as eloquent as those which were composed in the Nile Valley."[24] The designs illustrated—the Elements, the Thunderbird, the Storm, the Forest, and the Happy Hunting Grounds—were intended to be stenciled on a "canvas like fabric with dyes." These patterns were inspired by pictographs of the Hopi Indians, in northern Arizona, and the symbolic meaning of the designs was fully recounted.[25] In 1911, an ad appeared for "India Drugget Rugs—Craftsman Design." They are described as "firm, heavy handwoven rugs, made especially for us in India, of bullocks' wool, and are reversible. We carry these in colors and patterns perfectly suitable to harmonize with Craftsman furnishings." The illustrated example shows a rug with the so-called Nile pattern. Available on a natural background color in blue and brown, it also came in a "scroll" pattern. The smallest size available, three-by-three feet, sold for $5.50; the largest, fifteen-by-twelve feet, for $95.00.[26]

These untapped resources did not go unnoticed. In an article in *House and Garden*, "American Indian Art in the Home," Charles Francis Saunders suggested that Native American artifacts were the ideal solution to furnish a California bungalow or an informal country house. Contrary to *The Craftsman* advertisement, blankets were not suggested for floor use; they were too fragile. Only the Navajo rug was to be used on the floor, as it "wears indefinitely and is easily cleaned."[27] Also advertised in *The Craftsman* were "Alaska Fur Rugs" from the Hudson Bay Fur Company. Described as "the finest specimens of the big game in Alaska, perfectly mounted in rich rugs," these items could be ordered from the company, in Seattle, Washington.[28]

Magazines report that another foreign influence, batik, a Far Eastern technique, was in use in America around 1910.[29] Among its exponents in this country were Bertram Hartman, Mira Burr Edson, and Charlotte Busck. Busck, a member of the National Society of Craftsmen, was well known for her leatherwork. She studied, worked, and experimented with Professor Charles E. Pellew, who taught at Columbia University, in New York, and who wrote an article, in 1909, on the technique for *The Craftsman*.[30] Another artist who became known for her silk murals in batik was Lydia Bush-Brown, a student at the Pratt Institute of Fine and Applied Art, in Brooklyn, New York, and thereafter a student of Professor Pellew's, in Washington, D.C. Her 1920s work is well represented in the collection of New York's Cooper-Hewitt Museum. Marguerite Zorach did a series of batiked silk panels between 1918 and 1920 that, today, are part of the Metropolitan Museum of Art's holdings.[31]

Women were particularly encouraged to become interior decorators. Candace Wheeler's *Principles of Home Decoration with Practical Examples*, published in 1903, was a guide for those entering the profession or anyone interested in interiors. In the December 1907 *Craftsman*, "Pioneer Work of Women in Tasteful and Economical Interior Decoration" elaborates on this new profession: "Now that women are accepted as competent wage earners and forced to face responsibility without advice, they are, along certain lines where their experience has been greatest, proving themselves more definitely original, more fearless of tradition than men have been in the same field."[32]

The article further observes that in economically tight situations, it was the female decorator, working along with modern architects, who was able to resolve at far less cost the needs for the common, smaller home. Treatment of ceilings and floors; treatment and decoration of walls; the use of tapestry, leather, and wallpaper; concern for color and in relation to light—all were issues that began to matter. A science was applied to the interior, and women, now professionally trained and aided by their naturally intuitive responses, were the best people to assist with such issues.

Another development that began to influence issues of taste and application was the formation of societies throughout the United States. Although New York led with the New York Society of Decorative Art, numerous societies and organizations were founded at this time and became important. In 1895, the Chalk and Chisel Club was established in Minneapolis; by 1899, it became the Minneapolis Arts and Crafts Society. In 1897, both the Chicago and the Boston Arts and Crafts societies were founded, and in 1899, the Industrial Art League was formed in Chicago. In 1902, the Handicraft Guild was introduced in Minneapolis, and the Society of Arts and Crafts was established in Grand Rapids. A year later, William Twyman set up the Morris Society in Chicago, and in 1907, the National League of Handicraft Societies was founded in Boston.

Often, societies were connected with major museums, and they began to sponsor annual craft exhibitions that included various kinds of textiles.[33] Among them were the Arts and Crafts exhibitions of The Art Institute of Chicago, which began in 1898 and continued through 1921. In 1907, the Chicago Arts and Crafts Society cosponsored, with the Architectural League, an important exhibition of English and American Arts and Crafts at the Art Institute. Both the Cleveland and Detroit museums of art had similar programs, although their impact was more regional and did not span as many years.[34]

Some organizations were very focused—among them, the Deerfield Society of Blue and White Needlework. Founded by Margaret Whiting and Ellen Miller, in 1896, in Deerfield, Massachusetts, its members had to be residents of the Deerfield community. Initially, the society was founded to ensure the revival of colonial needlework designs.[35] To identify these copies clearly with their originals, members worked, at first, only with blue yarn on a white linen ground. As other colors were added, though, the organization's name became somewhat misleading. All pieces were marked with the letter *D*, surrounded or contained within a spinning wheel. Although the society dyed its own yarns, it never wove its own fabrics. The fabrics were ordered from Berea College, in Kentucky, and McCutcheon's, in New York City. The yarns used in the needlework were imported from Scotland.

Whiting and Miller found inspiration in the teachings of John Ruskin, the social reformer and art critic. Although the society became a profit-making enterprise, initially its aim was to imitate the eighteenth century out of sheer pleasure, with equal pay for its designers and needleworkers. The society was also very clear in separating craftsmanship from social reform, for, as Margaret Whiting once wrote, "It is not charity but art which founds and maintains a craft."[36] The ill health of both of its founders brought the society to an end in 1926.

Aside from needlework and textile references, issues of decoration achieved through such textile printing techniques as stenciling began to emerge during this period. In December 1903, an article appeared in *The Craftsman* entitled "Stenciled Fabrics in Combination with Peasant Embroidery." In character, the work consisted of appliqué with "stencilwork in patterns conventionalized from natural forms."[37] It was an inexpensive and relatively fast way of creating patterned fabrics. The appliqué, attached to the background fabric, subsequently was outlined with worsted cording. The stenciling that followed had to harmonize in coloration. The colors were to be mixed with white lead and turpentine into a thick, creamy substance, which was then rubbed or pounced through a stencil plate made of "tough, thin paper" that had been previously treated with paraffin so that the color would not be absorbed by the paper. Even cotton velvet fabrics were used for wall friezes and portieres, and, thereafter, fashioned into wall hangings.[38] Window curtains were also decorated with stenciled patterns. The recommended fabric was "sheer white crossbarred muslin" and "ecru etamine of open mesh and firm, crisp weave."[39] Matching designs could be stenciled on rough handwoven linen, which gave the cloth an uneven texture, to be used for portieres and couch covers. Needlework was not recommended for window curtains, as the sheerness demanded a light, airy, and transparent design. As far as maintenance, washing was recommended "if reasonable care is used."[40] Stenciling was considered most appropriate for Craftsman houses, bungalows, and country houses; inappropriate, though, were brocaded fabrics, lace, and heavily woven tapestries. Stencils were easily accessible; they could be purchased in art supply stores or ordered from paint company catalogues or magazines.[41] A vast array of fabrics was recommended upon which to

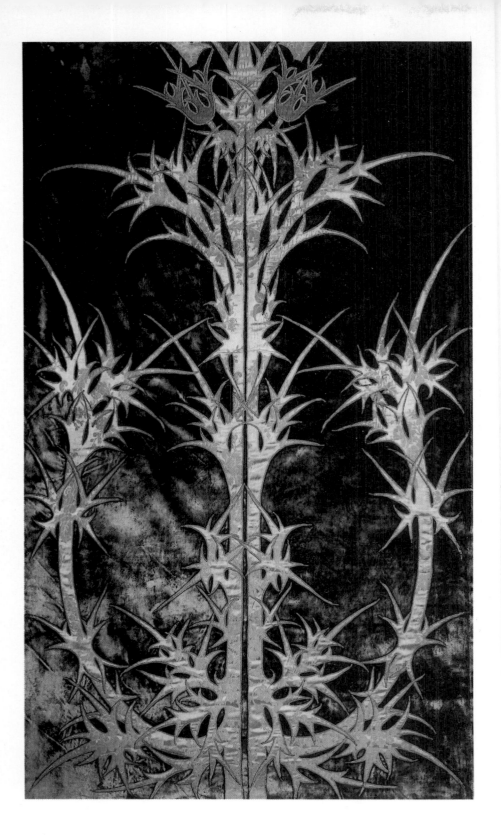

George Washington Maher and Louis J. Millet. Portiere. 1901. Designed for and used in James A. Patten House, Evanston, Illinois. Silk, cotton, velvet, linen, and gilt-metal-strip-wrapped linen, 80¹/8 × 48". Collection The Art Institute of Chicago. Restricted gift of The Antiquarian Society of The Art Institute of Chicago

stencil; even leather was suggested. To complete the interior, one could stencil on matting rugs as well as plaster walls. Screens and lamp shades were on the list, along with such accessories as pillows and runners.[42] Unfortunately, cheap fabrics like jute and burlap often were used, and if washing indeed took place, it is easy to understand why hardly any of these artifacts have survived. Despite such hazards, it was a quick way of turning living quarters into inexpensive, attractive interiors.

A number of American architects and designers made an important contribution to textiles. George W. Maher and Louis J. Millet did the James A. Patten House, in Evanston, Illinois. Extant textiles are two portieres.[43] The theme for the house was the thistle; the illustrated portiere, of 1901, carries this motif, appliquéd to a heavy, cotton velvet curtain to tie in

John S. Bradstreet. Curtain panels for the yellow bedroom of the William Prindle House. 1905. Cotton, linen, silk; each panel 53¹/₂ × 21″. Collection The Art Institute of Chicago. Gift of David A. Hanks in Memory of George B. Young

with the painted and stenciled wall decorations throughout the house.[44] John Scott Bradstreet, another midwestern designer, together with the architect William Hunt, designed the interior of the William Prindle House, in Duluth, Minnesota. A set of curtains dating from 1905 was part of the furnishing fabric of the house's yellow bedroom.

Issues of unifying motifs concerned the architect George Grant Elmslie. Born in Scotland, by 1889 he was part of the Adler and Sullivan firm, in Chicago. By 1903, Elmslie had established himself as its chief designer, and he was very much involved when the Henry B. Babson House, in Riverside, Illinois, was remodeled, in 1912. The original Babson House had been designed by Sullivan's office, under Elmslie's supervision, in 1908–9. The carpet, and the matching ones in the hall passages between the major first-floor rooms, was probably produced at that time.

Extant carpets also can be found in the Gamble House, in Pasadena, California. The house, designed by the Greene brothers, Charles Sumner Greene and Henry Mather Greene, was completed in 1908.

Frank Lloyd Wright's concern for textiles is well documented in one of his Fellowship lectures.[45] He advocated unifying design in architecture, as well as in the treatment of the interior and all its components. This approach is very much in evidence when one studies Wright's architectural drawings for a number of his houses, or if one looks at the still extant pieces of textiles or carpets. The drawing for the vaulted, two-story living room of the Susan Lawrence Dana House, in Springfield, Illinois, dating from 1902, includes a textile design superimposed in part over the architectural rendering.[46] In his design for the living room of the Avery Coonley residence, of 1907, in Riverside, Illinois, Wright included the carpet.[47] In the F. C. Bogk House, of 1916, in Milwaukee, Wisconsin, several of the actual carpets and their designs are still in existence. The carpet designs, in the archives of the Frank Lloyd Wright Foundation, at Taliesin West, are dated 1914 and 1915, respectively.[48] The common bond in these houses is that the architect selected an interior designer and, together, they settled on a unifying theme or, what Maher called, the "motif-rhythm theory."

Through education, the relationship among design, craft, and industry was being explored. Colleges with workshops and handicraft schools were established throughout the United States to concentrate on the teaching of weaving, needlework, and lacemaking. Mentioned here are a select few that made a substantial contribution to the development of American textiles.

Newcomb College, founded in 1886 at Tulane University, in New Orleans, and known for its pottery, was actively involved with needlework. After having won the Paris Exposition Medal in November 1900, the founder, Mrs. Josephine Louise LeMonnier Newcomb, decided to broaden the curriculum to include crafts and to build a separate building to pursue this new endeavor. Although Mrs. Newcomb died in 1901, the plan went through, and in the fall of 1902, "the textile class" began.[49] The class was taught by Mrs. Gertrude Roberts Smith, an assistant professor of drawing and painting. The simplest of materials were to be combined with good design, color, and four basic stitch techniques—"darning, buttonhole, satin, and outline."[50] The program was a great success, and such items as church vestments, panels and screens, table coverings and napkins, as well as clothing accessories, were made. In 1904, courses in weaving and spinning were added, and, frequently, the woven fabrics were embroidered. All pieces that passed a jury carried the Newcomb seal. A relatively large number of pieces have survived and are part of the Louisiana State Museum Collection.

Berea College, in Kentucky, was founded in 1855. In 1893, it established Student Craft Industries. A student-operated program known as Berea Fire-

Babson House carpet detail

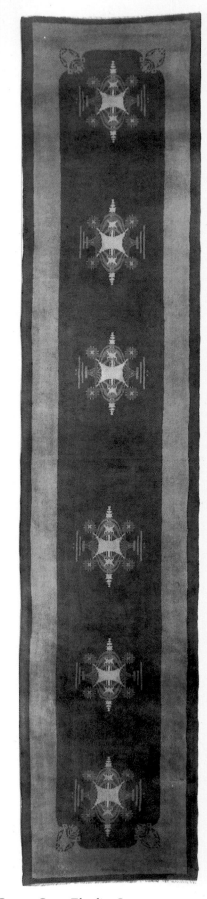

George Grant Elmslie. Carpet. 1908–12. Designed for the Henry B. Babson House, Riverside, Illinois. Linen, cotton, and wool; plain weave with "Ghiordes knots" cut pile, $220^{1}/_{2} \times 45^{1}/_{2}$". Collection The Art Institute of Chicago. Restricted gift of Mrs. Theodore D. Tieken

side Industries was the first to be introduced. Initially, the program produced handwoven coverlets as a means of making money.[51] Student Craft Industries is still in existence today.

The School of the California Guild of Arts and Crafts (what later became the California College of Arts and Crafts) was established by Frederick H. Meyer, in Oakland, in 1907. The school experimented by combining the arts and crafts into a single curriculum. Students who took courses became active in the field of design as interior designers, architects, or graphic artists, or they entered the profession as manual-training teachers. As such, their influence was considerable.

In a 1902 *Craftsman* article, "Art in Industries and the Outlook for the Art Student," Caryl Coleman wrote: "The future of 'Art in Industries' is largely in your hands, for it is within your office to create, not artists, for they are born, but to raise up an appreciative public, from the youth entrusted to your care, by implanting in their minds a knowledge of form, of color, of composition, of the motives of design, and the history of ornament; by stimulating their curiosity to know the reason why one picture is better than another, why one style of ornament in a particular case is better than another; by revealing to them their own talent, if they have any, or if they have not, by making them more modest in their judgment in matters of art."[52]

To Coleman, the problem lay in the methods of teaching, which tried to cover too vast a field in too short a time. "Would it not be better to insist upon good draughtsmanship, and when that is acquired, and only then, to allow the student to study exhaustively one subject, and not the whole field of design; guiding him in the course for which he shows a special aptitude."[53]

Oscar Lovell Triggs, an instructor at the University of Chicago in 1902, the year he wrote "The Workshop and School," was equally eloquent: "The art we try to keep alive in a poor, thin fashion was originally provided for the noble and leisure classes of Europe, and is still an incident of wealth and luxury. What can be more undemocratic than the principle of 'art for art's sake,' according to which most of our art is produced, and by the acceptance of which those gifted with special aesthetic taste defend their exclusiveness?" He found the answer in "the workshop . . . where materials shall be shaped into the things we use. It will be a 'studio,' where work shall be creative and not devoid of a sense of beauty."[54]

The following year Triggs wrote "A School of Industrial Art." The concept of his new school was geared "to bring art and labor into necessary association—labor to give substance, art to yield pleasure. . . . To associate art and industry; to change the character of labor so as to make industry educative, and to develop the instinct of workmanship and elicit the pleasure belonging to good workmanship so as to make the industrial life complete— such may be said to be the aims of industrial education."[55] The subject of textiles appeared as the tenth topic to be taught in workshops, along with decoration, printing and bookbinding, construction in wood, metal, leather, paper, stone, and glass.[56] The workshops were to be equipped with hand and power tools, so that "all the constructive processes" could be carried out.[57]

Although the history of critical response is recorded in the pages of *The Craftsman*, the textiles themselves remain the primary resource for our understanding of a period shaped by the architect, the professional artist, and the homemaker—the female homemaker, in particular. Native Americans and members of the Shaker communities, as well, made textiles that contributed significantly to the foundation of the American craft movement. But it was the rise of Arts and Crafts societies, the awakening interest of museums, and the commitment of colleges and universities that ensured a promising future for textiles in the ensuing decades of the twentieth century.

The Arts and Crafts in American Houses and Gardens

by James D. Kornwolf

SOURCES AND CHARACTERISTICS OF AMERICAN ARTS AND CRAFTS ARCHITECTURE

Craft and craftsmanship in American design in the period 1900 to 1920, especially in the design of house and garden, were dominated by the influence of England's Arts and Crafts movement, and were toasted at the outset by the greatest American practitioner of the movement, Frank Lloyd Wright, in his 1901 lecture "The Art and Craft of the Machine," given at Jane Addams's Hull-House, in Chicago. The movement was highly idealistic and basically Romantic, although it possessed major realist tenets and important ramifications for Modernism. It emerged in the United States around 1900, mainly as a response to newly created work by a second generation of English followers of William Morris—C. R. Ashbee, M. H. Baillie-Scott, Edwin Lutyens, and C.F.A. Voysey, among them. In the United States, the movement was the most progressive catalyst in architecture, interior design, and landscape and town planning in the first two decades of this century, and Wright was its most original designer.

Dozens of Arts and Crafts societies were organized from coast to coast. Wright played an active role in the Chicago Arts and Crafts Society, one of the few organizations he ever deigned to join. The impact of the Arts and Crafts was seen further in a slew of new magazines that emerged around 1900, among them *House Beautiful, House and Garden, Country Life in America, Indoors and Out, The Garden, The Craftsman,* and *The Ladies' Home Journal.* So, too, is its influence seen in *Landscape Architecture,* the publication of the American Society of Landscape Architects, founded in 1899.[1] The primary focus of these magazines was suburban or country houses and gardens, inspired by the model that Gertrude Jekyll and Edwin Lutyens together had created for Jekyll with Munstead Wood, in Surrey, England, in 1896.[2] The Munstead Wood ideal predominated in such magazines well past World War I. Their Deanery Gardens (1899) was fittingly called by one writer, "a single interpenetrating conception—parts roofed over, others open to the sun, with the garden walks leading right into and about the house . . . at once formal and irregular . . . Miss Jekyll's naturalistic planting wedded to Lutyens's geometry in a balanced union of both principles."[3]

Most helpful to bear in mind is that the Arts and Crafts movement constituted a state of mind, an attitude that did not therefore produce a style but a variety of styles with consonant principles. The emphasis of the Arts and Crafts was clearly upon ethics, craftsmanship, and a vernacular, traditional, indigenous aesthetic milieu that was but one aspect of a more encompassing social and environmental program. When Morris impugned English capitalists for their pollution of the environment, he claimed that "their love of art is a mere pretense: how can you care about the image of a landscape when you show by your deeds that you don't care for the landscape itself."[4]

Wright was the most outstanding of those who saw an ethical, as well as aesthetic, message in Morris's visions of a new, more equitable and artistically sensitive society. *The Craftsman,* begun by Gustav Stickley in 1901, with

Library of "A Bradley House."
Illustration by Will Bradley as reproduced
in *The Ladies' Home Journal* (1902)

worshipful articles on John Ruskin and Morris, attempted to bring the social
message of the English movement to the United States. The magazine featured
modest houses inspired by those in *The Studio*, which began publication, in
London, in 1893. The houses and gardens were intended, like Wright's first
truly Arts and Crafts designs in *The Ladies' Home Journal*, in 1901, to appeal
to ordinary people. With the almost immediate international acclaim given to
Barry Parker and Raymond Unwin's versions of the Garden City, whether at
Letchworth or Hampstead, influence from these Arts and Crafts manifestations had by 1920 spread from coast to coast. One especially American
dimension was the short-lived Country Life movement, which sought to bring
a new vitality and beauty to once-rural areas of America, that part of the land
suffering most in quality of life from the unbridled process of urbanization
and industrialization that absorbed the country in the latter years of the
nineteenth century.[5] World War I delivered a fatal blow to the Arts and Crafts
movement worldwide, but for two decades, sweeping changes were made in
the art and craft of house, garden, and neighborhood.

THEORY AND DESIGN
OF AMERICAN ARTS AND CRAFTS ARCHITECTURE

American Arts and Crafts architects from 1900 to 1920 firmly built upon
previous architectural achievements associated with both the Aesthetic and
English Arts and Crafts movements.[6] And yet they departed from earlier
ideas, moving in eight separate directions. Four of these directions are ethical
in nature; the remaining four are aesthetically significant.

From an ethical point of view, the ordinary person became, in theory, the undisputed focal point of Arts and Crafts designers. In the United States especially, women not only played major roles in the movement but, because of its nature, were intrinsic to it. The ideal of a balanced acceptance of both sexes embodies one of the organic bases of the American Arts and Crafts

The dining room of the Gustav Stickley home at 438 Columbus Avenue, in Syracuse, New York, designed in 1902–3

movement. Vida Dutton Scudder, professor at Wellesley College, Socialist, and pupil of Ruskin, held, in 1903, that "the beautiful only exists as found in use, as it springs from the common life of all and ministers to the common life of all." Gustav Stickley's mentor, Irene Sargent, a professor at Syracuse University, is credited with having led him away, in about 1898, from "imitation" furniture to that based upon Arts and Crafts models. She wrote five articles on Morris in the first issue of *The Craftsman*.7

The ethical search for simpler, more direct solutions to problems at all levels is well seen in the one-person campaign, led by the editor of the *Ladies' Home Journal*, Edward Bok, "to take hold of the small American house and make it architecturally better" by publishing appropriate solicited designs from recognized designers. Bok himself claimed that President Theodore Roosevelt remarked that Bok was "the only man I ever heard of who changed, for the better, the architecture of an entire nation."8 Gustav Stickley made the dissemination of simple domestic designs, free for the writing, the hallmark of *The Craftsman*, claiming over twenty million dollars of construction of his Craftsman houses in 1915 alone.9 As Wright aptly said, "Simplicity in art . . . is a synthetic, positive quality, in which we may see evidence of mind, breadth of scheme, wealth of detail, and withal a sense of completeness found in a tree or a flower."10

A third ethical factor was the intellectual cast of most American Arts and Crafts theorists and architects, and many of their clients, who were steeped in the Emersonian and Ruskinian critical tradition. Wright, the Greene brothers, and Irving Gill, among others, certainly saw themselves as intellectuals who sought a design with a strong aesthetic and ethical base. Speaking at Hull-House, in 1901, Wright declared that "all artists love and honor William Morris. . . . That he miscalculated the machine does not matter. He did sublime work for it when he pleaded so well for the process of elimination its abuse had made necessary . . . when he preached the gospel of simplicity . . . imagine an Arts and Crafts society that may educate itself to prepare to make some good impression upon the machine, the destroyer of the present ideals and tendencies, their salvation in disguise."[11] As Wright acknowledged, Morris was the undisputed founder of this movement and drew worldwide attention to the reform of craft. It was also Morris's vision of a reformed built environment that inspired the urban dimension of the Arts and Crafts movement, that associated with the Garden City. Both developments greatly affected Wright and many other American architects and interior designers, as well as such landscape architects as Frederick Law Olmsted, Jr., Henry Vincent Hubbard, Walter Burley Griffin, and Irving Gill.[12] Wright's creation, after 1909, of his own home-workplace, Taliesin, in Wisconsin, and his Usonian, a utopian creation of Broadacre City, were certainly manifestations of his effort to realize these ideals.

Another reformer, Oscar Lovell Triggs, a professor at the University of Chicago, was one of the substantial number of American Arts and Crafts exponents who opted to limit machine production to the production of machines or to the production of goods best done by machines, returning furniture and similar objects to the craft shop.[13] Mabel Tuke Priestman, an interior designer, wrote on behalf of the cause. She reviewed exhibitions, traced the histories of various American Arts and Crafts societies, and, finally, expounded her own theories.[14] This intellectual orientation was clearly shown in a study that contrasted Wright's clients—intellectual, educated, middle-class inhabitants of Chicago's western suburbs—with those wealthier yet more bourgeois and socially striving clients of the city's northern lakefront suburbs.[15]

Clearly, the liberal, intellectual nature of protagonists of the movement helps to account for the fourth ethical stance of American Arts and Crafts theorists, the marked emphasis in the period upon social reform. The proper sociopolitical and economic background for Wright's architecture and urban theories involved Progressive leaders such as Robert La Follette, governor of Wisconsin, President Theodore Roosevelt, and Henry George, who advocated radical tax reform. Vida Dutton Scudder, active in many social programs in Boston, liked to quote Ruskin's view that "life without industry is guilt; industry without art is brutality."[16] Yet, it was precisely this view that helped bring about the demise of the Arts and Crafts movement after World War I.

From an aesthetic point of view, surfaces, whether of roofs or walls or of furniture and the decorative arts, were neutralized in order to produce a unified visual effect. White or cream stucco, a material favored for exteriors from Berlin to Pasadena, was first popularized by C.F.A. Voysey but more widely used by M. H. Baillie-Scott, whose accent was on the garden. Wright found Baillie-Scott's houses too "negative," meaning that they, like the human figure in a Maurice Denis painting, such as *April*, seemed ghostlike against the vividly planted gardens. In 1915, in his booklet *The Prairie Spirit in Landscape Gardening*, Wilhelm Miller attempted to summarize the achievements of Wright's generation, writing that it conserved or restored "native prairie scenery" and "local vegetation." All stressed the "repetition of a dominant, horizontal line—hallmark of the prairie style" and one of Ruskin's major principles.[17] Neutral surfaces also meant an unequivocal emphasis upon the particular nature of the material being used. Stucco must appear as stucco; the intrinsic nature of materials—whether wood, tile, terra-cotta, glass, or fabric—must be stressed in the execution of a design. Wood, therefore, was usually stained, not painted. This, in turn, led to a natural emphasis upon craftsmanship, for staining wood correctly calls attention to its grain as surely as a good paint job nullifies it. The importance of craftsmanship led to a concern for durability or permanence; oak was preferred to pine, leaded stained glass to plate glass. The new importance of materials achieved an astounding deemphasis of nineteenth-century stylistic revival.

This emphasis upon a neutral simplicity and deemphasis of style facilitated a second aesthetic breakthrough—an unprecedented, heightened degree of abstraction of form, line, texture, mass, and space. This is seen in Miller's point about the repetition of horizontal lines and in the continued exploration to effect new integrations of indoor-outdoor space. It could readily be shown, moreover, that the abstraction first emerging in Modernist painting with Henri Matisse and Pablo Picasso between 1905 and 1910 was well advanced in the decorative arts by those dates, whether in stained glass designed by Wright or in furniture designed by Will Bradley. Unlike the abstract floral designs characterizing much Arts and Crafts stained glass, what Wright designed was wholly nonobjective, as if in anticipation of the Dutch movement de Stijl and work by Piet Mondrian and Theo Van Doesburg around 1917. Wright's architecture becomes abstract because it also breaks with overt Romantic associationism, whether using English cottages, Pennsylvania farmhouses, or California missions as models. As viewed from outside, his Unity Temple, in Oak Park, Illinois (1908), could as well be a library, a bank, or a museum for all that it looks like a church.

A third aesthetic accomplishment of the American Arts and Crafts movement, largely achieved in domestic architecture, was a heightening of interpenetration of house and garden, of form and space. The intensified relationship between one room, or area, and another, if integrally designed, and between house and garden reached such an unexpected crescendo in the period from 1900 to 1914 that it is often difficult to know where one room or one building ends and another begins, or where a house ends and its garden begins. The three spaces shown in Harvey Ellis's drawing of interiors for a City House are highly integrated; the eye is forced to view all three simultaneously. If dimensions and dotted lines did not differentiate one housing unit from another in Francis Joannes's Multiple Housing at Hilton Village, the structure would seem to be a single, unified building. Wright himself wrote that "garden and building may now be one. In any good organic structure it is difficult to say where the garden ends and the house begins—and that is all as it should be, because organic architecture declares that we are, by nature, ground-loving animals."[18] Not surprisingly, with its ample use of exterior planters and garden walls linking enclosed spaces, he considered the Avery Coonley House, with gardens designed by Jens Jensen, to best epitomize his work by 1914.

The aforementioned three features explain the culminating aesthetic concept of the Arts and Crafts of "total design," wherein everything, from dinner fork to regional state plan, was made to conform to the same design principles. Again, Morris provided the most influential example. It has been shown convincingly how hexagonal patterns in his wallpaper were utilized by Parker and Unwin in designing subdivisions for the Garden City, which broke radically from the tyranny of uniformly monotonous rectangular urban blocks.[19] Greene and Greene's indelible signature was visible on all facets of their work, which consisted of such materials as lovingly sanded woodblocks held in place by inset wood plugs, presumably masking screws. Gill's white stucco designs, like Baillie-Scott's, whether in small, single or large, multiple dwellings, consistently reduce architecture to a mere, somewhat inert backdrop against which are played the ever-changing and continually growing gardens.

KEY MANIFESTATIONS OF ARTS AND CRAFTS
IN AMERICAN ARCHITECTURE

The impact of the Arts and Crafts is well perceived in the East, Midwest, and in California, especially in domestic architecture. As might be expected, the East was most conservative, the Midwest, with Wright and others, most original. In burgeoning California, the contrasts are greatest because eastern and midwestern influences confronted, commingled, or merged with direct English, Spanish, Oriental, or indigenous traditions. The East is well represented by Will Bradley, of New Jersey; Harvey Ellis, of New York; and Wilson Eyre, William Price, and Walter Mellor and Arthur Meigs, all of whom worked in or near Philadelphia. The landscape, Garden City dimension of the movement is best seen in the work of two Boston-area landscape architects, Frederick Law Olmsted, Jr., and Henry Vincent Hubbard, who collaborated with architects.

Some of the earliest, overtly Arts and Crafts houses in America are those that Gustav Stickley, building upon Bok's example, had Will Bradley and Harvey Ellis design for *The Craftsman*, beginning in 1901. They drew unabashedly from earlier and similarly illustrated articles by Baillie-Scott in *The Studio*, yet both designers clearly exhibited their own styles. "A Bradley House," illustrated in the *Ladies' Home Journal* in 1903, reveals a taut, linear style typical of the artist. The full accoutrement of Arts and Crafts elements is present; Bradley designed all objects, and virtually all media and basic

Grosvenor Atterbury, Frederick Law Olmsted, Jr., et al. *Drawing of Station Square*. Forest Hills Gardens, New York, 1904–9. Collection Russell Sage Foundation

materials are represented. Uniquely Arts and Crafts is the unequivocal emphasis upon the horizontal and the way that decorative elements are made structural, structural elements are made decorative. As a designer rather than an architect, Bradley, with a sense of *horror vacuii*, filled virtually every available surface. Harvey Ellis, on the other hand, with almost Japanese restraint, left broad surfaces unadorned inside and out, features well seen in his City House, illustrated in *The Craftsman* in 1903. The plan of this house almost overmaximizes its tight, urban site and rigorously locks together indoor and outdoor spaces. The architect even provided for a hidden "Auto Way."[20]

Wilson Eyre's stucco walls, of such designs as the Rogers House, at Spring Lake, New Jersey, dating to 1908, affirm his neutralizing treatment of both house and garden. Eyre was a founder and editor of *House and Garden*, first published, in Philadelphia, in 1901. This magazine illustrated many Arts and Crafts houses and expounded many of the movement's principles into the 1920s.[21] William Price founded an Arts and Crafts community, in nearby Rose Valley, that produced Arts and Crafts furniture; between 1903 and 1907, he published *The Artsman*.[22] Philadelphia boasted other skilled Arts and Crafts designers. Edmund Gilchrist, who trained with Eyre, and Walter Mellor and Arthur Meigs were among them. Mellor and Meigs's Morris House, in Haverford, dated 1915, is more picturesque and English than work by Price or Eyre. The freehand rendering, stucco surfaces, large chimneys, and half-timbered porch chamber are remindful of work by Baillie-Scott. Hundreds of similar houses were built coast to coast in the period.[23]

Wilson Eyre, Grosvenor Atterbury, and other architects collaborated in typical Arts and Crafts fashion in designing houses and shops for the Forest Hills Gardens, on Long Island, of Frederick Law Olmsted, Jr. The community was inspired by the contemporary, widespread publicity given English garden cities and suburbs like Hampstead, recently designed by Parker and Unwin. As construction of Forest Hills began, in 1909, Stickley wrote on behalf of the concept in *The Craftsman*, and between 1910 and 1913 he published twenty-nine articles by Parker. Forest Hills, although designed on 142 acres for "people of moderate income," appears to have been too costly for this income level. Instead, it attracted more affluent people, often of intellectual cast, who were impressed with the quality of design achieved at reasonable cost. Forest Hills was hardly alone among attempts in the United States to implant Garden City principles. As with Roland Park, in Baltimore, many other cities, like Boston, New York, and Pittsburgh, saw such neighborhoods or suburbs built.[24] Perhaps the one that came closest to fulfilling the ideal of social reform was Hilton Village, in Newport News, Virginia, designed by Hubbard and Joannes, in 1918, on a 200-acre site.

Hilton Village is a milestone: It is the earliest example in the United States of federally funded and legislated housing, planned to accommodate some five hundred skilled workers and their families. Its construction was predicated on the country's entry into World War I and the need for expanded employment in the Newport News Shipbuilding and Drydock Company. Olmsted was asked to prepare the plan but recommended, instead, Henry Vincent Hubbard, who was professor of landscape architecture at Harvard University. Every effort was made to keep Hilton Village affordable. The majority of tenants, whether riveters, boilermakers, or ship carpenters, earned from $125 to $182 monthly. From these figures, the architects computed an affordable monthly rent that ranged from $24 to $36; the houses were designed accordingly. The planning concept was clearly derived from Parker and Unwin's Letchworth, England's first Garden City (1903), and Hampstead Garden Suburb, in London (1907), where Baillie-Scott designed a number of well-publicized single- and multiple-family dwellings that Joannes used as models. Existing Warwick Boulevard, a major artery into Newport News, was accepted as Hilton's Main Street and became home to the village's shops and stores, much as Finchley Road was to Hampstead. A square was laid out against Warwick Boulevard, flanked by two churches, again much like Hampstead. A second square was built adjacent to the nearby railway station, where a large playfield helped distance houses from the railroad. Most houses, whether single, double, or multiple, were built in white stucco between Warwick Boulevard and the James River. Houses in the middle of lateral blocks were set back to relieve any sense of monotony. The school and playground were built in parkland against the river, preventing its shoreline from being consumed entirely by private houses. A pier and swimming area were also created.[25]

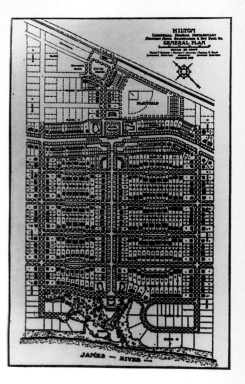

Henry Vincent Hubbard and Francis Y. Joannes. Drawing of *General Plan of Hilton Village*. Newport News, Virginia, 1918

In the Midwest, Arts and Crafts architects were in greatest strength in or near Chicago, but Cincinnati, Detroit, Milwaukee, Minneapolis, and St. Louis were also major centers of Arts and Crafts resolve. A foretaste of the impending impact of Arts and Crafts design was seen in 1896 when William Gannett began publication of *House Beautiful*. Wright designed its first cover, much as Voysey had done for *The Studio* three years before. Apart from Wright, other key Arts and Crafts designers at work in Chicago included Robert Spencer, Jens Jensen, George W. Maher, Walter Burley Griffin, Marion Mahony, and William Purcell and George Grant Elmslie. Wright's first two illustrated articles, "A Home in a Prairie Town" and "A Small House with 'Lots of Room' In It," appeared in the *Ladies' Home Journal* in 1901; they were among his first designs to reveal the new Arts and Crafts influence from England.[26] Key features of these two houses were their low hipped roofs, banks of leaded casement windows, stucco surfaces, integral planters, and emphasis upon a two-story living room focused on the hearth and flanked on either side by a spatially integrated library and dining room. Wright included built-in bookcases and cabinets, and his signature is recognized in the vertical, linear, and rectilinear furniture, probably designed for construction in oak. Most characteristic of Wright are the unprecedented horizontal emphasis of the roofs, the low sprawling profile, and the integration of mass and volume.

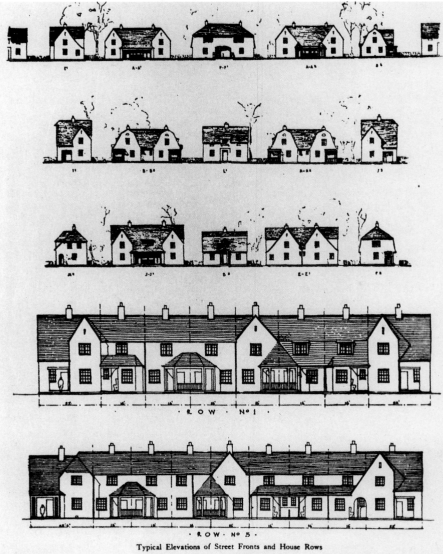

Typical Elevations of Street Fronts and House Rows

HILTON VILLAGE.—A Housing Development Near Newport News, Va., for the Newport News Shipbuilding & Dry Dock Co. Francis Y. Joannes, Architect

Hubbard and Joannes. *Hilton Village Street Fronts and House Rows*, 1918

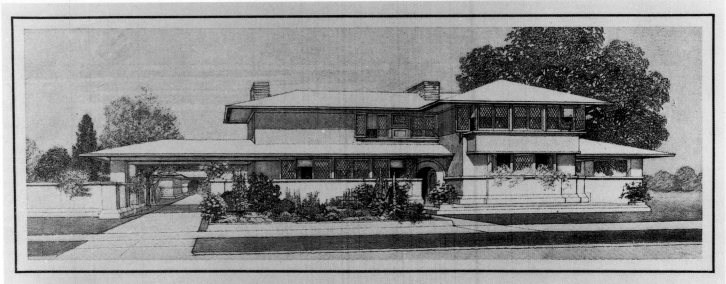

CITY man going to the country puts too much in his house and too little in his ground. He drags after him the fifty-foot lot, soon the twenty-five-foot lot, finally the party wall; and the home-maker who fully appreciates the advantages which he came to the country to secure feels himself impelled to move on.

It seems a waste of energy to plan a house haphazard, to hit or miss an already distorted condition, so this partial solution of a city man's country home on the prairie begins at the beginning and assumes four houses to the block of four hundred feet square as the minimum of ground for the basis of his prairie community.

The block plan to the left, at the top of the page, shows an arrangement of the four houses that secures breadth and prospect to the community as a whole, and absolute privacy both as regards each to the community, and each to each of the four.

and broad eaves are designed to accentuate that quiet level and complete the harmonious relationship. The curbs of the terraces and formal inclosures for extremely informal masses of foliage and bloom should be worked in cement with the walks and drives.

Cement on metal lath is suggested for the exterior covering throughout, because it is simple, and, as now understood, durable and cheap.

The cost of this house with interior as specified and cement construction would be seven thousand dollars:

Masonry, Cement and Plaster	$2800.00
Carpentry	3100.00
Plumbing	400.00
Painting and Glass	325.00
Heating — combination (hot water)	345.00
Total	$6970.00

IN A HOUSE of this character the upper reach and

Wright's Avery Coonley House, in Riverside, Illinois, dramatically shows how complete the interpenetration of house and garden design had become by 1908. The gardens are the work of Jens Jensen.[27] Wholly abstract, sculptural elements, both vertical and horizontal, begin to dissolve the earlier, clearer distinction between one story and another, between wall and roof. The scheme is really a small farm, for it comprises the main house, a very unbarnlike barn—with quarters for a worker as well as for horses, a cow, and chickens—and an adjacent gardener's cottage. All are linked by gardens, whether for use or for delight, and by pergolas, walks, planters, and other devices. The large living room dominates and focuses on the hearth and on a large pool, connected to it by an expansive, walled terrace. House and garden are welded into such a balanced integration that even Lutyens and Jekyll would be hard-pressed to surpass it.

Robert Spencer collaborated with Jensen in designing the Magnus House and its accompanying garden, in Winnetka, Illinois, about 1905. Spencer practiced in a more obvious Voyseyan Arts and Crafts mode before Wright, prior to 1900, although the two appear to have been apprised of each other's style around that very time. The Magnus House, now gone, was stuccoed, had a low hipped roof, and featured banks of casement windows. Window and wall were integrated by the creation of wood-enframed panels, derived from English half-timbering. Unlike Wright and more like Eyre, Spencer and Jensen kept house aloof from garden, but both featured the native prairie hawthorn, a favorite specimen of Jensen. The stained glass on the first story featured native hawthorn in winter, with small red berries; the second-story casement windows depicted it in summer, with green leaves and small white blossoms. Walter Burley Griffin and Marion Mahony worked in Wright's office until 1911. That year, they married and collaborated on a number of projects, including New Trier neighborhood, in Winnetka.

Frank Lloyd Wright. Perspective of *"A Home in a Prairie Town."* From *The Ladies' Home Journal* (1901)

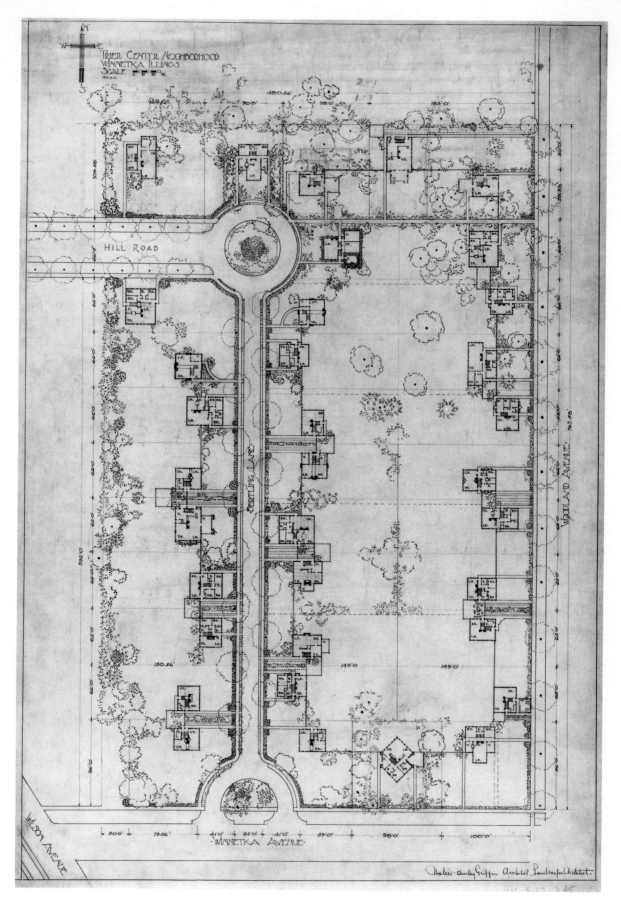

Walter Burley Griffin. Trier Center Neighborhood, Winnetka, Illinois. 1913. Site plan
with house plans and landscaping. Ink on linen. Collection The Art Institute of Chicago.
Gift of Marion Mahony Griffin through Eric Nicholls

George Washington Maher. *Rockledge,* Homer, Minnesota. c. 1914

Griffin's plot plan of the entire scheme shows three dozen small houses, more modest in scale than is usual with Wright. Some houses face two existing gridiron streets; a new "lane," entered through a semicircular entrance, leads to a full circle and to the remaining houses in the scheme. Other houses are detached, still others are semidetached, but most are linked by garden walls. The gardens appear to have been left quite open for ready communal enjoyment. Griffin's first house for New Trier built upon Wright's abstract, increasingly nondomestic style. It is a symmetrical block, with a raised two-story core that opens to a covered veranda and two terraces on either side that, together, comprise more than half of the "roof." Bold, vertical piers divide wall surfaces and flank windows. The space-efficent plan has a combined living-dining area and a compact kitchen, with two bedrooms and a bath on the first floor, one bedroom and bath on the second.[28]

Arts and Crafts work in the Midwest, outside Chicago, is well seen in *Rockledge,* the George W. Maher design built for E. L. King, in Homer, Minnesota, about 1912. *Rockledge* is a monumental, stucco house of nine broad bays covered by a low hipped roof. It has similarities to the Magnus House, but is as subtly classical as the latter is medieval. The paired or triple casement windows have unusually large single panes. An expansive terrace links house to garden and maximizes a panoramic view. A low, segmental, abstracted Palladian arch enframes the entrance and is integrated with the tripartite window above, which is linked to the entrance by a planter. This Palladian motif is echoed within, as can be seen from the built-in sideboard and overmantel in the dining room. Maher's design for the dining table and chairs, as well as for the chandelier, features canted ends or legs, with the tops or backs terminated by segmental arches. Segmental curves in the rug also echo those executed in frame, stucco, or brick.[29]

Of California's leading architectural exponents of the Arts and Crafts, none was a native, and this contributed to the diversity in design to be found there. Ernest Coxhead, an immigrant from England and an admirer of Voysey, built some of California's earliest Arts and Crafts houses, in San Francisco.[30] Bernard Maybeck was a New Yorker who relocated to Berkeley about 1895 and became one of the University of California's first professors of architec-

ture. The Greenes, who came from a Virginia family, were raised in Cincinnati, educated in the Morris-inspired school that Calvin Milton Woodward
ran at Washington University, in St. Louis, and briefly studied—unhappily,
because of its Beaux-Arts design emphasis—at Massachusetts Institute of
Technology; they began their practice, in Pasadena, before 1895. Irving Gill, a
native of Syracuse, worked for Louis Sullivan, in Chicago, from 1890 until
1893, when he settled in San Diego.

From a strictly Arts and Crafts period point of view, Greene and Greene
were the consummate practitioners of the movement in the United States. In
their 1908 masterpiece, the Gamble House, in Pasadena, much of the boldly
shingled house is surrounded by terraces and sleeping porches and by an
extremely monumental entrance with a wide, low door and sidelights enriched with Tiffany glass, one of the most artfully original entrances ever
created. The broad passage leads directly to all the other rooms and to an
irregular terrace with lily pool that rises naturally from the site's outcroppings
of rock, between which nestle California poppies. Second-floor sleeping
porches enhance the indoor-outdoor emphasis and, with their projecting
joists and rafters, underscore the wood with which they were built. Wood
dominates Greene and Greene exteriors and interiors, just as plaster or stucco
spells Gill. The dining room of the Gamble House perfectly illustrates this
emphasis on wood. It enframes all other materials, whether glass, tile, plaster,

or textile. The focal point of the room is a Greene-and-Greene-designed table, supported by a massive base that enables its expansion. The slight curves of the tabletop are echoed in the back supports of the chairs; the straight legs echo the square form of the base. The walls are paneled to the height of the overmantel and windows. A heavy, wood cornice is separated from the paneling by a plain, plaster frieze, a foot in height, but joined to it by typically Greene and Greene diminishing consoles or "capitals." These are located above vertical "piers" that mark breaks in the surface, whether for corners or door entrances. Built-in cabinets, glass-paneled cupboards, and a handsome sideboard are integrated into the paneling. The sideboard is actually unified with a three-unit exterior window that is thereby transformed into furniture. The room is lit by an extremely simple frame and glazed light fixture.[31]

Irving Gill's Dodge House, built in Los Angeles in 1916, was, unfortunately, demolished. Its planning and massing of volumes reflect Gill's familiarity with Baillie-Scott's *Houses and Gardens*, published in 1906. The ample spatial flow through the principal rooms and into the adjacent patio, entry, court, side porch, and garden is most accomplished. The severe, cream-stucco elevations, with banks of casement windows, arched doorways, and flat roofs, are typical of Gill and are very similar to Ludwig Mies van der Rohe's houses of the 1920s. The equally severe interiors, as seen in the game room with plain, white plastered walls, are made to contrast sharply with floor-to-ceiling doors and windows and with a richly surfaced fireplace mantel and built-in bookcase. The architect's 1910 design for the flat-roofed Lewis Courts, in Sierra

Irving Gill. Dodge House, north elevation, Los Angeles, 1906

Irving Gill. Perspective drawing for
Casas Grandes project, Hollywood Hills,
Los Angeles, 1914–15

Madre, California, are identical in style but are far more modest structures.
They affirm his conviction "to provide," in his own words, "an orderly
environment for low-income groups."[32] Gill's Casas Grandes project for the
Hollywood Hills, dated 1912–15, is suggestive of a number of projects of
Baillie-Scott in the same period.[33] The bold forms of the buildings—their
massiveness—recall work by Louis Sullivan, Gill's mentor, or even earlier
Romantic work by Karl Friedrich Schinkel and Joseph Gandy, but they are
more abstract. The forms bring to mind such remote, distant structures as the
Dalai Lama's fortress, in Tibet, or the Incan fortress town of Machu Picchu.
Six structures are integrated by an elaborate series of terraces supported by
stucco retaining walls and filled with the ever-blooming flora of southern
California.

Gill's Lewis Courts and his Casas Grandes project are fitting conclusions
to what drama the Arts and Crafts movement created or hoped to create in the
United States. Steep English roofs did not interest Gill, whose flat roofs were
intended to express the Ruskin-Morris principle of indigenous, vernacular
expression without meriting the label Spanish Colonial revival and without
pioneering the flat roofs of the so-called International Style. Gill's houses are
contemporaneous with those of Adolf Loos, which, also covered by white or
cream stucco, feature flat or partially flat roofs. Although Loos has long been
held as a pioneer of the International Style, Gill has not, largely because his
very similar designs were not known to Walter Gropius or other Bauhaus
designers. Defending indigenousness and the rule of nature above art, Gill
wrote, in one of the last issues of *The Craftsman*: "There is something very
restful and satisfying to my mind in the simple cube house with creamy walls,
sheer and plain, rising boldly into the sky, unrelieved by cornices or overhang
of roof, unornamented save for the vines that soften a line or creepers that
weave a pillar or flowers that inlay color more sentiently than any tile could do.
I like the bare honesty of these houses, the childlike frankness, and the chaste
simplicity of them."[34]

William Price's Arts and Crafts Colony at Rose Valley, Pennsylvania

by George E. Thomas

At the end of the nineteenth century, sociologist Thorstein Veblen took a caustic look at the materialism of American society in *The Theory of the Leisure Class*. In an age when the popular taste demanded that every surface and material be embellished, Veblen observed that designers of overly ornamented facades, frilled dresses, and ornate furniture no longer sought beauty but instead expressed power as represented by financial wealth; the stresses induced by industrialization had transformed the very nature of the society.[1] Simultaneously, in the generation after the Civil War, America's cities became battlegrounds between political machines and reform movements. By the end of the century, it was clear that no amount of reform activity, no journalistic crusading, no activism by socialites or political novices could redeem the fundamental inequities of the industrial city.[2]

When American architects turned away from the cities, their arena in the 1870s and 1880s, to the suburbs and the country, they joined a national movement, one that cut across all social classes because it was rooted in national political and intellectual values. Over the previous two and a half centuries, a significant number of Europeans had emigrated to the New World to create new social systems. Pennsylvania Quakers and New England Shakers, among others, shaped an aesthetic of simplification that contrasted with the worldliness they rejected; later, communal experiments, such as the millennial-centered Harmonist Society and the secular Brook Farm, marked the ongoing continuum of New World social experiment. Thus, around 1900, when American architects and designers rediscovered the devices of simplification of form, expression of material, and representation of the manufacturing process, they gave the new movement a distinct national identity that could be seen in bungalows and cottages, in suburbs and villages, and in Mission furniture and interiors from the Atlantic to the Pacific.

In England, William Morris's Arts and Crafts movement sprang from similar aesthetic, political, and social conditions. Nurtured by the writings of Thomas Carlyle, John Ruskin, and Morris, its leaders had turned back to the medieval Christian past while advocating the reintegration of design and production. In contrast with modern industry, where design and production were separated, Morris's own workshops set new standards—design appropriate to the nature of the product, and produced in workplaces that were appealing and pleasant. A few other industrialists followed suit in such utopian industrial communities as Port Sunlight, outside Liverpool. For most, however, the stresses between life and work, politics and passion, were resolved in socialism and communism, the great political movements that have contested with capitalism in the twentieth century.

When followers of Morris, among them C. R. Ashbee, made contact with fellow social activists in the United States around 1900, their ideas fell on fertile ground.[3] Even before, Americans had celebrated the individual as the focus of the democracy, in the writings of Ralph Waldo Emerson and Walt Whitman and, later, in the theoretical writings of Andrew Jackson Downing.[4] By the 1890s, a new generation of Americans, perhaps responding to the millennial lure of the twentieth century, essayed experiments in political, industrial, and social reform, many of which took on the flavor and fervor of Morris's Arts and Crafts movement. They spanned the country, ranging from Massachusetts's Fellowship Farms, beginning in 1907, at Westwood, to the Beaux-Arts Village, in about 1900, on Washington's Puget Sound.[5]

The best known were Elbert Hubbard's Roycrofters, in East Aurora, New York, near Buffalo, and Gustav Stickley's Craftsman organization, in Eastwood, a suburb of Syracuse, New York. Both were established by charismatic leaders who had encountered William Morris in the waning years of the nineteenth century. In accordance with the essentially feudal social structure advocated by Morris, both the Roycrofters and the Craftsman organizations raised designers to the status of artists and, in turn, attempted to reestablish apprenticeship as the basis for industrial training. But the connection between work and the totality of the integrated life was not made in either place. Although the Roycrofters, for instance, established a broad cultural curriculum of lectures, drama, and sports, work was always separated from residence, management remained segregated from work force, and the true community of the American village was not achieved.

The lack of revolutionary intent of both Hubbard and Stickley was expressed in their similar commercial and economic goals. Neither established an original architecture nor founded communities that embodied a broad social vision. Instead, the vocabulary of East Aurora recalled the rugged simplification of Henry Hobson Richardson's medievalizing architecture of the generation before, while Stickley adapted the Adirondack cabin to his Craftsman Farm, his retreat near Morris Plains, New Jersey. Similarly, both men found inspiration in the medieval past, Hubbard going so far as to have himself depicted in medieval garb, with the title of "Fra Elbertus," while Stickley took as his slogan *Als ik kan,* a Flemish expression meaning "As I can," which was also Morris's personal motto. Ultimately, while both preached the gospel of reform, neither Hubbard nor Stickley envisioned much more than a paternally directed, work-centered mill town.

Rose Valley furniture shops, Rose Valley, Pennsylvania, c. 1904.

Price and McLanahan. Inglenook, Schoen House. Rose Valley, c. 1905

An alternative to the mill town was the art-centered resort, a Chautauqua for the artist, that developed in the Catskills, in Woodstock, New York. There, in the early twentieth century, a circle of New York–based writers, artists, potters, and sculptors constructed a suburb on the edge of the existing village. Merging the château and Adirondack lodge forms of vacation architecture with the aesthetic simplification of Japan, the best Woodstock architecture, such as Ralph Whitehead's Byrdcliffe (c. 1906), linked East Coast design to the architecture of Greene and Greene, in California. Still, Woodstock was a retreat, a twentieth-century Blythedale, but never a total community.

More audacious, although less well known, was the village established in the summer of 1901 at Rose Valley, Pennsylvania, by Philadelphia architect William L. Price.[6] Price had been an early convert to the ideas of economic reformer Henry George, who advocated a draconian single tax on land to force the breakup of large estates. By the end of the century, Price and two fellow visionaries had founded a single-tax colony in Arden, Delaware—where land was held in common, a system that survives to the present—along with a handful of tiny artists' cottages that recalled Morris's Red House. In 1901, Price persuaded Philadelphia financier John Gilmore; industrialist (and single-taxer) Joseph Fels; Edward Bok, publisher of the *Ladies' Home Journal*; and the trustees of Swarthmore College to provide the initial capital for a stock company to purchase land and several abandoned mills in the Ridley Creek Valley, near Media, Pennsylvania. There, Price intended to shape an experiment in community living that would overlay on the single-tax approach the celebration of personal creativity that underlay Morris's Arts and Crafts movement. In a 1903 article, "Is Rose Valley Worth While?" Price posed fundamental questions that the community was intended to answer:

What is the use of a culture and refinement built on a substratum out of touch with those who do the real work of life? What help is there in art or science? Must the artist always strive to express himself hampered by the discomfort around him, with no market for his works but galleries and museums, public or private? What relation to life does such art bear?[7]

Price had deeper motives, however, than the production of art in a pleasant place for a broader audience. Rose Valley was to form a first step toward the transformation of society in response to the "portents in the almost universal dissent" that he observed in the rejection of historical precedent in modern painting and architecture. Unlike English utopianism, which looked backward, Price proclaimed the importance of the present: "For this is America, and art is the utterance of the living and not the dead."[8] That such statements ring of the insights of Ralph Waldo Emerson and Walt Whitman was no accident. Price's associate in shaping Rose Valley was Horace Traubel, Whitman's longtime amanuensis and literary executor, who, from 1903 until 1907, joined Price in publishing the Rose Valley journal, *The Artsman*.[9] While Traubel and Price put the community's goals into words, Price's architectural partner and fellow investor M. Hawley McLanahan helped shape the economic course of the village. Together, they organized the purchase of the land, persuaded coworkers, friends, and family to form the community, and eventually established the first successful workshops for the production of furniture.

The origins were modest. The stockholders leased space in the principal asset of the property, a three-story, stone, mill building. Initially, it was used for the production of furniture and, later, for printing, bookbinding, and pottery. By adding new production facilities after the initial ventures stood on their own, the founders hoped to create a broader universe from a stable center. Work that met the high standards of the community was stamped with the seal of the association—a *V* superimposed on a primrose representing the valley, surrounded by a buckled leather belt symbolizing the bond of the association.[10]

With their goal of humanizing capitalism, the stockholders of Rose Valley expected to produce goods having real value. Most notable were the

Alice Barber Stephens. *Rose Valley String Quartet at Music Stand.* c. 1904. Graphite on paper

Rose Valley Shops. Sideboard. c. 1904. Oak

Rose Valley Shops. Chest. c. 1904. Oak

products of its furniture shop. These ranged from massive, richly carved pieces with a distinctly medieval flavor to more severe works derived from the Arts and Crafts or from Stickley's Mission or Craftsman style. Price, however, was as wary of unthinking simplification as he was of "unthinking ornamentation."[11] In a 1904 lecture entitled "Some Humors of False Construction," Price argued for aesthetic and constructive logic and condemned the literal revival of historic styles that made "precedent our guide, accepting our taste without analysis second hand." Price concluded: "When America finds itself we will have national arts and not until then."[12]

Despite Price's growing acceptance of the modern spirit, most of the furniture of the Rose Valley shops was medievalizing in character, no doubt because successful marketing depended upon accommodating contemporary taste. In this, it was less exotic than Frank Lloyd Wright's Japanese-influenced furniture designs, which looked as if they were made for machine production even though they were modeled on subtly handcrafted sources. But, despite the conservative styling, the production of the Rose Valley furniture was not anachronistic. Like Wright, Price accepted the machine—not as Bauhaus ideal but as a tool that was subservient to the user.

We have tried to draw a line between the machine that will aid and the machine that will hinder man's development. In a general way we define a good machine to be that machine, whether simple or complex, which remains a tool that a thinking man may work, shaping the product by his volition. A bad machine is that machine which is automatic in its operations, requiring only a human feeder, who must with deadly regularity supply it with the material from which it, not he, makes the product.[13]

The best furniture was of museum quality, but more modest pieces found their way into community houses. Still, such work was expensive—significantly limiting its market. Similarly, the print shop, under the direction of Carl DeMoll and, later, Will Roberts, produced works of high quality—but

William Jervis pottery shops, Rose Valley, c. 1905

at costs that also precluded popular success. William P. Jervis's pottery was equally well received and equally short-lived. Although Price explained the economic failure of the crafts shops as the result of unwillingness of Americans to pay the costs of furniture that would outlast the buyers, the real problem lay in Price's refusal to acknowledge the workings of the fashion-based marketing system that fuels the national economy. Costly furniture, even if it were offered on an installment plan, could not be readily retired to the attic when it looked dated. By 1907, the shops closed.

With their demise, a second mill building became more crucial to the

Price and McLanahan.
Alterations to Rose Valley
Guest House, c. 1905

community; nearer to the heart of the village, it served as a studio for artists, as the Guild Hall for governance, and as a theater, library, and community center. Built without pay by the members of the village, the Guild Hall epitomized the democratic spirit of the folk mote—the community's government. It was this participatory side of Rose Valley life that nurtured a mixed and varied population, forming the context for such adventures as the cooperative School in Rose Valley and, in the 1920s, Jasper Deeter's repertory company in the Hedgerow Theater, as the Guild Hall was renamed.

Among the other assets of the property was a row of mid-nineteenth-century mill-workers' houses that were converted into a hostel, or guest house, modeled on those described in Morris's *News from Nowhere*. It provided a place where visitors and potential members of the community could test their interest. Existing detached houses, originally constructed for the mill foremen, were converted into comfortable quarters for the craftsmen. Unlike the mill town or the artists' colonies, Rose Valley was inclusive, with artists and craftsmen, mill hands and corporate executives, living in close proximity to one another and sharing the governance and the activities of the community. This democratic village was an intentional consequence of Price's flirtation with the single tax and other ideas in the previous decade. After designing a number of turn-of-the-century commuter suburbs, including Wayne and Overbrook, near Philadelphia, and Roland Park, outside of Baltimore, Price had come to realize the liabilities of economically stratified communities of choice and the evil of ghettos and ethnically segregated neighborhoods. In his manifesto, "Is Rose Valley Worth While?" Price argued that true community would be attained only by people who shared common interests. There were no suburbs that encompassed an economic range from well-to-do industrialists to draftsmen and craftsmen. This would

Price and McLanahan. Alice Barber Stephens House, Rose Valley, 1904

have presented a striking contrast between ornate mansions and simple cottages, a difficulty Price was determined to overcome, arguing: "And why not? Certainly our fitness to associate together upon simple human conditions should not be gauged by our incomes. Here the tiniest cottage may be built side by side with a more spacious neighbor."[14]

For such economic and social diversity to be successful, it was necessary to establish a unifying architectural character. In an essay entitled "Choosing Simple Materials for the Home," Price recalled naturalist John Burroughs's theme that "a house should be built of materials picked up at hand . . . not only for sentimental and practical reasons but because it tends to produce types— tends towards a pleasing homogeneity in local style that is altogether good."[15]

Recalling the regional identity of each English shire, Price shaped an overriding architectural vocabulary of local materials—fieldstone and rough cast stucco over simple volumes of modern hollow tile, capped by roofs steep enough to shed snow and rain. Red roof tiles and ornamental accents of Mercer tile provided a link to another stalwart of the Arts and Crafts movement, Henry Chapman Mercer.

Properly selected, local materials had another advantage, enabling the architect to meet modern needs or, in Price's phrase, to "fit the living purpose, not the dead precedent."[16] This intention was reflected in many of the Rose Valley houses, beginning, in 1904, with the extension of an existing barn into a residence and studio for artists Charles and Alice Barber Stephens. Its plain stone base, stucco walls, and tile roof shared the vocabulary of the region's houses, while a tile thunderbird on the gable end and a thunderbird-shaped fireplace marked Price's effort to reflect the client's study of Native American arts. The exterior was intended to duplicate the old barn as closely as possible, while the interior marked a notable shift toward simplification, anticipating Charles Rennie Mackintosh's work. Price phrased his intentions in the moral tones of the movement: "All the detail is as simple and direct as possible, and the interior is finished in cypress stained to soft browns and greys and guilty of no finish other than wax or oil."[17]

In 1909, as the community's economic ventures ended, its leaders sought to reduce its debt by constructing a group of houses for sale; designed by Price to be an integral part of the valley, they were also intended to be expressions of modern life: "In regards to the houses individually, the nature of materials employed in their construction has been altogether preserved. No false impression is to be gathered from any of the details. Under a present day impulse new structural conditions as exemplified in concrete and hollow tile have been accepted. These demand a specific surface treatment and naturally point the way to the accomplishment of a plastic art whereby perhaps an indigenous expression, typically American, is to become established."[18]

Price and McLanahan. Alice Barber Stephens House stair, Rose Valley, 1904

Price and McLanahan. McLanahan House, Rose Valley, c. 1905

Reflecting sentiments rooted in the Arts and Crafts movement, which had stimulated Price for a generation, the Rose Valley Improvement Company houses contrasted in their modest cost, scale, and simplicity of detail with the geometric opulence of Frank Lloyd Wright's Oak Park houses. When C. R. Ashbee visited Rose Valley, in 1908, he perceived a shared commitment to the expression of the democracy and the modern spirit:

Rose Valley Price, the architect, is really fine; there is something prophetic about him. He has, like most of us who have studied the arts and crafts and feel the humanity underlying the movement, the conviction that if the movement is to find itself it must speak in a voice of its own and not in the language of back numbers, the beaux arts, the "Old Colonial". . . . He has no patience with the work of McKim and others who stand for traditional culture. He reminds me often of Lloyd Wright.[19]

Unlike Wright and the better-known Prairie School, whose work caught the imagination of elitist European Modernists, Price remained committed to the individual in the social sphere of the democracy. It was this theme that Price explored in a 1912 article, "The House of the Democrat," published in Stickley's journal *The Craftsman*.[20] Drawing on Emerson's imagery, Price envisioned a just society—a Rose Valley grown large:

Price and McLanahan, Rose Valley Improvement Co. House, 1909

When the Democrat has built his house, when free men have housed themselves to meet their present need and have no fear that the need of tomorrow shall cry—then shall . . . men and women find time and powers out of their work to write plays and play them, to write poems and sing them, to carve, to paint, to teach, to prophesy new philosophies and new sciences, to make, to give, to live.

Ironically, because of a half-century of European-influenced theory, Price and his contributions to an American aesthetic have been forgotten, but Rose Valley and Arden survive as monuments to Price's idealism and America's continuing social and political revolution.

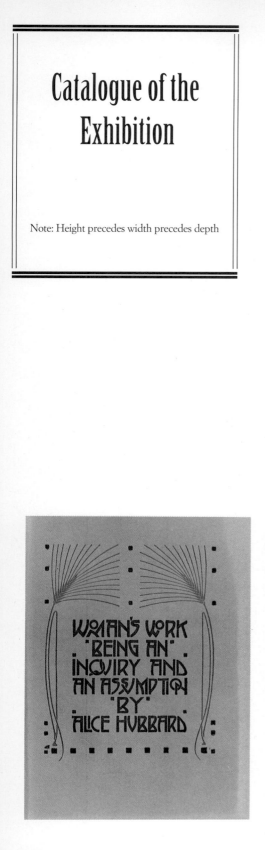

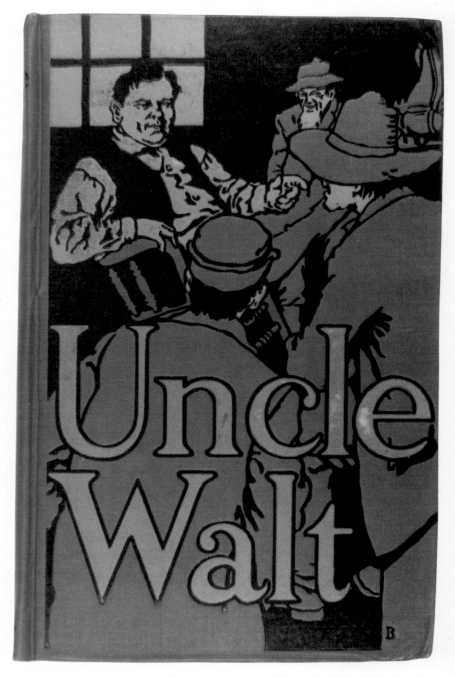

Alice Hubbard. *Woman's Work*
East Aurora, New York: The Roycroft Press,
1908.
Designed by Dard Hunter,
typography by Charles Rosen
Collection Wolfsonian Foundation, Miami

Walt Mason. *Uncle Walt: The Poet Philosopher*
Chicago: George Matthew Adams, 1910.
Designed by Will Bradley
Collection Wolfsonian Foundation, Miami

Elihu Vedder. *The Digressions of V*
Boston: Houghton, Mifflin and Company, 1910
Collection Wolfsonian Foundation, Miami

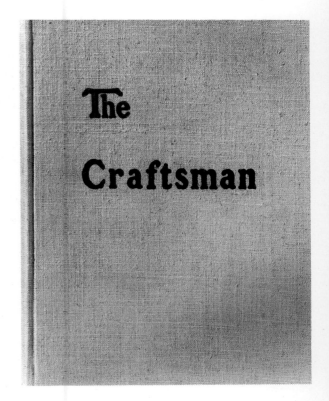

Gustav Stickley, ed. *The Craftsman*. v. 23, nos. 4–6
New York: United Crafts, 1913
Collection Winterthur Library,
Printed Books and Periodicals

Ceramics

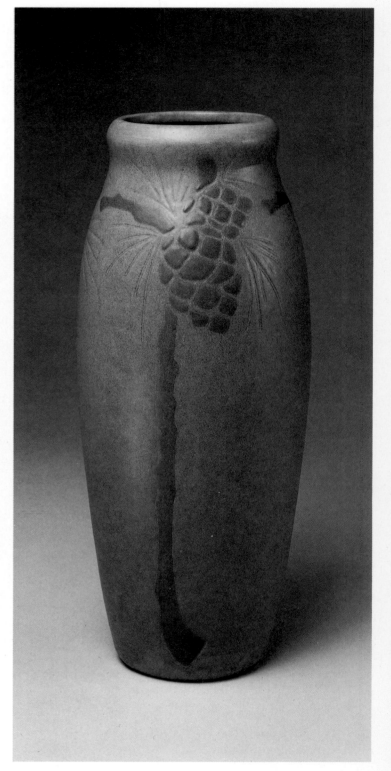

Charles Volkmar. *Vase.* c. 1910
Glazed earthenware, $6^1/8 \times 5^1/4 \times 5^1/4''$
Collection The Newark Museum, New Jersey

Arthur E. Baggs. *Vase.* c. 1907–9
Designed for Marblehead Pottery
Ceramic, $11^7/8 \times 5^1/2 \times 5^1/2''$
Private collection

Charles Fergus Binns. *Vase*. 1905
Stoneware, $7^5/8 \times 4^7/8 \times 4^7/8''$
Collection Museum of Ceramic Art at Alfred, Alfred University,
Alfred, New York

Charles Fergus Binns. *Vase*. 1916
Stoneware, $10^5/8 \times 5^3/4 \times 5^3/4''$
Collection Museum of Ceramic Art at Alfred, Alfred University,
Alfred, New York

Theophilus A. Brouwer, Jr. *Vase*. c. 1894–1911
Designed for Middle Lane Pottery
Ceramic, $11^1/_2 \times 7^1/_{16} \times 7^1/_{16}''$
Private collection

Grace Young. *Vase*. 1899
Produced at Rookwood Pottery
Ceramic, $15^1/_2 \times 6 \times 6''$
Collection The Brooklyn Museum.
Gift of Mr. and Mrs. Jay Lewis.
(84.176.4)

Matthew A. Daly. *Vase*. 1892
Produced at Rookwood Pottery
Ceramic, $24 \times 8^1/_2 \times 8^1/_2''$
Private collection

140

Taxile Doat. *Vase*. 1913
Produced at University City Pottery
Porcelain, 10¹/₄ × 8 × 8″
Private collection

Below:
Byrdcliffe Pottery. *Bowl*. 1917–18
Glazed earthenware, 2³/₄ × 5⁵/₈ × 5⁵/₈″
Collection The Newark Museum, New Jersey

Kataro Shirayamadani. *Vase*. 1898
Produced at Rookwood Pottery
Earthenware with electro-deposited copper,
$12^5/_{16} \times 4^1/_4 \times 4^1/_4''$
Collection Cooper-Hewitt Museum, National Museum of Design,
Smithsonian Institution, New York. Gift of Marcia and William Goodman

Henry Chapman Mercer. *Inkwell.* c. 1910
Produced at Moravian Pottery and Tile Works
Ceramic, $5^{1}/_{2} \times 5^{1}/_{2} \times 5^{1}/_{2}''$
Collection Dr. Thomas C. Folk

Henry Chapman Mercer
Tile (Persian Antelope). c. 1910
Produced at Moravian Pottery and Tile Works
Earthenware, $7 \times 5^3/4''$
Collection The Newark Museum,
New Jersey. Gift of Moravian
Pottery and Tile Works

Henry Chapman Mercer
Tile (Byzantine Four Flowers). c. 1910
Produced at Moravian Pottery and Tile Works
Red earthenware, $7^1/8 \times 5^7/8''$
Collection The Newark Museum, New Jersey.
Gift of Moravian Pottery and Tile Works

Mary Louise McLaughlin
Vase. c. 1898–1906
Ceramic, $6 \times 4^5/8 \times 4^5/8''$
Private collection

Opposite below:
Henry Chapman Mercer
Tile (Fluminus Impetus . . .). c. 1910
Produced at Moravian Pottery and Tile Works
Red earthenware, $7 \times 5^3/4''$
Collection The Newark Museum, New Jersey.
Gift of Moravian Pottery and Tile Works

145

Louis Comfort Tiffany
Water Lilies with Frogs. c. 1904
Designed for Tiffany Studios
Ceramic, $6^3/8 \times 7^1/2 \times 7^1/2''$
Collection Dr. Thomas C. Folk

Louis Comfort Tiffany
Vase (Fiddleheads). 1905–14
Designed for Tiffany Studios
Glazed earthenware, $9^{1}/_{4} \times 5 \times 5''$
Collection The Newark Museum, New Jersey.
Wallace M. Scudder Bequest Fund

Grueby Faience Company. *Vase.* c. 1905–12
Ceramic, 10^1/$_4$ × 9 × 9"
Private collection

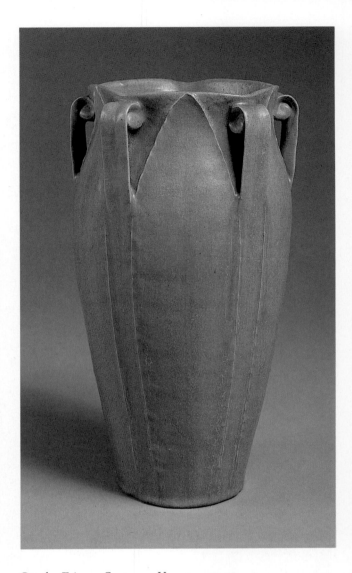

Grueby Faience Company. *Vase.* c. 1905–10
Matte-glazed earthenware, 10^1/$_2$ × 5^7/$_8$ × 5^7/$_8$"
Collection The Newark Museum, New Jersey

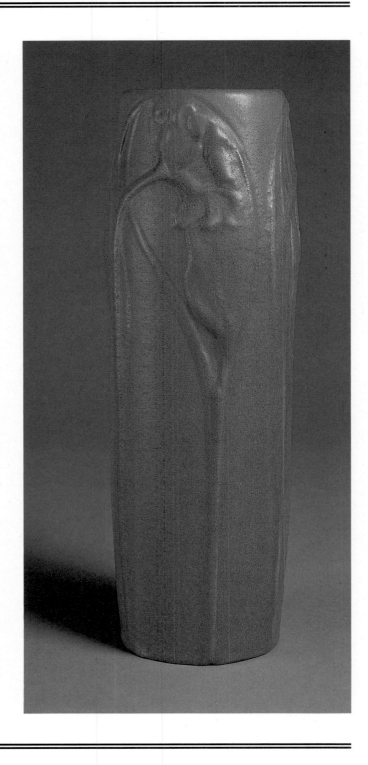

Artus Van Briggle. *Vase (Irises).* 1903
Glazed earthenware, 11⁵/16 × 4 × 4″
Collection The Newark Museum, New Jersey.
Estate of John Cotton Dana

Anna Marie Valentien. *Vase.* 1901
Produced at Rookwood Pottery
Ceramic, 14⁷/8 × 6¹/2 × 6¹/2″
Private collection

Saturday Evening Girls' Club
Bowl (with Rabbits). c. 1910
Produced at Paul Revere Pottery
Earthenware, $2^1/_4 \times 5^1/_2 \times 5^1/_2$"
Collection The Newark Museum,
New Jersey

Esther Huger Elliot
and Joseph Fortune Meyer
Humidor. c. 1904
Produced at Newcomb Pottery
Ceramic, $7^1/_2 \times 7 \times 7$"
Collection Dr. Thomas C. Folk

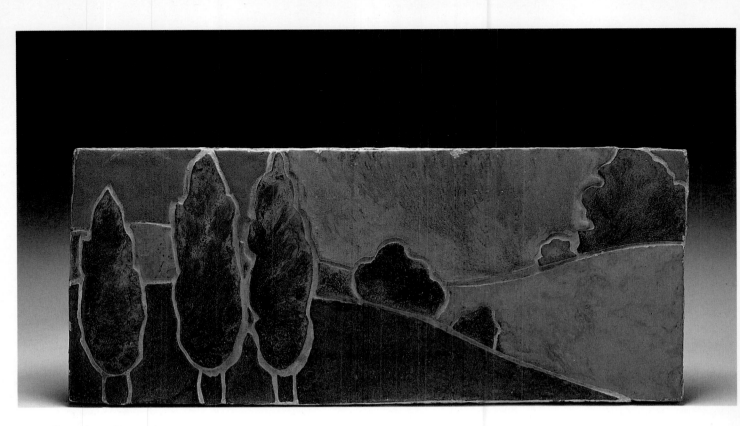

Mary Chase Perry (Stratton)
Tile Frieze. c. 1906
Designed for Pewabic Pottery
Ceramic, $16 \times 38^{1}/_{2}''$
Collection Pewabic Pottery

Maria de Hoa LeBlanc
and Joseph Fortune Meyer
Vase. c. 1910
Produced at Newcomb Pottery
Earthenware, $6^{1}/_{2} \times 5^{1}/_{2} \times 5^{1}/_{2}''$
Collection The Newark Museum, New Jersey

William A. Long. *Olla.* 1906–11
Produced at Clifton Art Pottery
Unglazed red earthenware,
$8^{1}/_{4} \times 14 \times 14''$
Collection The Newark Museum,
New Jersey.
Frank Conlin, Jr., Memorial Fund

John Kunsman
Teapot, Lid and Stand. 1909
Designed for Fulper Pottery
Stoneware, $9 \times 10 \times 7''$
Collection Dr. Thomas C. Folk

Charles Dean Hyten. *Mission Ware Vase.* c. 1910–20
Produced at Niloak Pottery
Marbled earthenware, 8³/₈ × 5 × 5″
Collection The Newark Museum, New Jersey.
Louis Bamberger Bequest Fund

Dard Hunter. *Dinnerware Service.* c. 1907–26
Ceramic, serving platter: 10¹/₄ × 10¹/₄″;
pitcher: 5¹/₄ × 5³/₄ × 5³/₄″; footed dish: 3³/₈ × 9 × 9″
Designed for the Roycroft Inn, Produced at Buffalo Pottery Company
Private collection

Maria Longworth Nichols (Storer). *Vase.* 1879–80
Produced at Rookwood Pottery
Stoneware, 10¹/₂ × 8⁵/₁₆ × 8⁵/₁₆″
Collection Cooper-Hewitt Museum,
National Museum of Design, Smithsonian Institution,
New York. Gift of Marcia and William Goodman

Maria Longworth Nichols (Storer)
Low Vase. 1882
Produced at Rookwood Pottery
Ceramic, 6⁷/₈ × 9 × 9″
Collection Dr. Thomas C. Folk

Opposite:
Maria Longworth Nichols (Storer)
Vase. 1895
Produced at Rookwood Pottery
Ceramic, 8¹/₂ × 3⁵/₈ × 3⁵/₈″
Private collection

George E. Ohr
Bowl with Handle and Spout. c. 1898–1909
Earthenware, $4 \times 7^5/8 \times 4^5/8''$
Collection Cooper-Hewitt Museum, National Museum of Design,
Smithsonian Institution, New York. Gift of Marcia and William Goodman

George E. Ohr. *Vase.* c. 1898–1909
Ceramic, $7^{1}/8 \times 5^{1}/8 \times 5^{1}/8''$
Private collection

George E. Ohr. *Vase.* c. 1898–1909
Ceramic, $9^{1}/2 \times 7^{1}/4 \times 7^{1}/4''$
Private collection

Opposite:
George E. Ohr
Teapot and Coffeepot. c. 1900
Earthenware, $7^{5}/16 \times 10^{5}/16 \times 7''$
Collection National Museum of American History, Smithsonian
Institution, Washington, D.C.

Mary Chase Perry (Stratton)
Monumental Vase. c. 1906–10
Designed for Pewabic Pottery
Ceramic, 28³/₄ × 15³/₄ × 15³/₄"
Collection Pewabic Pottery

Mary Chase Perry (Stratton). *Vase.* c. 1915–25
Designed for Pewabic Pottery
Ceramic, 18 × 13¹/₄ × 13¹/₄"
Collection Pewabic Pottery

Mary Chase Perry (Stratton)
Vase. c. 1912–20
Designed for Pewabic Pottery
Ceramic, 15 × 9 × 9″
Collection Pewabic Pottery

Cadmon Robertson. *Vase*. 1910
Designed for Hampshire Pottery
White earthenware, 11³/₄ × 5 × 5″
Collection The Newark Museum, New Jersey

Elizabeth Overbeck and Hannah Overbeck
Vase. c. 1910–31
Ceramic, 14¹/₂ × 10 × 10″
Collection Stephen Gray

Frederick Hurten Rhead
Vase. c. 1914–17
Designed for Rhead Pottery
Ceramic, $4 \times 3^{1}/_{2} \times 3^{1}/_{2}''$
Private collection

Opposite:
Hugh Robertson. *Vase.* c. 1885–88
Produced at Chelsea Keramic Art Works
Ceramic, 8 × 4³/8 × 4³/8″
Private collection

Hugh Robertson. *Vase.* c. 1885–89
Produced at Chelsea Keramic Art Works
Stoneware, 7¹/4 × 4 × 4″
Collection Cooper-Hewitt Museum,
National Museum of Design,
Smithsonian Institution, New York.
Gift of Marcia and William Goodman

Hugh Robertson. *Vase.* 1884–90
Produced at Chelsea Keramic Art Works
Ceramic, 7¹/2 × 2 × 2″
Collection The Brooklyn Museum.
Gift of Mrs. Charles Messer Stow

Hugh Robertson. *Vase.* 1885–88
Produced at Chelsea Keramic Art Works
Ceramic, 7¹/8 × 2 × 2″
Collection The Brooklyn Museum.
Gift of Arthur W. Clement

Adelaide Alsop Robineau. *Monogram Vase.* 1905
Porcelain, $12^1/_4 \times 5 \times 5''$
Collection Everson Museum of Art, Syracuse, New York

Adelaide Alsop Robineau. *Vase.* 1910
Porcelain, $11^1/_2 \times 2^3/_4 \times 2^3/_4''$
Collection Everson Museum of Art, Syracuse, New York

Adelaide Alsop Robineau. *Lantern.* 1908
Porcelain, $8 \times 6 \times 6''$
Collection Everson Museum of Art, Syracuse, New York

Jacques Sicard
Vase (with Beetles). 1904
Produced at Weller Pottery
Ceramic, $11^1/_2 \times 5^1/_2 \times 5^1/_2''$
Private collection

Kataro Shirayamadani. *Vase*. 1909
Produced at Rookwood Pottery
Earthenware, $13 \times 7 \times 7''$
Collection Dr. Thomas C. Folk

Opposite:
Lenore Asbury. *Vase*. 1917
Designed for Rookwood Pottery
Stoneware, $21^1/_2 \times 7 \times 7''$
Collection Cooper-Hewitt Museum,
National Museum of Design,
Smithsonian Institution, New York.
Gift of Marcia and William Goodman

Glass

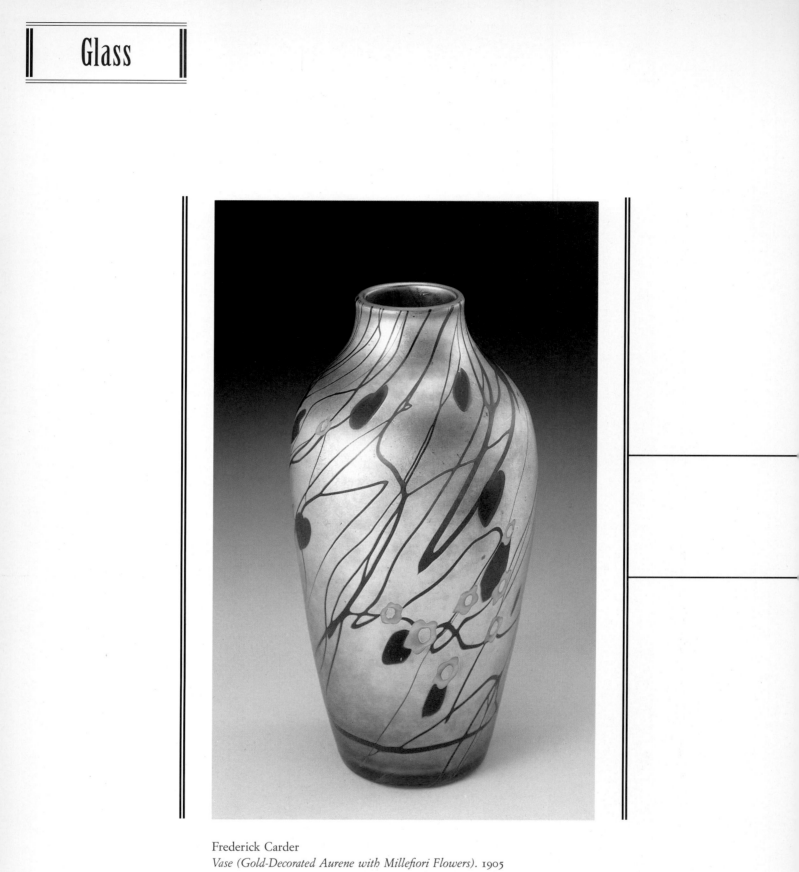

Frederick Carder
Vase (Gold-Decorated Aurene with Millefiori Flowers). 1905
Designed for Steuben Glass Works
Glass, $11 \times 8^{1}/_{2} \times 8^{1}/_{2}''$
Collection Stephen Milne

Frederick Carder
Vase (Blue Aurene). c. 1905–33
Designed for Steuben Glass Works
Glass, $8^{1}/_{4} \times 8^{1}/_{4} \times 8^{1}/_{4}''$
Collection Stephen Milne

Frederick Carder
Vase (Gold Aurene). c. 1904–33
Designed for Steuben Glass Works
Glass, $7 \times 4 \times 4''$
Collection Stephen Milne

169

Martin Bache. *Vase.* c. 1890
Designed for Quezal Art Glass and Decorating Company
Glass, $7^1/_2 \times 3^3/_4 \times 3^3/_4$″
Collection The Brooklyn Museum. Gift of Mrs. Alfred Zoebisch
(59.143.16)

Louis Comfort Tiffany
Vase (Opaque). 1913–20
Designed for Tiffany Furnaces
Glass, $9^5/_8 \times 5 \times 5$″
Collection The Brooklyn Museum.
Gift of Charles W. Gould (14.739.15)

Opposite:
Louis Comfort Tiffany
Vase (Trumpet). c. 1900
Designed for Tiffany Glass and Decorating Company
Glass, $18^1/_4 \times 5^1/_4 \times 5^1/_4$″
Collection The Brooklyn Museum.
Gift of Mary Berman in memory of
Mr. and Mrs. Harry Berman (59.78.1)

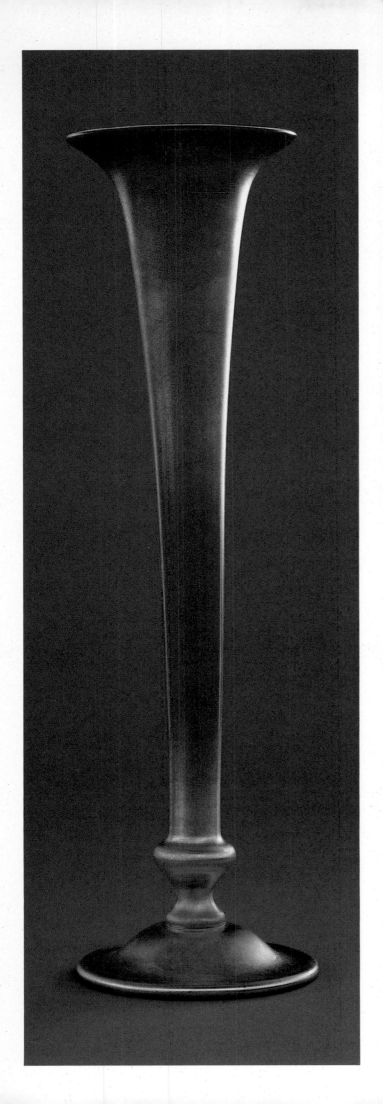

Louis Comfort Tiffany. *Vase.* c. 1917
Designed for Tiffany Furnaces
Favrile glass, $12^5/_{16} \times 4^{11}/_{16} \times 4^{11}/_{16}''$
Collection The Metropolitan Museum of Art, New York

Louis Comfort Tiffany
Vase (Peacock Feather). c. 1892–1902
Designed for Tiffany Glass and Decorating Company
Favrile glass, 10³/₄ × 6 × 6″
Collection The Metropolitan Museum of Art, New York

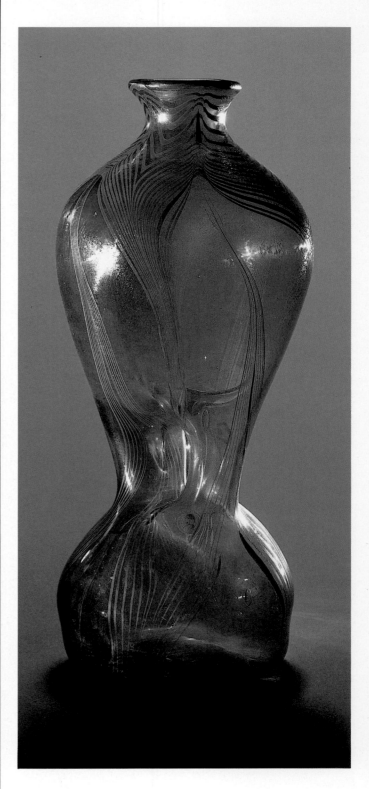

Louis Comfort Tiffany
Vase (Pinched Green). c. 1900
Designed for Tiffany Glass and Decorating Company
Glass, 10 × 3¹/₄ × 3¹/₄″
Collection The Brooklyn Museum. Gift of Mrs. Anthony
Tamburro in memory of her father, Rene de Quelin (64.246.7)

Louis Comfort Tiffany
Vase (Pressed & Cased). c. 1900
Designed for Tiffany Glass and Decorating Company
Glass, $8^5/8 \times 2^1/2 \times 2^1/2''$
Collection The Brooklyn Museum. Gift of Mrs. Anthony
Tamburro, in memory of her father, Rene de Quelin (62.262.8)

Louis Comfort Tiffany
Vase (Peacock). c. 1900
Designed for Tiffany Glass and Decorating Company
Glass, $13^1/2 \times 4 \times 4''$
Collection The Brooklyn Museum.
Gift of Charles W. Gould (14.739.8)

Louis Comfort Tiffany
Vase (Irregular). c. 1896–1900
Designed for Tiffany Glass and Decorating Company
Glass, $6^{1}/_{2} \times 5^{1}/_{4} \times 5^{1}/_{4}''$
Collection The Brooklyn Museum. Gift of Charles W. Gould

Louis Comfort Tiffany
Vase (Pinched). 1896–1919
Designed for Tiffany Furnaces
Glass, 8 × 5 × 5″
Collection The Brooklyn Museum. Bequest of Laura L. Barnes
(67.120.114)

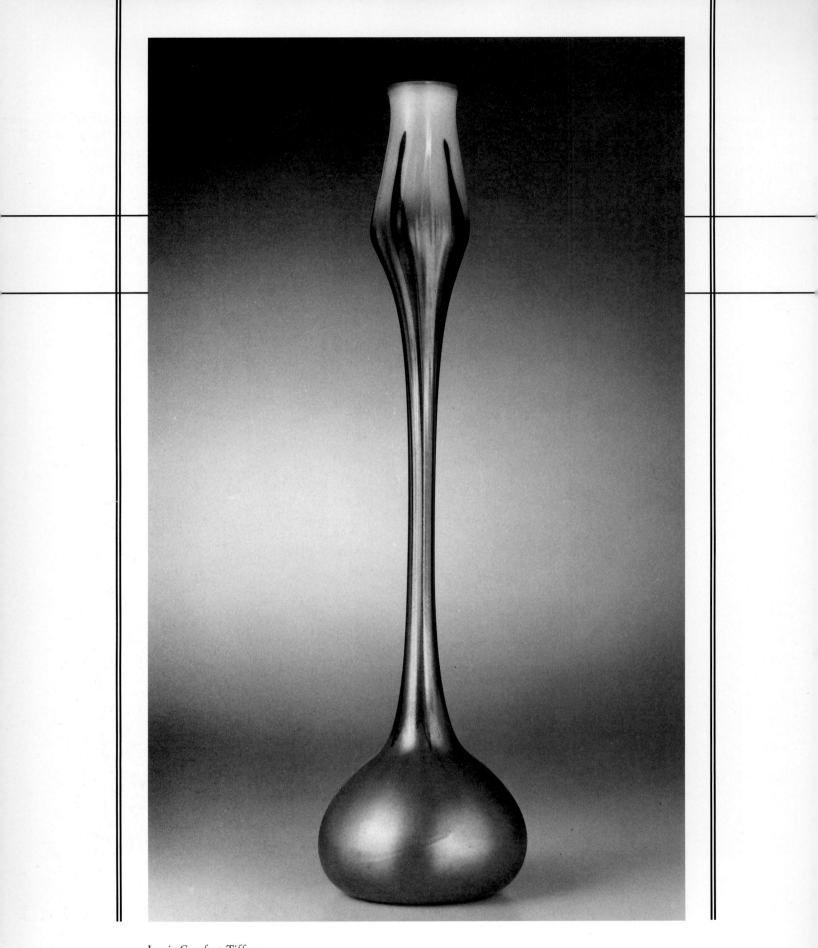

Louis Comfort Tiffany
Egyptian Onion Flower-Form Vase. c. 1900
Designed for Tiffany Glass and Decorating Company
Glass, $21^3/_4 \times 5^1/_2 \times 5^1/_2$"
Private collection

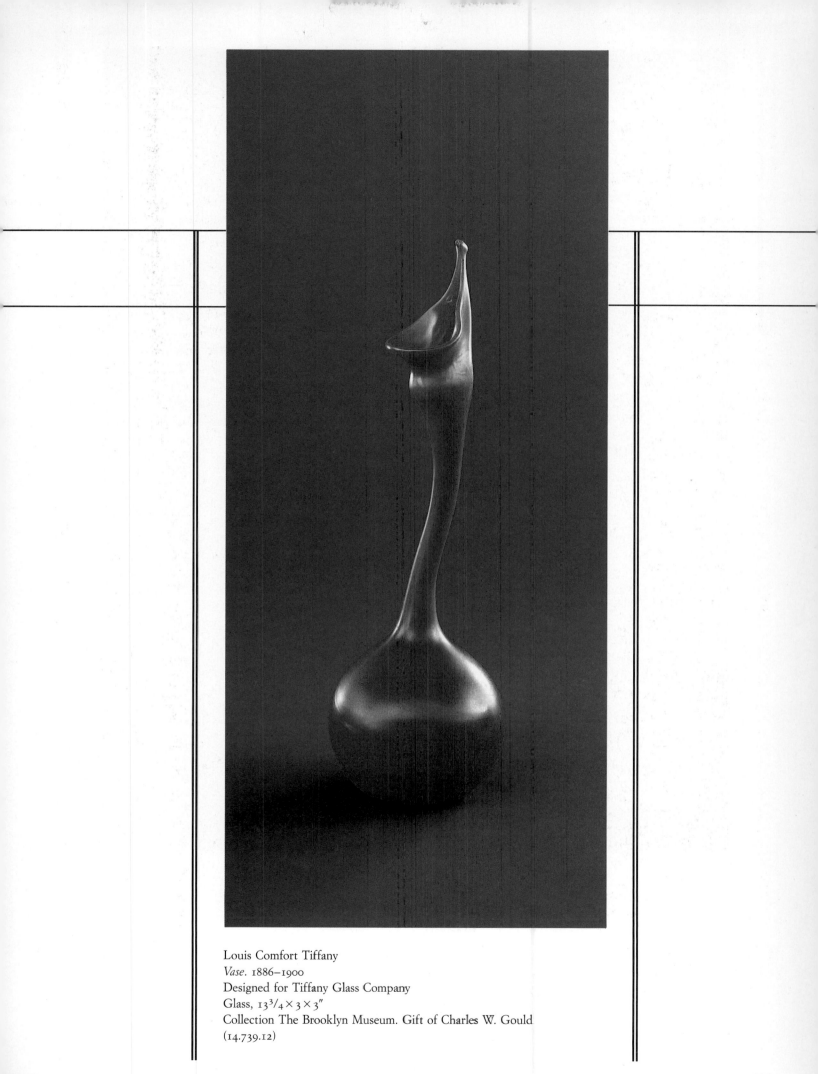

Louis Comfort Tiffany
Vase. 1886–1900
Designed for Tiffany Glass Company
Glass, 13³/₄ × 3 × 3"
Collection The Brooklyn Museum. Gift of Charles W. Gould
(14.739.12)

John La Farge
Samoan Girl Dancing the Siva. 1909
Fused cloisonne stained glass, 18 × 14″
Collection Mary and Oliver Hamill

John La Farge
Joshua Commanding the Sun to Stand Still. 1909
Fused cloisonne stained glass, 18 × 14″
Collection Mary and Oliver Hamill

Louis Comfort Tiffany. *Window (Landscape Scene with Iris and Flowering Magnolia)*. c. 1905
Designed for Tiffany Studios. Stained glass, 60¹/₄ × 42″
Collection The Metropolitan Museum of Art, New York

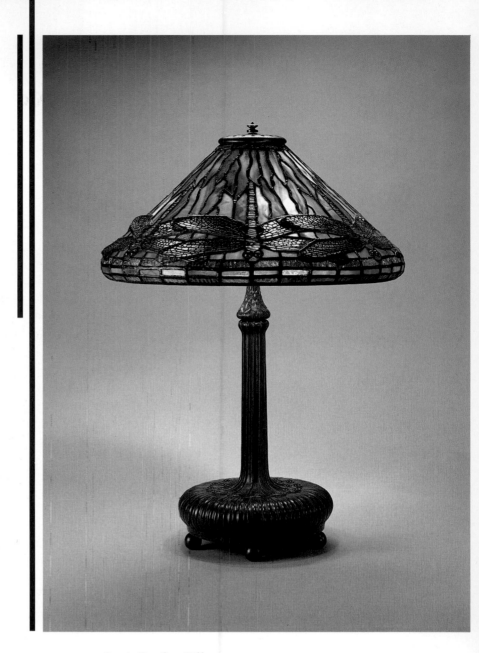

Louis Comfort Tiffany
Purple Winged Dragonfly Shade and Bronze Table Lamp. 1900–1910
Designed for Tiffany Studios
Leaded glass, patinated bronze, metal filigree, 22 × 16 × 16″
Courtesy The Neustadt Museum of Tiffany Art, New York

Dard Hunter
Flower Motif Window. c. 1907
Designed for the Roycroft Inn
Stained glass, lead, wood,
33 1/2 × 28 1/8 × 1 3/4″
Private collection

Louis Comfort Tiffany. *Vase (Lava)*. 1915
Designed for Tiffany Furnaces
Favrile glass, 3⁷/₈ × 3³/₈ × 3³/₈″
Collection The Metropolitan Museum of Art, New York

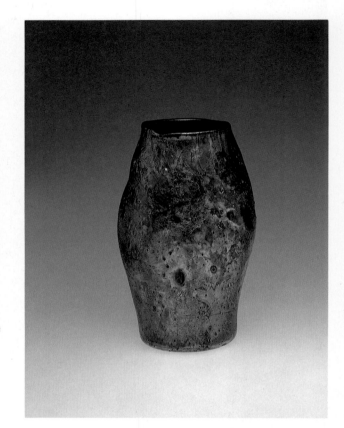

Louis Comfort Tiffany
Vase (Lava). c. 1893–1925
Designed for Tiffany Furnaces
Favrile glass, 5¹/₁₆ × 3 × 3″
Collection The Metropolitan Museum of Art, New York

Louis Comfort Tiffany. *Vase (Lava).* 1915
Designed for Tiffany Furnaces
Favrile glass, $5^{3}/_{16} \times 3 \times 3''$
Collection The Metropolitan Museum of Art, New York

Metals

Dirk Van Erp. *Table Lamp.* c. 1912
Copper, mica, 20 × 18 × 18″
Collection Norwest Corporation, Minneapolis

Art Crafts Shop, Buffalo
Candlesticks. c. 1910
Copper, enamel,
26³/₄ × 9⁷/₈ × 8⁵/₈″ each
Collection Elaine Dillof

Art Crafts Shop, Buffalo
Jewelry Box. c. 1905
Copper, enamel,
3³/₄ × 7³/₄ × 5"
Collection John Markus

Elizabeth Eaton Burton
Lamp. c. 1905
Copper, abalone shells,
32¹/₂ × 24³/₄ × 24³/₄"
Collection Tazio Nuvolari

Roycroft Shops
Vase. c. 1910
Copper, silver, $66^{3}/_{4} \times 3^{1}/_{2} \times 2^{1}/_{2}''$
Collection Kurland-Zabar

Elizabeth Eaton Burton
Book Cover. c. 1905
Suede, copper, $10 \times 7^{1}/_{2}''$
Private collection. Courtesy David Rago

Elizabeth E. Copeland. *Box*. c. 1914
Silver, enamel, $2^{1}/_{2} \times 3^{1}/_{8} \times 3^{1}/_{8}''$
Collection The Brooklyn Museum (96.1)

Carence Crafters. *Plant Holder*. c. 1910
Copper, silver wash, $10^{7}/_{8} \times 5^{1}/_{2} \times 2^{1}/_{8}''$
Collection Ira Simon

Marcus & Company. *Humidor*. c. 1915–20.
Copper, silver, arrowheads, $8 \times 6^1/_4 \times 6^1/_4''$
Collection Norwest Corporation, Minneapolis

Forest Craft Guild
Desk Set. c. 1910
Copper, obsidian glass,
letter rack: $4^1/_2 \times 6 \times 2''$; pen tray: $11 \times 3^5/_{16}''$
Collection Don Marek

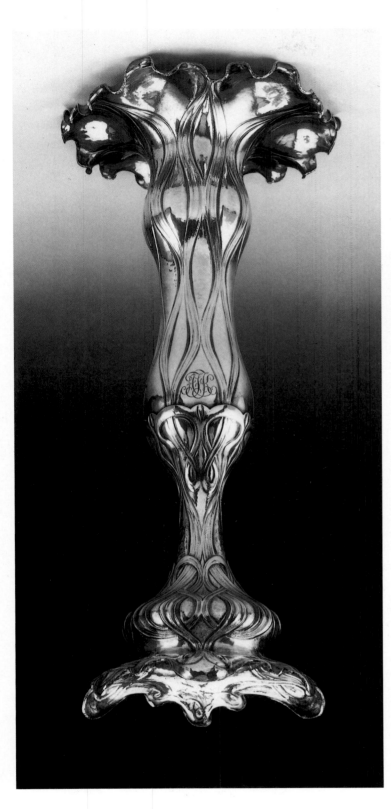

Gorham Manufacturing Company
Martelé Vase. 1898
Silver, gold wash, 15 × 7 × 7″
Courtesy Historical Design Collection, Inc., New York

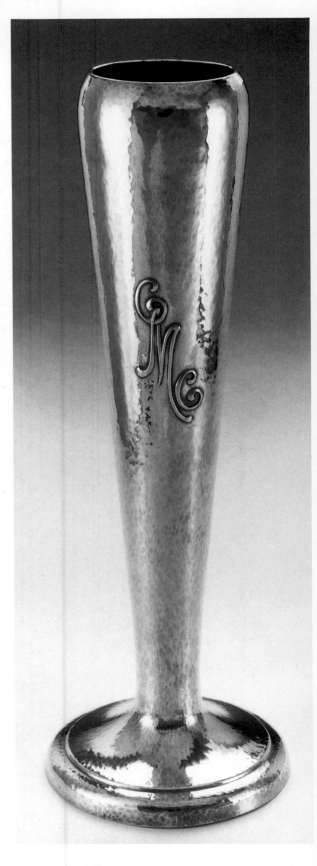

Clemens Friedell. *Vase.* 1915
Silver, 17¼ × 6 × 6″
Private collection

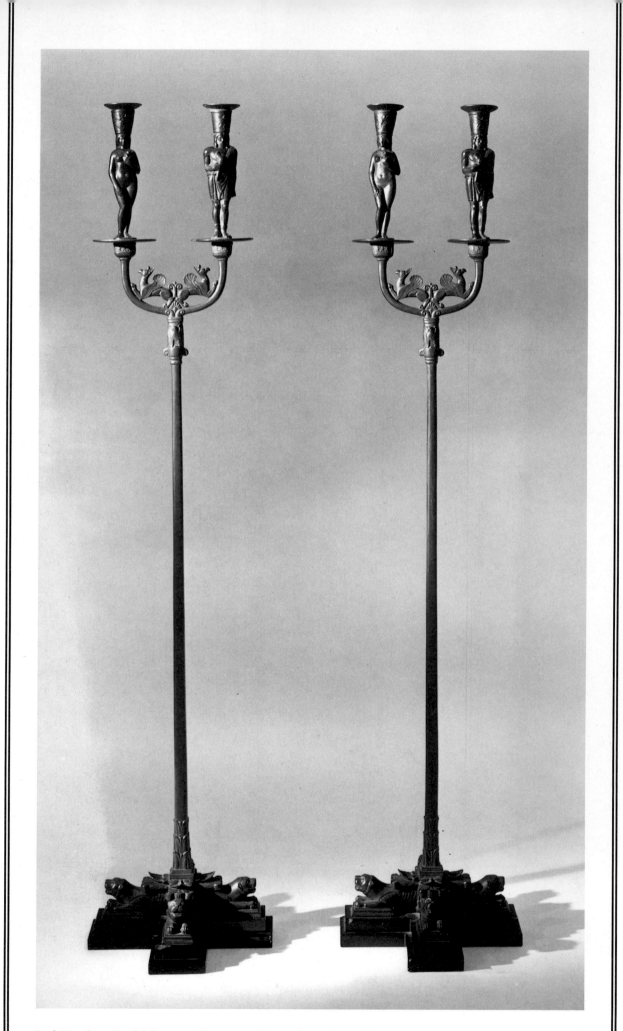

Paul Manship. *Candelabra*. 1916. Bronze, 58$^{1}/_{2}$ × 12$^{1}/_{2}$ × 12$^{1}/_{2}$″ each
Collection Cranbrook Academy of Art Museum, Bloomfield Hills, Michigan. Gift of George and Ellen Booth

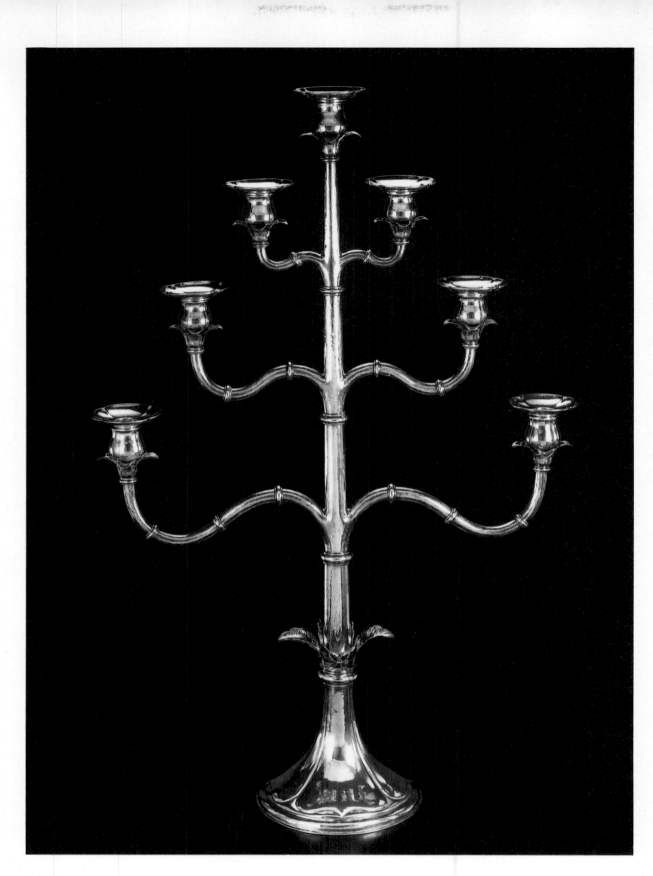

Kalo Shop
Candelabrum. c. 1910
Silver, 28^1/$_2$ × 19^1/$_2$ × 6^1/$_4$″
Private collection

George Washington Maher. *Urn*. 1912
Designed for *Rockledge*
Bronze, copper, $30^{1}/_{2} \times 12^{1}/_{2} \times 12^{1}/_{2}''$
Collection Norwest Corporation, Minneapolis

Madeline Yale Wynne
Belt Buckle. c. 1900
Copper, $2^3/8 \times 9^1/2$″
Collection Pocumtuck Valley Memorial Association, Memorial
Hall Museum, Deerfield, Massachusetts

Jessie M. Preston
Jewelry Box. c. 1904–7
Bronze, $1^7/8 \times 4^1/4 \times 2^1/2$″
Private collection. Courtesy ARK Antiques, New Haven, Connecticut

Theodore Hanford Pond
Vase. c. 1910
Copper, $17^1/2 \times 4^1/4 \times 4^1/4$″
Collection Norwest Corporation,
Minneapolis

Dirk Van Erp. *Vase.* c. 1911
Hammered copper, 24 × 10 × 10″
Collection Susan Fetterolf and Jeffrey Gorrin

Jessie M. Preston
Candlesticks. c. 1915
Bronze, 12³/₄ × 7³/₄ × 7³/₄″ each
Collection Elaine Dillof

Robert R. Jarvie
Candlesticks. c. 1910
Bronze,
average height: 14″;
average base: 7″
Collection Ira Simon

Robert R. Jarvie. *Tray*. c. 1906
Copper, $5^5/8 \times 11^1/8 \times 11^1/8''$
Collection Ira Simon

Gustav Stickley. *Tray*. c. 1905
Copper, $15 \times 15''$
Private collection

Attributed to Eva Macomber
Box. c. 1907
Produced by Society of Arts and Crafts, Boston
Copper, enamel, $4^{1}/_{2} \times 6^{3}/_{8} \times 6^{3}/_{8}''$
Collection Museum of Fine Arts, Boston.
Gift of Lois and Stephen Kunian

Attributed to
Frank J. Marshall
Box. c. 1910
Produced by Society of Arts
and Crafts, Boston
Copper, enamel,
$1^{1}/_{2} \times 4^{1}/_{2} \times 4^{1}/_{2}''$
Collection Museum
of Fine Arts,
Boston. Gift of Lois
and Stephen Kunian

Karl E. Kipp. *Planter.* 1905
Copper, $3^1/_4 \times 5^3/_4 \times 5^3/_4''$
Collection Marilee Boyd Meyer

Mary Catherine Knight. *Bowl.* c. 1903
Silver, enamel, $1^{15}/_{16} \times 4^1/_4 \times 4^1/_4''$
Collection The Cleveland Museum of Art.
John L. Severance Fund

Samuel Yellin. *Gothic Chest.* 1918
Wrought iron, $34^{1}/_{2} \times 18^{1}/_{2} \times 11''$
Collection Yellin Metalworkers, Philadelphia

Marie Zimmermann. *Candelabra*. c. 1920
Bronze, crystal, 28^1/$_8$ × 30^7/$_8$ × 8^5/$_8$"
Collection Mitchell Wolfson, Jr. Courtesy Wolfsonian Foundation, Miami

Arthur J. Stone
Tea Service. 1907
Sterling silver, ivory, gold wash,
Kettle: $9^1/4 \times 10^1/8 \times 7^1/8''$;
teapot: $5^1/4 \times 11^5/8 \times 5^{15}/16''$; creamer: $4 \times 6 \times 4''$
Collection Museum of Fine Arts, Boston. Gift of a Friend of
the Department of American Decorative Arts and Sculpture,
John H. and Ernestine A. Payne Fund, and Curator's Fund

Julius Olaf Randahl
Pitcher. 1915
Silver, $8^7/8 \times 8^1/8 \times 4^7/8''$
Collection The Art Institute of Chicago. Twenty-fifth
Anniversary Gift of Mr. and Mrs. Louis Marks, Gift of
Mr. and Mrs. Lawrence S. Dreiman

Shreve and Company
Punch Bowl. c. 1910–20
Silver, $10^{1}/8 \times 13^{1}/_2 \times 13^{1}/_2''$
Collection Milwaukee Art Museum. On loan from Warren Gilson

Tiffany & Company
Tea and Coffee Service "Special Hand Work." c. 1915
Sterling silver,
kettle on stand with lamp: $17^7/8 \times 9 \times 4''$;
coffeepot: $9 \times 8^1/2 \times 4''$; creamer: $3^7/8 \times 5 \times 3^1/2''$
Collection Museum of the City of New York.
Gift of Ms. Claire Lewis

Louis Rorimer
Coffee and Tea Service. c. 1910
Designed for the Rokesley Shop
Silver, moonstones, ebony,
coffeepot: $11^1/8 \times 9^3/4 \times 5''$; teapot: $7^1/8 \times 10\ ^7/8 \times 5''$;
sugar bowl: $3^3/4 \times 8^{13}/16 \times 3''$
Collection The Cleveland Museum of Art. Gift in memory of
Louis Rorimer, from his daughter, Louise Rorimer Dushkin, and
his granddaughter, Edie Soeiro

Katherine Pratt
Creamer, Sugar Bowl, and Tray. c. 1900–1920
Hand-raised sterling silver,
tray: $8^1/_4 \times 5''$; creamer: $5^1/_8 \times 4^3/_4 \times 4''$
Private collection

Karl F. Leinonen
Bowl and Spoon. c. 1900–1920
Hand-raised sterling silver,
bowl: $1^3/_4 \times 5^7/_8 \times 5^7/_8''$;
spoon length: $6^1/_4''$
Private collection

Robert R. Jarvie
Hot Beverage Service. c. 1915. Sterling silver
coffeepot: $7^3/_4 \times 7^1/_2 \times 3^1/_4''$; creamer:
$5 \times 6 \times 2^3/_4''$; tray: $21 \times 15^3/_4''$
Collection Museum of Fine Arts, Boston. Gift of a friend of
the Department of American Decorative Arts and Sculpture,
John H. and Ernestine A. Payne Fund, and Curator's Fund

George Porter Blanchard. *Bowl.* c. 1904
Sterling silver, $3^1/4 \times 10^1/8 \times 10^1/8''$
Private collection. Courtesy ARK Antiques,
New Haven, Connecticut

George Washington Maher. *Coffee and Tea Service.* 1912
Designed for *Rockledge*
Silver, tray: $24^1/2 \times 20''$; coffeepot: $9^1/2 \times 8^1/2 \times 8^1/2''$;
creamer: $5 \times 5^1/4 \times 5^1/4''$
Private collection

Mildred Watkins. *Teapot.* c. 1913
Sterling silver, $11^1/2 \times 9^3/16 \times 4^3/8''$
Collection Yale University Art Gallery, New Haven.
Gift of ARK Antiques

James H. Winn. *Lavaliere.* 1895–1917
Silver, gold, turquoise, length: 16¼"
Collection The Art Institute of Chicago. Restricted gift of
Warren L. Batts, Mrs. Jacob H. Biscof, Mrs. Arthur S. Bowes,
and the Art Rental and Sales Gallery

Mildred Watkins. *Pendant and Chain.* c. 1904–14
Silver, enamel, pendant: 1¾ × 1½"
Collection The Art Institute of Chicago. Dr. Julian Archie
Endowment; Neighbors of Kenilworth, Edgar J. Schoen, and
Village Associates of the Women's Board of the Art Institute
of Chicago Funds

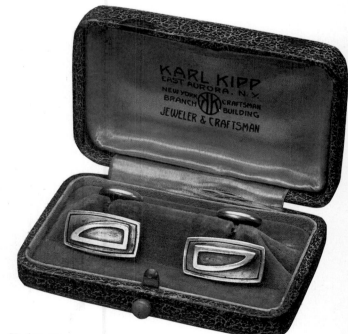

Karl E. Kipp
Cufflinks. c. 1910
Sterling silver, box: 3 × 2½ × 1½"
Collection Bill Drucker

Margaret Rogers
Necklace and Earrings. c. 1920
Gold, cornelian,
necklace: $17^1/_2"$; earrings: $^1/_2 \times {}^1/_2"$
Collection Marilee Boyd Meyer

Forest Emerson Mann
Necklace. c. 1906
Silver filigree, amazonstones, California pearls,
chain: $14^1/_2"$; pendant: $2^7/_8 \times 2"$
Collection Don Marek

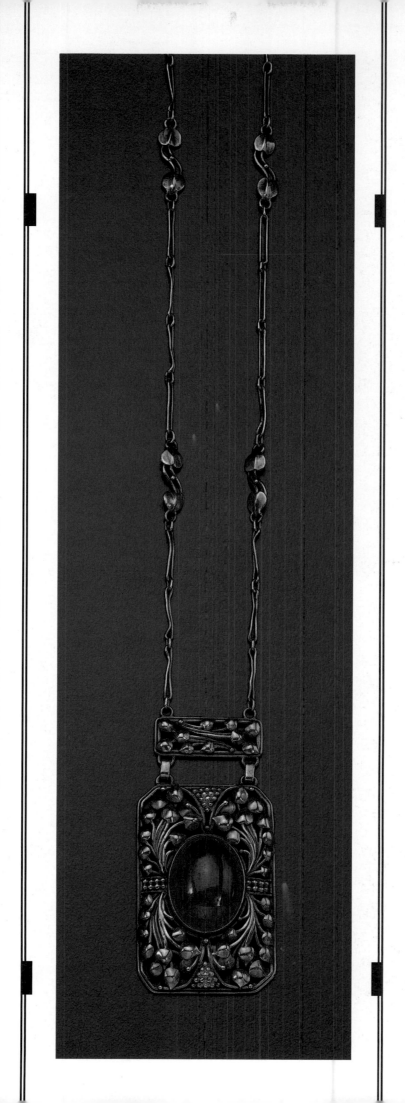

Josephine Hartwell Shaw
Pendant Necklace. c. 1900–1920
Gold, jelly-opal, length: 16″
Collection Joyce Jonas

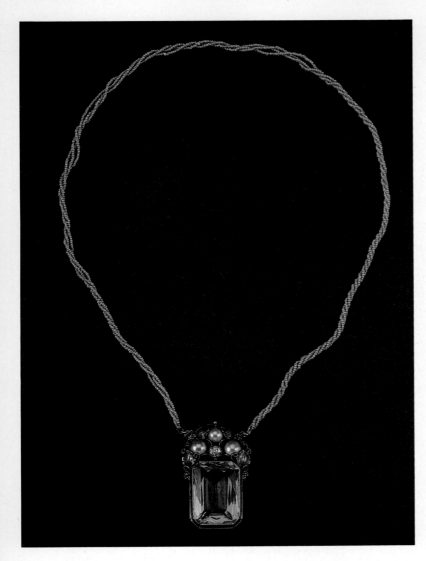

Edward Everett Oakes
Necklace. c. 1920
Aquamarine, pearl, gold,
chain: $15^3/_4''$; pendant: $1^1/_2 \times {}^1/_4''$
Collection Marilee Boyd Meyer

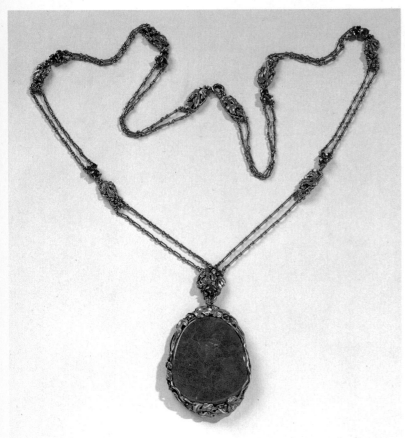

Louis Comfort Tiffany
Necklace. c. 1918
Black opal, 18k gold, sapphires, green garnets
Chain: $14^1/_2''$; pendant: $1^1/_2 \times 2^1/_2''$
Collection Ira Simon

Kalo Shop. *Necklace*. c. 1905
Gold, semiprecious stones, length: 16″
Private collection

Elverhoj Colony. *Necklace.* c. 1900–1920
Gold, pearl, tourmaline, length: 14″
Collection Joyce Jonas

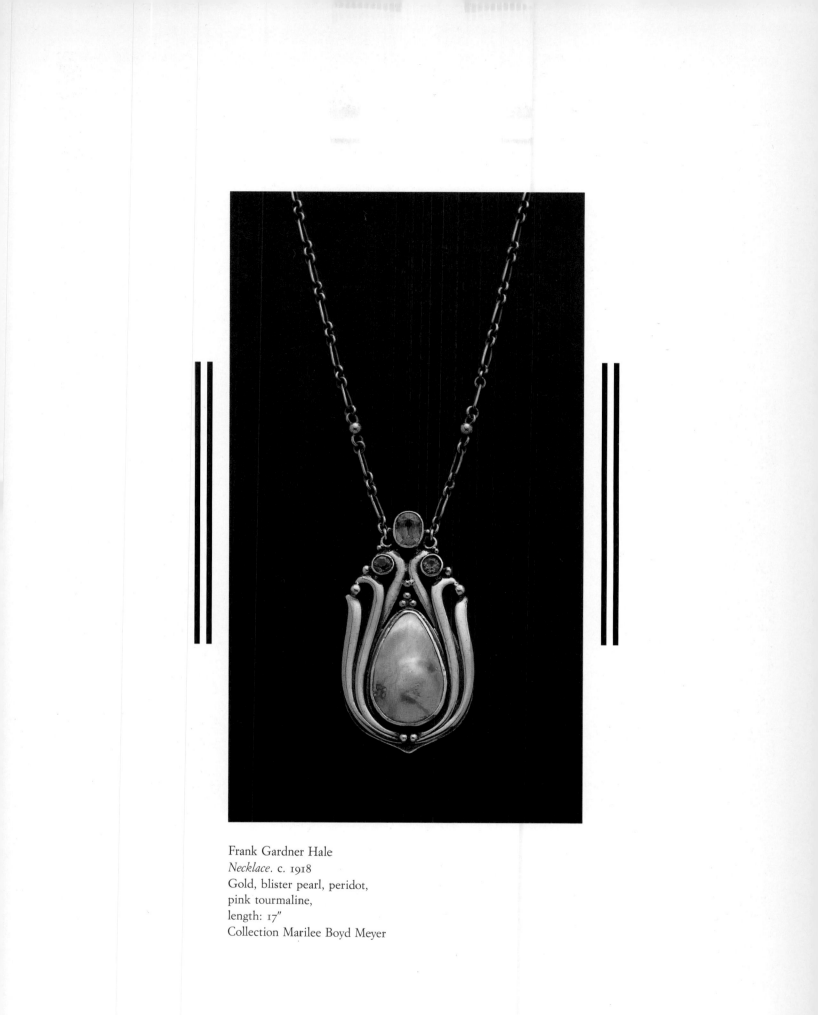

Frank Gardner Hale
Necklace. c. 1918
Gold, blister pearl, peridot,
pink tourmaline,
length: 17″
Collection Marilee Boyd Meyer

Textiles

Margaret Whiting
Door Curtain (detail). 1899
Linen, 8′3″ × 6′4″
Collection Pocumtuck Valley
Memorial Association,
Memorial Hall Museum,
Deerfield, Massachusetts.
Gift of Gertrude Cochrane Smith

Nonoluck Silk Company
*Partially-worked Panel Intended
as a Pillow.* c. 1910–15
Stenciled linen embroidered with
cotton, 23³/₄ × 24¹/₈″
Collection The Art Institute of Chicago

Anonymous. *"Collars and Cuffs" Sack Kit.* c. 1910
Linen, 14 × 12"
Collection John Bryan

Anonymous. *Workbag.* c. 1910
Linen, 22¹/₈ × 14"
Collection John Bryan

Deerfield Society of Blue and White Needlework. *Wall Hanging.* c. 1910 Linen, 37 × 36¹/₂"
Collection Pocumtuck Valley Memorial Association, Memorial Hall Museum, Deerfield, Massachusetts

H. E. Varren Company
Panel Intended as a Pillow, Design No. 215. c. 1910
Stenciled, painted cotton, 22⅞ × 17½″
Collection The Art Institute of Chicago

Gustav Stickley. *Carpet.* c. 1905
Cotton, wool, soft wood paper fibers,
6′10¾″ × 3′10⅞″
Collection The Art Institute of Chicago

Madeline Yale Wynne
Witch Basket. c. 1901–10
Raffia, $7^7/_8 \times 6^1/_8 \times 6^1/_8''$
Collection Pocumtuck Valley
Memorial Association,
Memorial Hall Museum,
Deerfield, Massachusetts

Mrs. Carrie E. Clapp. *Basket.* c. 1905
Palm leaves, $4^1/_4 \times 8 \times 8''$
Collection Pocumtuck Valley Memorial Association,
Memorial Hall Museum, Deerfield, Massachusetts

Roycroft Shops. *Doily.* c. 1910
Leather, $17^1/_2 \times 17^1/_2''$
Collection Raymond Groll

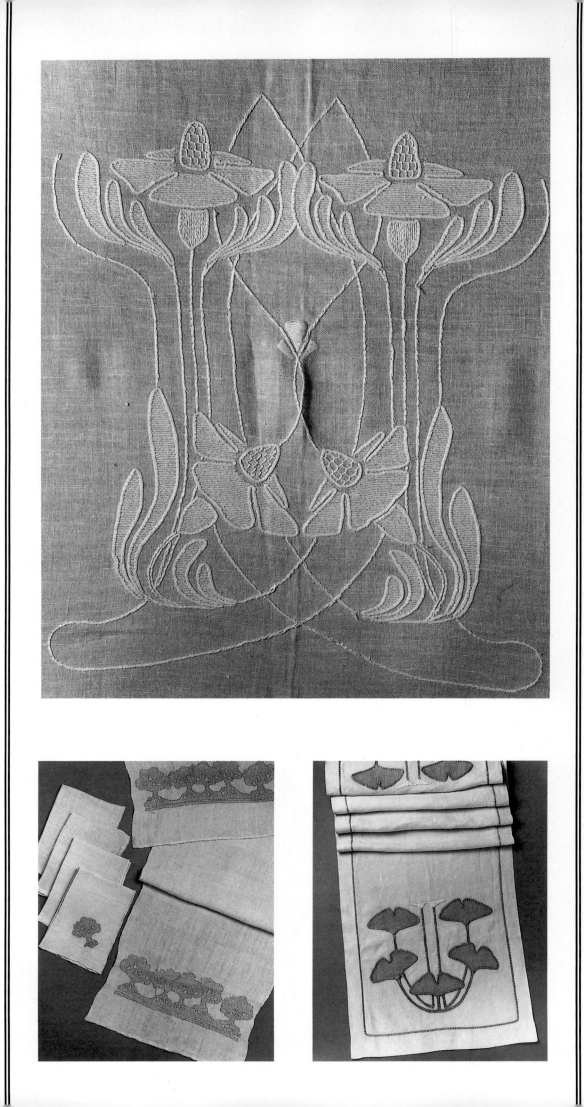

Richardson Silk Company
Pillow Sham, Design No. 525. c. 1910
Linen embroidered with silk, 23¹/₂ × 16¹/₂"
Collection The Art Institute of Chicago

Richardson Silk Company
Partially-worked Panel Intended as a Pillow,
Design No. 2951. c. 1910–15
Stenciled cotton embroidered with silk,
16³/₄ × 21¹/₈"
Collection The Art Institute of Chicago

Opposite above:
Gustav Stickley. *Bedspread.* c. 1912
Linen, 9'6" × 6'10"
Collection John Bryan

Opposite below left:
Gustav Stickley
Table Runner with Napkins. c. 1905
Linen runner: 71¹/₄ × 15¹/₄"
Collection John Bryan

Opposite below right:
Gustav Stickley
Table Runner. c. 1905
Linen, 90 × 15"
Collection John Bryan

John S. Bradstreet
Center table. c. 1904
Designed for William Prindle House
Cypress with *jin-di-sugi* finish,
27^1/$_4$ × 30 × 30"
Collection Tazio Nuvolari

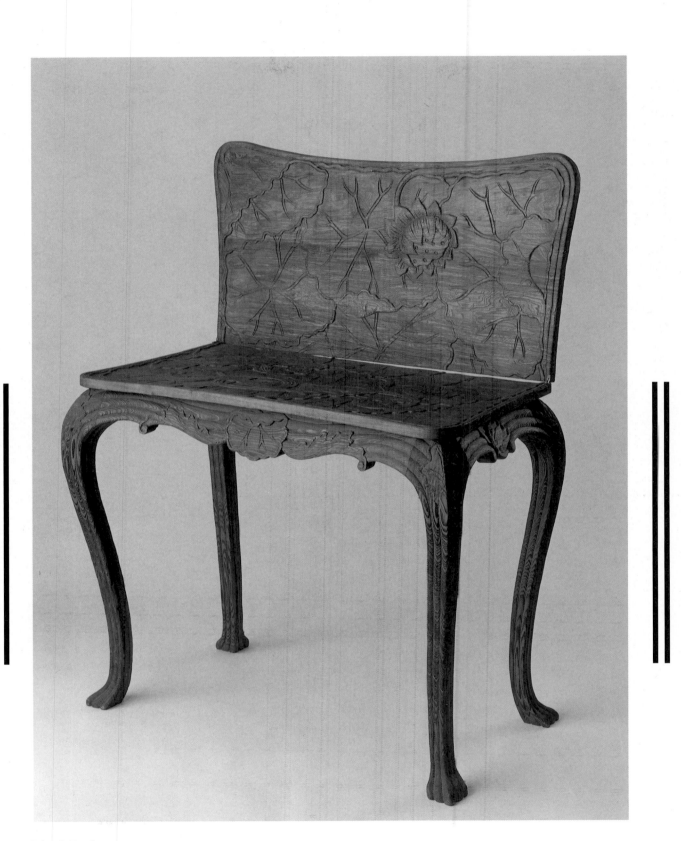

John S. Bradstreet
Flip-top card table. c. 1904
Designed for William Prindle House
Cypress with *jin-di-sugi* finish,
$30^{1}/_{4} \times 35^{1}/_{2} \times 19^{3}/_{4}''$
Collection The Minneapolis Institute of Arts.
Gift of Wheaton Wood

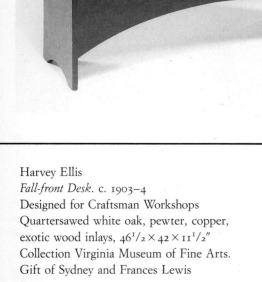

Harvey Ellis
Fall-front Desk. c. 1903–4
Designed for Craftsman Workshops
Quartersawed white oak, pewter, copper,
exotic wood inlays, $46^{1}/_{2} \times 42 \times 11^{1}/_{2}''$
Collection Virginia Museum of Fine Arts.
Gift of Sydney and Frances Lewis

George M. Niedecken. *Dainty (Curio) Cabinet.* 1907
Curly birch, metal-capped feet, plate glass, $53 \times 37 \times 17''$
Collection David and Jean Sullivan.
Courtesy Milwaukee Art Museum

George M. Niedecken
Upholstered Armchair. 1907
Walnut, walnut veneer, velour upholstery,
$46^{1}/_{2} \times 25^{1}/_{4} \times 25^{3}/_{4}''$
Collection Nicole Teweles

Charles Sumner Greene and Henry Mather Greene
Chiffonier. c. 1909
Designed for Gamble House master bedroom
Black walnut, ebony, lignum vitae, semiprecious stone inlay,
$62 \times 37^{1}/_{2} \times 21''$
Collection Gamble House

Charles Rohlfs
Rocking Chair. c. 1900
Carved quartersawed oak, leather, 31 × 24 × 34"
Collection Susan Fetterolf and Jeffrey Gorrin

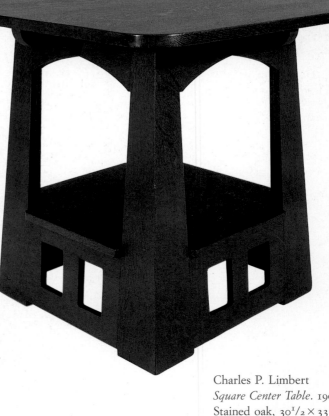

Charles P. Limbert
Square Center Table. 1904
Stained oak, 30^1/$_2$ × 33^1/$_2$ × 33^1/$_2$"
Courtesy Struve Gallery, Chicago

Charles P. Limbert
Bench #243. 1905
Oak, 24 × 30 × 18"
Collection Victorian Chicago Arts and Crafts Antique
Gallery

Charles P. Limbert
Wastebasket. c. 1908
Quartersawed oak,
17^3/$_4$ × 11 × 11"
Collection David Rago

George Washington Maher
Armchair. c. 1914
Designed for *Rockledge*
Oak with studded, padded leather upholstery,
$59^1/_4 \times 33 \times 26^3/_8''$
Collection The Metropolitan Museum of Art, New York.
Purchase Theodore R. Gamble, Jr. Gift in honor of his
mother, Mrs. Theodore Robert Gamble

George Washington Maher
Standing Clock. 1912
Designed for *Rockledge*
Oak, copper, silk, brass
$80 \times 31^1/_2 \times 15^1/_8''$
Collection Tazio Nuvolari

Charles Rohlfs. *Candelabra*. 1900–1902
Wood, copper, lapis shells, $17^{1}/_{4} \times 18^{1}/_{4} \times 8^{3}/_{8}''$
Collection Mr. Donald Magner

Frank Jeck
Infant's Crib. 1922
Hand-carved cherry,
velvet hangings, $64^{1}/_{2} \times 44^{1}/_{4} \times 24^{1}/_{4}''$
Collection Glencairn Museum,
Bryn Athyn, Pennsylvania

Charles Rohlfs. *Plant Stand*. 1901
Fumed quartersawed oak, hammered copper,
brass bucket, $48 \times 18 \times 18''$
Collection Beth Cathers

226

William Roth. *Umbrella Stand.* 1910
Designed for Roycroft Shops
Quartersawed oak, hammered copper,
$30 \times 13^{1}/_{2} \times 13^{1}/_{2}''$
Private collection

Charles Rohlfs. *Fall-front desk.* 1902
Carved quartersawed oak, $54^{1}/_{8} \times 14 \times 35^{1}/_{4}''$
Collection Tazio Nuvolari

William L. Price. *Music Stand.* c. 1901–6
Carved, stained oak, $43^{1}/_{2} \times 20 \times 16''$
Collection Mr. and Mrs. Hyman Myers

Lucia Kleinhaus Mathews
"Young Girl in White." c. 1900–1915
Oil on wood panel; carved,
painted wood frame, $22^{1}/_{16} \times 20^{1}/_{4} \times 2^{1}/_{8}''$
Collection The Oakland Museum.
Gift of Harald Wagner

Lucia Kleinhaus Mathews
Clock. c. 1906–15
Painted, gilded wood; metal, glass, $14^{3}/_{4} \times 6 \times 4''$
Collection The Oakland Museum. Gift of the Concours
d'Antiques, The Art Guild

Lucia Kleinhaus Mathews
Figural box. 1916
Painted wood, $4^{1}/_{4} \times 13^{1}/_{8} \times 8^{3}/_{8}''$
Collection Donald Magner

Roycroft Shops
Picture Frame with Portrait of Elbert Hubbard.
c. 1912
Stained oak, gelatin silver print,
glass, 26 × 23³/₈ × ³/₄"
Private collection

Roycroft Shops
Funereal Box. c. 1910
Mahogany, copper,
8¹/₄ × 14¹/₄ × 12¹/₈"
Collection Tazio Nuvolari

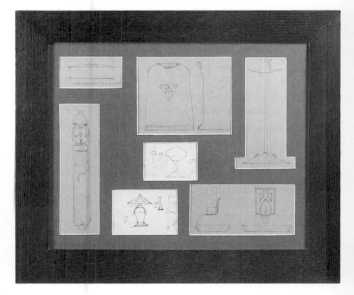

Roycroft Shops
Picture Frame with Drawings
Attributed to Karl Kipp.
c. 1910–12
Stained oak, Roycroft paper matte,
graphite on paper, 20³/₄ × 24³/₄"
Private collection

Roycroft Shops. *Child's chest*. 1912. Designed for Elbert Hubbard's granddaughter Lynette. Quartersawed oak, copper, mirror, $33^3/_4 \times 25^3/_4 \times 11''$.
Private collection

Roycroft Shops
Magazine stand. c. 1906–12
Oak, $63^1/_4 \times 21^3/_4 \times 17^3/_4''$
Collection Tazio Nuvolari

Roycroft Shops. *Wastepaper Basket*.
c. 1910 Mahogany, copper, $13 \times 11 \times 11''$
Collection Tazio Nuvolari

Roycroft Shops
Wastepaper Basket. c. 1910
From the home of Ralph Waldo Emerson
Maple, $13 \times 12^1/_4 \times 12^1/_4''$
Collection Tazio Nuvolari

Gustav Stickley
Corner Cupboard.
c. 1902
Designed for
the Stickley home
Oak, wrought iron,
$72 \times 42 \times 29^{1}/_{2}''$
Collection
Mrs. Barbara Fuldner

Harvey Ellis
Side Chair. c. 1903–4
Designed for United Crafts
Stained curled maple, pewter, wood inlays,
$40^{1}/_{2} \times 16^{1}/_{2} \times 15^{1}/_{2}''$
Collection The Newark Museum, New Jersey. Sophronia Anderson
Bequest fund

Gustav Stickley
Round Table. c. 1907–8
Quartersawed oak,
30 × 35¹/₂ × 35¹/₂″
Collection Sydney and Frances Lewis. Courtesy Virginia
Museum of Fine Arts

Frank Lloyd Wright. *Table.* 1904
Wood, 27 × 27 × 26¹/₄″
Collection Albright-Knox Art Gallery, Buffalo.
Gift of Darwin R. Martin, 1968

Gustav Stickley
Settle. 1901–2
Oak, 40¹/₄ × 60 × 27″
Collection Barbara Taff and Alan Sachs

Gustav Stickley
Three-panel Screen. c. 1904
Oak, $59^1/_4 \times 75^1/_2''$
Collection Beth Cathers

Gustav Stickley
Sideboard. c. 1905–10
Oak, copper, $47^1/_2 \times 56 \times 21^3/_4''$
Collection Yale University Art Gallery.
Gift of Dr. and Mrs. Matthew Newman

Ernest Stowe. *Desk.* c. 1900–1911
Varnished pine, white birchbark, yellow birch, cedar,
54 1/2 × 43 5/8 × 25"
Collection Adirondack Museum, Blue Mountain Lake, New York. Warren W. Kay Collection

Resource List

Artists' Biographies
Communities
Exhibitions
Guilds and Societies
Periodicals
Production Centers
Schools
Settlement Houses
Small Presses

This resource list is a select compendium of the most prominent American artists, Arts and Crafts communities, educational facilities, major exhibitions, important publications, and influential production centers of the period 1900–1920. To our knowledge, this is the first attempt to amass resource information on the inception of the American craft movement.

As a first step, the information was gathered by research scholars from every region of the country, since each region was to be represented. The material was reviewed, edited, and collated by the American Craft Museum curatorial staff. As the project proceeded, the need for further scholarship became increasingly evident. This listing that follows, therefore, is offered as an introductory outline rather than a conclusive document.

Our guideline was to present information for future study in as useful a format as possible. The information is limited to what could be gathered from the most reliable sources—even though these sources were on occasion contradictory. Often, a founding date is provided, but the closing date is uncertain. Some listings are still active, and these are indicated by the word "present." The categories are presented in alphabetical order, as are the listings within each category.

J. K.

ARMSTRONG, DAVID MAITLAND
Born April 15, 1836, Danskammer,
New York; died May 26, 1918, New
York, New York.
Muralist, glass artist

An artist working in mosaic glass in
New York City, in 1878 Armstrong
served as director of the American art
department at the Paris Exposition, for
which he received France's Legion of
Honor. Although not a member of
Louis C. Tiffany and Associated Artists, he worked for the firm in 1879–80
on the decoration of the Veterans'
Room of the Seventh Regiment Armory; he also worked on the chapel at
Biltmore, George Vanderbilt's estate, in
North Carolina. Armstrong was responsible for the stained-glass
decoration in hundreds of churches,
public buildings, and private houses in
the United States.

ASBURY, LENORE
Born 1866; died 1933.
Ceramist, decorator

Asbury was one of the most accomplished decorators at the Rookwood
Pottery Company, where she was active
from 1894 to 1931. Known for her
softly rendered naturalistic floral subjects, Asbury, like almost all of the
Rookwood decorators, received her
early instruction at the Art Academy
of Cincinnati.

BACHE, MARTIN
Born 1870s, Alsace-Lorraine, France;
died 1924.
Glass manufacturer

Bache worked as a batch mixer for the
Tiffany Glass and Decorating Company, in Corona, New York, from 1894
to 1901. In 1901, he set up his own
plant, Quezal Art Glass and Decorating
Company, in Brooklyn, New York, together with another former Tiffany
employee, Thomas Johnson. Bache
used his knowledge of Tiffany's glass
melts and lustering compounds to
make identical glass mixtures, which
Johnson, a skilled glassblower, transformed into art glass that virtually
duplicated the characteristic iridescent
finish of Tiffany glass. Faulty equipment and the incompatibility of the

glasses used by Quezal resulted in great
waste, limiting useful output. The firm
closed in 1925.

BAGGS, ARTHUR EUGENE
Born October 27, 1886, Alfred, New
York; died 1947.
Ceramist, educator

Baggs trained under Charles Fergus
Binns in the ceramics program at Alfred University. In 1904, Dr. Herbert J.
Hall founded the Handicraft Shop, in
Marblehead, Massachusetts, as a therapeutic community for convalescing
patients, and Baggs was chosen to direct the ceramics program. When the
demands of the pottery became too
difficult for the patients, it changed to
a professional enterprise known as
Marblehead Pottery. Baggs took owner-
ship of Marblehead in 1915, and
produced ceramics noted for their simple lines, matte finishes, and incised
decoration. The pottery lasted until
1936. In 1928, Baggs became professor
of ceramic arts at Ohio State University, where he taught until 1947.

BARRON, JANE CARSON
Born January 26, 1879, Cleveland,
Ohio.
Metalworker

Barron, who received her training at
the School of the Museum of Fine
Arts, Boston, was a Master member of
the Society of Arts and Crafts, Boston.
She won several awards for her metalwork and enamels, among them a silver
medal at the Louisiana Purchase International Exposition.

BATCHELDER, ERNEST ALLEN
Born January 22, 1875, Nashua, New
Hampshire; died August 1957.
Writer, teacher, ceramist

In 1901, Batchelder published *The
Principles of Design*. From 1904 until
1910, he taught at the Minneapolis
Handicraft Guild and, later, at the
Throop Polytechnic Institute, in Pasadena, California. He established his
own School of Arts and Crafts in Pasadena in 1909, and was renowned for
his ceramic tiles. His articles appeared
in *The Craftsman* and *Handicraft*.

BINNS, CHARLES FERGUS
Born October 4, 1857, Worcester, En-
gland; died December 4, 1934, Alfred,
New York.
Ceramist, educator

Binns spent his early years in England,
working at the Worcester Royal Porcelain Works. In 1900, he was
appointed the first director of the New
York School of Clayworking and Ceramics at Alfred University, in Alfred,
New York, where he remained until his
death. Binns's specialty became high-
fired stoneware vessels inspired by
early Chinese pottery, but he was important primarily for establishing the
idea of the "studio potter" in this
country and for his writing. His books
Ceramic Technology (1897) and *The Potter's Craft* (1922) are classics in the field.

BLANCHARD, PORTER GEORGE
Born February 28, 1886, Boston,
Massachusetts; died 1973.
Silversmith

Trained by his father, the silversmith
George Porter Blanchard, Porter
George founded the Arts and Crafts
Society of Southern California in 1924.
His early silverwork was based on
American colonial examples; later, his
work reflected more progressive European styles. Blanchard's work always
showed the marks of handwork; his
flatware was hammered by hand and
his hollowware was spun.

BOK, EDWARD WILLIAM
Born October 9, 1863, Den Helder,
the Netherlands; died January 9, 1930.
Editor, design reformer

One of the chief promoters of well-
designed and economical middle-class
housing, Bok was also editor of the
Ladies' Home Journal. Beginning in
1895, he commissioned prominent architects to provide model house plans
to his readers at a nominal fee; after
1900, Frank Lloyd Wright, Robert
Spencer, and Ralph Adams Cram were
among those who responded. Bok's
other reform activities included the
Rose Valley community, which he,
William Price, and other prominent
Philadelphians helped to found in 1901.

BOWLES, JANET PAYNE
Born June 29, 1882, Indianapolis, Indiana; died July 18, 1948, Indianapolis.
Metalsmith, jeweler

In 1899, Bowles moved from Indianapolis to Boston, where she learned the rudimentary techniques of metalsmithing at a local shop. She moved to New York City in 1907 and established a studio; there, prestigious commissions for jeweled ornaments, gold spoons and plates, and other metalware enabled her to refine her skills. In 1912, she won first prize at the competition of London and Paris Jewelers and, the following year, a prize from the Paris International Goldsmiths. Bowles returned to Indianapolis in 1914, where she produced metalware and jewelry for the next two decades. She continued to teach courses in metalsmithing until 1942, when she retired.

BRADLEY, WILL H.
Born July 10, 1868, Boston, Massachusetts; died January 25, 1962, Pasadena, California.
Designer, illustrator

Bradley became well known as a freelance designer through his covers and posters for Stone and Kimball's *Chap-Book*, the periodical that launched the little-magazine movement in 1894. The next year, he established Wayside Press, in Springfield, Massachusetts, to design trade books and limited editions. After 1900, as an independent designer without equal in the field, he became one of the highest-paid commercial artists in the country. Recognized by his flat, two-dimensional massings of black and white and his swirling curvilinear lines, Bradley was profoundly influenced by Aubrey Beardsley, as well as William Morris and his Kelmscott Press books.

BRADSTREET, JOHN SCOTT
Born 1845; died 1914.
Designer

The New England–born Bradstreet moved to Minneapolis in 1873, where he established John S. Bradstreet and Company, "Manufacturers of Artistic and Domestic Furniture of Modern Gothic and Other Designs," featuring the popular Neo-Gothic style that reflected the influence of the English Arts and Crafts movement. By 1883, the expanding firm of Bradstreet, Thurber and Company responded to popular demand by stocking decorative accessories that reflected Moorish and Japanese influences. After his company was destroyed by fire in 1893, Bradstreet created a crafts center, consisting of a community of carvers, gilders, painters, and furnituremakers. It was during this period that he invented a process to simulate the Japanese practice of aging wood, *jin-di-sugi*. In 1899, he opened the Minneapolis Crafthouse, which was both a workshop and a salesroom. Bradstreet absorbed and adapted many influences in his search for an American style, and he was a major force in the artistic growth of both his adopted city and his time.

BRIGHAM, LOUISE
Social activist, furniture designer

After studying art in various European cities, Brigham designed furniture to be constructed with wood discarded from packing crates. Much of it, quite sophisticated in design, was done in the Arts and Crafts style. She used her designs in her settlement house, Sunshine Cottage, in Cleveland, and in other American cities to teach disadvantaged children how to produce furniture in an effort to better themselves.

BRIGHAM, WALTER COLE
Born 1870; died 1941.
Glass artist, painter

In 1900, Brigham established the Harbor Villa Studio on Shelter Island, New York, at the eastern tip of Long Island. There, he used seashells, stones, and glass to create a "marine mosaic," which he defined as the artistic adaptation of fragments of "common things . . . from the fields, the beach and the sea" strongly cemented to form "effects beautiful in color and unusual in design." From 1900 to 1915, Brigham's marine mosaics rivaled stained-glass windows in popularity and gained a wide following. He also fashioned jewelry, lamp shades, and fire screens of the same materials at his studio, which became a fashionable stop at the flourishing summer oceanfront resort.

BROUWER, THEOPHILUS ANTHONY, JR.
Born 1864; died 1932.
Ceramist

In 1893, Brouwer established the Middle Lane Pottery, in East Hampton, New York, and began experimenting with luster glazes. He developed a series of rich, iridescent glazes with various textures, controlling the desired effects through the manipulation of the kiln. The majority of his vases were of simple shapes, but his ware occasionally took animal and vegetable forms. After 1910, Brouwer's interest turned to sculpture executed in concrete.

BURTON, ELIZABETH EATON
Born Paris, France.
Metalworker

Working in several media, including wood, leather, and metal, Burton produced a series of large, decorative screens featuring elaborately carved leather. She is primarily known for her electric lamps constructed of copper tubing and various natural shells in the form of flowers. She worked with her father, Charles Frederic Eaton, in Santa Barbara, California.

BUSH-BROWN, LYDIA
Born November 5, 1887, Florence, Italy; died 1984.
Weaver

Bush-Brown trained at Pratt Institute, in Brooklyn, New York, and studied batik techniques with Charles Pellew in Washington, D.C. Particularly known for her silk murals, made in the 1920s and 1930s, she wrote several articles on their potential use in interior decoration.

CARDER, FREDERICK
Born September 18, 1863, Brockmoor, Kingswinford, Staffordshire, England; died December 10, 1963, Corning, New York.
Glass artist

Carder worked for various Staffordshire potteries and glass factories before becoming a designer, in 1881, for Stevens and Williams of Brierley Hill, in England. In 1902, he emigrated to the United States, where he was able to give free rein to his inventive genius. In 1903, he established the Steuben Glass Works, in Corning, New York; the following year, he developed and began producing an art glass known as Aurene, which was usually iridescent gold or brilliant blue. These vessel forms were highly competitive with Tiffany's products. In 1918, the factory was taken over by Corning Glass Works, where Carder was art director from 1932 until his retirement, in 1959.

CAULKINS, HORACE JAMES
Born July 12, 1850, Oshawa, Ontario, Canada; died July 15, 1923, Detroit, Michigan.
Manufacturer, merchant

As president and manager of his own dental supplies firm in Detroit, Caulkins also manufactured dental and high-heat furnaces. In 1892, he began Revelation Kilns, a company that manufactured china kilns and furnaces marketed to professional potteries throughout the United States. Caulkins's interest in ceramics led to a partnership in 1903 with Mary Chase Perry

(Stratton). Their company, Pewabic Pottery, produced art pottery and tiles for church floors and altars, fountains, fireplaces, and swimming pools.

CLAPP, CARRIE E.

Born 1844, Millers Falls, Massachusetts; died 1922.
Basketmaker

Clapp made her home in Montague Center, in the Pocumtuck Valley, Massachusetts, where, in 1901, she became one of the principal founders of the Montague Arts and Crafts Society. She was instrumental in reviving the use of palm leaves and reeds for basketmaking, a cottage industry that had declined in the area.

COBURN, FREDERICK W.

Born August 6, 1870, Nashua, New Hampshire; died December 14, 1953.
Critic

Coburn was a critic for the *Boston Transcript*, *The Nation*, and *The New York Times Literary Supplement*. He served as treasurer of the Winchester Handicraft Society.

CONNICK, CHARLES J.

Born September 27, 1875, Springboro, Pennsylvania; died December 28, 1945, Boston, Massachusetts.
Stained-glass artist

Connick founded a studio, in 1912, that he modeled on the medieval craft tradition. Three years later, his work was exhibited at the Panama-Pacific International Exposition, in San Francisco, and won a gold medal. Major commissions included windows for the Cathedral of St. John the Divine, in New York City, the chapel and Proctor Hall at Princeton University, and the National Shrine of the Immaculate Conception, in Washington, D.C. From 1934 to 1939, he served as president of the Boston Society of Arts and Crafts. Writer, lecturer, editor, and craftsman, Connick played a leading role in the revitalization of stained glass in America.

COPELAND, ELIZABETH E.

Born 1866, Boston, Massachusetts; died 1957.
Enamelist, silversmith, jeweler

Copeland studied at Cowles Art Academy, in Boston, from 1896 to 1900. In 1904, after a brief period at the Handicraft Shop, she established a studio on Boylston Street, where she worked until retiring in 1937. Jewelry and enameled objects with repoussé ornament formed a large part of her early work, the latter inspired by the jeweled and enameled reliquaries of the Middle

Ages. In 1915, she won a bronze medal at the Panama-Pacific International Exposition, and in 1916, she received the Medalist award from the Boston Society of Arts and Crafts.

COXHEAD, ERNEST

Born 1863, England; died March 27, 1933.
Architect

Coxhead emigrated to the United States in 1886. In 1890, he designed the English Lutheran Church, in Los Angeles, in a Queen Anne style that incorporated Richardsonian features. After moving to San Francisco that same year, he began designing shingle houses, in a version of the Queen Anne style, and some of the earliest Arts and Crafts houses in the city. A number of these were markedly abstract and free of both ornament and historical, stylistic references.

CRAM, RALPH ADAMS

Born December 16, 1863, Hampton Falls, New Hampshire; died September 22, 1942, Boston, Massachusetts.
Architect, medievalist

With Bertram Grosvenor Goodhue, Cram designed religious architecture, using the English medieval church as a model. Designed in 1891, All Saints' Church, Boston, the first of Cram's Episcopal churches, influenced American religious architecture for the next fifty years. In 1912, Cram and Goodhue designed a church for the Swedenborgian community in Bryn Athyn, Pennsylvania, which was completed—with modifications to Cram's original design—in 1919.

Cram promoted the establishment of guilds to revive crafts. In works ranging from All Saints of Ashmont to the Cathedral of St. John the Divine, in New York City, he strove to unify the architect and the artisan by facilitating the collaboration of stained-glass makers, wood- and stone-carvers, embroiderers, and metalworkers. In 1914, Cram was appointed head of the School of Architecture at the Massachusetts Institute of Technology.

CROWNINSHIELD, FREDERIC

Born November 27, 1845, Boston, Massachusetts; died September 13, 1918, Capri, Italy.
Mural painter, stained-glass designer, teacher

Crowninshield was instructor of drawing and painting at the Museum of Fine Arts, Boston, from 1879 to 1885. He encouraged students to make drawings after decorative objects in the school's collection, and he supervised the decoration they made of their

lunchroom in an Egyptian style. He influenced the expansion of traditional art schools and academies into more practical training programs that taught such skills as illustration and decorative painting. His specialties were mural painting and stained-glass windows.

DALY, MATTHEW A.

Born 1860, Cincinnati, Ohio; died 1937.
Ceramist, decorator

One of the first decorators to join the Rookwood Pottery Company, Daly had been a student of Benn Pitman's at the Art Academy of Cincinnati. A leading Rookwood decorator from 1882 to 1903, he left to head the art department at the United States Playing Card Company.

DAY, LEWIS FOREMAN

Born 1845, London, England; died April 18, 1910.
Design critic

A member of the Arts and Crafts Exhibition Society, Day was the author of numerous books on design, among them *The Planning of Ornament* and *Ornament & Its Application*.

DENNETT, MARY WARE

Born April 4, 1872, Worcester, Massachusetts; died July 25, 1947, Valatie, New York.
Reformer, gilt-leather worker

As an artist working in gilt leather who was strongly committed to the social ideals of Ruskin and Morris, Dennett was influential in the founding of the Boston Society of Arts and Crafts. A member of the society's governing council, she advocated the combination of craftwork with agriculture, the cooperative salesroom, and various educational and information bureaus. Dennett left the society in 1905, protesting the group's preference for art objects over condition of craftsmanship. She continued to fight for industrial and social reform through her involvement in the Single-Tax League, Free Trade League, Anti-Imperialist League, and Consumers' League. Later, she was influential in the women's suffrage and birth-control movements.

DIXON, HARRY SAINT JOHN

Born June 22, 1890, Fresno, California; died 1967, San Francisco, California.
Metalworker

Dixon studied with Dirk Van Erp in 1908. For the next decade, he worked in various metal shops in San Francisco, before opening his own in 1920. His work, which generally used motifs from nature, was marked with a punch showing a man forging a bowl. His major work was the elevator doors for the San Francisco Stock Exchange, executed about 1930.

DOAT, TAXILE
Born 1851, Albi, France; died 1939, France.
Ceramist

Trained at Sèvres, Doat developed new glazes and formulas for the production of porcelain. The author of *Grand Feu Ceramics* (1905), he traveled in 1909 to the United States and became director of University City Pottery, an educational program in ceramics, founded by Edward Gardner Lewis, in St. Louis, Missouri. Most instruction was given by correspondence courses, but a small group of women studied personally with Doat—among them Adelaide Alsop Robineau. During its brief existence, the University City Pottery produced some of the finest porcelain in the United States, noteworthy both for body and glazes. Although Lewis's program soon disbanded, Doat continued to work at a reorganized University City Pottery until 1915, when he returned to France.

DONALDSON, DOUGLAS
Born August 24, 1882, Detroit, Michigan; died 1972, California.
Metalworker, teacher

Donaldson studied with James H. Winn and exhibited at the Boston Society of Arts and Crafts and the Detroit Society of Arts and Crafts. In 1909, he went to California, where he taught metalworking at a school established by Ernest A. Batchelder. From 1912 to 1919, he headed the art department of the Manual Arts High School of Los Angeles. In 1921, he and his wife, Louise, opened a metalworking and enameling studio in Hollywood.

DOW, ARTHUR WESLEY
Born April 6, 1857, Ipswich, Massachusetts; died December 13, 1922.
Educator, artist

Dow was a landscape painter who had been profoundly influenced by Japanese art. In accordance with its principles, he taught that art was constructive rather than imitative. In his book *Composition* (1899), he used diagrams to demonstrate how to construct a picture in empathetic response to nature. This book and his teaching programs at Pratt Institute, in Brooklyn, New York, and Columbia University Teachers College ultimately became the basis of art education across America. In 1900, he founded

the Ipswich Summer School of Art, which embraced the philosophy of the Arts and Crafts movement, particularly its emphasis on the value of hand labor. Dow believed that the modern factory system was "not only killing art—but people." His "natural method" of teaching ceramics, weaving, dyeing, and basketmaking entailed the imitation of the primitive artist's direct approach to nature's materials and simple formative processes.

DOWNES, WILLIAM HOWE
Born March 1, 1854, Derby, Connecticut; died February 19, 1941, Brookline, Massachusetts.
Writer, art critic for the *Boston Transcript*

Downes wrote *Twelve Great Artists* (1900), *Life and Works of Winslow Homer* (1911), and *John S. Sargent: His Life and Work* (1925), as well as numerous magazine articles. He retired from active journalism in 1922.

DRISCOLL, CLARA
Glass artist

Driscoll began working at the Tiffany Glass Company in 1887. As head of the design department, at an annual salary of more than ten thousand dollars, she was one of the highest-paid designers in the country, and responsible for many of Tiffany's important lampshade patterns. Her Dragonfly lamp, one of Tiffany's most successful models, won a prize at the 1900 Paris Exposition. As with other models, this lamp was produced in various sizes and color combinations and with different sculptural bases. Other successful designs by Driscoll included the Rose lamp and the Butterfly lamp.

ELLIOT, ESTHER HUGER
Ceramist, decorator

Elliot enrolled as a special art student at Sophie Newcomb Memorial College, in New Orleans, in 1890. She was active as a decorator at Newcomb Pottery from 1896 to 1905.

ELLIS, HARVEY
Born 1852, Rochester, New York; died January 2, 1904, Syracuse, New York.
Architect, furniture designer

Ellis worked in architectural offices in New York State, St. Louis, and St. Paul. During visits to the American Southwest, he became impressed with Pueblo and Mission architecture. Working periodically with his brothers, who were also architects, in Rochester, New York, he returned there in 1894 and became active in art circles, helping to found the Rochester Arts and

Crafts Society in 1897. Ellis created a personalized version of the Richardsonian Romanesque, the Queen Anne, and the modernized Colonial. His pen drawings were well known to readers of architectural magazines of the period. Between 1903 and January 1904, he created some of Gustav Stickley's most important furniture. His designs for houses, furniture, and wall decorations were published in *The Craftsman*.

ELMSLIE, GEORGE GRANT
Born 1871, near Huntley, Scotland; died 1952, Chicago, Illinois.
Architect, designer

Emigrating to the United States in 1884, Elmslie worked alongside Frank Lloyd Wright and George W. Maher in the Chicago office of the architect J. L. Silsbee in 1887. From 1889, he worked under Louis Sullivan, acting as his chief designer from 1895 to 1909, when he went into partnership with two other architects. As with other Prairie School architects, Elmslie was concerned with creating an interior that was harmonious with the whole. He designed complete sets of household furnishings, including carpets, often ornamented with prickly, stylized plant motifs similar to those found on buildings by Sullivan.

EYRE, WILSON
Born 1858, Florence, Italy; died 1944, Philadelphia, Pennsylvania.
Architect

Eyre was the leading member of the regional school of architecture that developed among Philadelphia-based architects. From 1878 to 1881, he worked with the architect James P. Sims, in New York City. In 1881, he began a practice in Philadelphia, where his main efforts were concentrated in the Chestnut Hill section of the city. Eyre's work, reminiscent of Richard Norman Shaw, his English counterpart, covered a number of idioms, from Queen Anne to shingle style, American Colonial, English plaster, and Georgian. The strong horizontality of his designs reflects the influence of C.F.A. Voysey.

FOGLIATI, A.
Metalsmith, enamelist

Evidence suggests that Fogliati was trained in England before coming to Chicago in about 1903 and working as master metalsmith and enamelist at Hull-House. Along with Isadore V. Friedman, he helped organize the Hull-House Shops, where jewelry, brass and copper vessels, and other ware were exhibited and sold until the late 1930s.

FRIEDELL, CLEMENS

Born 1872, New Orleans, Louisiana;
died 1963.
Silversmith

Friedell worked for the Gorham Manufacturing Company before moving to
California in 1908. His workshop made
tableware, trophies, and portrait reliefs,
often using floral forms as ornaments.
His specialties were embossed mono-
grams and repoussé work. He won a
gold medal at the Panama-California
Exposition, in San Diego, in 1915.

GAW, ELIZABETH ELEANOR
D'ARCY

Born 1868, Montreal, Quebec, Canada;
died 1944, California.
Metalworker, interior decorator

Gaw trained at the Art Institute of
Chicago and at C. R. Ashbee's Guild
and School of Handicraft, in London.
For a period of eleven months, ending
in January 1911, she worked with Dirk
Van Erp, the San Francisco metalworker, at his Copper Shop. Their
names appeared together on a windmill
trademark that he adopted as a mark
of their partnership. Although the
partnership lasted only a short time,
Gaw has been credited with introducing a new sophistication into Van Erp's
work—and because the Copper Shop
produced the same designs for several
years after her departure, her influence
continued. In 1911, Gaw returned to
her former profession as an interior
decorator and weaver.

GEBELEIN, GEORGE CHRISTIAN

Born November 6, 1878, Wivesten-
selbitz, Oberfranken, Bavaria; died
January 25, 1945, Wellesley Hills,
Massachusetts.
Metalsmith

From 1893 to 1896, Gebelein apprenticed with Goodnow and Jenks, silver
manufacturers, in Boston, and later
with Tiffany & Company, in New York
City. In 1903, he joined Boston's Handicraft Shop, where he taught Katherine
Pratt, Mildred Watkins, and other talented apprentices. With the help of
David Mason Little, a pupil, Gebelein
opened his own shop, Gebelein Silversmiths, in Boston, in 1906, which
continues to this day. Gebelein specialized in handcrafted silver in the
Colonial revival style, distinguishing
himself with numerous reproductions
and interpretations of silver by Paul
Revere.

GERMER, GEORGE ERNEST

Born May 26, 1868, Berlin, Germany;
died December 8, 1936.
Metalsmith

After apprenticing and working at the
Kunstgewerbemuseum, in Berlin,
Germer emigrated to the United States
in 1893. For the next twenty years, he
worked as a designer, modeler, and
chaser for major silver manufacturers
in Boston, Providence, and New York
City. Joining the Boston Society of
Arts and Crafts in 1912, Germer
devoted his career to liturgical metalwork, often executed in Gothic revival
style.

GILL, IRVING JOHN

Born 1870, Syracuse, New York; died
October 7, 1936, Carlsbad, California.
Architect

After working for architects in both
Syracuse and Chicago, Gill joined the
Chicago firm of Adler and Sullivan in
1891. Two years later, he went to San
Diego and established his own practice. Over the next thirteen years, his
work moved in a number of directions,
including English cottage, Beaux-Arts
classicism, Prairie School, bungalow,
and Mission styles. Drawing on them
all, Gill developed a simple, austere,
cubic idiom, which predominated after
1907. This anti-ornamental architectural style was an outgrowth of his
passionate interest in construction. In
his concrete buildings, all extraneous
features—interior moldings, exterior
trim, and ornament—were eliminated.
His homes celebrated the California
climate and landscape through the
skillful design of windows and arches
and the extensive use of such outdoor
spaces as pergolas and terraces.

GOODHUE, BERTRAM
GROSVENOR

Born April 28, 1869, Pomfret, Connect-
icut; died April 23, 1924, New York,
New York.
Architect

Goodhue began his career, in 1884, as
a draftsman with the New York City
firm of Renwick, Aspinwall & Russell,
where he was exposed to the Gothic
revival style, of which James Renwick
was a leading exponent. In 1889,
Goodhue moved to Boston and became head draftsman for Cram and
Wentworth, which, in 1896, became
Cram, Goodhue, and Ferguson. The
firm specialized in ecclesiastical architecture, designing a great many
churches throughout the East. Goodhue's wide-ranging travels led him
occasionally to incorporate Byzantine,
Romanesque, and Spanish Baroque
stylistic elements into his churches, but
the Gothic style, with a Romantic medieval interpretation, was the hallmark
of his work. During the 1890s, influenced by the English Arts and Crafts

movement, Goodhue designed a number of books in the fashion of William
Morris.

GREENE, CHARLES SUMNER

Born October 12, 1868, Brighton Station, Ohio; died June 11, 1957, Carmel,
California.

GREENE, HENRY MATHER

Born January 23, 1870, Brighton
Station, Ohio; died October 2, 1954,
Altadena, California.
Architects, designers

After graduating from the Massachusetts Institute of Technology School of
Architecture in 1891, the Greene
brothers established an architectural
practice in Pasadena, California. They
built numerous private houses—from
small bungalows to large estates—in a
wholly original way. For affluent clients, the Greenes designed every detail
of the furniture and decoration, with
an emphasis on fine woodwork. Their
furniture designs often revealed an
Oriental influence. Some decorative
elements—panels of glass and lamps—
were supplied by the Tiffany Studios,
while others, such as rugs, were made
to their design specifications in England. Their most important buildings
and furnishings were executed before
1910. The Gamble House (1907–9), in
Pasadena, one of their most notable designs, is now a museum of their work.

GRIFFIN, WALTER BURLEY

Born November 24, 1876, Maywood,
Illinois; died February 11, 1937, Luck-
now, India.
Architect

Griffin was a leading Prairie School architect. In 1899, he graduated from the
University of Illinois, where he studied
landscape gardening and architecture.
From 1901 to 1905, he worked for
Frank Lloyd Wright, in Chicago. In
1911, he married his associate, Marion
Mahony. The following year, Griffin
won the international competition for a
new capital city in Canberra, Australia.

GRUEBY, WILLIAM HENRY

Born 1867; died February 23, 1925,
New York, New York.
Ceramist

In 1894, Grueby established the Grueby Faience Company to produce tiles
in a variety of styles. Four years later,
the company introduced a line of
boldly sculptural matte-glazed vases
decorated with modeled leaf forms. In
1901, at the Buffalo Pan-American Exposition, Grueby exhibited with
Gustav Stickley, who highly com-
mended Grueby's ware in *The Craftsman*. Grueby's vases were commis-

sioned by Tiffany as lamp bases to be covered with glass shades. In 1911, his art-pottery operation ceased, although it continued to produce architectural terra-cotta and tile work until 1919, when the company was sold to C. Pardee Works, a tile company in Perth Amboy, New Jersey.

GYLLENBERG, FRANS J. R.
Born 1883, Sweden; died after 1946.
Metalsmith

As an early member of Boston's Handicraft Shop, Gyllenberg executed designs by Mary Catherine Knight. In 1906, the Boston Society of Arts and Crafts admitted him as a Craftsman member; in 1929, the society elected him a Medalist craftsman, its highest honor. By 1926, Gyllenberg had formed a partnership at the Handicraft Shop with his younger assistant, Alfred Henry Swanson. Their well-crafted silver, in alternately simple, fluted, or Colonial revival style, was a significant part of the shop's operations. Gyllenberg and Swanson actively continued to produce silver as late as 1946.

HALE, FRANK GARDNER
Born November 13, 1876, Norwich, Connecticut; died September 19, 1945, Salem, Massachusetts.
Metalworker

Hale studied at the School of the Museum of Fine Arts, Boston, and at C. R. Ashbee's Guild of Handicraft, in London. He was dean of the Guild of Jewelers, Boston Society of Arts and Crafts. Hale was known for his hand-wrought reproductions of fifteenth- and sixteenth-century metalwork and for his enameling. With his brother-in-law, the painter Orlando Rolland, he established the Marblehead Association, a group of craftsmen and artists.

HEINIGKE, OTTO
Born 1851, Brooklyn, New York; died July 1, 1915, Brooklyn.
Stained-glass designer, craftsman

Trained as a painter at the Brooklyn Polytechnic Institute, Heinigke's first job was as a designer of carpets. By the mid-1880s, though, he was designing and making stained glass. In 1890, he formed a partnership with Owen J. Bowen. Architects were impressed with Heinigke and Bowen's designs and craftsmanship, and the firm received a considerable number of important commissions in churches throughout the East Coast—perhaps the most important being for the Church of the Pilgrims, in Brooklyn, New York.

HICKOX, ELIZABETH CONRAD
Born 1873; died 1947.
Basketmaker

A Native American basketweaver in northwestern California, Hickox produced most of her work from 1890 to 1930. Although raised as a weaver in the Karuk tradition, a nation living in the inland mountains, she was half-German and half-Wiyot. The Wiyot were a nation that lived along the coast in and around Humboldt Bay. Native American baskets of northwestern California were produced from natural fibers that included hazel, willow, and woodwardia fern, which were considered gifts from ancient spirit beings. Using these sacred fibers as the raw material for baskets made them important cultural symbols that were actively included in traditional ceremonies. Approaching her work with reverence, Hickox developed an individual style through the innovative use of color and dramatic figure/ground relationships. Her specialties included the ceremonial cap and lidded trinket baskets, many of which were sold through Grace Nicholson, the preeminent dealer in Native American baskets, in Pasadena, California.

HORTI, PAUL
Born 1865, Hungary; died 1907, Hungary.
Furniture designer, educator

Oscar Onken, founder of the Shop of the Crafters, in Cincinnati, was impressed by an exhibition of Austro-Hungarian Secessionist furniture at the Louisiana Purchase International Exposition in 1904, in particular the inlaid designs of Paul Horti. In 1906, Onken hired Horti to work at the shop, where he introduced inlay into Onken's furniture.

HUBBARD, ALICE G.
Born 1861; died May 7, 1915, aboard the *Lusitania*.
Social activist, writer

Alice Hubbard wrote *Woman's Work* (1908), a book that questioned the traditional role assigned to women. It was one of many she wrote, ranging from those on social issues—designed to awaken the consciousness of both men and women—to nature conservancy and collections of children's poems. She was married to Elbert Hubbard, founder of the Roycrofters.

HUBBARD, ELBERT G.
Born June 19, 1856, Bloomington, Illinois; died May 7 1915, aboard the *Lusitania*.
Writer, publisher, businessman

Two years after retiring from the Larkin Soap Company, Hubbard founded the Roycrofters, in East Aurora, New York, in 1893. Utilizing the principles of William Morris, this community established a successful printing press as well as workshops for the production of metalwork, leatherwork, and furniture—the simple oak benches, tables, and chairs known as Mission furniture. The Roycroft workshops survived until 1938, well after Hubbard's death, under the direction of Hubbard's son, Elbert, Jr.

HUBBARD, HENRY VINCENT
Born August 22, 1875, Taunton, Massachusetts; died October 6, 1947, Milton, Massachusetts.
Landscape architect

Hubbard was the first person in the United States to receive a college degree in landscape architecture, which he earned from Harvard University in 1901. Professionally, he divided his time between his design work for Olmsted Brothers, Brookline, Massachusetts, and his teaching responsibilities at Harvard. In 1929, Harvard created a Department of Regional Planning, the first in the country, and appointed Hubbard the Charles Dyer Norton Professor of Regional Planning. He wrote extensively on landscape architecture and city planning, publishing such books as *An Introduction to the Study of Landscape Design* (1917) and *Our Cities of Today and Tomorrow* (1929). He was also the founder of the journals *Landscape Architecture*, in 1910, and *City Planning*, in 1925.

HUNTER, DARD
Born November 29, 1883, Steubenville, Ohio; died February 20, 1966, Chillicothe, Ohio.
Book designer and -maker, leaded-glass designer

Hunter worked intermittently in the Roycroft community between 1903 and 1910. After spending several months in Vienna in 1908, he returned with a new sense of line, color, and pattern, the influence of his study of the Wiener Werkstätte and Glasgow styles. Best known for his book design and production, Hunter became a world authority on hand papermaking. Among his masterpieces for Roycroft were the books *Justinian and Theodora* (1906) and *White Hyacinths* (1907). He began making windows, lamp shades, and lighting fixtures of leaded glass for the Roycroft Inn and Shops, after learning the craft from the New York firm of J. & R. Lamb. On leaving the Roycroft community, he continued to design and construct stained-glass windows at his studios in New York, Connecticut, and Ohio.

HYTEN, CHARLES DEAN
Born 1887; died 1944.
Ceramist

Under the direction of Hyten, the Niloak ("kaolin" spelled backwards; a key ingredient of porcelain) Pottery, of Benton, Arkansas, produced luxurious pottery. Niloak's process, which was eventually patented, used a mixture of local clays of different colors that when thrown on the wheel produced interesting patterns—the only decoration on Niloak pottery. Following the closing of Niloak in the mid-1930s, Hyten became a salesman for Camark Pottery, of Camden, Arkansas.

JAMES, GEORGE WHARTON
Born September 27, 1858, Gainsborough, Lincolnshire, England; died November 8, 1923, St. Helena, California.
Writer, ethnologist

James spent his literary career writing about North American Indians, intensively studying tribes in California, Nevada, Utah, Arizona, and New Mexico. Among his craft books are *Indian Basketry* (1900), *How To Make Indian and Other Baskets* (1903), and *Indian Blankets and Their Makers* (1914). From 1904 to 1905, James was associate editor of *The Craftsman*.

JARVIE, ROBERT RIDDLE
Born 1865, Schenectady, New York; died 1941, North Riverside, Illinois.
Metalsmith

In 1904, Jarvie resigned his post at the Chicago Department of Transportation to open the Robert Jarvie Shop. His line soon included several styles of candlesticks and lanterns and an array of hand-beaten accessories. A few years later, he began to work in gold and silver and, after 1912, to design trophies and other presentation pieces. His work shows the influence of Louis Sullivan's geometric arabesque ornament and Charles Rennie Mackintosh's linear, right-angle fret ornament. In 1911, John Petterson executed many of the splendid candlesticks and trophies that made Jarvie's workshop famous. Jarvie had difficulty sustaining his shop through World War I, eventually closing it before 1920.

JECK, FRANK
Born Czechoslovakia.
Woodworker

Jeck worked on the Romanesque addition to Ralph Adams Cram's Gothic-style cathedral in the Swedenborgian community of Bryn Athyn, near Philadelphia. His method shows how the Romanticism of the reform movement could still draw upon historical methods to produce a desired effect.

JENSEN, JENS
Born September 13, 1860, Dybbøl, Schleswig, Denmark; died October 1, 1951, Ellison Bay, Wisconsin.
Landscape architect

Jensen emigrated to the United States in 1884. Two years later, he took a job as a day laborer for the West Chicago Park System; over the next fourteen years, he rose to become superintendent of Humboldt Park. From 1909 until the early 1930s, Jensen directed a large, private practice, landscaping estates for the country's financial and industrial leaders, among them, Julius Rosenwald, Ogden Armour, and Henry and Edsel Ford. Jensen developed the theory of the prairie garden, a form specifically adapted to the Midwest. His insistence on the use of native plant materials and his rejection of imported varieties made him a remarkably pure landscape architect.

KIPP, KARL E.
Born 1882; died 1954.
Metalsmith

In 1908, Kipp, a former banker, came to the Roycroft campus, in East Aurora, New York, and began his artistic career creating bookbindings. Soon after, he was made head of the Roycroft Copper Shop by the colony's founder, Elbert Hubbard. In 1911, Kipp and his first assistant, Walter U. Jennings, left Roycroft to establish their own art-metal enterprise, the Tookay Shop, also in East Aurora. Following the death of Elbert Hubbard, in 1915, Kipp returned to Roycroft at the request of Hubbard's son, who began to establish Roycroft outlets across the country. Kipp remained at Roycroft until he retired in the early 1930s.

KNIGHT, MARY CATHERINE
Born 1876.
Metalsmith

Knight studied under Mary Ware Dennett at Philadelphia's Drexel Institute. She worked as a designer at Gorham Manufacturing Company before joining the Boston Society of Arts and Crafts' Handicraft Shop, where she supervised craftsworkers. Her own silver designs, with tooled and enameled decoration, were executed by her alone or in collaboration with other craftsmen in the shop.

KOEHLER, FLORENCE D.
Born 1861, Jackson, Michigan; died 1944, Rome, Italy.
Jeweler, enamelist, metalworker

Koehler worked as a potter at Rookwood. From 1898 to 1904, she taught decorative porcelain painting at Chicago's Atlan Ceramic Art Club. Her jewelry designs were influenced by historical examples she studied in European museum collections.

KORALEWSKY, FRANK L.
Born Straalsund, Germany.
Metalsmith

Koralewsky was a prominent figure in the Arts and Crafts revival of wrought iron. After apprenticing and studying ironwork in German shops, he emigrated to Boston. There he began working for Frederick Krasser's ironworking firm, which executed commissions for Harvard University and the Cathedral of St. John the Divine, in New York City. In 1913, Koralewsky became director of the firm. A highly ornamental, tour-de-force iron lock executed by Koralewsky between 1905 and 1911 won the Boston Society of Arts and Crafts Medalist award in 1914 and, later, a gold medal at the 1915 Panama-Pacific Exposition. Examples of his ironwork, including screens, door hinges, knockers, locks, and latches, are in the collection of the Detroit Institute of Arts.

KUNSMAN, JOHN
Born 1864; died 1946.
Ceramist

Introduced to pottery through his father, a German immigrant who started his own pottery company in Johnsonville, Pennsylvania, in 1880, Kunsman left the family business in 1889 and joined the Fulper Pottery, in Flemington, New Jersey, where he became its leading thrower and master craftsman. He produced original stoneware pieces that echoed early American themes, and in 1909, he began to work in a style more aligned with the Arts and Crafts movement. He was closely associated with the development of Fulper's popular Vasekraft line, which was introduced the same year.

LA FARGE, JOHN
Born March 31, 1835, New York, New York; died November 14, 1910, Providence, Rhode Island.
Painter, stained-glass designer, decorator, writer

After studying painting in Paris, La Farge returned to New York City in 1858 and embarked on a career as a painter of landscapes and murals. His most significant commission came from H. H. Richardson, who invited La Farge to produce a series of murals and architectural motifs for Holy Trinity Church, in Boston. In the 1870s, he began to experiment with glass, and by 1879, he had opened his own shop in New York City. The following year, La Farge received a patent for opalescent glass. In 1883, he set up the short-lived La Farge Decorative Art Company to produce his glass, but from 1885, it was made by John Calvin and Thomas Wright. His window *The Sealing of the Twelve Tribes* earned him a medal at the 1889 Paris Exposition. At this time, his glass combined a strong Japanese influence with brilliant technical effects. La Farge wrote a number of books and theoretical treatises on art. His importance to glass in this period is rivaled only by Louis Comfort Tiffany.

LAMB, FREDERICK STYMETZ

Born June 24, 1863, New York, New York; died July 9, 1928, Berkeley, California.
Mural painter, stained-glass artist

F. S. Lamb was the son of Joseph Lamb, who emigrated from England to found J. & R. Lamb Studios in 1857. Specializing in ecclesiastical and memorial work, Lamb Studios was famous in the late nineteenth century for its stained-glass windows, mosaics, and murals. With his brother, Charles Rollinson Lamb, Frederick took over the family business in the 1880s. His chef d'oeuvre was *Religion Enthroned*, a stained-glass window commissioned by the United States government for the Central Pavilion of the Paris Exposition of 1900, for which gold medals were given to F. S. Lamb for design and to J. & R. Lamb Studios for execution. The window is in the collection of the Brooklyn Museum.

LEBLANC, MARIA DE HOA

Born 1870s; died 1954.
Ceramist, decorator, embroiderer

A highly esteemed decorator at Newcomb Pottery, LeBlanc served as Arts Craftsman from 1908 to 1914. In 1904, her pottery was awarded a bronze medal at the Louisiana Purchase International Exposition; in 1915, her pottery and embroidery were exhibited at the Panama-Pacific International Exposition.

LEINONEN, KARL F.

Born 1866, Turku, Finland; died 1957.
Metalsmith

Leinonen enjoyed a long and distinguished career at Boston's Handicraft Shop, which he helped to manage and where he provided bench space for lo-cal silversmiths. In 1918, the Boston Society of Arts and Crafts elected him a Medalist craftsman, its highest honor. About 1925, he formed a partnership with his son, K. Edwin Leinonen, that lasted well into the 1950s, as they produced silver that drew largely on the Handicraft Shop's early silver designs.

LIMBERT, CHARLES P.

Born 1854; died 1923.
Furniture designer and manufacturer

Limbert started manufacturing an extensive line of Mission-style furniture under his own name in Grand Rapids, Michigan, in 1902. Four years later, he moved his offices and factory to Holland, Michigan, to escape from the overly commercial character of Grand Rapids. By this time, Limbert was prominent in the American Arts and Crafts movement. His factory catalogues featured many oak pieces derived from Gustav Stickley and comparable craftsmen, but with occasional details showing an awareness of continental work.

LOW, WILL HICOK

Born May 31, 1853, Bronxville, New York; died November 27, 1932, Albany, New York.
Mural painter, stained-glass designer, book illustrator

Low is best known for his mural paintings dating from the 1890s and the first two decades of the twentieth century. From 1880 to 1882, he assisted John La Farge with the decoration of the Union League Club, the Water-Color Room and the dining room of the Cornelius Vanderbilt II House, and the William H. Vanderbilt House. His most important commission comprised thirty-two murals of allegorical subjects created for the New York State Education Building, in Albany, between 1913 and 1918.

LUMMIS, CHARLES FLETCHER

Born 1859, Lynn, Massachusetts; died 1928, Los Angeles, California.
Newspaperman, antiquarian

Educated at Harvard and trained as a journalist, Lummis's first major position was city editor of the *Los Angeles Times*. A period of recuperation after a severe illness enabled him to travel throughout the Southwest, and he became one of America's foremost spokesmen for the preservation of Spanish missions. In 1895, he formed the California Landmarks Club.

MACOMBER, EVA

Metalsmith, enamelist

Macomber studied metalworking and enameling. She gained the rank of craftsman in the Boston Society of

Arts and Crafts in 1905; in 1916, she became a Master craftsman. She developed exceptional technical and compositional skills, which were already in evidence when she participated in the Tenth Anniversary Exhibition of the society in 1907.

MAHER, GEORGE WASHINGTON

Born December 25, 1864, Mill Creek, West Virginia; died September 12, 1926, Kenilworth, Illinois.
Architect, designer

Maher served his apprenticeship in Chicago with Bauer and Hill, and later with J. L. Silsbee, as a draftsman alongside Frank Lloyd Wright and George Grant Elmslie. He entered private practice in 1888. Maher's work was inspired by the modern movements in Europe, particularly the Austrian Secessionist architecture he had seen at the Louisiana Purchase International Exposition in 1904.

MAHONY, MARION

Born 1871, Chicago, Illinois; died 1962.
Architect, renderer, designer

Mahony, a graduate of the Massachusetts Institute of Technology program in architecture, became the first woman licensed as an architect in the state of Illinois. She worked intermittently for Frank Lloyd Wright and was responsible for many architectural renderings, notably those of the Rock Crest-Rock Glen development, in Mason City, Iowa (1912), and the Joshua G. Melson House (1912–14). When Wright left for Europe in 1909 and Mahony was placed in charge of the firm's commissions, she designed several houses on her own. It is often suggested that Mahony designed much of the furniture for her employer. In 1911, she married the architect Walter Burley Griffin.

MANN, FOREST EMERSON

Born March 6, 1879, Portland, Maine.
Metalsmith

Trained at Pratt Institute, in Brooklyn, New York, Mann was active in the National Society of Craftsmen. Later, he was director of the Forest Craft Guild.

MANSHIP, PAUL

Born 1885, Minnesota; died 1966.
Sculptor

Manship went to Philadelphia in 1905, where he worked with several sculptors. In 1909, he won the Prix de Rome. For the next three years, as a student at the American Academy in Rome, he fell under the spell of antiquity. The stylizations of archaic Greek art had a profound influence on his decorative art objects. His functional objects were particularly well crafted, using the cast-bronze technique, and demonstrated his mastery of form and material. His best-known sculpture is the gilded bronze *Prometheus* (1933), for the fountain in New York City's Rockefeller Plaza.

MARSHALL, FRANK J.
Metalsmith, enamelist

Marshall became a craftsman member of the Boston Society of Arts and Crafts in 1907 and exhibited at its Tenth Anniversary Exhibition the same year. In 1913, he became a Master craftsman of the society. An enamelist of considerable technical skill, he produced superb and distinctive copper boxes with enamel discs.

MASON, WALT
Born 1862, Canada; died 1939.
Poet-philosopher, humorist

Mason came to this country in 1880 with little more than a grade-school education. He started working as a telegraph editor for the *Emporia Gazette*, in Emporia, Kansas, and later became an editorial writer. His column, "Rippling Rhymes," was an immediate success, and his rhymes appeared daily in some two hundred newspapers in the United States, Canada, and other countries. In his writing, Mason often championed social causes that shared the ideals of the Arts and Crafts movement.

MATHEWS, ARTHUR FRANK
Born October 1, 1860, Markesan, Wisconsin; died February 19, 1945, San Francisco, California.
Painter, architect, interior decorator, furniture designer

Trained as an architectural draftsman and painter in Oakland, California, Mathews was a leader of the Arts and Crafts movement in San Francisco. In 1890, he became director of the California School of Design, and later in the decade, he married a pupil, Lucia Kleinhans [Kleinhaus], with whom he worked in close collaboration for the rest of his life. In the late 1890s, Mathews began to design and execute mural decorations and paintings on furniture, and after the 1906 earthquake, he continued such work primarily for San Francisco houses and public buildings. That same year, he and his wife founded the Furniture Shop. Its purpose: to do complete schemes of interior decoration and to make and market unique pieces of furniture, tapestries, stained-glass windows, ornamental boxes, and picture frames. Much of Mathews's work is preserved in the Oakland Museum.

MATHEWS, LUCIA KLEINHANS [KLEINHAUS]
Born August 29, 1872, San Francisco, California; died 1955, Los Angeles, California.
Painter, furniture and woodwork decorator, wood-carver

After studying at the California School of Design and the Mark Hopkins Institute of Art, in San Francisco, she established the Furniture Shop, in 1906, with Arthur Mathews, whom she had married a decade earlier. Assisting with the design of the workshop's furniture and decorative accessories, she also supervised color choices and carving. Her work included many unique, richly painted and gilded boxes, candlesticks, lamps, frames, and other accessories, examples of which are in the collection of the Oakland Museum. The Mathewses were the founders of the Philopolis Press, in 1906, as well as the magazine *Philopolis*, for which they provided stories and illustrations.

MAYBECK, BERNARD RALPH
Born February 7, 1862, New York, New York; died October 3, 1957, Berkeley, California.
Architect

Maybeck learned wood-carving and cabinetry from his German father. He attended the Ecole des Beaux-Arts, in Paris, and then worked a few years for John Merven Carrère and Thomas Hastings on the Ponce de Leon Hotel, in St. Augustine, Florida. After settling in the San Francisco Bay Area in 1890, Maybeck worked for A. Page Brown on the Swedenborgian Church in San Francisco. His mature architectural expression encompassed a number of idioms, from his use of Gothic, Swiss, and Japanese in a totally unconventional manner for the First Church of Christ, Scientist, in Berkeley, in 1910, to a personalized classicism for the Palace of Fine Arts at the 1915 Panama-Pacific International Exposition.

McHUGH, JOSEPH P.
Born 1854; died 1916.
Designer, retailer

In 1884, McHugh established the Popular Shop in New York City. It not only stocked the latest wallpaper, fabrics, and household furnishings but offered a complete decorating service. In 1893, McHugh began producing his own furniture, and by the turn of the century, he was offering a large variety in the Mission style. His furnishings won awards at the Pan-American Exposition, in 1901, and at the South Carolina Interstate and West Indian Exposition, in 1902.

McLAUGHLIN, MARY LOUISE
Born 1847, Cincinnati, Ohio; died 1939, Cincinnati.
Ceramist, wood-carver, metalworker

McLaughlin studied drawing, wood-carving, and china painting at the University of Cincinnati School of Design from 1873 to 1877. Soon after, she began a series of experiments to master the underglaze colored slip decoration she had admired on French *barbotine* ware exhibited at the Philadelphia Centennial International Exposition of 1876. In 1879, McLaughlin helped found the Cincinnati Women's Pottery Club. When the club disbanded in 1890, she formed the Associated Artists of Cincinnati, a group of ceramics decorators and metalworkers. Largely because of McLaughlin's activities, underglaze slip decoration was widely practiced. By the mid-1880s, it had become synonymous with pottery decoration in Cincinnati.

MEIGS, ARTHUR INGERSOLL
Born June 29, 1882, Philadelphia, Pennsylvania; died June 9, 1956, Radnor, Pennsylvania.
Architect

In spite of a lack of formal architectural training, Meigs became one of the leading architects of the Philadelphia School. His social prominence assured a substantial clientele of wealthy, elite Philadelphians for the firm that he and Walter Mellor founded in 1906. Suburban and country houses in an eclectic style, much in the tradition of Wilson Eyre, was its forte.

MELLOR, WALTER
Born April 25, 1880, Philadelphia, Pennsylvania; died January 11, 1940, Philadelphia.
Architect

Mellor studied architecture at the University of Pennsylvania, and then worked for T. P. Chandler, a local architect. In 1906, he went into partnership with Arthur Meigs and became one of the leading architects of the Philadelphia School. Mellor and Meigs were involved primarily with the design of suburban and country residences for the rich. Much of their work was in the Main Line area, near Philadelphia, where they created regional expressions from architectural precedents set in England.

MERCER, HENRY CHAPMAN
Born June 24, 1856, Doylestown, Pennsylvania; died March 9, 1930, Doylestown.
Founder of Moravian Pottery and Tile Works, designer

Although trained as a lawyer, Mercer became an archaeologist on the staff of the University Museum, in Philadelphia. His involvement in ceramics was an outgrowth of both his interest in American pioneer handcraft tools and his discovery that the Pennsylvania German pottery tradition was almost extinct. In 1898, Mercer founded the Moravian Pottery and Tile Works, in Doylestown, named after the Moravian cast-iron stove plates that inspired his first tile designs. Later design sources included medieval English floor tiles and eighteenth-century German tiles. Between 1910 and 1912, after the original pottery had burned down, Mercer designed a larger structure of reinforced concrete. Between 1914 and 1916, he built a museum, also of reinforced concrete, to house his collection of more than six thousand hand tools. Mercer's Moravian tiles were used on the floors of Fenway Court (now the Isabella Stewart Gardner Museum, in Boston); in the Pennsylvania State Capitol, in Harrisburg; and in buildings designed by many leading architects of the Arts and Crafts movement, including Stanford White, Julia Morgan, and Ward Wellington Ward.

MEYER, FREDERICK HENRY

Born November 6, 1872, Hamelin, Germany; died January 6, 1961, Oakland, California.
Educator

Meyer came to this country in 1888. He served as superintendent of drawing for the Stockton, California, public schools from 1898 to 1902 and as professor of applied art at the California School of Design for the next four years. In 1907, he founded a school, which, some years later, in 1924, became the California College of Arts and Crafts. Meyer served as president and trustee until his retirement in 1944.

MEYER, JOSEPH FORTUNE

Born 1848, France; died 1931.
Ceramist

Meyer settled in Biloxi, Mississippi, and operated his own pottery. In 1886, he became the first potter at the New Orleans Art Pottery Company and, in 1896, joined Newcomb Pottery at Sophie Newcomb Memorial College, where he remained as principal thrower until 1925.

MILLER, ELLEN

Born 1854; died 1929.
Textile artist

After studying painting in New York City, Miller settled with Margaret Whiting in Deerfield, Massachusetts, in 1896. Together they revived the tra-

ditional, early eighteenth-century embroidery that had flourished in New England in colonial times. What emerged from their shared interest was the Deerfield Society of Blue and White Needlework, which was associated more closely with the Colonial revival than the Arts and Crafts movement. Miller and Whiting sought patterns and ideas in the community's surviving embroidery. The traditional embroidery was worked in crewel wools, but the women substituted flax for the thread and imported Russian linen for the earlier homespun wool foundation. Designs were derived from early colonial bed covers, embroidered in the mid-eighteenth century. The industry flourished for twenty years, and Deerfield Blue and White became famous across America. Problems of importing linen were created by the advent of World War I, and by 1925, the industry had died out.

MUNDIE, WILLIAM BRYCE

Born 1863, Canada; died 1939.
Architect, ceramist, designer
Mundie, an architect, moved to Chicago in 1884, where he became a designer for the pioneering architect William LeBaron Jenney. Seven years later, he became his partner in the renamed firm of Jenney & Mundie. Along with a number of other architects in the Chicago area, Mundie designed early Teco Pottery forms. Teco Pottery is a designation of Gates Potteries, founded in 1886, as the art line of the American Terra Cotta and Ceramic Company.

NASH, ARTHUR J.

Born 1849, England; died 1934.
Glass artist
Before emigrating to the United States in 1892, Nash had managed the White House Glassworks, in Stourbridge, England, founded in 1837 by Thomas Webb, a leading English pioneer of modern glass. With Louis Comfort Tiffany, Nash set up the Stourbridge Glass Company, later known as Tiffany Furnaces; Nash was both vice president and manager. He supervised the building of the factory at Corona, New York, where he and his glassblowers created vases, bowls, and lamp shades of iridescent glass, later called Favrile. Some of the flower-form vases, such as the jack-in-the-pulpit, were probably brought over from Stourbridge by Nash. When he retired, in 1919, he was succeeded as manager by his son, A. Douglas Nash.

NICHOLS (STORER), MARIA LONGWORTH

Born March 20, 1849, Cincinnati, Ohio; died April 30, 1932, Cincinnati.
Ceramist

Nichols studied with Maria Eggers in the first china-painting classes offered, in 1874, at the University of Cincinnati School of Design, which her first husband, George Ward Nichols, had helped to found. She later experimented in ceramics decoration at the commercial pottery of Frederick Dallas, in Cincinnati. Nichols made her most important contribution to the arts after visiting the Japanese pottery exhibit at the 1876 Philadelphia Centennial International Exposition; four years later, she founded Rookwood, Ohio's first art pottery. There, she developed and patented a glaze that gave her pottery a rich, deep tone, and later, she won a gold medal for her work at the 1889 Paris Exposition. In 1890, Nichols turned over Rookwood Pottery to an associate.

NIEDECKEN, GEORGE MANN

Born August 16, 1878, Milwaukee, Wisconsin; died November 3, 1945, Milwaukee.
Designer, interior decorator

Niedecken received his early training at Milwaukee art schools and at the Art Institute of Chicago. In 1898, he left Chicago for further study abroad, which included working with Alphonse Mucha, in Paris. After returning to America, he concentrated on design and interior decoration, and by 1904, he was working for Frank Lloyd Wright. In 1907, Niedecken and John Walbridge founded the Niedecken-Walbridge Company, a firm of interior architects that specialized in interior design, custom-furniture design, mural painting, and art glass. Niedecken's Prairie-style work continued through the early 1920s, highlighted by collaborations with Louis Sullivan, Frank Lloyd Wright, Spencer and Powers, Purcell and Elmslie, and William Drummond, among others. Noted collaborations that he undertook with Wright included the Robie, Coonley, and Dana houses.

NUTTING, WALLACE

Born November 17, 1861, Marlboro, Massachusetts; died July 19, 1941, Framingham, Massachusetts.
Antiquarian, manufacturer, photographer

A leading figure of the Colonial revival in the 1920s, he owned and operated the Wallace Nutting chain of Colonial Houses, his own antiques-furnished restorations that were open to the public. Nutting produced copies of period furniture; his early reproductions were of oak furniture of the seventeenth century, country pieces of the eighteenth, and Windsor chairs. He wrote more than twenty books, including *Antique Treasury* and *Furniture of the Pilgrim Century*.

OAKES, EDWARD EVERETT

Born March 5, 1891, Boston, Massachusetts; died 1961.
Silversmith, jeweler

Oakes, who apprenticed with Frank Gardner Hale, is known for his jewelry designs—clusters of leaves and flowers that were fabricated separately and then assembled. Oakes made his own alloys for the jewelry.

OHR, GEORGE EDGAR

Born 1857, Biloxi, Mississippi; died 1918, Biloxi.
Ceramist

The son of a blacksmith, Ohr learned potterymaking from Joseph F. Meyer, who was later associated with Newcomb Pottery. From 1883 to 1907, or thereabouts, Ohr designed and crafted highly unusual earthenware pieces from local clays at his Biloxi Art Pottery. A bold experimenter and thrower of extraordinary skill, he constructed vessels with walls as thin as eggshell porcelain, which he then twisted, squeezed, and folded into irregular shapes, often adding strangely curved handles. In the same experimental style, Ohr glazed his vessels with interesting, often bizarre, combinations of colors. He was the subject of a retrospective at the American Craft Museum in 1989.

OLMSTED, FREDERICK LAW, SR.

Born 1822, Hartford, Connecticut; died August 28, 1903, Waverley, Massachusetts.
Landscape architect

OLMSTED, FREDERICK LAW JR.

Born 1870, Staten Island, New York; died 1957, Malibu, California.
Landscape architect

Olmsted, Sr.'s plan for New York's Central Park, in 1857, had a threefold effect. It established the precedent for parks in urban areas, it initiated the profession of landscape architecture in this country, and it launched him on his career as a planner. Olmsted planned hundreds of parks and recreation areas in New York, Chicago, Washington, D.C., Detroit, Boston, Montreal, and other cities. This extraordinary innovator laid out America's first regional metropolitan park system, created the nation's first planned garden suburb, and influenced campus planning throughout the country, most notably that of Stanford University. Olmsted helped lay the foundation for a national park system, and he campaigned to save Niagara Falls, the California Redwoods, and other features of America's natural landscape from abuse and destruction.

Upon his father's retirement, in 1895, Frederick, Jr., joined the Olmsted Brothers firm as a partner. He continued to champion the ideals of his father as one of the nation's premier landscape architects. His notable commissions in New York City included the Cloisters and Forest Hills Gardens, Queens. In Washington, D.C., he designed the White House grounds, Lafayette Park, Washington Monument Gardens, and Jefferson Memorial Gardens.

PERRY (STRATTON), MARY CHASE

Born 1867, Detroit, Michigan; died 1961, Detroit.
Ceramist

In 1903, Perry founded the Pewabic Pottery, in Detroit. Influenced by the work of William Grueby and Louis Comfort Tiffany, and by the fine Oriental pottery in the collection of Charles L. Freer, Perry produced vases, at first, in the Art Nouveau style, but, later, in very simple shapes decorated with iridescent and luster glazes.

PETTERSON, JOHN PONTUS

Born May 15, 1884, Göteborg, Sweden; died December 30, 1949.
Metalsmith

After studying silversmithing at the Royal School of Arts and Crafts, in Norway, Petterson emigrated to New York City in 1905 and worked for Tiffany & Company. In 1911, he moved to Chicago to work in the Jarvie Shop, where he executed many of the splendid candlesticks and trophies that made it famous. In 1914, he opened his own business, the Petterson Studio. There, he and his assistants made hammered copper ware and produced handwrought silver flatware, hollowware, jewelry, and other special-order items. In 1937, Petterson won a silver medal at the Paris Exposition Internationale des Arts et des Techniques.

POND, THEODORE HANFORD

Born September 27, 1873, Beirut, Lebanon; died November 3, 1933, Akron, Ohio.
Metalworker, educator, museum director

As writer, lecturer, and craftsman, Pond played a major role in directing the course of Arts and Crafts education in America. He spent his youth in Europe and the Middle East before attending Pratt Institute, in Brooklyn, New York, from 1888 to 1892. Shortly after, he worked as a designer of stained glass and interior decoration for Louis Comfort Tiffany. In 1902,

Pond left the faculty of the Rhode Island School of Design to found the Department of Applied and Fine Arts at the Rochester Athenaeum and Mechanics Institute, in Rochester, New York. To this institution, Pond brought such craftspersons as Frederick Walrath, Lulu Scott Backus, and M. Louise Stowell. In 1908, he went to Baltimore to create and head the Department of Design and Applied Arts at the Maryland Institute. There, from 1911 to 1914, he organized and directed the Pond Applied Art Studios.

POTTER, HORACE E.

Born December 10, 1873, Cleveland, Ohio; died 1948.
Metalsmith

Potter graduated from the Cleveland School of Art in 1898. He remained there as a teacher of design and historic ornament while establishing himself as a designer and craftsman with studios in the Rose Building. From 1903 to 1904, he studied both in Boston and at C. R. Ashbee's Guild and School of Handicraft, in London. In Cleveland, Potter began a workshop at his family's farm, where he collaborated with Wilhelmina Stephan, a local artist and craftsperson. About 1908, Potter and a group of assistants established another workshop. This eventually became the Potter Studio, which, in turn, became the prestigious Cleveland firm of Potter and Mellen that continues today.

PRATT, KATHERINE

Born August 3, 1891, Boston, Massachusetts; died 1978.
Metalsmith

After graduating from the School of the Museum of Fine Arts, Boston, in 1914, Pratt apprenticed under George C. Gebelein. From about 1917, she began crafting hollowware and other silver objects at Boston's Handicraft Shop, where she continued the conservative designs of the previous generation of silversmiths, often drawing inspiration from colonial examples. In 1931, the Boston Society of Arts and Crafts selected her as a Medalist craftsman, its highest honor. Pratt's work received a gold medal in 1937 at the Paris Exposition Internationale des Arts et des Techniques.

PRESTON, JESSIE M.

Born Oak Park, Illinois.
Jeweler

One of the Midwest's most famous jewelrymakers, she showed all over the United States. Preston specialized in handwrought jewelry. Looking to nature and naturalistic forms for inspiration, she incorporated rock and pebbles into her work, which included jewelry, lamps, candlesticks, and candelabras.

PRICE, WILLIAM L.
Born 1861, Philadelphia, Pennsylvania; died October 15, 1916, Philadelphia.
Architect, furniture designer, reformer

Price founded a utopian crafts community, the Rose Valley Association, near Philadelphia in 1901. Because he felt that Americans had already lost their craft skills to machinery, he hired immigrant wood-carvers. Hand-carving and exposed joinery were intrinsic parts of Price's designs for Rose Valley furniture, as were Gothic motifs. He described craft as being "the art that is life." Despite his idealism, the success of Rose Valley was short-lived; in 1906, production ceased, and by 1909, the community had disbanded.

RANDAHL, JULIUS OLAF
Born 1880, Sweden; died 1972.
Silversmith

Randahl worked at the Kalo Shop, in Park Ridge, Illinois, from 1907 to 1910. In 1911, he founded his own firm, the Randahl Shop. Before World War I, the Randahl Shop made bowls, tea sets, and other silverware reflecting the Kalo influence. Following the war, Randahl developed a national reputation, and in 1937, he won a silver medal at the Paris Exposition Internationale des Arts et des Techniques. In 1950, Randahl and his two sons formed the Randahl Company; in 1957, they purchased Cellini Craft. After 1965, the company concentrated on jewelry, and is still in existence, in the Chicago area, as Randahl Jewelers.

RHEAD, FREDERICK HURTEN
Born 1880, Hanley, Staffordshire, England; died 1942, Newell, West Virginia.
Ceramist

After working with Roseville Pottery and Jervis Pottery, Rhead moved to southern California in 1913. There, he organized Rhead Pottery, in Santa Barbara's Mission Canyon, whose foremost decorating technique was the inlay process. As a complement to the pottery, Rhead began *The Potter*, a monthly magazine specializing in the art of potterymaking. Both *The Potter* and Rhead Pottery were abandoned in 1917, when Rhead became director of research for the American Encaustic Tiling Company, of Zanesville, Ohio. In 1927, Rhead left to direct the Homer Laughlin China Company, in Newell, West Virginia, where he remained until his death.

RICHARDSON, HENRY HOBSON
Born September 29, 1838, Priestley Plantation, Louisiana; died April 27, 1886, Brookline, Massachusetts.
Architect

Richardson studied at Harvard University and in Paris before settling in Brookline, Massachusetts, in 1874. He developed a unique style of masonry building, well suited to the New England landscape, which served to free American architects from the series of European revivals that dominated the nineteenth century. His work included a number of churches, such as Trinity, in Copley Square, Boston, as well as railroad stations and public libraries.

ROBERTSON, ALEXANDER W.
Born 1840, Wolviston, Durham County, England; died 1925.
Ceramist

A supply of fine, iron-rich red clay in the vicinity of the Snake River attracted Robertson to Chelsea, Massachusetts. There, in 1866, he established a firm to produce flowerpots, ferneries, matchboxes, and other simple brown ware. Joined by his father, James, and his brother, Hugh, Robertson began to produce art pottery under the name Chelsea Keramic Art Works in 1872. Most of the work was in a simple Greek style until the 1880s, when they developed incising, impressing, carving, and other elaborate techniques. In 1884, Alexander left for San Francisco, where, in 1899, he founded the Roblin Art Pottery.

ROBERTSON, CADMON
Died 1914.
Ceramist, chemist

Robertson joined the Hampshire Pottery in 1904 and, soon after, became its superintendent. A notable chemist who introduced more than nine hundred glaze formulas, he was responsible for a great variety of matte glazes, from green and peacock to old blue, gray, bronze, brown, and yellow.

ROBERTSON, HUGH CORNWALL
Born 1845, Wolviston, Durham County, England; died 1908, Dedham, Massachusetts.
Ceramist

Along with other family members, Robertson was responsible for founding the Chelsea Keramic Art Works. After visiting the Philadelphia Centennial International Exposition in 1876, he began to experiment with glazes, honeycomb patterns, incised intaglio designs, and other new methods of surface decoration. Experiments with the Oriental *sang-de-boeuf*, or ox blood,

glaze consumed his energies in the late 1880s. Robertson's work later won awards at the World's Fairs of 1900, 1904, and 1915.

ROBINEAU, ADELAIDE ALSOP
Born 1865, Middletown, Connecticut; died February 18, 1929, Syracuse, New York.
Ceramist

Robineau taught china painting in New York City, where she studied painting with William Merritt Chase and exhibited as a watercolorist and miniaturist. In 1899, she, her husband, and George Clark bought the magazine *China Decorator*; renaming it *Keramic Studio*, they began publication, in Syracuse. The editorship of the magazine elevated Robineau to national prominence; it also provided financial support for her artwork. About 1903, she made the important change from china painter to ceramist, and soon began the practice of excising decoration, which led to the finely perforated ware that became her hallmark. In 1910, she became associated with the ceramics school in St. Louis, Missouri, where she taught for a year before returning to Syracuse. In 1911, her display of fifty-five pieces at the International Exposition of Decorative Arts, in Turin, Italy, received a grand prize.

ROGERS, MARGARET
Born Boston, Massachusetts.
Jeweler

Working primarily in Boston, Rogers created handwrought jewelry using colored, semiprecious stones. A member of the Boston Society of Arts and Crafts, she received its bronze medal for excellence.

ROHLFS, CHARLES
Born February 15, 1853, New York, New York; died June 29, 1936, Buffalo, New York.
Designer, furnituremaker

Rohlfs was a Shakespearean actor prior to training at the Cooper Union for the Advancement of Science and Art, in New York City. About 1890, he set up a small workshop in Buffalo, whose output ranged from simple, Mission-style pieces to more intricate work with abstract Art Nouveau ornament, for which he is best known today. Rohlfs showed furniture at the 1901 Pan-American Exposition, in Buffalo, the 1902 International Exhibition of Modern Decorative Arts, in Turin, and the Louisiana Purchase International Exposition in 1904. Winning widespread acclaim in Europe, he received commissions from Buckingham Palace. Rohlfs was associated with Elbert

Hubbard and lectured to the Roycrofters, until he retired in the mid-1920s.

RORIMER, LOUIS
Born September 12, 1872, Cleveland, Ohio; died November 30, 1939, Cleveland.
Furniture and interior designer

Rorimer studied decorative arts in Munich at the Kunstgewerbeschule and in Paris at the Academie Julian. Working in a wide range of decorative styles, he drew from historic models for his later work, which was occasionally influenced by modern French and English decorative design. In 1919, Rorimer received recognition for his furniture and interior design at the Cleveland Museum of Art's first annual exhibition of local artists and craftsmen. For eighteen years, he served on the faculty of the Cleveland School of Art.

ROSS, DENMAN WALDO
Born January 10, 1853, Cincinnati, Ohio; died September 12, 1935, London, England.
Educator, design teacher, writer

Ross graduated from Harvard in 1875 and was a founding member of the Boston Society of Arts and Crafts in 1897. That same year, he exhibited in its "First Exhibition of the Arts and Crafts." The author of *A Theory of Pure Design: Harmony, Balance, Rhythm* (1907), his journals are in the archives of Harvard's Fogg Art Museum.

ROTH, WILLIAM
Born 1874; died 1944.
Builder, furnituremaker

Roth lived and worked at the Roycrofters, in East Aurora, New York. He was a builder and occasionally made furniture for the Roycroft Shops, where he worked for Elbert Hubbard and, later, his son, Elbert, Jr.

SHAW, JOSEPHINE HARTWELL
Jeweler, metalsmith

In the late 1890s, Hartwell studied at Massachusetts Normal School of Art, in Boston, and at Pratt Institute, in Brooklyn, New York. Later, she taught drawing courses in Providence and near Philadelphia. In 1906, she married the silversmith and sculptor Frederick A. Shaw. Beginning in 1908, she showed her work at eleven annual Art Institute of Chicago Arts and Crafts exhibitions. In 1914, she received the Boston Society of Arts and Crafts Medalist award. Her work is in the collection of the Museum of Fine Arts, Boston.

SHIRAYAMADANI, KATARO
Born 1865, Japan; died 1948.
Ceramics decorator and designer

Shirayamadani was one of a group of Japanese artists and craftsmen touring the United States in 1887 when he was invited to join the decorating staff of Rookwood Pottery. Except for a ten-year return to Japan, he stayed at Rookwood until his death, in 1948. One of its finest artists, he is credited with developing the electrodeposit method of surfacing ceramics with metal and with designing many of the standard Rookwood shapes.

SICARD, JACQUES
Born 1865, France; died 1923, France.
Ceramics designer

Sicard came to the Weller Pottery, in Zanesville, Ohio, to continue his experiments in metallic luster glaze effects. There, he developed an art ware called Sicardo-Weller, decorated with floral and other motifs painted in metallic lusters over predominantly molded forms. One of the few examples of American art pottery made in the Art Nouveau style then popular in Europe, the Sicardo-Weller inventory was marketed through 1912, five years after Sicard returned to France.

SIMPSON, ANNA FRANCES
Born 1886; died 1930.
Textile artist, ceramics decorator

After receiving her diploma in art in 1906 from Sophie Newcomb Memorial College, in New Orleans, Simpson chose to stay on as a textile designer. She later became a prolific ceramics decorator, and many of the characteristic motifs of Newcomb pottery are attributed to her. Her pottery and textile works were often exhibited together.

SMITH, FRANCES BARNUM
Metalsmith

Smith studied at the Cleveland School of Art and later at the School of the Museum of Fine Arts, Boston, prior to establishing a workshop, in 1901, in Cleveland, with Jane Carson Barron. The shop, which employed only women, became known for decorative table and toilet articles featuring fancy enameling and fine hammered work in gold, silver, and copper. Smith and Barron exhibited together at the annual Art Institute of Chicago Arts and Crafts Exhibition, and they won a silver medal for jewelry and metalwork at the Louisiana Purchase International Exposition in 1904.

STICKLEY, GUSTAV
Born March 9, 1858, Osceola, Wisconsin; died April 21, 1942, Syracuse, New York.
Furniture designer, theorist, publisher

Stickley learned furnituremaking as an apprentice in his uncle's chair factory, in Gardner, Massachusetts. In 1898, he met C.F.A. Voysey and other notable designers in Europe; the following year, he established the United Crafts, in Eastwood, New York, the forerunner of Craftsman Workshops, which he founded in 1904. Stickley began to make sturdy tables and cupboards, as well as chairs with slat backs, usually of oak, with exposed joinery and plain leather or canvas upholstery; this work became known as Mission furniture. In 1901, he founded a periodical, *The Craftsman*; espousing theories derived from John Ruskin and William Morris, it became a strong voice in the American Arts and Crafts movement. Stickley patented several of his designs and issued catalogues of his products that reached a wide market. One of the most prolific writers and propagandists for the Arts and Crafts movement, Stickley used modern tools and machines in his workshops.

STICKLEY, ALBERT (1863–1928)
STICKLEY, CHARLES (1865–1928)
STICKLEY, LEOPOLD (1869–1957)
STICKLEY, JOHN GEORGE (1871–1921)
Furniture designers and manufacturers

There were five Stickley brothers, all of whom manufactured furniture in a variety of partnerships. The oldest was Gustav Stickley, who started the first family business, with Charles and Albert, in 1884—the Stickley Brothers Company, in Binghamton, New York. Operating together until 1890, they soon organized separate ventures. Charles remained in Binghamton, directing the Stickley and Brandt Chair Company, from 1891 to 1919; in 1891, Albert and John George, minus Gustav, founded a new Stickley Brothers Company, in Grand Rapids, Michigan, whose furniture paralleled that of their older brother and the Cotswold School. Their furniture line, Quaint, introduced around 1900, had a strong English Arts and Crafts influence and was successfully marketed in London and Europe. Inlay furniture, introduced in 1901, featured the work of master craftsman Timothy A. Conti and revealed the influence of Japanese art and design. Their company remained in business until the advent of World War II.

In 1902, Leopold and John George founded their own firm, L. and J. G.

Stickley, in Fayetteville, New York. They modeled the company and its products after Gustav's United Crafts, the forerunner of his Craftsman Workshops. Leopold and John George Stickley were the less flamboyant brothers, and their furniture designs are generally considered of lesser importance than Gustav's work. In 1918, when the two brothers absorbed the bankrupt Craftsman Workshops, they suspended the Craftsman style in favor of Colonial revival products, which the company continues to manufacture to this day.

STONE, ARTHUR J.
Born 1847, Sheffield, England; died 1938, Gardner, Massachusetts.
Metalsmith

Trained at Sheffield, Stone was one of America's major silver craftsmen. An offer to establish a hollowware department at F. W. Smith and Company brought him to Gardner, where he remained the rest of his life. Noted for its spare use of ornament and smooth surfaces, Stone's work at F. W. Smith soon began to rival the most acclaimed American silverwork. Widespread promotion by the Boston Society of Arts and Crafts helped to ensure the shop's success.

STOWE, ERNEST
Carpenter, rustic-furniture maker

Stowe lived and worked in the Saranac Lakes district of New York, where a number of elaborate vacation camps were constructed between the 1890s and World War I. In addition to helping construct camp buildings, Stowe produced a quantity of rustic furniture characterized by close attention to detail and an adaptation of rustic materials to forms derived from traditional cabinetwork. For most of his furniture, Stowe used white birchbark, yellow birch rounds, and unbarked cedar.

SULLIVAN, LOUIS HENRY
Born September 3, 1856, Boston, Massachusetts; died April 14, 1924, Chicago, Illinois.
Architect

Sullivan studied architecture under William Robert Ware, before moving to Chicago in 1873. As a partner in Adler and Sullivan, he designed some of the earliest skyscrapers, creating a style that synthesized monumental geometric forms and ornament. His creations, including the Auditorium Building (1887–89) and the Getty Tomb (1890), helped to establish the city's international reputation as a center of modern architecture.

THRESHER, BRAINERD BLISS
Born 1870; died 1950.
Metalsmith

In addition to jewelry, Thresher executed furniture, screens, and pictorial wood panels. He was greatly influenced by the reverence for nature found in Japanese art and by Edward Colonna, the leading exponent of the style in the United States. Like other cultured upper-class craftsmen, Thresher responded to William Morris's philosophy not so much by returning art to work as by bringing it to leisure. In Ohio, he helped to found the Dayton Society of Arts and Crafts and the Dayton Art Institute, where he instituted a program to circulate paintings and sculpture in the manner of a library, a practice widely emulated today.

TIFFANY, LOUIS COMFORT
Born February 18, 1848, New York, New York; died January 17, 1933, New York.
Painter, stained-glass designer, decorator

Trained as a painter, Tiffany, in 1879, founded a professional interior decorating firm, Louis C. Tiffany and Associated Artists. Important commissions included the Veterans' Room of the Seventh Regiment Armory, in New York City, the Samuel L. Clemens House, in Hartford, and several rooms in the White House. Tiffany devoted much of the next two decades to the design and production of stained glass, patenting luster glass in 1881 and founding the Tiffany Glass Company in 1885. He also developed and, in 1894, patented Favrile (meaning handmade), an iridescent glass used for blowing bowls and vases. After 1900, Tiffany Studios, an outgrowth of the glass company, produced a panoply of decorative objects, from enameled boxes and jewelry to tableware, clocks, and desk sets. In 1918, he founded the Louis Comfort Tiffany Foundation, which made Laurelton Hall, his Oyster Bay, New York, country house, available as a retreat for young artists.

TILLINGHAST, MARY ELIZABETH
Born 1845, New York, New York; died December 1912, New York.
Embroiderer, stained-glass artist, designer

Tillinghast studied in Paris under Émile-Auguste Carolus-Duran and Jean-Jacques Henner. She also studied with John La Farge, with whom she later collaborated on textiles for his decorating commissions. Tillinghast was responsible for a celebrated group of embroidered panels commissioned for Cornelius Vanderbilt II's New York City residence. Her stained-glass works include the Hutton window, in Grace Church, and the *Revocation of the Edict of Nantes* window, in the New-York Historical Society Building. She received a gold medal at the Chicago World's Columbian Exposition in 1893 and both gold and bronze medals at the Cotton States Exposition in 1895.

TODD, EMERY W.
Silversmith, jeweler

Todd studied and worked at the Kalo Shop, in Chicago, founded by Clara Barck Welles. With Clemencia C. Cosio, he founded the TC Shop, which operated from 1910 to 1923. There, Todd and Cosio designed and fashioned jewelry and handwrought table silver. He taught at the Art Institute of Chicago from 1927 to 1930.

TRIGGS, OSCAR LOVELL
Born October 2, 1865, Greenwood, Illinois; died November 1930.
Educator, writer

Triggs pursued an academic career, teaching English literature at the University of Chicago, where he was awarded his Ph.D. in 1895. His involvement with the Arts and Crafts movement took many forms. He was secretary of Chicago's Industrial Art League, an organization that promoted the industrial arts through the teaching of Arts and Crafts classes. The league provided shops, tools, and materials for the use of guilds of artists and craftsmen, furnishing a place for them to exhibit and sell their work. Triggs's book *Chapters in the History of the Arts and Crafts Movement* (1902) was published by the league.

VALENTIEN, ANNA MARIE BOOKPRINTER
Born 1862, Cincinnati, Ohio; died 1947.
Ceramist

While studying at the Art Academy of Cincinnati in 1884, Bookprinter joined the Rookwood Pottery. Three years later, she married Albert Robert Valentien, Rookwood's first full-time decorator and head of the decorating department. Together, they traveled to Europe, where they studied under French sculptors—among them, Auguste Rodin. Returning to Rookwood, they remained there until the early years of the twentieth century. In 1907, they moved to San Diego, California, and in 1911, established the Valentien Pottery, which featured Anna Marie's relief-modeled forms and Albert's painted decorations.

VAN BRIGGLE, ARTUS

Born March 21, 1869, Felicity, Ohio; died July 4, 1904, Colorado Springs, Colorado.
Ceramist

Van Briggle studied at the Art Academy of Cincinnati. In 1893, he received a two-year scholarship to study at the Academie Julian, in Paris. Three years later, he returned to Cincinnati, to resume work as an underglaze painter for Rookwood, where he continued to experiment with matte glazes. After 1899, Van Briggle, who suffered from tuberculosis, moved to Colorado Springs. He made a remarkable number of vases, distinctly Art Nouveau in form and decoration, covered with matte glazes of subtle texture and delicate, subdued color.

VAN ERP, DIRK

Born 1859, Leeuwarden, the Netherlands; died 1933, San Francisco, California.
Metalsmith

After training in his family's hardware business, Van Erp emigrated to the United States in 1886. In 1900, he began crafting vases out of shell casings while working as a marine coppersmith at the Navy shipyard in Mare Island, California. Van Erp opened the Copper Shop, in Oakland, in 1908. Two years later, the shop moved to San Francisco, where he remained for the rest of his life. His oeuvre was perhaps the most original produced in America. Entirely handwrought, his vases were left with a rough hammered surface, which formed their only decoration. On occasion, this was accompanied by a red finish, achieved by heating the copper during the annealing process. Van Erp's copper and mica lamps were the ideal accompaniment to the oak furniture of the Arts and Crafts interior.

VEDDER, ELIHU

Born 1836, New York, New York; died 1923.
Designer, illustrator

A painter, illustrator, and poet who introduced images of mystery and fantasy into his paintings, Vedder's work has become recognized as a precursor of Surrealism. After returning to New York City from studies in Europe, he eked out a meager existence by designing greeting cards and comic valentines and by illustrating books and magazines. During the Civil War, he produced his most inventive work.

VOLKMAR, CHARLES

Born August 21, 1841, Baltimore, Maryland; died February 6, 1914, Metuchen, New Jersey.
Ceramist

Trained in France, Volkmar established his first pottery in Tremont (the Bronx), New York, in 1881, where he produced plaques, tiles, and vases, generally with landscape decoration. In 1895, he formed the Volkmar Ceramic Company. The following year, he began to produce his most advanced art pottery, under the name Crown Point. In 1903, he formed the Volkmar Kilns, in Metuchen, New Jersey, with his son, Leon. Volkmar was active in the Salmagundi Club, in New York City, where he directed the members' ceramic activities and produced special commemorative ware for the club.

WALKER, CHARLES HOWARD

Born November 9, 1857, Boston, Massachusetts; died April 17, 1936, Boston.
Architect, educator, critic

A founding member of the Boston Society of Arts and Crafts, Walker lectured to the society in 1900 on "Principles of Design Illustrated by the Crafts" and, two years later, on "Some Impressions of the Arts and Crafts Movement in England and on the Continent." He served as director of the School of Drawing and Painting at the Museum of Fine Arts, Boston, and was founder of the city's School of Fine Arts, Crafts, and Decorative Design.

WARREN, HERBERT LANGFORD

Born March 29, 1857, Manchester, England; died June 27, 1917, Boston, Massachusetts.
Architect, professor, design critic

A founding member of the Boston Society of Arts and Crafts, his published articles included "The Craftsman in the Middle Ages" (1900) and "The Qualities of Carving" (1901). Warren lectured widely on the Arts and Crafts.

WATKINS, MILDRED G.

Born July 21, 1882; died 1968.
Metalsmith

A graduate of the Cleveland School of Art, Watkins belonged to a group of Cleveland artists who were among the nation's earliest practitioners of handcrafted enamels, jewelry, and metalwork. About 1904, she apprenticed under George Gebelein at Boston's Handicraft Shop. In 1907, she exhibited work at the decennial exhibition of the Boston Society of Arts and Crafts and was awarded Master craftsman standing by the society. Watkins collaborated with Jane Carson Barron, Frances Barnum Smith, and other Cleveland craftswomen, but after 1907, she also produced and exhibited on her own—jewelry, boxes, small tableware, and serving pieces.

WHEELER, CANDACE THURBER

Born 1827, Delhi, New York; died August 5, 1923, New York, New York.
Textile and wallpaper designer, writer

Wheeler was an amateur painter until 1876. On seeing the Royal School of Art Needlework exhibition at the Philadelphia Centennial International Exposition, she was inspired to create a comparable institute in the United States. With Mrs. David Lane, she founded the New York Society of Decorative Art in 1877, to sponsor decorative-arts competitions and to help craftswomen support themselves. Two years later, she joined Louis Comfort Tiffany, Lockwood de Forest, and Samuel Colman in founding Associated Artists, an interior decoration firm that planned the decor of several rooms in the White House and the Hartford home of Samuel L. Clemens, as well as many other houses and buildings. As textile specialist, she designed embroidery, textiles, and wallpaper—mainly floral designs with a strong Japanese influence. Wheeler and her family ran the firm from 1883 to 1907. In 1893, she designed the furniture and textiles for the Women's Building at the Chicago World's Columbian Exposition. She was the author of several important books, including *Principles of Home Decoration with Practical Examples* (1903).

WHITEHEAD, RALPH RADCLIFFE

Born 1854, Yorkshire, England; died February 23, 1929, Santa Barbara, California.
Woodworker

Whitehead was the heir of a British industrialist. In 1901, he founded Byrdcliffe, an artists' colony, just outside Woodstock, New York. Artists and craftspersons came as both teachers and pupils, staying for varying amounts of time and producing paintings, pottery, furniture, textiles, and metalwork. Since intricate handwork made the furniture prohibitively expensive, Whitehead closed the woodworking shops in 1905 and encouraged the development of other, less costly, crafts, such as pottery, weaving, and framemaking. For a time, Byrdcliffe continued to attract famous visitors—among them, Jane Addams and C. R. Ashbee—but by 1915, it had become a private estate kept by Whitehead. In the years that followed, he and his wife turned their attention to pottery.

WHITING, FREDERIC ALLEN

Born January 26, 1873, Oakdale, Tennessee; died 1959.
Design critic

Whiting was secretary of the Boston Society of Arts and Crafts from 1903 to 1912. In 1904, he was in charge of the Arts and Crafts display in the Palace of Art at the Louisiana Purchase International Exposition. He served as secretary-treasurer of the National League of Handicraft Societies from 1907 to 1909 and as editor of *Handicraft* from 1910 to 1911.

WHITING, MARGARET
Born 1860; died 1946.
Textile artist

After studying fine arts in New York City, Whiting moved to Deerfield, Massachusetts, in 1896, to revive the art of early colonial, blue-and-white crewel embroidery. With Ellen Miller, she acquired the Godfrey Nims Homestead, in 1900, to serve as the home of the Deerfield Society of Blue and White Needlework. The designs used for the blue-and-white work were derived from early colonial bed covers, embroidered about 1750 in New England. These and other historic artifacts were collected or sketched by Whiting, who also experimented with old dye formulas. Most of the embroidery designed by Whiting—and worked by Deerfield women under her direction—was utilitarian in character. Luncheon sets, scarves for dressers, hangings, and bedspreads were the pieces executed in greatest number.

WILLET, WILLIAM
Born 1866, New York, New York; died 1921, Philadelphia, Pennsylvania.
Mural painter, stained-glass window designer

Willet studied with William Merritt Chase and John La Farge. His work included windows at West Point Military Academy; Proctor Hall, Princeton University; Mather Memorial, Trinity Cathedral, Cleveland; and St. Paul's Cathedral, Pittsburgh. In Pittsburgh, he also painted murals in St. Alvernia's Convent; Presbyterian Hospital Chapel; and Thaw Memorial, Third Presbyterian Church. In New York City, he executed a memorial mural painting in Greenwood Cemetery Chapel.

WILSON, FREDERICK
Born November 3, 1858, England.
Stained-glass designer

For a period of nearly thirty years, Wilson was one of the most important designers of stained-glass windows for Louis Comfort Tiffany. He was particularly responsible for commissions in which figures were the major elements; he also designed mosaics. Wilson created free-lance designs that utilized glass made by Tiffany's firm but were not done under its aegis.

WINN, JAMES H.
Born 1866, Chicago, Illinois; died 1940.
Jewelry artist

Winn was a highly influential, Chicago-born jewelrymaker and an alumnus of the School of the Art Institute of Chicago. Although many of his pieces possessed the heavy, substantial qualities of Arts and Crafts designs, he also produced pieces with the fine sinuous lines associated with Art Nouveau.

WRIGHT, FRANK LLOYD
Born June 8, 1867, Richland Center, Wisconsin; died April 9, 1959, Phoenix, Arizona.
Architect, designer

Wright began his career, in Chicago, as chief draftsman to Louis Sullivan. The furniture he designed for his own use in these early years remains his most notable, but he continued to design furniture for most of his important houses. Wright emphasized natural wood and simple function; he also designed metal grilles and lamps and stained-glass windows with elaborate geometrical leading. This work was closely related to the Arts and Crafts movement. Although he advocated machine-made furnishings, his reverence for wood and other natural materials and his reliance upon forthright structures make him an influential figure in the American craft movement. His most important contribution to design came in 1904 with his uncompromising rectilinear furniture of painted metal for the Larkin Administration Building, in Buffalo, New York. Wright's effect on architectural and industrial design theory was profound, in Europe as well as the United States.

WYNNE, MADELINE YALE
Born September 25, 1847, Newport, New York; died 1918, Ashville, North Carolina.
Metalworker, enamelist, jeweler

Wynne established a studio in Chicago and helped found the Chicago Arts and Crafts Society in 1897. A well-known art metalsmith of gold and silver jewelry, with obvious hammer marks and unusual textures and colors, her interest in craft extended to furniture, leather, needlework, photography, and basketry.

YELLIN, SAMUEL
Born March 12, 1885, Mogilev-Podolski, Russia; died October 3, 1940, New York, New York.
Metalworker

In Philadelphia, Yellin received commissions for metalwork from such prestigious architectural firms as McKim, Mead and White. His Arch Street Metalworkers Studio included a showroom, library, museum, drafting room, and forge space for two hundred workers. Instrumental in the revival of wrought iron in America, he was considered its foremost master craftsman.

YOUNG, GRACE
Born 1869, Kentucky; died 1947.
Ceramist, decorator

After studying at the Art Academy of Cincinnati, in 1886 Young became a decorator at Rookwood Pottery. A fine painter, she is credited with being among the first to place portraits on vases. Young left Rookwood in 1904 to return to the Art Academy of Cincinnati to teach.

ZIMMERMANN, MARIE
Born 1878; died 1972.
Metalworker, jeweler

Zimmermann was a painter and sculptor, but it was in metalwork and jewelry that she garnered national acclaim. By 1903, she had completed her studies at the Art Students League, in New York City, and exhibited work at the Art Institute of Chicago. In 1915 and 1916, she began to show at New York City's Ehrich Galleries. Throughout the 1920s, Zimmermann received prestigious commissions for architectural metalwork in the East and Midwest. Her metalwork was distinguished by highly skillful chemical treatments, gilding, and plating, which created a broad range of color and textural effects.

ZORACH, MARGUERITE THOMPSON
Born September 25, 1887, Santa Rosa, California; died June 27, 1968, Brooklyn, New York.
Painter, printmaker, weaver

Trained in Paris as a painter, Thompson married the sculptor William Zorach in 1912. She showed at the 1913 Armory Show, in New York City, and other major exhibitions. Her style ranged from Fauvism and Cubism in her early years to realism later in her career. In addition to painting and etching, Zorach was noted for the clothing and accessories she designed and made from cloth that she wove. She received considerable publicity for a tapestry of the Rockefeller family, commissioned by Mrs. John D. Rockefeller, Jr. Her work is in the permanent collections of the Metropolitan Museum of Art, Whitney Museum, and Brooklyn Museum.

COMMUNITIES

THE ACADIANS

Mid-1700s–c. 1925
Louisiana Gulf Coast

Immigrants from Canada developed a regional textile tradition, spinning and weaving cotton, *"coton jaune,"* and brown cotton. Acadians showed at the Art Institute of Chicago Arts and Crafts Exhibition in 1910.

ARDEN

1900–1901
Arden, Delaware
Founders: William L. Price, Frank Stephens, Joseph Fels

This short-lived experiment in communal living was revived soon after its demise in the more successful Rose Valley Association.

ATASCADERO COMMUNITY

c. 1912
Atascadero, California
Founder: Edward J. Lewis

After the collapse of his People's University, in St. Louis, Lewis planned a self-sufficient community on twenty-three thousand acres north of San Luis Obispo, with farms, agricultural processing, and educational facilities. Owned by a holding company, residences and lots were sold to individuals. Garden City, Beaux-Arts, and Arts and Crafts principles guided Lewis's vision.

BEAUX-ARTS VILLAGE

c. 1910
Puget Sound, near Seattle, Washington

Its aim was to maintain an art school and workshop facilities, but it had only rustic bungalows for a few Seattle artists.

BRYN ATHYN

1897–present
Bryn Athyn, Pennsylvania

In 1897, the Swedenborgian community of Bryn Athyn, near Philadelphia, was established as a religious and educational center of the Church of the New Jerusalem. Between 1912 and 1926, the congregation undertook the construction of a cathedral. With the financial backing of Raymond Pitcairn, the community hired Ralph Adams Cram and Bertram Grosvenor Goodhue, the leading American designers of Gothic churches. The Boston firm designed a perpendicular-style cathedral, but Pitcairn altered the plans to his own specifications and the cathedral was completed in 1919. A second phase was begun the following year, adding a wing, tower, and council hall, and it was completed in 1926. For these building projects, the church maintained six craft shops—for drafting, modeling, stone-carving, woodworking, metal, and stained glass—which were organized in emulation of the shops that had built medieval cathedrals.

BYRDCLIFFE COLONY

1902–15
Woodstock, New York
Founders: Ralph Radcliffe Whitehead, Hervey White, Bolton Coit Brown

Whitehead provided financial support for thirty buildings, where crafts were combined with cultural and physical activities. Ultimately, the furniture proved too expensive to produce and attention was paid to less costly craft media, such as handbuilt pottery.

CHETIMACHEZ INDIANS

c. 1900
Avery's Island, Louisiana

This group showed handwoven baskets and mats at the Art Institute of Chicago Arts and Crafts Exhibition in 1910.

THE ELVERHOJ COLONY

1913–n.d
Milton-on-the-Hudson, near Poughkeepsie, New York
Founders: Johannes Morton, A. H. Anderson

The colony offered courses in printing, etching, jewelry, weaving, metalwork, and bookbinding. It was known for gold and silver jewelry that incorporated semiprecious stones into designs based upon local flowers.

FELLOWSHIP FARMS

1907–18
Westwood, Massachusetts
Founder: The Rev. George Emery Littlefield

Founded on Socialist Unitarian beliefs, Fellowship Farms failed as a center for Arts and Crafts. It succeeded, however, as a means by which the colonists, many of whom maintained jobs in nearby towns, could purchase land at cheap prices. Fellowship Farms published the journal *Ariel.*

GERMAN SETTLEMENT SOCIETY

1836–early 20th century
Hermann, Missouri
Founder: The Settlement Society of Philadelphia

This colony of German immigrants settled in an area dubbed the "Missouri Rhineland." The geographic isolation caused them to rely on their own crafts: baskets, tinware, rag rugs, weavings, pottery, and handmade furniture.

LONGWOOD ART INDUSTRIAL AND STOCK COMPANY

1902–n.d.
Longwood, Illinois
Founder: George L. Schreiber

This community combined craft and agriculture in an old church that was equipped to make furniture, pottery, textiles, and metalwork. In addition, it grew flax in local fields for its work.

MISSION INN

1901–present
Riverside, California

This luxury hotel, owned by Frank A. Miller, exhibited an unusual art collection and promoted craft ideals of craft and traditional art. While the hotel was being built, workshops were set up on the site to produce many of the fixtures and ornaments. Other artists were later brought in to build furniture and make ceramics for furnishings and souvenirs for tourists.

NEW CLAIRVAUX

1902–8
Montague, Massachusetts
Founder: The Rev. Edward Pearson Pressey

Pressey brought together a group of college-educated men and women to produce crafts and to work the land.

The philosophy was based upon a Romantic return to the simple life, with minimal reliance on wages and trade with the outside world. The New Clairvaux Plantation was founded in 1904 as a crafts school to train apprentices. Pressey also founded the Montague Arts and Crafts Society, which he based upon the nearby Deerfield Society. The village shop sold the colony's output: woodworking, basketry, weaving, dyed goods, and printing. Pressey wrote, with Carl Purington Rollins, *The Arts & Crafts & the Individual* (1904). New Clairvaux published a journal, *Country Time and Tide: A Magazine for a More Profitable Country Life* (1902).

ROSE VALLEY ASSOCIATION
1901–9
Moylan, Pennsylvania
Founder: William L. Price

With financial backing by Philadelphia philanthropists and trustees from Swarthmore College, the architect Will Price founded Rose Valley in 1901. A group of middle-class families, many of them members of the Society of Friends (Quakers), joined Price in his utopian experiment and settled in a group of abandoned textile mills outside Philadelphia. Beginning in 1901, Rose Valley craftsmen produced furniture, bookbindings, and pottery. Because the use of machine tools was limited, Rose Valley furniture is noted for handcrafted features, carving, and exposed joinery in the Gothic, Renaissance, and Colonial styles. The Rose Valley Association published a journal, *The Artsman: The Art That Is Life* (1903–7). The shops were closed in 1906 as a result of labor disputes, and the community was disbanded after 1909.

ROYCROFT
1895–1938
East Aurora, New York
Founder: Elbert G. Hubbard

More capitalistic than many of the other colonies founded during this period, Roycroft produced printed and bound books, leather goods, and furniture. By 1906, more than four hundred people were at work. The venture succeeded primarily through Hubbard's marketing abilities. Roycroft published the journal *The Philistine* (1896) and a magazine, *The Fra: For Philistines and Roycrofters* (1908–17). After Hubbard and his wife died, on the *Lusitania,* in 1915, the business was continued by their son, Elbert Hubbard, Jr.

SHAKERS
1787–present
Founder: Ann Lee

The United Society of Believers in Christ's Second Appearing established nineteen communities in New England and the Midwest, which became known for furniture, baskets, wooden boxes, rugs, and other products. Members were celibate and property was held in common. In retrospect, the spare utilitarian objects produced by the Shakers were congruous with Arts and Crafts principles of forthright construction and lack of ornament. The community at Mount Lebanon, New York, was a center of Shaker chair production.

SUNLAND COMMUNITY
c. 1900–1910
Sunland, California

Bolton Hall was built by George Harris to serve as an example to the community. An architect, his method of natural construction employed boulders and natural wood.

EXHIBITIONS

ALASKA-YUKON-PACIFIC EXPOSITION
1909
Seattle, Washington

At the exposition, the House of Hoo-Hoo exhibited finely crafted wood furniture by Ellsworth Stoney, a Seattle architect.

THE ART INSTITUTE OF CHICAGO ARTS AND CRAFTS EXHIBITION
1897–1921
Chicago, Illinois
Founders: Chicago Arts and Crafts Society (Jane Addams, Frank Lloyd Wright, Madeline Yale Wynne, Oscar Lovell Triggs)

In 1897, the Chicago Arts and Crafts Society began to sponsor an Arts and Crafts exhibition at the Art Institute. In 1902, the Alumni Association of Decorative Designers of the School of the Art Institute took over the exhibition for a year. The show proved so successful that the museum assumed its sponsorship, and annual exhibitions were held at the museum for more than twenty years. These were among the premier Arts and Crafts exhibitions in the United States. Displaying mostly American work, every important name in craft appeared here.

ART STUDENTS' LEAGUE OF BUFFALO, BUFFALO CHAPTER AMERICAN INSTITUTE OF ARCHITECTS, BUFFALO SOCIETY OF ARTISTS THE JOINT ANNUAL EXHIBITION
April 16–28, 1900
Buffalo, New York

An exhibition of both fine arts and decorative crafts, it included examples of the work of Dedham, Rookwood, and Biloxi Art potteries.

ARTS AND CRAFTS EXHIBITION; EXHIBITION OF ART CRAFTSMANSHIP
March 23–April 4, 1903, Syracuse, New York
April 15–April 25, 1903, Rochester, New York

The exhibition was first presented under the auspices of Stickley's United Crafts at the Craftsman Building, in Syracuse. It then moved to the Mechanics Institute, in Rochester, as an "Exhibition of Art Craftsmanship." Shown were Native American weaving and basketry, American Arts and Crafts, school exhibits, furniture by C.F.A. Voysey, and objects from Samuel Bing's Salon de l'Art Nouveau, in Paris. Claude Bragdon designed the cover for the Rochester catalogue.

CALIFORNIA EXHIBITION OF APPLIED ARTS
1916

Los Angeles, California; Buffalo, New York; Boston, Massachusetts; New York, New York; Chicago, Illinois
Founder: Douglas Donaldson

After the Panama-California Exposition in San Diego closed, Donaldson organized an exhibition of California crafts to travel under the auspices of the Los Angeles Society of Arts and Crafts.

CLEVELAND MUSEUM OF ART
EXHIBITION OF WORK BY ARTISTS & CRAFTSMEN OF THE WESTERN RESERVE (ALSO KNOWN AS THE MAY SHOW)

1919–present
Cleveland, Ohio

An enthusiastic commitment to the promotion of contemporary Arts and Crafts led the museum's first director, Frederic Allen Whiting, to establish the May Show. Since 1919, this popular exhibition has presented work annually by Cleveland-area artists.

DETROIT MUSEUM OF ART
GEORGE LELAND HUNTER:
LOAN EXHIBITION OF TAPESTRIES

April 1919
Detroit, Michigan

This exhibition covered tapestry from the fifteenth century to current examples of American work.

GRAND RAPIDS FURNITURE EXPOSITION ASSOCIATION
GRAND RAPIDS FURNITURE MARKET

1878–c. 1950
Grand Rapids, Michigan

This exposition attracted numerous buyers to see the latest in furniture design. Gustav Stickley's "New Furniture" was first offered in 1900.

JOHN HERRON ART INSTITUTE OF INDIANAPOLIS
ANNUAL EXHIBITION OF WORKS BY INDIANA ARTISTS

1908–n.d.
Indianapolis, Indiana

This exhibition showed work in the fine and decorative arts.

LOS ANGELES COUNTY MUSEUM OF HISTORY, SCIENCE, AND ART
EXHIBIT OF DECORATIVE LANDSCAPES AND TEXTILES

1919
Los Angeles, California

The exhibit included work by Fannie M. Kerns, Vivien F. Stringfield, and Marjorie Hodges.

LOUISIANA PURCHASE INTERNATIONAL EXPOSITION (ALSO KNOWN AS ST. LOUIS WORLD'S FAIR)

April 30–December 1, 1904
St. Louis, Missouri

This fair, celebrating the centenary of the purchase of the Louisiana Territory, introduced Mission and Arts and Crafts styles to a large and impressionable American audience. By registering in the Department of Fine Arts, a craftsperson could be displayed in the Palace of Fine Arts.

METROPOLITAN MUSEUM OF ART
THE HUDSON-FULTON CELEBRATION

September–November 1909
New York, New York

This celebration of America's past featured an extensive exhibition of American decorative arts, which included furniture, silver, ceramics, glass, and textiles. In all, 606 decorative objects were shown.

MINNESOTA STATE ART SOCIETY
ANNUAL EXHIBITION OF THE MINNESOTA STATE ART SOCIETY

1903–7
Various sites in Minnesota, including Minneapolis, St. Paul, and Mankato

The Minnesota State Art Society was created by legislative action in 1903. Its purpose was to "advance the interests of the fine arts, to develop the influence of art in education and to foster art in manufactures." Craftwork displayed in the society's Annual Exhibition included metalwork, pottery, bookplates and bookbindings, leatherwork, glassware, embroidery, and lace.

MONTCLAIR ART MUSEUM
STATE-WIDE CRAFTS EXHIBITION

April 15–May 20, 1956
Montclair, New Jersey

A committee of selection, drawn from the New Jersey Designer-Craftsmen group and the Montclair Art Museum, chose 256 craft pieces by forty-seven New Jersey craftspersons. The media were limited to woodwork, ceramics, metalwork, and textiles.

NATIONAL TERRA COTTA SOCIETY
CLAY PRODUCTS SHOW

1912
Chicago, Illinois

This show was initiated to acquaint architects and builders with architectural terra-cotta products.

PAN-AMERICAN EXPOSITION

1901
Buffalo, New York

An exhibition of Arts and Crafts was held in the central court of the Manufacturers and Liberal Arts Building. Stickley, Tiffany, Gorham, and Grueby exhibited. The entry from the National Arts Club included pottery by Newcomb Pottery, Volkmar, and Robineau. Gold medals went to Grueby, Rookwood, and Tiffany; silver to Tiffany, Newcomb College, and the National Arts Club; bronze to Charles Volkmar.

PANAMA-CALIFORNIA EXPOSITION

1915–16
San Diego, California

Held in Balboa Park, San Diego, it introduced Spanish Colonial revival architecture. The Foreign and Domestic Arts Building displayed European, American, and Asian objects, while the Indian Arts Building exhibited contemporary and historic Native American crafts. In 1916, part of the exposition was open for a second season.

PANAMA-PACIFIC INTERNATIONAL EXPOSITION

1915
San Francisco, California

Craft was displayed everywhere at this celebration of the opening of the Panama Canal—in the Department of Fine and Applied Arts, the Palace of Varied Industries, and the Palace of Manufacturers, among other locations. Newcomb College earned the grand prize for its combined exhibit of pottery, embroidery, and jewelry.

PHILADELPHIA MUSEUM OF ART
AN EXHIBITION OF TILES

October 1915
Philadelphia, Pennsylvania

Organized by Edwin Atlee Barber, the exhibition featured 179 objects drawn primarily from the museum's collection. Examples ranged from Roman, Chinese, and Persian tiles to those produced by the Moravian Pottery and Tile Works, in nearby Doylestown.

SOCIETY OF ARTS AND CRAFTS, BOSTON

1897–present
Boston, Massachusetts

The society held several major exhibitions at Boston's Copley Hall: "First National Exhibition," April 5–16, 1897, at which four hundred objects by one hundred craftsmen were shown; "Second National Exhibition," April 4–15, 1899, which displayed works by Louis

Comfort Tiffany, Alfred Stieglitz, and Maxfield Parrish; and "Third National Exhibition," February 5–26, 1907. Beginning in 1901, the society held smaller exhibitions, often focusing on one medium. In May 1911, the society held the first of a series of exhibitions at the Museum of Fine Arts, Boston. In 1907, the society became part of the National League of Handicraft Societies.

THE SOCIETY OF PRINTERS FOR THE STUDY AND ADVANCEMENT OF THE ART OF PRINTING
THE DEVELOPMENT OF PRINTING AS AN ART

January 1–29, 1906
Boston, Massachusetts

This exhibition, which commemorated the two-hundredth anniversary of Benjamin Franklin's birth, traced the history of printing in both Europe and America. One section, "Modern Print-ing," showed the influence of William Morris's Kelmscott Press and provided a showcase for work by contemporary American presses, including Riverside, Gillis, and De Vinne.

TEXAS WOMEN'S ASSOCIATION

c. 1915
Houston, Texas

Billed as "the first exclusive women's fair ever held," it included competitions for many kinds of craftwork.

GUILDS AND SOCIETIES

AGUA CALIENTE

c. 1903
Warner's Ranch, San Diego County, California
Founder: Mrs. J. H. Babbitt

Babbitt, a teacher at a Native American school, was a collector of baskets. She organized a group of basketmakers among the Kupa Indians, also known as the Cupeño or Agua Caliente Indians.

AMERICAN CERAMIC SOCIETY

1899–c. 1930s
Columbus, Ohio
Founders: Edward Orton, Jr., Theodore Randall

Randall was the editor of *The Clay-Worker*, the official organ of the National Brick Manufacturer's Association of the U.S.A. The society was formed to combat European competition.

AMERICAN WOMEN'S LEAGUE

1907–15
St. Louis, Missouri
Founder: Edward J. Lewis

The league's goal was to educate women in various pursuits, especially potterymaking. The league started University City Pottery.

ANTIQUARIAN SOCIETY OF THE ART INSTITUTE OF CHICAGO

1877–present
Chicago, Illinois

Beginning as the Chicago Society of Decorative Arts, this group of socially prominent women set aside funds to found a collection of tapestries, embroidery, lace, china, and pottery.

ARROYO GUILD OF CRAFTSMEN

c. 1909–15
Pasadena, California

This society was inspired by the ideal of a medieval guild. Its members proclaimed that they were ready to create architecture, stained glass, carpeting, metalwork, vases, books, sculptured leather, tiles, and landscape architecture on commission. A single issue of *Arroyo Craftsman,* a magazine associated with the guild and edited by George Wharton James, was published in 1909.

ATLAN CERAMIC ART CLUB

1893–present
Chicago, Illinois
Founder: Florence Pratt Steward

The most prestigious and influential china-painting club in Chicago, it was allied with the National League of Mineral Painters. Its members won numerous gold awards at international expositions and held annual shows at the Art Institute of Chicago.

AT THE SIGN OF THE LIVE OAK

Oakland, California
Founders: Charles and Louise Keeler

This informal crafts guild operated out of the Keelers' home. Charles printed his own poems and constructed furniture based on Louise's designs.

THE BASKET FRATERNITY

c. 1903–4
Pasadena, California
Founder: George Wharton James

The society published the periodical *The Basket* as well as books by James, including *Practical Basketmaking; How To Make Indian and Other Baskets*; and *George Wharton James's Beadwork Book*. It ran basketry competitions and distributed model Native American basket designs. Books, a slide library, and basket exhibits were loaned to members throughout the United States.

THE BOHEMIA GUILD

1902–4
Chicago, Illinois
Founder: Industrial Art League

The guild was a model workshop of the Industrial Art League. Inspired by the league's founder, Oscar Lovell Triggs, it was organized along the lines of a medieval craft guild. Changing the nature of work and the lot of the worker, and placing the best possible product on the market, was the guild's primary purpose, subordinate to making money. The guild organized the experimental School of Industrial Art and Handicraft in 1902, under the direction of sculptor Julia Bracken, bookbinder Gertrude Stiles, and printer Frederic W. Goudy. The school operated workshops from artists' studios in the Academy of Fine Arts. There, apprentices learned metalwork, potterymaking, bookbinding, and wood carving, as well as other crafts. The guild maintained a showroom, from which it sold this student work to the public. Although highly productive, the guild discontinued its work in 1904 when the Industrial Art League disbanded.

CAHUILLA BASKETMAKERS

c. 1903
Southern-central California

Maria Los Angeles, Felipa Akwaka, Rosario Casero, and Maria Antonia, as well as other members of the Cahuilla tribe, wove baskets of grass, husks of squaw weed, skunk weed stalks, and tule roots. The colors were the natural white, yellow, and brown of the materials, and black, created by being soaked in mud from the sulphur springs.

CALUMET COPPER MINE WOMEN

c. 1913–19
Calumet, Michigan
Founder: Clare L. Grierson

Wives of copper miners in northern Michigan produced needlework for competitive shows.

CENTRAL ART ASSOCIATION

1894–c. 1910
Chicago, Illinois
Founders: T. Vernette Morse, Hamlin Garland, Lorado Taft

A Chautauqualike organization to promote "good art," it offered china-painting classes, attracting three thousand members in four years.

CHICAGO CERAMIC ASSOCIATION

1892–c. 1905
Chicago, Illinois

Founded by 260 professionals and socialites to unite china painters and ceramics workers, the association offered courses of study and annual exhibitions at the Art Institute of Chicago.

CINCINNATI POTTERY CLUB; LATER, PORCELAIN LEAGUE OF CINCINNATI

1879–present
Cincinnati, Ohio
Founder: Mary Louise McLaughlin

The first club of its kind, and a model for pottery associations in Chicago and New York City, it contributed to the growth of the women's art movement. This group provided study and inspiration for its prestigious members. In 1894, the club became the Porcelain League of Cincinnati.

CLIFF DWELLERS CLUB OF CHICAGO

1907–present
Chicago, Illinois
Founders: Hamlin Garland, Lorado Taft

The club provided purely social gatherings for its membership of artists, writers, architects, and connoisseurs.

THE CRAFTERS

1901–6
Chicago, Illinois
Founders: Elizabeth Eleanor D'Arcy Gaw, Mary Mower, Lawrence Buck

A cooperative organized to design wall decorations, furniture, and light fixtures, it showed at the Art Institute of Chicago Arts and Crafts exhibitions in 1902 and 1903.

CRAFTSMAN'S GUILD

Early 1900s
Chicago, Illinois

The group made animal toys and children's furniture that were sold through a salesroom and restaurant in Chicago.

DAYTON SOCIETY OF ARTS AND CRAFTS

1902–c. 1904
Dayton, Ohio

Classes in crafts and design were offered by Forest Emerson Mann. Pottery was made from Miami River clay and fired at the Miami Pottery.

THE DEERFIELD SOCIETY OF BLUE AND WHITE NEEDLEWORK

1896–c. 1916
Deerfield, Massachusetts
Founders: Ellen Miller, Margaret Whiting

Using textile examples found in the Deerfield Historical Society, Miller and Whiting began a program in which local women revived the eighteenth-century needlecraft tradition of the Connecticut River Valley. The earliest products were bed curtains, coverlets, and tablecloths. The society showed at several Art Institute of Chicago Arts and Crafts exhibitions.

DEERFIELD SOCIETY OF VILLAGE INDUSTRIES

1899–1934
Deerfield, Massachusetts

Following the success of the Deerfield Society of Blue and White Needlework, a group of townspeople began producing baskets, and then expanded into the production of weavings, rugs, photographs, baskets, wrought iron, jewelry, and furniture. Begun as the Deerfield Society of Arts and Crafts, the name of the group was eventually changed to the Deerfield Society of Village Industries. The group, which held annual exhibitions of its work, was prominent in producing historical pageants and furthering the growing interest in the history of the community of Deerfield. The Deerfield Society figures prominently in Arts and Crafts literature of the period.

FOREST CRAFT GUILD

1907–17
Grand Rapids, Michigan
Founder: Forest Emerson Mann

The Forest Craft Guild was founded by Forest Emerson Mann in 1907. Mann had been a student at the Pratt Institute, in Brooklyn, New York, in the late 1890s and later taught Arts and Crafts at Chautauqua, New York, and Dayton, Ohio, before relocating to Grand Rapids in 1904. There he directed the Society of Arts and Crafts and taught classes in design, composition, and technical processes. Mann expanded these activities to create the Forest Craft Guild, which concentrated on the commercial production and sale of jewelry, wrought metal, and leatherwork. Much of the guild's work was inspired by medieval designs and revealed Mann's detailed study of historic styles and workmanship.

GRACE UNITED METHODIST CHURCH QUILTING CLUB

1897–present
Austin, Texas

This quilting group, the oldest in Texas, has been in continuous operation.

GUILD OF ALLIED ARTS, BUFFALO

1910
Buffalo, New York
Founder: Clara B. Sackett

Patterned after medieval guilds, it provided instruction and maintained a salesroom.

GUILD OF ARTS AND CRAFTS

c. 1896–1920
San Francisco, California

The guild held its first exhibition of bookbinding, illumination, graphics, and posters at J.A.G. Cartinton's studio in 1896.

GUILD OF BOOK WORKERS

1906–n.d.
New York, New York
Founders: Charles Dexter Allen, Dr. Charles W. Boyes, Sarah J. Freeman, Frederic and Bertha Goudy, Emily Preston, Wilbur Macy Stone, Caroline Alden Weir

The group held meetings and exhibitions on books, bookbinding, and bookplates.

GUILD OF HANDICRAFT INDUSTRIES

1911–n.d.
New York, New York

The guild was founded through a union of the Society of Craftsmen, Cooper Union, Metropolitan Museum of Art, and the School of Industrial Arts at Columbia University, Teachers College.

HANDICRAFT GUILD OF INDIANA

c. 1920
Indiana

The guild exhibited printed and batiked fabrics at the Art Institute of Chicago Arts and Crafts Exhibition in 1921.

HILLSIDE CLUB

c. 1897–1923
Berkeley, California

This civic-improvement association was founded by the women of Berkeley to encourage the well-being of local citizens through good fellowship and a happy home life. Its shingle-covered clubhouse—designed by Bernard Maybeck, whom the club actively promoted—celebrated European vernacular designs and craft practices and natural local materials.

INDUSTRIAL ART LEAGUE

1899–1904
Chicago, Illinois
Founder: Oscar Lovell Triggs

The league fostered the Skokie and Quisiana shops, Longwood Art Industrial and Stock Company, South Park Workshop, and the Bohemia Guild, and sponsored manual-training classes in public schools.

LOCKPORT VILLAGE COOPERATIVE

c. 1920s
Lockport, Illinois
Founder: Edward F. Worst

Worst, the supervisor of manual training for Chicago's elementary schools, organized needy Swedish women into a village co-op that built its own looms and wove linens using local flax.

LOS ANGELES SOCIETY OF ARTS AND CRAFTS

c. 1905–20
Los Angeles, California

Its first annual exhibition, in 1916, organized by Douglas Donaldson, subsequently traveled to other locations in the United States.

MINNEAPOLIS HANDICRAFT GUILD

1900–1915
Minneapolis, Minnesota

It sponsored regular and summer-school classes in bookbinding, pottery, metalwork, and leather, and exhibited the work of its members in the Art Institute of Chicago Arts and Crafts exhibitions.

MORRIS SOCIETY

1903–c. 1905
Chicago, Illinois
Founders: Joseph Twyman, Richard Green Moulton, Oscar Lovell Triggs

The society sponsored lectures, publications, and exhibitions that expounded on William Morris's ideals. It initiated Morris study circles as far away as Billings, Montana, and helped create at least one Arts and Crafts organization—the William Morris Society, of Columbus, Ohio. From 1903 to 1905, the society published the *Bulletin of the Morris Society*.

NATIONAL ARTS CLUB

1898–present
New York, New York
Founders: Charles de Kay, Charles Rollinson Lamb, Louis Comfort Tiffany, Spencer Trask

The National Arts Club was founded as a private club for artists. In the early years of the twentieth century, it held exhibitions in the Arts and Crafts manner, including one in 1900, and it had an entry in the 1901 Pan-American Exposition. The club also sponsored an exhibition of pictorial photography in 1902. In 1906, the club held an important exhibition of Arts and Crafts ceramics entitled "The Art of the Fire." By then, most activities had been taken over by the National Society of Craftsmen.

NATIONAL LEAGUE OF HANDICRAFT SOCIETIES

1907–present
Boston, Massachusetts
Founder: Herbert Langford Warren

The league was founded in 1907 on the tenth anniversary of the Boston Society of Arts and Crafts. Societies from various states set standards for work and organized exhibitions. Two traveling libraries of books on the Arts and Crafts circulated throughout the country under the aegis of the league, providing information to isolated craftsmen. A stated goal of the league's formation was its activation of *Handicraft,* which

the Boston society had published between 1902 and 1904. The league published *Handicraft* from 1910 to 1912, and along with articles on crafts and the craft ideal, the magazine provided a chronicle of member Arts and Crafts societies throughout the United States, giving their histories and activities.

Note: For selected listings of the constituent societies of the National League of Handicraft Societies, see Allen H. Eaton's *Handicrafts of New England*. Between 1910 and 1912, the monthly issues of *Handicraft* included profiles of the local Arts and Crafts societies that formed the league. These articles generally provide the founding date of the organization and a description of each group's activities, although the founders of the societies usually are not given.

NATIONAL LEAGUE OF MINERAL PAINTERS

1891–present
Founder: Susan Stuart Goodrich Frackelton

Frackelton gave instruction and information to small china–painting societies throughout the United States. The league published *Keramic Studio*, an influential magazine that provided designs and information on obtaining materials. It afforded an excellent record of American Arts and Crafts exhibitions and societies during the early years of the twentieth century.

NATIONAL SOCIETY OF CRAFTSMEN

1906–n.d.
New York, New York
President: Spencer Trask

The society took over the exhibition and information service of the National Arts Club. It published the *Bulletin of Arts and Crafts.*

NEW ULM LACEMAKERS

c. 1910–13
New Ulm, Minnesota

It exhibited Bohemian pillow laces at the Art Institute of Chicago Arts and Crafts exhibitions.

NEW YORK SOCIETY OF DECORATIVE ART

1877–n.d.
New York, New York
President: Mrs. David Lane; Corresponding Secretary: Candace Wheeler

Prominent New York society matrons founded the society to provide financial independence for women through the production of needlework. Louis Comfort Tiffany and John La Farge were judges who reviewed submissions. Wheeler became disenchanted with the society and in 1878 formed the Women's Exchange, which is still in existence today.

NEW YORK SOCIETY OF KERAMIC ART

1892–c. 1912
New York, New York
Founders: Marshall T. Fry, Elizabeth Hardenberg, Anna B. Leonard, Maude Mason, Edith Penman, Mrs. L. Vance Philips, Adelaide Alsop Robineau, Charles Volkmar

The society organized exhibitions and promoted high quality in ceramic work. In 1912, it became part of the National Society of Craftsmen.

NORMAL COLLEGE ARTS AND CRAFTS CLUB

1907–n.d.
New York, New York
President: Verena Bustroem

The club provided instruction in leatherwork, bookbinding, metalwork, china painting, basketry, and pottery.

PROVIDENCE HANDICRAFT CLUB

c. 1910
Providence, Rhode Island
Founder: Mrs. Arnold Talbot

Talbot brought together four Portuguese weavers to produce peasant crafts.

ROCHESTER ARTS AND CRAFTS SOCIETY

1897–n.d.
Rochester, New York
Founders: Harvey Ellis, M. Louise Stowell, Charles F. Bragdon, John F. Dumont, Thillman Fabray

The society presented its first two exhibitions shortly after its incorporation: Japanese prints and modern French posters, in May 1897, and "artistic photography" the following month.

SATURDAY EVENING GIRLS' CLUB

1905–42
Boston, Massachusetts
Founders: Edith Brown, Mrs. James Storrow, Edith Guerrier

This association of young women, most of whom were born to immigrant parents in the Boston area, met on Saturday evenings for reading and craft activities, which, after 1906, included ceramics. This led to the establishment of the Paul Revere Pottery, a name adopted in 1912, which provided employment for the club members under the direction of the designer Edith Brown. The products, the best known of which were children's breakfast sets, were sold under the name of the Bowl Shop. The women's mark, S.E.G., was placed on each piece.

SCHOOL CRAFTS CLUB

1903–n.d.
New York, New York
Founder: James P. Haney

The club provided instruction in Arts and Crafts and held exhibitions.

SOCIETY OF ARTS AND CRAFTS, BOSTON

1897–present
Boston, Massachusetts
Founding President: Charles Eliot Norton

The Society of Arts and Crafts, Boston, was the preeminent voice for the promulgation of the Arts and Crafts aesthetic in America. Its focus was precious, unique objects, with a jury overseeing the materials offered in its salesroom at 1 Somerset Street. The society modeled itself on medieval craft guilds. At one time, there were special uniforms for the various media in which members worked. From 1902 to 1904, the society published the magazine *Handicraft*, which served as a manifesto of its Arts and Crafts ideas.

WISCONSIN DESIGNER-CRAFTSMEN

1916–c. 1970s
Milwaukee, Wisconsin

This group, which began as the Wisconsin Craft Workers, embraced Arts and Crafts tenets. It offered studio and exhibition space.

YE HANDICRAFTERS

c. 1904
Brooklyn, New York
Founders: Mary A. Buston, (Miss) O. S. Douglas, Mrs. George R. Westbrook

The group conducted exhibitions and maintained workrooms and a salesroom.

PERIODICALS

AMATEUR WORK

1901–7
Publisher: F. A. Draper Publishing Company, Boston, Massachusetts

The magazine advertised as "containing illustrated articles descriptive of electrical and mechanical apparatus, furniture and other useful articles, games, photography, wood turning, book-binding, mechanical drawing, toys, etc." It is a good example of one way that Americans learned handicrafts. In 1907, it was absorbed into *Electrician and Mechanic.*

THE AMERICAN CHAP-BOOK

September 1904–August 1905
Publisher: American Type Founders Company, Jersey City, New Jersey

Under the direction of Will Bradley, one of America's most influential typeface designers, the magazine was a house organ for the American Type Founders Company and provided important instruction to the growing numbers of printers throughout the United States. It also influenced the future design of American periodicals. Many of the typefaces introduced were used by small presses working in the Arts and Crafts tradition.

ARCHITECTURAL RECORD

July 1891–1948
Publisher: F. W. Dodge Corporation, New York, New York

Architectural Record sought to be the journal of record for architecture in

the United States, as well as providing European examples from which architects might find inspiration.

ART AND PROGRESS; later, THE AMERICAN MAGAZINE OF ART

1909–53
Publisher: American Federation of Arts, Washington, D.C.

After appearing as *Art and Progress*, the magazine's name was changed in 1916. A monthly, it included activities and exhibitions of such craft societies as the National Arts Club and the National Society of Craftsmen.

THE ARTSMAN: The Art That Is Life

1903–7
Publisher: Rose Valley Association Press, Moylan, Pennsylvania

The journal of William Price's Rose Valley community.

BRUSH AND PENCIL
1897–1907
Publisher: Phillips and Company, Chicago, Illinois
Editors: Charles Francis Browne (1897–1900), Fredrick William Morton (1900–1907)

The magazine's masthead read, "An Illustrated Magazine of the Arts and Crafts." It emphasized the fine arts, particularly in the Midwest, and featured articles on Dedham pottery.

BULLETIN OF ARTS AND CRAFTS
November 1911–March 1912
New York, New York

This short-lived journal, published by the National Society of Craftsmen, was taken over by the River School of Art, in Johnville, Bucks County, Pennsylvania, and renamed *Arts and Crafts Magazine*.

THE BUNGALOW MAGAZINE
1909–10
Los Angeles, California
Editor: Henry Lawrence Wilson

The magazine provided plans for inexpensive retreats—small-scale, individual residences known as bungalows. In 1907, Wilson wrote *The Bungalow Book*.

THE CRAFTSMAN
1901–16
Publisher: The United Crafts, Eastwood, New York; Syracuse, New York; New York, New York
Founder and Editor: Gustav Stickley

Created by Gustav Stickley in 1901, and it became the most important American journal of the Arts and Crafts style and contained articles dealing with the English founders of the movement. *The Craftsman* provided plans and instructions for houses and furniture in the approved Stickley style.

FINE ARTS JOURNAL
1899–1918
Publisher: Fine Arts Journal Company, Chicago, Illinois
Editors: Marian Ainsworth White (1899–1905), Evelyn Marie Stuart (1905–10), James William Pattison (1911–18)

A Chicago magazine promoting the Arts and Crafts.

THE FRA: For Philistines and Roycrofters
1908–17
Publisher: Roycroft Press, East Aurora, New York

Founder and Editor: Elbert G. Hubbard

Larger in format and graphically more ambitious than Hubbard's *The Philistine*, *The Fra* was able to offer longer articles, more writers, and greater advertising space.

GOOD HOUSEKEEPING
1885–present
Publisher: Clark W. Bryan & Company, Holyoke, Massachusetts; Springfield, Massachusetts; New York, New York

The magazine espoused the Colonial revival as the major American style, and provided suggestions for the efficient management of a household.

HANDICRAFT
1902–4; 1910–12
Boston, Massachusetts; New York, New York

Published by the Boston Society of Arts and Crafts from 1902 to 1904, *Handicraft* was a manifesto of Arts and Crafts ideas. The National League of Handicraft Societies took over the magazine from 1910 to 1912, using it to provide information on craft societies and exhibitions. It was then absorbed by *Industrial Arts* magazine.

HOUSE BEAUTIFUL
1896–present
Chicago, Illinois; New York, New York
Founder: Herbert S. Stone

A progressive magazine that promoted Arts and Crafts ideals and advanced interior decoration, it had a circulation of forty thousand by 1905. As a record of American upper-class taste around the turn of the century, it featured the work of Frank Lloyd Wright and interiors in the Arts and Crafts style.

THE INTERNATIONAL STUDIO
1897–1931
Publisher: John Lane, New York, New York
Editor: Charles Holme

"An Illustrated Magazine of Fine and Applied Art," it reported on American and European art movements. *Connoisseur* absorbed it in 1931.

KERAMIC STUDIO
1899–1924
Publisher: Keramic Studio Publishing Company, Syracuse, New York
Editors: Adelaide Alsop Robineau, Anna B. Leonard

Robineau's magazine responded to the tradition of china painting. It reported on the activities of the National League of Mineral Painters, with each

issue containing numerous design diagrams and instructions. It was a source of information on American Arts and Crafts, covering exhibitions and individual potteries such as Marblehead and Rookwood. By 1905, it featured instruction in crafts other than ceramics, such as leatherworking and wood burning. After 1924, the name changed to *Design*.

THE KNIGHT ERRANT
1891–92
Publisher: Elzevin Press, Boston, Massachusetts
Founders: Bertram Grosvenor Goodhue, Ralph Adams Cram

Architects Goodhue and Cram dealt with the emerging Arts and Crafts.

LADIES' HOME JOURNAL
1883–present
Publisher: Curtis Publishing Company, Philadelphia, Pennsylvania
Editor: Edward William Bok

In 1889, Cyrus H. K. Curtis invited Edward Bok to be editor of the *Ladies' Home Journal*. Under Bok's leadership, the magazine became an important voice for the concerns of women; other sections were devoted to home design, decoration, and backyard gardening. Bok maintained high literary standards and pursued articles and artwork by such well-known writers and artists as Mark Twain and Kate Greenaway. He also covered such provocative issues as women's suffrage, and carried serious pieces by important public figures.

LANDSCAPE ARCHITECTURE
1910–present
Publisher: Lay, Hubbard & Wheelwright, Harrisburg, Pennsylvania; New York, New York
Founders: Charles Downing Lay, Henry Vincent Hubbard, Robert Wheelwright

The official organ of the American Society of Landscape Architects, it comprehensively covers landscape architectural design, technology, and trends. The earliest issues included articles on gardens for large estates and city planning.

LE DERNIER CRI
1916–17
Grand Rapids, Michigan
Founder: Forest Emerson Mann

A short-lived quarterly for craft shops.

PALETTE AND BRUSH
1907–10
Publishers: Keramic Studio Publishing Company, Syracuse, New York; Lewis

Publishing Company, University City, Missouri
Editors: Adelaide Alsop Robineau (1908–10), Grace W. Curran (1910)

"A Monthly Book for Art Lover, Student, and Craftsman," it provided monthly "classes" in fine arts and crafts for the student unable to attend formal sessions.

THE PHILISTINE
1895–1915
Publisher: Roycroft Press, East Aurora, New York
Founder and Editor: Elbert G. Hubbard

An inexpensive little magazine of literature and polemics, by 1910 *The Philistine* was selling more than two hundred thousand copies a month. Hubbard published mottoes and book reviews, along with the poems of Stephen Crane and his own essays. Hubbard's "A Message to Garcia" promoted obedience in the workplace and was reprinted and distributed by the president of the New York Central Railroad, among others.

POPULAR MECHANICS
1902–present
Publisher: Popular Mechanics Company, Chicago, Illinois

The magazine contained sections on home craftsmanship, aimed at small-town readers dissatisfied with local retailers.

THE POTTER
1916–17
Santa Barbara, California
Founder: Frederick Hurten Rhead

For one year, Rhead edited and published a monthly magazine that specialized in the art of potterymaking.

POTTERY AND GLASS
1908–15
Publisher: Pottery and Glass Publishing Company, New York, New York

It reported on the American glass, pottery, and brass industries, and featured work of current art potteries. It was absorbed by *Pottery, Glass and Brass Salesman*.

THE SKETCH BOOK
1902–7
Chicago, Illinois
Founder: School of the Art Institute of Chicago

The school's student publication, it promoted the Arts and Crafts and urged the integration of art and life.

PRODUCTION CENTERS

 CERAMICS

ALBERHILL POTTERY
1912–14
Riverside, California
Founder: Alberhill Coal and Clay Company

Alexander W. Robertson worked for the small Alberhill Coal and Clay Company, experimenting with clays and showing their suitability for potterymaking. Sculptural ornament adorned vases, and several pieces won a gold medal at the 1915 Panama-California Exposition, in San Diego.

AMERICAN ENCAUSTIC TILING COMPANY
1875–1936
Zanesville, Ohio

One of the first producers of decorative wall and floor tile in the country, its displays won international awards. Frederick H. Rhead was in its employ from 1917 to 1927.

AMERICAN TERRA COTTA AND CERAMIC COMPANY; GATES POTTERIES
1881–1966
Crystal Lake, Illinois
Founder: William Day Gates

American Terra Cotta produced tile and architectural terra-cotta. Gates Potteries, a subsidiary founded in 1886, produced Teco, the famous Arts and Crafts line. Teco pottery received many awards, and some of the Teco Green glazed ware was designed by Prairie School architects Frank Lloyd Wright and William LeBaron Jenny.

AREQUIPA POTTERY
1911–18
Fairfax, California
Founder: Dr. Philip King Brown

The pottery was established to provide craft therapy for patients recovering from tuberculosis at the Arequipa Sanatorium. Frederick H. Rhead developed the use of local clays, with raised decoration and matte glazes, during his directorship (1911–13). Albert L. Solon, the next director (1913–16), focused on carved decoration and glossy glazes and experimented with tile production. Frederick H. Wilde, during his tenure (1916–18), developed more tile manufacture and marketing strategies and introduced translations of Spanish designs.

BARNET POTTERY
c. 1910
Chicago, Illinois
Founder: Belle Barnet Vesey

Vesey founded and operated this pottery, producing tiles and vases in floral and geometric designs. She showed work at the Art Institute of Chicago Arts and Crafts Exhibition in 1910.

BATCHELDER TILE COMPANY
1909–32
Pasadena, California; Los Angeles, California
Founder: Ernest A. Batchelder

Batchelder built a small kiln and shop behind his house in Pasadena, planning to develop this into a school of design and handicraft. When he moved to a more industrial location in 1912, it expanded into a major tile manufactory. Handpress-molded tiles were based on paper designs, often depicting the California landscape, stylized medieval motifs, or adaptations of Mayan iconography. The tiles eventually were available throughout the United States.

BILOXI ART POTTERY
c. 1883–c. 1907
Biloxi, Mississippi
Founder: George Edgar Ohr

Master potter George Ohr produced some of the most advanced art pottery of his time, with eccentric forms and glazes. Discouraged by lack of public interest in his work, he stopped potting early in the century, and placed six thousand pieces in storage. These were discovered in 1972 in a warehouse.

BRAGDON AND THOMAS; LATER, THE TILE SHOP; LATER, CALIFORNIA FAIENCE

1916–c. 1950
Berkeley, California
Founders: William V. Bragdon, Chauncey R. Thomas

The firm made handpress-molded tiles, often with a brick-red relief contour line and shiny glazes. The name changed to the Tile Shop in 1922, and in 1924 it became California Faience.

BUFFALO POTTERY; LATER, BUFFALO CHINA, INC.

1901–present
Buffalo, New York

Buffalo Pottery was established to satisfy the china and pottery needs of the Larkin Soap Company, of Buffalo. The distinctive olive-green color of the Deldare line, which was developed by William Rea in 1905, is found on many styles produced between 1905 and 1909. In 1911, Emerald Deldare was introduced; today, it is the most sought after of the Buffalo ware because of its limited production and superior design and decoration. Buffalo Pottery, which became Buffalo China, Inc., in 1956, also produced dinnerware for the Roycroft Inn, in East Aurora, New York.

BYRDCLIFFE POTTERY

1903–28
Woodstock, New York
Founders: Edith Penman, Elizabeth R. Hardenberg, Mabel Davidson, Charles Volkmar

Part of Ralph Radcliffe Whitehead's Byrdcliffe Colony, Byrdcliffe Pottery produced pieces characterized by pure handicraft; no wheels or molds were used and later pieces were fired in open-air kilns. The most noteworthy colors were Byrdcliffe blue, apple green, and withered rose. The pottery continued production even after the colony itself closed.

CAMBRIDGE ART POTTERY

1900–1933
Cambridge, Ohio
Founder: Charles L. Casey

A maker of art pottery, with red, brown, and mulberry glazes on local clays for jardinieres, pedestals, umbrella stands, and tankards, Cambridge produced the Terrhea, Oakwood, Guernsey, Acorn, and Otoe lines.

CLEVELAND POTTERY AND TILE COMPANY; LATER, COWAN POTTERY STUDIO

1913–31
Cleveland, Ohio
Founder: R. Guy Cowan

Early in his career, Cowan won many awards, including first prize at the Art Institute of Chicago Arts and Crafts Exhibition in 1917. After World War I, Cowan Pottery produced high-fired porcelain and figurines.

CLIFTON ART POTTERY; LATER, CLIFTON PORCELAIN TILE COMPANY

1905–11
Newark, New Jersey
Founders: Fred Tschirner, William A. Long

The factory was known for two products: Crystal Patina, a pale green glaze over a white body, giving the effect of oxidized bronze, and Clifton Indian ware, unglazed redware, decorated with motifs based on Native American pottery, but with a glazed interior. After 1911, production of art ware was phased out; by 1914, the firm produced only glazed floor tiles. The name was changed to Clifton Porcelain Tile Company.

COOK POTTERY

1897–c. 1926
Trenton, New Jersey
Founders: Charles Howell Cook, W. S. Hancock

It was the first firm to produce Belleek ware in America and reproductions of Dutch faience. About 1906, Cook produced Nippur ware, softly muted pieces based on those found at Nippur, in ancient Babylonia. In addition, the firm produced Metalline ware, featuring metallic glazes.

CRAVEN ART POTTERY

1904–8
East Liverpool, Ohio
Founders: Leonard Forester, Allen Fink, M. A. Sutton, Walter B. Hill, Albert L. Cusick

The firm's best-known ware was matte-glazed earthenware, designed by William P. Jervis and made of Ohio yellow clay.

CROSSWARE POTTERY

1905–c. 1911
Chicago, Illinois
Founders: Nellie Agnes Cross and sons Richard, Jr., and Charles

This pottery showed work at the Art Institute of Chicago Arts and Crafts Exhibition in 1911. Nellie Cross served several times as the president of the National League of Mineral Painters.

DEDHAM POTTERY

1891–1943
Dedham, Massachusetts
Founders: Arthur A. Carey, Hugh Robertson

Dedham Pottery began as Chelsea Pottery, a revitalization of the defunct Chelsea Keramic Art Works. In 1895, the pottery moved to Dedham, Massachusetts, and the name was changed. Hugh Robertson continued his experiments in glazes, and the crackle glaze was synonymous with the work produced at Dedham. All decoration was freehand.

DURANT KILNS

1911–30
Bedford Village, New York
Founder: Mrs. Clarence C. (Jean) Rice

Rice trained under Leon Volkmar, one of the leading ceramists of the period. Together, they produced table and art ware in the style of sixteenth-century Italian enamels. Rice maintained a salesroom in New York City from 1913 to 1918. After her death the following year, Volkmar continued the business, finally purchasing it in 1924.

FLORENTINE POTTERY

1901–19
Chillecothe, Ohio
Founder: W. E. Eberts

The pottery perfected a bronze luster glaze for a line called Effeco, which was shown in 1904 at the Louisiana Purchase International Exposition.

FRACKELTON CHINA AND DECORATING WORKS

1883–1902
Milwaukee, Wisconsin
Founder: Susan Stuart Goodrich Frackelton

Frackelton, a major early figure in the china-painting movement, formed the National League of Mineral Painters, in Chicago, in 1892. She was the author of Tried by Fire (1885), the standard reference of china painters. Frackelton won numerous awards, developed overglaze paints, and was the first to work with salt-glazed stoneware for art pottery.

FULPER POTTERY COMPANY; SUCCEEDED BY STANGL POTTERY

1860–1972
Flemington, New Jersey
Founder: Abra(ha)m Fulper

In 1860, Fulper bought a pottery from Samuel Hill, who had established it in 1814. Fulper died in 1881, and his sons, George W., William H., Charles, and Edward B., continued the operation, incorporating in 1899 as Fulper Pottery Company. In 1909, they introduced Vasekraft art pottery, a series of simple shapes, decorated with a variety of matte and shiny glazes; the most famous of the glazes was Famille Rose, developed by William H. Fulper, Jr. In

1930, Stangl acquired the firm, and changed its name at that time. Although art ware continued to be produced until 1935, emphasis shifted primarily to the production of dinnerware. There are important collections of Fulper pottery at the Newark Museum and at the New Jersey State Museum, in Trenton.

GRAND FEU POTTERY

1912–16
Los Angeles, California
Founder: Cornelius Brauckman

The firm won a gold medal at the Panama-California Exposition, in San Diego, in 1915, and was a participant in the first Los Angeles Annual Arts and Crafts Salon, in 1916. Its white stoneware, *grès-cerame*, was fired at a temperature high enough to fuse the body and the glaze simultaneously. Shapes tended to be classical, without applied or painted decoration, but variegated glazes made each piece unique. Hand-thrown pieces were identified as Grand Feu art pottery; cast pieces were identified as Brauckman art pottery.

GRUEBY FAIENCE COMPANY; LATER, GRUEBY FAIENCE AND TILE COMPANY

1894–1911
Boston, Massachusetts
Founders: William H. Grueby, William H. Graves, George P. Kendrick

The name Grueby is synonymous with green matte-glazed art pottery. Grueby Faience Company was founded, in Boston, in 1894, for the production of architectural ceramics. In 1897, production was expanded to produce art pottery, characterized by simple, thrown shapes and decorated with matte glazes; the green glaze was the most successful. The body of the pottery was quite thick, based on the original architectural ware. In 1909, the company was declared bankrupt, but Grueby immediately started another company, Grueby Faience and Tile Company, in the same factory. He continued to produce art ware until 1911, when the firm again succumbed to financial failure.

HALCYON ART POTTERY

1910–13
Halcyon, California
Founder: Alexander W. Robertson

Halcyon, California, was colonized in 1903 as a utopian settlement by a group of Theosophists that came to call itself the Temple of the People. Incorporating as Temple Home Association, it aimed at social, political, and economic regeneration. The pottery was created in 1910 as a means of income for the association's projects. Local red-burning clays, carved or modeled decoration, and unglazed finishes were characteristic of the pieces.

HAMPSHIRE POTTERY

1871–1923
Keene, New Hampshire
Founders: James Scholly Taft, James Burnap

Hampshire was notable in the late nineteenth century for its production of souvenir ware for tourist sites throughout the United States. Known primarily for redware and stoneware, the firm also experimented with numerous glazes and produced a line of art ware.

JERVIS POTTERY

1908–12
Oyster Bay, New York
Founder: William P. Jervis

Jervis produced primarily utilitarian products, including redware. There was always an emphasis on subdued colors.

LENOX, INCORPORATED

1889–present
Trenton, New Jersey
Founder: Walter Scott Lenox

The Ceramic Art Company, which produced fine porcelain china services for America's tables, was renamed Lenox, Incorporated, in 1906. The company received a major commission from President Woodrow Wilson in 1917 for a china service for the White House, which became the first official American service.

LESSELL ART WARE

1911–12
Parkersburg, West Virginia
Founder: John Lessell

The firm produced ceramics in imitation of copper and bronze.

LINDEROTH CERAMIC COMPANY; LATER, ALHAMBRA CERAMIC WORKS

1898–n.d.
Chicago, Illinois
Founder: Sven Linderoth

Linderoth, a Swedish architect, produced blank pottery shapes for decoration by the prestigious Atlan Ceramic Art Club, of Chicago. The company, which changed its name to Alhambra Ceramic Works in 1907, offered a line of art pottery with intricately carved surfaces.

LOS ANGELES PRESSED BRICK

c. 1887–1926
Los Angeles, California

The company produced high-grade pressed building and fire bricks. In 1906, Frederick H. Robertson, the son of Alexander W. Robertson, of Chelsea Keramic Art Works, was hired. Production of decorative ceramic tiles probably began about 1910. Robertson left in the early 1920s, and the company merged with Gladding McBean in 1926.

J. AND J. G. LOW ART TILE WORKS; LATER, LOW TILE COMPANY

1878–1909
Chelsea, Massachusetts; incorporated in Maine
Founder: John Gardner Low

John Gardner Low, with his father, the Honorable John Low, founded the J. and J. G. Low Tile Works in Chelsea. They were joined by George Robertson, from Chelsea Keramic Art Works, and Arthur Osborne. In 1882, Osborne began designing art pottery, and Robertson oversaw the glazes. During the early years of the twentieth century, in order to generate new capital so that the firm could produce Chelsea ware, it incorporated in Maine under the name Low Tile Company. The new line, based on Japanese pottery, featured a white body and applied glazes, often somber in tone. None of the pottery was marked. Low Tile Company suspended its charter in 1909. The National Museum of American History, of the Smithsonian Institution, and the Brooklyn Museum have major collections of Chelsea pottery.

MARBLEHEAD POTTERY

1904–36
Marblehead, Massachusetts
Founders: Arthur E. Baggs, Dr. Herbert J. Hall

Production, which began as therapy for convalescing patients, was abandoned quickly when the patients were unable to meet production demands that reached two hundred pieces a week. After changing to a professional operation, the pottery mainly produced simple, molded pieces, particularly vases, jardinieres, and lamps.

MARKHAM POTTERY

1905–21
Ann Arbor, Michigan; National City, California
Founders: Herman C. Markham, Kenneth S. Markham

The pottery, after moving from Ann Arbor to National City in 1913, became famous for its textured glazes and won a gold medal at the Panama-Pacific International Exposition in 1915. Each piece created was a unique work of art that was numbered sequentially.

J. W. McCOY POTTERY

1899–1925
Roseville, Ohio; Zanesville, Ohio
Founder: James W. McCoy

McCoy, who came from four generations of potters in Ohio, first produced utilitarian ware, then art lines such as Mont Pelee, Loy-Nel-Art, Venetian, and Green Woodland. In 1925, the name changed to Brush Pottery.

MERRIMAC POTTERY

1897–1908
Newburyport, Massachusetts
Founders: Thomas S. Nickerson, W. G. Fisher

The pottery began with the production of inexpensive ware for florists. In 1898, when Fisher joined the firm, the emphasis shifted to art ware. Its most famous product was Arrhelian ware, begun in 1903; it imitated Arretine redware, which was produced throughout the Roman Empire in its early years. Forms of the pottery were based on original molds owned by the Museum of Fine Arts, Boston.

MIDDLE LANE POTTERY; LATER, BROUWER POTTERY

1894–1911
East Hampton, New York; Westhampton, New York
Founder: Theophilus Anthony Brouwer, Jr.

Although Brouwer had no formal training in ceramics, he developed a highly refined series of glazes and produced all of the pieces himself. By 1900, at his pottery on Middle Lane, in East Hampton, Brouwer was producing a series of ware that he called "fire painting," in which glazes of various colors interacted on the surface of the pottery, and Gold Leaf underglaze, which combined the glazes with layers of pure gold. In 1902, he moved to Westhampton, changed the name to Brouwer Pottery, and produced Flame Ware, using a combination of various techniques and glazes.

MORAVIAN POTTERY AND TILE WORKS

1899–1964
Doylestown, Pennsylvania
Founder: Henry Chapman Mercer

Mercer tried to produce work in direct imitation of eighteenth-century ware, but his experiments were unsuccessful. He then turned to architectural tiles. Popular and in demand in Arts and Crafts interiors, Mercer designed these tiles so that they could be combined into large friezes. The subjects that inspired him included nature, the Bible, and historical figures. Mercer created the process for

manufacturing his architectural tiles, and he also produced some art pottery.

G. E. MORIN STUDIO

1897–1911
Los Angeles, California
Founder: G. E. Morin

A teacher of china painting, Morin also sold her own work.

NIELSON POTTERY

1905–8
Zanesville, Ohio
Founder: Christian Nielson

A maker of stoneware and majolica art pottery.

NILOAK POTTERY

1909–42
Benton, Arkansas
Founder: Charles Dean Hyten

Kaolin, a fine white clay used in the manufacture of porcelain, was spelled backward, and Niloak became the name of the pottery, which was founded to make art ware. Different colored Arkansas clays were swirled into pot shapes on the wheel. Originally, it was called Mission pottery.

NORSE POTTERY

1903–13
Edgerton, Wisconsin; Rockford, Illinois
Founders: Thorwald P. A. Samson, Louis Ipson

Norse produced art pottery designed after bronze Scandinavian relics, with a dull metallic glaze.

NORTHWESTERN TERRA COTTA COMPANY

Late 1870s–1956
Chicago, Illinois
Founders: Employees of the Chicago Terra Cotta Company

The firm, founded by the employees of the Chicago Terra Cotta Company in the late 1870s, and then incorporated in 1888, produced architectural terra-cotta. By 1927, it had become the largest such manufacturer in the United States, furnishing terra-cotta facades for many important Chicago buildings. It also produced the art-pottery line Norweta.

OAKWOOD POTTERY

1877–1926
Dayton, Ohio
Founders: Bernard Goetz and sons Isidore and Louis

The Goetzes made earthenware and stoneware and, occasionally, art ware. In 1904, the firm sent a piece of matte-green pottery to the Louisiana Purchase International Exposition.

OMAR KHAYYAM POTTERY

c. 1914
Candler, North Carolina
Founder: Oscar Louis Bachelder

Bachelder was one of the first North Carolina folk potters to achieve a national reputation as an art potter in the utilitarian tradition. He worked forty years, in twenty-eight states and territories, but became known for his North Carolina shop, which produced Albany slip ware.

OVERBECK POTTERY

1911–55
Cambridge City, Indiana
Founders: Mary Frances, Margaret, Hannah, and Elizabeth Overbeck

A small family pottery, it produced unusual incised inlaid art ware with specially developed glaze colors.

J. B. OWENS POTTERY COMPANY; ZANESVILLE TILE COMPANY

1885–c. 1907
Roseville, Ohio; Zanesville, Ohio
Founder: J. B. Owens

Owens made art pottery between 1886 and 1906, creating a rivalry among the three most notable Zanesville potteries: Owens, Weller, and Roseville. Owens produced slip-painted underglaze art ware, examples of which were Utopian, Lotus, Alpine, Henri Deux, and Corona, among others. In 1905, Owens expanded into tile, calling this part of the company the Zanesville Tile Company.

JOHN PATTERSON AND SONS POTTERY COMPANY; LATER, PATTERSON BROTHERS COMPANY

1882–1971
Wellsville, Ohio
Founder: John Patterson

Started as John Patterson and Sons Pottery Company in 1882, it reorganized in 1900 as the Patterson Brothers Company and produced underglaze decorated art ware, designated as Oakwood Art Pottery in ads.

PAUL REVERE POTTERY

1908–42
Boston, Massachusetts; Brighton, Massachusetts
Founders: Edith Guerrier, Edith Brown, Mrs. James Storrow

An outgrowth of the Saturday Evening Girls' Club, a Boston association for the education of immigrants, it produced tableware, lamps, vases, bookends, and inkwells. Popular objects produced were children's breakfast sets and a series of thirteen tiles representing Paul

Revere's historic ride. In 1915, the factory moved to Brighton.

PAULINE POTTERY

1882–1909
Chicago, Illinois; Edgerton, Wisconsin
Founder: Pauline Bogart Jacobus

Jacobus founded one of the first art potteries in Chicago, but moved to Edgerton in 1888 to be closer to a clay source. She produced earthenware majolica, and showed her work at the Louisiana Purchase International Exposition in 1904.

PETERS AND REED POTTERY

1898–1921
South Zanesville, Ohio
Founders: John D. Peters, Adam Reed

It produced red earthenware flowerpots and occasional art lines, such as Moss Aztec, Pereco, Sandsun, Chromal, and Persian. In 1921, the name changed to Zane Pottery Company.

PEWABIC POTTERY

1903–present
Detroit, Michigan
Founders: Mary Chase Perry (Stratton), Horace James Caulkins

Pewabic was an important art pottery that became famous for its tile work for churches and museums. It also produced iridescent and luster-glazed pottery designed by Perry.

PICKARD CHINA STUDIO; LATER, PICKARD, INC.

1898–n.d.
Chicago, Illinois; Antioch, Illinois
Founder: Wilder A. Pickard

Pickard tried to create a social environment, based upon William Morris's workshops, for his china-painting firm. Employing as many as fifty artists, by 1908 Pickard china was carried by more than one thousand of the most prestigious retail outlets.

POILLON POTTERY

1901–28
Woodbridge, New Jersey
Founders: Mrs. Cornelius Poillon, Mrs. Howard A. Poillon

Producing art ware made of earthenware with matte and gloss glazes, the pottery first exhibited at the New York Society of Keramic Art, in December 1901.

REDLANDS POTTERY

c. 1904–9
Redlands, California
Founder: Wesley H. Trippett

The self-trained Trippett began production of tiles and pots using local red and white earthenware clays. He often employed a burnished bisque finish and decorated his ware with molded local flora and fauna.

REVELATION KILNS

1892–1969
Detroit, Michigan
Founder: Horace James Caulkins

This company produced some of the modern overglaze china-decorating kilns and pottery kilns used throughout the country. Caulkins began a business partnership with Mary Chase Perry (Stratton) in 1903, which became Pewabic Pottery later that year.

RHEAD POTTERY

1914–17
Santa Barbara, California
Founder: Frederick Hurten Rhead

Rhead founded his own pottery, originally called Camarata Pottery. Ware included large pots for garden ornaments as well as smaller pieces. Rhead concentrated on design and decoration, using inlaid patterns, and developed a mirror-black glaze that imitated ancient Chinese ware.

ROBINEAU POTTERY

1904–16
Syracuse, New York
Founder: Adelaide Alsop Robineau

Robineau produced a small but very sophisticated body of porcelain, remarkable for its matte finishes and intricate, carved effects. She showed her work at the Louisiana Purchase International Exposition in 1904. The Newark Museum began collecting Robineau's work in 1914. She was also active as a teacher and a writer. In 1899, she founded the important journal *Keramic Studio*.

ROBLIN ART POTTERY

c. 1898–1906
San Francisco, California
Founder: Alexander W. Robertson

The pottery used California materials for its clay, slip, and glaze. Robertson was responsible for potting and firing; his usual ornamentation included fine handles and feet, beading, and a high-quality, high-gloss glaze. His associate, Linna Irelan, executed modeled decoration of plants and animals.

ROOKWOOD POTTERY

1880–1967
Cincinnati, Ohio
Founder: Maria Longworth Nichols (Storer)

Rookwood was one of the most successful and famous art potteries, producing Cincinnati faience and employing many famous potters and designers. It won numerous awards and introduced many new techniques and glazes, such as its Standard, Sea Green, and Vellum.

ROSEVILLE POTTERY COMPANY

1890–1954
Roseville, Ohio; Zanesville, Ohio
Founder: George F. Young

Roseville was one of the competitive "big three" potteries in Zanesville, rivaling Weller and Owens. It won a number of awards at expositions. Its art-pottery lines included Rozane, Cornelian I and II, Donatello, and Pine Cone.

SHAWSHEEN POTTERY

1906–c. 1911
Billerica, Massachusetts; Mason City, Iowa
Founders: Edward and Elizabeth Burnap Dahlquist, Gertrude Singleton Mathews

Recalling Etruscan pottery and bronzes, early Shawsheen vessels were hand-coiled, patterned with geometric decoration, and fired to a warm black color with tones of bronze and copper. The Dahlquists moved the pottery to Mason City, Iowa, in 1907. Edward taught at the Memorial University until 1909 or 1910, and both he and Elizabeth gave ceramics classes at the pottery and in their home. While in Iowa, much of the pottery's work was done by students, and most of the pieces were wheel-thrown. The pottery did not continue after the Dahlquists moved to Chicago in 1911, but Elizabeth continued to produce pottery for the HoHo Shop, which she opened in 1915.

NELLIE SHELDON

1903–8
Los Angeles, California
Founder: Nellie Sheldon

Sheldon was a ceramist and china painter trained at the Art Institute of Chicago. She maintained a studio in Los Angeles before moving to Iowa in 1908.

TIFFANY POTTERY

1904–17
Corona, New York
Founder: Louis Comfort Tiffany

Although not the main emphasis of Tiffany's artistic endeavors, pottery was produced as part of his exploration of every form of art. Experiments with ceramics began at the Tiffany Furnaces, and the first examples were shown at both the Louisiana Purchase International Exposition and the New York Society of Keramic Art in 1904. The first commercial offerings were made in 1905, when Tiffany's father, Charles Lewis Tiffany, opened the Tiffany & Company store on New York City's Fifth Avenue.

TRENTVALE POTTERY

1901–2
East Liverpool, Ohio

This short-lived pottery produced art ware similar to Rookwood's Standard.

C. B. UPJOHN POTTERY

1904–5
Zanesville, Ohio
Founder: Charles Babcock Upjohn

Upjohn's new two-kiln plant produced art pottery for less than a year. The company had been undercapitalized and was sold to other Zanesville interests.

VALENTIEN POTTERY

c. 1911–13
San Diego, California
Founders: Albert and Anna Marie Valentien

The Valentiens opened their pottery in buildings designed by Irving John Gill. Arthur Dovey, a former Rookwood employee, assisted them. The pottery was known for energetic, low-relief modeling executed in earthenware with a matte glaze, and ornamented by figures emerging from the vases.

VAN BRIGGLE POTTERY COMPANY

1902–present
Colorado Springs, Colorado
Founder: Artus Van Briggle

The pottery manufactured earthenware covered with semimatte glazes. Definitive molded forms were often embellished with molded decoration in simple, strong floral patterns. The potter's wife, Anne Gregory Van Briggle, carried on after his death, in 1904. The company passed into other hands in 1912, and it continues today.

VANCE FAIENCE COMPANY; LATER, AVON FAIENCE COMPANY; LATER, WHEELING POTTERIES COMPANY

1900–1902; 1902; December 1902–8
Tiltonville, Ohio; Wheeling, West Virginia
Founders: J. Nelson Vance, J. D. Culbertson, Charles W. Franzheim

In 1900, Vance Faience Company was incorporated by several West Virginia businessmen with the intention of making it a large manufacturer of high-grade art ware. By 1902, when the name was changed to Avon Faience Company, William P. Jervis was named manager, and the pottery began producing Art Nouveau–inspired pieces. Later that year, Avon was absorbed by the Wheeling Potteries Company and continued as a department of the Wheeling firm at the Tiltonville, Ohio, plant, until all art-

work production ceased in 1905. Wheeling Potteries continued for another three years, when it went into receivership in late 1908.

VOLKMAR KILNS

1903–11
Metuchen, New Jersey
Founders: Charles Volkmar, Leon Volkmar

Father and son, Charles and Leon Volkmar were important teachers of pottery. They produced art ware primarily, and tiles and panels particularly, and were known for their simple Oriental forms and monochrome glazes.

A. M. WAGNER STUDIO

1892–1912
Los Angeles, California
Founder: A. M. Wagner

Wagner painted fine china and porcelain. She won a prize at the California State Fair, in Sacramento, in 1900.

WALRATH POTTERY

1908–18
Rochester, New York
Founder: Frederick E. Walrath

Trained by Charles Fergus Binns, Walrath had a teaching position at the Mechanics Institute, in Rochester, New York, where he used the school's ceramics studio to produce his own restrained and stylized work. He received a bronze medal at the Louisiana Purchase International Exposition in 1904.

WELLER POTTERY

1882–1948
Zanesville, Ohio
Founder: Samuel A. Weller

A huge pottery, it achieved a near monopoly of the mass-produced art-pottery market with its Louwelsa Weller line. It attracted French ceramist Jacques Sicard, who invented Sicardo lusterware.

WHEATLEY POTTERY COMPANY

1903–27
Cincinnati, Ohio
Founders: T. J. Wheatley, Isaac Kahn

The company produced the art-line Wheatley Ware. It attempted to patent the Limoges method of slip decoration discovered by Mary Louise McLaughlin, but the patent did not withstand a court test.

WHITE PINES POTTERY

1915–35
Woodstock, New York
Founder: Ralph Radcliffe Whitehead

Whitehead founded the Byrdcliffe Colony. After he left, he and his wife,

Jane, produced cast and glazed work, exhibiting their pottery throughout the United States.

HUGO EBERHARDT AND COMPANY

1891–mid-1950s
Chicago, Illinois
Founder: Hugo Eberhardt

Manufacturers of stained glass.

FLANAGAN AND BIEDENWEG COMPANY

1885–1953
Chicago, Illinois
Founders: Joseph E. Flanagan, William E. Biedenweg

By 1900, this firm was the largest Chicago maker of art glass for residences and churches.

GIANNINI AND HILGART

1889–n.d.
Chicago, Illinois
Founders: Orlando Giannini, Fritz Hilgart

This firm specialized in art glass and mosaics during its earliest years. It also executed glass for Frank Lloyd Wright and leaded-glass lamp shades for Teco Ware bases.

LINDEN GLASS COMPANY; LATER, THE LINDEN COMPANY

1882–1909; 1910–34
Chicago, Illinois
Founders: Frank L. Linden, Ernest J. Spierling

Excelling in fresco painting and stained glass, the company was famous for the stained-glass work in Frank Lloyd Wright's Dana House.

THE PIKE STAINED GLASS STUDIOS

1909–n.d.
Rochester, New York
Founder: William J. Pike

Pike apprenticed with Louis Comfort Tiffany before establishing his own firm in 1909. He produced both secular and religious designs and executed commissions for Ralph Adams Cram. He lectured extensively on medieval methods of stained-glass production.

QUEZAL ART GLASS AND DECORATING COMPANY

1901–25
Brooklyn, New York
Founders: Martin Bache, Thomas Johnson, Percy Britton, William Weidebine

Working for Louis Comfort Tiffany as a glass mixer, Bache knew the secret Tiffany glass formula. Johnson, trained as a glassblower, had also worked for Tiffany. Their work imitated Tiffany's glass.

STEUBEN GLASS WORKS; LATER, STEUBEN DIVISION OF CORNING GLASS WORKS

1903–present
Corning, New York
Founders: Frederick Carder, Thomas G. Hawkes, Samuel Hawkes, Townsend Hawkes

In 1903, Frederick Carder, an English glassmaker, came to Corning, New York, to work with Thomas G. Hawkes, president of T. G. Hawkes and Company, a factory noted for its cut and engraved glass. Willing to arrange for most of the financial backing, Hawkes offered Carder the opportunity of establishing his own glass factory to produce the blanks upon which glass artisans then decorated. This was the beginning of Steuben. In 1918, the Corning Glass Works purchased Steuben and adapted its facilities to emergency war use. The Steuben Division of Corning Glass Works was formed, and at the end of the war, it reverted to its peacetime activity of manufacturing art glass.

Carder developed a gold metallic luster glass, which he patented as Aurene. This glass was an immediate success, and he soon brought out its counterpart, Blue Aurene. Gold and Blue Aurene were made between 1904 and 1930. It was the spray of chemical salts dissolving under heat that gave the glass a soft, lustrous surface. When Carder retired, in 1932, the Steuben Division was reorganized under the direction of Arthur A. Houghton, Jr.

STURDY-LANGE STUDIOS

c. 1905–15
Los Angeles, California
Founders: Emil Lange, Harry Sturdy

The firm manufactured architectural and decorative stained glass. Its leaded glass appeared in lighting fixtures, doors, and windows. Lange was hired by architects Greene and Greene for the H. M. Robinson House and other commissions. He trained at Tiffany Studios, in New York, and often worked with Tiffany glass.

TEMPLE ART GLASS COMPANY

1903–33
Chicago, Illinois
Founder: Henry J. Nerthart

The company manufactured art glass for Frank Lloyd Wright's Harvey P. Sutton House and Francis W. Little House.

TIFFANY GLASS COMPANY; LATER, TIFFANY GLASS AND DECORATING COMPANY; LATER, TIFFANY STUDIOS; STOURBRIDGE GLASS COMPANY; LATER, TIFFANY FURNACES

1885–1938
Corona, New York
Founder: Louis Comfort Tiffany

Reorganizing the interior decorating firm that he founded in 1879, Louis C. Tiffany and Associated Artists, Tiffany established the Tiffany Glass Company, in Corona, New York, in 1885, to accommodate his expanding glass business. In 1892, this enterprise was renamed Tiffany Glass and Decorating Company. Arthur J. Nash, a glass innovator from England, joined Tiffany in opening a glassworks, the Stourbridge Glass Company, in 1893, with Nash as operations manager of the shops. In 1902, these companies were reorganized into two basic concerns: Tiffany Studios, which manufactured a variety of products in addition to stained glass and lamps, and Tiffany Furnaces, which primarily produced blown glass in the form of glassware and the iridescent art glass known as Favrile (meaning handmade). Tiffany retired in 1919, although he continued as a financial partner. After Tiffany Studios declared bankruptcy in 1932, the business in the various Tiffany shops continued marginally until 1938.

METALS

APOLLO STUDIOS

c. 1909–25
New York, New York
Founder: Apollo Silver Company

Apollo produced metalworking kits for brass, copper, and jewelry.

ART CRAFTS SHOP; LATER, HEINTZ ART METAL SHOP

c. 1900–1930
Buffalo, New York
Founders: Otto L. Heintz, Edwin A. Heintz

The Heintz brothers joined a flourishing jewelry business around the turn of the century, which, by 1906, was known as the Heintz Art Metal Shop. It developed a reputation for handcrafted copper or bronze bowls, vases, lamps, desk sets, trophies, and picture frames as well as gold and silver jewelry. Production continued until the early years of the Depression.

ART METAL COMPANY

c. 1905–15
Los Angeles, California

The company worked on commissions from architects Charles and Henry Greene. In 1914, it made the bronze fire screen for the Robert R. Blacker House.

JOHN O. BELLIS

c. 1906–40
San Francisco, California
Founder: John O. Bellis

Bellis, a silversmith, trained at Shreve and Company. He created medieval revival designs with obvious hammer marks, rivets, and banded borders resembling the Shreve medieval line.

CARENCE CRAFTERS

Early 20th century
Chicago, Illinois

A little-known metal workshop, identifiable with Chicago Arts and Crafts, Carence produced copper, brass, and silver vessels acid-etched in naturalistic designs.

THE CELLINI SHOP

c. 1914–69
Evanston, Illinois
Founder: Ernest Gerlach

Gerlach, a maker of copper bowls before 1920, was also a seller of other artists' work, including jewelry and silver flatware.

CLEWELL METAL ART

c. 1900–c. 1942
Canton, Ohio
Founder: Charles W. Clewell

Clewell was a metalworker who experimented with bronze and silver coatings on pottery, producing objects inspired by Roman bronzes. He was named a Master craftsman by the Boston Society of Arts and Crafts.

THE COPPER SHOP; LATER, DIRK VAN ERP STUDIOS

1908–c. 1977
Oakland, California; San Francisco, California
Founder: Dirk Van Erp

Van Erp opened the Copper Shop, in Oakland, in 1908, and moved it to San Francisco two years later. Elizabeth Eleanor D'Arcy Gaw was a partner and designer from 1910 to 1911; Thomas McGlynn and Edna Hall also designed for the shop. Van Erp's children, Agatha and William, were among its crafters. Van Erp retired in 1929, but William maintained the operation until at least 1944, under the name of Dirk Van Erp Studios. The shop was known for quality work in copper lamps, with strong lines and subdued naturalistic forms, often with coated isinglass for the shades.

THE COPPER SHOP OF THE ROYCROFTERS

1903–38
East Aurora, New York
Founder: Elbert G. Hubbard

Hubbard established the Copper Shop to produce metal hinges for his furniture. Between 1908 and 1911, the work was directed by Karl E. Kipp, who left to form the Tookay Shop.

FORVE, PETTEBONE COMPANY

c. 1905–10
Los Angeles, California

The firm designed and manufactured art metalwork and gas and electric lighting fixtures. Many of its chandeliers were used in houses designed by J. J. Blick.

GORHAM MANUFACTURING COMPANY

1831–present
Providence, Rhode Island
Founder: Jabez Gorham

An important presence in American silver for several decades, Gorham began producing a new line of handmade silver in 1896. It was first shown publicly the following year at the Waldorf-Astoria Hotel, in New York City, and at the Boston Society of Arts and Crafts exhibition. William Codman and Edward Holbrook were responsible for the line, named Martelé, which ranged from small toilet articles to furniture. The two men provided the craftsmen with rough sketches, which they were encouraged to interpret, making the silver the product of a union between designer and craftsman. Pieces were in the Art Nouveau style and retained hammer marks to show that they were handmade. Martelé production ended in 1912, with special orders taken until 1920, or thereabouts.

GRAND RAPIDS ARTS AND CRAFTS SHOP

1907–n.d.
Grand Rapids, Michigan

This shop manufactured handwrought metalwork.

THE HANDICRAFT SHOP

1901–c. 1940
Boston, Massachusetts; Wellesley Hills, Massachusetts
Founders: Arthur A. Carey, Frederic Allen Whiting, Mary Ware Dennett, Mary Catherine Knight

Founded as an offshoot of the Boston Society of Arts and Crafts, the Handicraft Shop began operation as a workshop for wood-, leather-, and metalworking. By 1906, it produced metalwork exclusively, particularly in silver. A collaboration between several silversmiths, many of its products were based upon American colonial prototypes.

THE JARVIE SHOP

1890s–1920
Chicago, Illinois
Founder: Robert R. Jarvie

A prominent metalsmith interested in interior illumination, Jarvie created candlesticks and lanterns, as well as copper bowls. By 1906, he had outlets for his candlesticks in more than ten states. By 1910, he was considered a major silversmith of trophies.

THE KALO SHOP

1900–1970
Chicago, Illinois
Founder: Clara Barck Welles

This workshop became Chicago's largest producer of handwrought silverware, serving generations of customers. Clara Barck began an all-female venture that produced weaving and leather goods but switched to silversmithing when she married George Welles. Their trademark designs were rounded, organic curves.

LEBOLT AND COMPANY

1899–present
Chicago, Illinois
Founder: J. Myer Lebolt

In 1912, this metal shop developed a series of distinctive hand-hammered tea and coffee services and flatware patterns in Arts and Crafts styles. It later expanded, opening retail outlets in Paris, New York, Chicago, and Milwaukee.

MARCUS & COMPANY

1878–present
New York, New York
Founder: William Marcus

Marcus & Company was one of New York's two great jewelry firms at the turn of the century, the other being Tiffany & Company. The firm was founded by William Marcus, the son of Herman Marcus, a German immigrant, who was employed by Tiffany & Company after he arrived in New York in 1850. One of the few American firms to produce silver inspired by the progressive designs of C. R. Ashbee for his Guild of Handicraft, Marcus & Company became well known for the jewelry designs of Marcus's second son, George E. Marcus, which were shown at the initial exhibitions of the Boston Society of Arts and Crafts, in 1897 and 1899. The company achieved an international reputation and is still active today.

MARSHALL FIELD AND COMPANY CRAFT SHOP AND CRAFTSMAN SHOWROOM

1902–c. 1950
Chicago, Illinois
Founder: Marshall Field

In 1902, the department store opened a special showroom for Stickley Mission furniture. Two years later, it changed its silverware and jewelry department into a workshop on the tenth floor, to combine hand craftwork with machinery to produce Arts and Crafts metalwork for a mass public. It made silver flatware, trays, plates, and jewelry.

METAL OFFICE FURNITURE COMPANY; LATER, STEELCASE

1912–present
Grand Rapids, Michigan
Founder: Peter Wege, Sr.

Wege, who invented a method of bending steel to make furniture, became well known for his rolltop desks. Frank Lloyd Wright designed special metal office furniture that was executed by Steelcase.

JAMES A. MILLER AND BROTHER

1874–n.d.
Chicago, Illinois
Founder: James A. Miller

A roofer of slate, tin, and iron, Miller also executed copper bowls and vases for Frank Lloyd Wright.

PALMER COPPER SHOP

c. 1910–18
San Francisco, California
Founder: Lillian MacNeill Palmer

The shop adapted Asian vases into lamps and made objects incorporating handpainted wire mesh. Harry Saint John Dixon joined Palmer as a metalworker from 1912 to 1918, after leaving Dirk Van Erp's workshop.

THE POTTER STUDIO

1915–21
Cleveland, Ohio

This studio designed and produced art jewelry, showing at the Art Institute of Chicago Arts and Crafts exhibitions in 1916, 1919, and 1921.

ROKESLEY SHOP

c. 1913–14
Cleveland, Ohio
Founders: Carolyn Hadlow Vinson, Ruth Smedley, Mary Blakeslee

This shop, which produced metalwork and jewelry, exhibited at the Art Institute of Chicago Arts and Crafts exhibitions in 1913 and 1914.

SHREVE AND COMPANY

1852–present
San Francisco, California
Founder: George R. Shreve

Shreve and Company, founded in 1852 as a jewelry store, established itself as a leading silver manufacturer after 1883. The fully mechanized company, which produced a large variety of ware, was especially noted for a line of silver developed by George R. Shreve and characterized by hand-hammered surfaces added to machine cutout designs. In the late 1890s, the company introduced its most distinctive craftsman line, evoking medieval hardware with applied strapwork and simulated rivets suggestive of preindustrial metalwork. Although the ornament, now commonly called "Shreve Strap," was purely decorative, it suggested a constructional purpose that reflected the design philosophy of the Arts and Crafts movement and was an effective compromise between craft and assembly-line techniques. Still active today, the original Shreve factory was destroyed in the San Francisco earthquake of 1906.

TIFFANY & COMPANY

1837–present
New York, New York
Founder: Charles Lewis Tiffany

This leading silver company was started in 1837 when Charles Lewis Tiffany and John B. Young opened a stationery store in New York City. They began to manufacture silver after 1868 when they acquired the shop and silverware of Edward C. Moore, who exerted a major influence on Tiffany throughout the nineteenth century. The firm, which developed an international reputation as a gem dealer, exhibited at expositions and featured the world renowned "Tiffany setting" for diamond solitaires. Tiffany was one of the first companies to use Native American materials, designs, and themes.

THE TOOKAY SHOP

1911–15
East Aurora, New York
Founder: Karl E. Kipp

After training with Elbert Hubbard at Roycroft, Kipp left and formed his own shop, where he produced designs reminiscent of the Vienna Secession. Eventually, he returned to Roycroft.

TRE'O SHOP

1908–15
Evanston, Illinois
Founders: Hope McMaster, Margery Woodworth, Clara C. Finn

Three graduates of the School of the Art Institute of Chicago, they produced handwrought metal objects and showed at the Art Institute Arts and Crafts exhibitions from 1908 to 1915.

THE VAN DORN IRONWORKS

1872–n.d.
Cleveland, Ohio
Founder: James H. Van Dorn

Beginning as an individual metalworker, Van Dorn turned his company into one of the largest firms in Ohio making ornamental ironwork. He manufactured Frank Lloyd Wright's metal office furniture designs for the Larkin Administration Building, in Buffalo, New York.

THE VOLUND SHOP

1914–15
Park Ridge, Illinois
Founders: Grant Wood, Kristopher Haga

Wood and Norwegian silversmith Haga produced handmade silver and gold jewelry. They exhibited at the Art Institute of Chicago Arts and Crafts Exhibition in 1914. Wood then went to Iowa, where he later established his reputation as a painter, and Haga to the Kalo Shop, in Chicago.

WINSLOW BROTHERS COMPANY

1887–1921
Chicago, Illinois
Founder: William Herman Winslow

Winslow, an inventor, developed bronze- and iron-casting processes and invented the Winslow window, a pioneering variety of movable sash. He executed ironwork for Frank Lloyd Wright and other Prairie School architects.

‖ TEXTILES ‖

ABNAKEE RUG INDUSTRY

1897–n.d.
Pequahet, New Hampshire
Founder: Helen R. Albee

Albee initiated a program for local women to produce hooked rugs. She produced *Mountain Playmates*, a tract on her work.

CHENEY BROTHERS

1838–1955
Manchester, Connecticut; Hartford, Connecticut
Founders: Ralph Cheney, Ward Cheney, Rush Cheney, Frank Cheney

By the end of the nineteenth century, the firm was America's leading maker of decorative silk. It produced designs

by Candace Wheeler and Associated Artists.

GROSVENOR STUDIO

c. 1900–1910
Los Angeles, California
Founder: Fredrika Grosvenor

Grosvenor was a tapestry artist.

HANDICRAFT SHOP FOR ITALIAN NEEDLECRAFTS

1917–n.d.
Philadelphia, Pennsylvania
Founder: Katharine Davis

The shop was one of several that sought to perpetuate the traditions of Italian lacemaking by employing immigrant women.

LOULIE HIGGINS

1913–17
Columbus, Georgia
Founder: Loulie Higgins

Higgins was a frequent exhibitor at the Art Institute of Chicago Arts and Crafts exhibitions, showing not only her embroidery and fiberwork but that of others.

STEARNS AND FOSTER COMPANY; LATER, STEARNS TECHNICAL TEXTILES COMPANY

1846–n.d.
Cincinnati, Ohio; Cleveland, Ohio
Founders: George Stearns, Seth Foster

This company, run by the husbands of quilters, produced special batting for quiltmakers and published how-to books on quiltmaking.

THREAD AND THRUM WORKSHOP

c. 1905, Hyannis, Massachusetts
c. 1909, Auburn, New York

The workshop manufactured woolen and camel's-hair rugs designed to blend with Arts and Crafts furniture.

H. E. VARREN COMPANY

c. 1900

A large wholesaler of needlework kits, Varren produced thread for embroidery, sewing, and knitting. It was the manufacturer of Royal Society trademark products and a supplier to the Valley Supply Company, a mail-order firm offering textile kits.

‖ WOOD ‖

JOHN W. AYERS COMPANY

1887–1913
Chicago, Illinois

Founder: John W. Ayers

This company executed furniture designed by Frank Lloyd Wright in the early 1900s for the B. Harley Bradley House, the Warren Hickox House, and the Frank L. Smith bank.

F. H. BRESLER COMPANY

1900–n.d.
Milwaukee, Wisconsin
Founder: Frank H. Bresler

Bresler was hired by the Niedecken-Walbridge design firm to execute furniture for two Frank Lloyd Wright projects, the Avery Coonley and Frederick Robie houses.

THE FURNITURE SHOP

1906–20
San Francisco, California
Founders: Lucia and Arthur Mathews

The shop created furniture and decorative objects in a variety of styles. Arthur and his assistant Thomas A. McGlynn designed most of the pieces, while Lucia assisted with design, supervised the carving and coloring of many pieces, and carved and colored her own pieces. The firm was known for its richly painted and gilded work and its flat floral and fruit panel decorations, displaying California's bounty. At the height of their production, more than twenty workers assisted the Mathewses.

FURNITURE SHOP OF THE ROYCROFTERS

1893–1938
East Aurora, New York
Founder: Elbert G. Hubbard

The first furniture produced at Roycroft was for the Roycroft Inn. Furniture, copper accessories, lamps, and leather bookends were available by mail order by 1909. Roycroft was both a school and a factory. Hubbard was a very successful businessman.

PETER HALL MANUFACTURING COMPANY

c. 1905–10
Pasadena, California
Founders: John Hall, Peter Hall

Architects Charles and Henry Greene, admiring the firm's renovation work, helped the Halls set up their own shop. It executed commissions for furniture and woodwork for the Greenes from 1905 through the period of Greene and Greene's most significant projects.

INDIAN SPLINT MANUFACTURING COMPANY

1909–13
Geneva, New York

The company produced Arts and Crafts furniture as well as furniture and paneling made of splint wood, in emulation of Native American handicrafts.

JOHN FURNITURE

1866–1944
New Braunfels, Texas
Founder: Johan Michael John

A German immigrant cabinetmaker who made beautifully crafted walnut furniture, John also assembled furniture pieces from other factories.

CHARLES P. LIMBERT AND COMPANY

1894–1944
Grand Rapids, Michigan
Founder: Charles P. Limbert

Undaunted after the dissolution of the Limbert and Klingman Chair Company in 1892, two years later Limbert launched Charles P. Limbert and Company, which initially produced furniture combining Art Nouveau and the rectilinear Arts and Crafts style. Limbert named his line Dutch Arts and Crafts. From 1902, notable works were executed in ash with bolted construction. Later works, including lines made of oak with ebony inlays, were produced in Holland, Michigan, as the company expanded. After his death, in 1923, the company continued its operations until 1944.

MATTHEWS BROTHERS FURNITURE COMPANY

1857–1937
Milwaukee, Wisconsin
Founders: Eschines P. Matthews, Alonzo R. Matthews

Frank Lloyd Wright hired the firm to make furniture for the Darwin D. Martin House. Matthews Brothers became one of the largest furniture manufacturers in the Midwest. Items were made to order, mostly by hand.

JOSEPH P. McHUGH AND COMPANY

1884–c. 1920
New York, New York
Founder: Joseph P. McHugh

Although several other designers are credited with furniture designs that came to be known as the Mission style, McHugh was probably the first to market the furniture on a broad scale. The company maintained a group of retail outlets known as the Popular Shop. One, located at Forty-second Street and Fifth Avenue, in New York City, sold products from Liberty of London, Morris chintzes, and McHugh's Mission furniture.

MICHIGAN CHAIR COMPANY

1893–n.d.
Grand Rapids, Michigan

This company, which produced Arts and Crafts furniture as early as 1898, attracted many innovative designers. It eventually became a major manufacturer, with fifteen hundred designs.

CARL ENOS NASH COMPANY

c. 1900–1910
Los Angeles, California
Founders: J. D. Nash, C. E. Nash

The firm manufactured fine furniture, mantels, and interior woodwork. It also sold ceramic tiles, often employed in houses designed by J. J. Blick.

OLD HICKORY CHAIR COMPANY

1898–1940
Martinsville, Indiana
Founder: Edmund Llewellyn Brown

This was the first and most important of the Indiana factories producing hickory furniture chairs, rockers, and settees that were sent by the thousands to warm-weather houses in the Adirondacks. Brown received a patent for his bark-splitting machine.

THE QUISIANA WORKSHOP

1902–n.d.
La Porte, Indiana
Founder: Industrial Art League of Chicago

This cooperative, organized along the lines of a medieval craft guild, produced Arts and Crafts furniture.

CHARLES ROHLFS WORKSHOP

1898–1928
Buffalo, New York
Founder: Charles Rohlfs

In the Arts and Crafts tradition, with ornament inspired by China, Art Nouveau, and the Middle Ages, Rohlfs made custom furniture based upon standardized models. His business was extremely successful; Marshall Field mounted an exhibition in 1900. The furniture was also very popular in Europe; Rohlfs made a suite of furniture for Buckingham Palace.

RUSTIC HICKORY FURNITURE COMPANY

1902–33
La Porte, Indiana
Founder: E. H. Handley

A competitor of the Old Hickory Chair Company, this was one of the firms making Adirondack furniture for the eastern United States.

THE SHOP OF THE CRAFTERS

1904–19
Cincinnati, Ohio
Founder: Oscar Onken

Onken was a prominent businessman who was introduced to the Arts and Crafts influence at the Louisiana Purchase International Exposition in 1904. His shop produced handmade furniture of oak and leather with metal fittings. The finest work was designed by Paul Horti.

STICKLEY BROTHERS COMPANY

1891–1940
Grand Rapids, Michigan
Founders: Albert Stickley, John George Stickley

Albert and John George split from their famous brother, Gustav, to form this company. Specializing in Arts and Crafts and Art Nouveau designs, it was one of the first American furniture companies to open salesrooms in Europe. It also produced a line of lighting fixtures.

L. AND J. G. STICKLEY

1902–present
Fayetteville, New York
Founders: Leopold Stickley, John George Stickley

The brothers founded the Onondaga Shops, which operated between 1902 and 1910, where they produced furniture in the style of their brother Gustav. In 1918, they absorbed the bankrupt Craftsman Workshops, but they abandoned the Craftsman style to produce Colonial revival furniture. Recently, the firm introduced a line based on the old Arts and Crafts designs.

TOBEY FURNITURE COMPANY; TOBEY AND CHRISTIANSON CABINET COMPANY

c. 1860–c. 1927
Chicago, Illinois
Founder: Charles Tobey

This was one of the first American retailers to aggressively market factory-made Arts and Crafts furniture using modern advertising techniques. Tobey and Christianson, the subsidiary, turned out a special hand-carved line known as Tobey Handmade Furniture. In 1900, Tobey introduced Gustav Stickley's oak "New Furniture," and a year later promoted Art Nouveau forms.

GENERAL

ALLEN-HIGGINS COMPANY

Worcester, Massachusetts

The company, which advertised in *The Craftsman* and *Interior Decorator*, produced wallpaper that catered to the aesthetic of the Arts and Crafts movement.

HEYWOOD BROTHERS AND COMPANY

1883–1930
Chicago, Illinois
Founder: Henry Heywood

A maker of Arts and Crafts rattan furniture.

THE J. & R. LAMB STUDIOS

1857–present
New York, New York
Founder: Joseph Lamb

The firm's specialty was religious artwork based upon Arts and Crafts methods of craftsmanship. In the late nineteenth century, it was famous for its stained-glass windows, mosaics, and murals. Today, Lamb is the oldest existing stained-glass manufacturer in the United States.

W. H. LAU AND COMPANY

1898–1924
Chicago, Illinois
Founder: Willy H. Lau

Lau executed lighting fixtures for Frank Lloyd Wright's B. Harley Bradley House, and designed and executed lighting for George W. Maher, another Prairie School architect.

NIEDECKEN-WALBRIDGE COMPANY

1907–c. 1917
Milwaukee, Wisconsin
Founder: George Mann Niedecken

A decorating firm, it hired and supervised workshops to execute Frank Lloyd Wright's furniture, rugs, upholstery, and draperies. Niedecken also designed his own furniture.

ROYCROFTERS LEATHER SHOP

1903–n.d.
East Aurora, New York

The leather shop, headed by Frederick C. Kranz, who joined the community in 1903, produced fine hand-tooled bindings for the many books that were produced by the Roycroft Press.

THE UNITED CRAFTS; LATER, CRAFTSMAN WORKSHOPS

1899–1916
Eastwood, New York; New York, New York
Founder: Gustav Stickley

Gustav Stickley was among those most responsible for popularizing furniture in the Arts and Crafts style in America. His furniture factory, United Crafts, began, near Syracuse, in 1899, and he showed the first furniture in the Arts and Crafts style at the Grand Rapids Furniture Market in 1900. The firm's name changed to Craftsman Workshops in 1904, and it expanded to produce metalwork, lighting, and textiles. The furniture, made of quartersawed oak, was massive in scale, to denote stability. Stickley used machinery to produce the furniture; the textiles and metalwork continued to be handmade. From 1901 to 1916, he published *The Craftsman*, a magazine responsible for the spread of the Arts and Crafts style among the middle class. Because of changes in fashion, the firm declared bankruptcy in 1915. It tried to reorganize the following year, but in 1918, it was absorbed by L. and J. G. Stickley, of Fayetteville, New York.

SCHOOLS

ALFRED UNIVERSITY, NEW YORK SCHOOL OF CLAYWORKING AND CERAMICS

1900–present
Alfred, New York
Director: Charles Fergus Binns

The New York School of Clayworking and Ceramics, the ceramics program at Alfred University, offered two- and four-year programs in clay technology, clay testing, and graphic and decorative arts. Courses included painting and decorative arts, clayworking, and over- and underglaze decoration. The school was chartered by the State of New York to train ceramists and to "conduct experiments for commercial purposes of clays and shales of New York State." Charles Fergus Binns, who apprenticed under his father at Worcester Royal Porcelain, in England, headed the school from 1900 to 1931. The students held an annual exhibition of their work, reported in the pages of *Keramic Studio*.

THE ART CRAFT INSTITUTE

c. 1900
Chicago, Illinois
Founders: Chicago retailers and metalsmiths

Several Chicago jewelers and merchants organized to teach good design, especially in jewelry. Corporate members offered scholarships and work-study programs. By 1904, two hundred graduates had been placed in jobs.

SCHOOL OF THE ART INSTITUTE OF CHICAGO, DEPARTMENT OF DECORATIVE DESIGN

1886–present
Chicago, Illinois
Founder: Louis J. Millet

Millet, a well-known metalworker who executed designs for Louis Sullivan, founded and served as head of the Department of Decorative Design. The school soon expanded, offering a Department of Applied Design.

ART STUDENTS LEAGUE

1875–present
New York, New York

The league was founded by a group of students who broke away from the National Academy of Design and began to hold art classes under the direction of Professor Lemuel Wilmarth. In 1889, it joined with several other prominent New York City arts organizations to form the American Fine Arts Society. Throughout its history, the league has been prominent in American art education and in providing scholarships.

BILTMORE INDUSTRIES

1901–15
Asheville, North Carolina
Founders: Eleanor P. Vance, Charlotte L. Yale

Woodworkers Vance and Yale took a cottage on the Biltmore estate and organized a wood-carving class for young boys. Mrs. George Vanderbilt, who was interested in the project, helped them expand the classes to metalwork, weaving, and raising sheep.

BRADLEY POLYTECHNIC INSTITUTE

1896–n.d.
Peoria, Illinois
Founder: William Rainey Harper

Harper and other University of Chicago faculty members developed a manual-arts curriculum in Peoria. Its most singular feature was a training program in watch- and jewelrymaking for more than three thousand students. The Bradley students and faculty formed an Arts and Crafts society, and, through the Manual Arts Press, the institute published books on woodworking.

SCHOOL OF THE CALIFORNIA GUILD OF ARTS AND CRAFTS; LATER, CALIFORNIA SCHOOL OF ARTS AND CRAFTS; LATER, CALIFORNIA COLLEGE OF ARTS AND CRAFTS

1907–present
Berkeley, California; Oakland, California
Founder: Frederick Henry Meyer

After his furniture studio was destroyed in the San Francisco earthquake, Meyer founded a school. Courses included drawing, composition, design, wood-carving, pottery, jewelrymaking, weaving, and embroidery. Fine-arts courses were added later. In 1908, the name was changed from the School of the California Guild of Arts and Crafts to the California School of Arts and Crafts. The school created a model artist's studio in the Palace of Education building at the 1915 Panama-Pacific International Exposition, in San Francisco. Most of its furniture was designed by Marjory Wheelock and made by students. The school moved to Oakland in 1924 as the California College of Arts and Crafts.

CALIFORNIA SCHOOL OF DESIGN; LATER, MARK HOPKINS INSTITUTE OF ART; LATER, CALIFORNIA SCHOOL OF DESIGN OF THE SAN FRANCISCO INSTITUTE OF ART; LATER, CALIFORNIA SCHOOL OF FINE ARTS

1874–present
San Francisco, California
Founder: San Francisco Art Association

The school was founded to hold courses in applied arts. Frederick H. Meyer was professor of applied art from 1902 to 1906.

SYBIL CARTER LACE ASSOCIATION

1890–c. 1915
White Earth, Minnesota
Founder: Sybil Carter

Carter was invited by an Episcopalian bishop to teach lacemaking to Objibway Indians in Minnesota. She then started schools on the reservations of six tribes, in California, Minnesota, New Mexico, New York, and Wisconsin. The lace won many awards at international expositions.

CHAUTAUQUA SUNDAY SCHOOL ASSEMBLY; LATER, THE CHAUTAUQUA INSTITUTION

1874–present
Lake Chautauqua, New York
Founders: John H. Vincent, Lewis Miller

Originally planned to train Sunday-school teachers in a scenic location, the Chautauqua concept expanded to include lectures, discussions, and home readings. By 1878, the Chautauqua Literary and Scientific Circle was a four-year home-reading plan, emphasizing American, European, and classical history and literature. Books were supplemented by the *Chautauquan*, a monthly magazine published from 1880 to 1914. Beginning in 1883, under the direction of William Rainey Harper, the Chautauqua summer-school department offered courses for credit, while art courses, including metalwork, basketry, leatherwork, bookbinding, and pottery, were offered on a noncredit basis. In 1902 it was renamed the Chautauqua Institution. For nearly a century, the Chautauqua movement influenced the development of adult education in the United States.

COLUMBIA UNIVERSITY, TEACHERS COLLEGE, DEPARTMENT OF FINE ARTS

1897–present
New York, New York

During its earliest years, the Department of Fine Arts included courses in decorative arts in the Arts and Crafts tradition.

THE COOPER UNION FOR THE ADVANCEMENT OF SCIENCE AND ART

1857–present
New York, New York

Cooper Union offered women a daytime program of courses in art and design; an evening program for working men provided occupational training. Courses for both included drawing and modeling, advertising and costume design, painting and sculpture, and architectural design. The Cooper Union Museum for the Arts of Decoration was located at the school.

FOUR WINDS SUMMER SCHOOL

1912–14
Syracuse, New York
Founders: Adelaide Alsop Robineau, Kathryn E. Cherry, Henry Rankin Poore

This school, in Robineau's studio, gave instruction in china painting, pottery, sketching, jewelry, metalwork, leatherwork, basketry, carving, and gilding.

GRAND RAPIDS ARTS AND CRAFTS SCHOOL OF DESIGN

1905–6
Grand Rapids, Michigan
Founder: Forest Emerson Mann

Mann established this short-lived school. He also operated a summer school for crafts at Port Sherman, on Lake Michigan.

ART SCHOOL OF THE JOHN HERRON ART INSTITUTE OF INDIANAPOLIS

1902–n.d.
Indianapolis, Indiana
Founder: Art Association of Indianapolis

The school opened in 1902 with instruction in wood-carving. By 1911, it had an applied arts department.

HUMBOLDT STATE NORMAL SCHOOL; LATER, HUMBOLDT STATE UNIVERSITY

1914–present
Arcata, California

The school's ceramics program was begun by Horace Jenkins.

IOWA STATE UNIVERSITY, CERAMICS ENGINEERING PROGRAM

1907–present
Ames, Iowa
Founder: State of Iowa

Iowa State was offering a degree in ceramics engineering by 1907. The school attracted well-known ceramists—among them, Paul Cox, of Newcomb College.

LAKESIDE PRESS; LATER, R. R. DONNELLEY AND SONS

1864–present
Chicago, Illinois; Crawfordsville, Indiana
Founder: Richard Robert Donnelley

In 1908, the company started a school to train apprentice craftsmen for the composing room and pressroom. The program included training in artistic bookbinding, with leather binding, gold leaf, and finishing.

MANUAL ARTS HIGH SCHOOL OF LOS ANGELES

1911–19
Los Angeles, California

Douglas Donaldson, a jeweler and metalsmith, headed the art department and taught craft techniques to high school students.

MINNEAPOLIS HANDICRAFT GUILD

1900–1915
Minneapolis, Minnesota

The guild sponsored the Summer School of Design Applied to Crafts as well as regular classes in pottery, metalwork, leather, and bookbinding.

MINNEAPOLIS SCHOOL OF ART, DEPARTMENT OF HANDICRAFT; LATER, MINNEAPOLIS COLLEGE OF ART AND DESIGN

1905–present
Minneapolis, Minnesota
Founder: Minneapolis Society of Fine Arts

In 1905, the school started a handicraft section within its School of Decorative Design; by 1907, it had expanded to a Department of Handicraft. This included classes in embroidery and lace, leather illumination, bookbinding, jewelrymaking, wood carving, and leaded glass. The school continues today as the Minneapolis College of Art and Design.

SCHOOL OF THE MUSEUM OF FINE ARTS, BOSTON

1877–present
Boston, Massachusetts
Founders: William Morris Hunt, John La Farge

In 1894, the school began classes in decoration. Many decorators at Grueby Faience Company were graduates of the school.

NATIONAL ACADEMY OF DESIGN

1825–present
New York, New York

The academy was established as an honorary arts organization for American artists and architects. Modeled after England's Royal Academy, new members were required to present the academy with a self-portrait within the first year of election. As a result of this requirement, the permanent collection now consists of more than seven thousand watercolors, drawings, graphics, paintings, and pieces of sculpture that are principally gifts of its members, a significant collection of American art from the mid-nineteenth century to the present.

NAVAJO SCHOOL OF INDIAN BASKETRY

c. 1903

Los Angeles, California
In 1903, the school published the book *Indian Basket Weaving*.

NEW YORK SCHOOL OF APPLIED DESIGN FOR WOMEN

1892–n.d.
New York, New York
Superintendent: Ellen J. Pond

The school provided instruction in stained glass, wallpaper design, architecture, painting, and illustration, and maintained a salesroom.

OHIO STATE UNIVERSITY, CERAMICS ENGINEERING PROGRAM

1894–present
Columbus, Ohio
Founder: State of Ohio

In 1894, Ohio State established the first university ceramics engineering program in the United States. Its director, Edward Orton, Jr., garnered many substantial gifts from the ceramics industry for the program.

OREGON SCHOOL OF ARTS AND CRAFTS

1906–present
Portland, Oregon
Founder: Julia Hoffman

The school was established to teach seven disciplines in the Arts and Crafts, including metalwork and textiles. Today, some of the school's courses are bookplates and bindings, calligraphy, carpets and rugs, ceramics, embroidery, furniture, and glass. The Hoffman Exhibition Gallery features the work of national and international craftspersons.

OTIS ART INSTITUTE

1918–present
Los Angeles, California
Founder: Los Angeles County Museum of History, Science, and Art

The institute had both fine-arts and crafts departments. Pottery, textile decoration, and wood-carving were offered. In 1919, Douglas Donaldson began teaching metalwork, jewelry, and decorative-design classes.

PENNSYLVANIA MUSEUM SCHOOL OF INDUSTRIAL ART; LATER, PHILADELPHIA COLLEGE OF ART; LATER, PHILADELPHIA COLLEGES OF THE ARTS; LATER, THE UNIVERSITY OF THE ARTS

1876–present
Philadelphia, Pennsylvania

Founded as the Pennsylvania Museum School of Industrial Art under the aegis of the present Philadelphia Museum of Art, it was renamed the Philadelphia College of Art when it became an independent art college in 1964. It has educated craftspersons in all media since the Philadelphia Centennial International Exposition in 1876.

PEOPLE'S INDUSTRIAL COLLEGE

c. 1907
Saugatuck, Michigan
Founder: Oscar Lovell Triggs

Triggs, a former University of Chicago professor, tried to organize this school according to the tenets of William Morris. Classes were to include cabinetmaking and beekeeping, but the enterprise folded when Triggs moved to California.

RHODE ISLAND SCHOOL OF DESIGN

1877–present
Providence, Rhode Island
Founder: Helen Metcalf

The school was founded to provide theoretical and practical training for artisans and to promote public art education. Exhibitions of student and alumni work were an important part of the school's program. In 1895, the focus changed from training industrial artists to providing crafts and fine-arts education.

ROCHESTER ATHENAEUM AND MECHANICS INSTITUTE; LATER, ROCHESTER INSTITUTE OF TECHNOLOGY

1902–present
Rochester, New York
Founder: Theodore Hanford Pond

The Department of Decorative Arts of the Rochester Athenaeum and Mechanics Institute provided classes in carpetweaving, metalwork, furnituremaking, stained glass, book design, pottery, and embroidery. In 1944 the name was changed to the Rochester Institute of Technology.

RUTGERS UNIVERSITY, NEW JERSEY SCHOOL OF CLAYWORKING AND CERAMICS

1902–n.d.
New Brunswick, New Jersey
Director: C. W. Parmelee

An important institution, it was founded for the training of ceramics workers.

THROOP POLYTECHNIC INSTITUTE

1904–10
Pasadena, California

Interested in teaching the historical foundations of good craftsmanship, the school equally emphasized engineering and the humanities. An Arts and Crafts department was organized by Ernest Batchelder, who supervised the workshop and taught design courses. Other classes included drawing and drafting, wood, metal, clay, leather, and sewing. In 1910, when Throop reorganized as the California Institute of Technology, the department was discontinued.

TROY SCHOOL OF ARTS AND CRAFTS

1907–n.d.
Troy, New York
Director: Emile C. Adams

The school provided instruction in all media. A summer school was established in 1916.

TULANE UNIVERSITY, SOPHIE NEWCOMB MEMORIAL COLLEGE FOR WOMEN

1886–present
New Orleans, Louisiana
Founder: Josephine Louise LeMonnier Newcomb

In 1895, Sophie Newcomb Memorial College for Women began Newcomb Pottery as a practical training ground for women students to earn a living.

The ceramics produced became world famous and won many awards as examples of art with a southern motif. The school expanded into the teaching and production of other crafts: metalwork, glasswork, embroidery, weaving, and calligraphy.

UNIVERSITY OF CINCINNATI SCHOOL OF DESIGN; LATER, ART ACADEMY OF CINCINNATI

c. 1873–present
Cincinnati, Ohio
Founder: Cincinnati Museum Association

The School of Design was turned over to the Museum Association in 1884, becoming the Art Academy of Cincinnati. Under the aegis of Henry L. Fry, William H. Fry, and Benn Pitman, the academy fostered an unusual wood-carving program as well as courses in china painting.

UNIVERSITY CITY POTTERY

1910–15
St. Louis, Missouri
Founder: Edward J. Lewis

Conceived for women's education, Lewis recruited a notable group of ceramics artists: Adelaide Alsop Robineau, Taxile Doat, and Frederick H. Rhead. The pottery produced art porcelain, for which it won numerous prizes.

UNIVERSITY OF ILLINOIS, CERAMICS ENGINEERING PROGRAM

1905–present
Champaign-Urbana, Illinois
Founder: State of Illinois

The university, in 1905, was one of the first to offer a degree in ceramics engineering.

UNIVERSITY OF NORTH DAKOTA, CERAMICS DEPARTMENT

1919–n.d.
Grand Forks, North Dakota
Founder: State of North Dakota

In 1919, the university ceramics department showed ten pieces of pottery, designed and made by Margaret Cable, at the Art Institute of Chicago Arts and Crafts Exhibition.

UNIVERSITY OF WASHINGTON, DESIGN DEPARTMENT

1916–present
Seattle, Washington

The design department offered courses in pottery, metalwork, and needlework. Grace Denny organized a textile history program that included technical instruction.

SETTLEMENT HOUSES

GREENWICH HOUSE

1905–present
New York, New York
Founder: Mary L. Aldrich

Organized after Chicago's Hull-House, Greenwich House provided social services for immigrants as well as handicraft instruction, exhibitions, and a picture library.

HENRY STREET SETTLEMENT

1915–present
New York, New York
Founders: Alice Lewisohn, Irene Lewisohn

One of several private institutions founded in New York City during the early decades of the twentieth century to provide social services to recently arrived immigrants, it became an important center for the visual and performing arts. Both Isadora Duncan and Martha Graham appeared there.

HULL-HOUSE

1889–present
Chicago, Illinois
Founders: Jane Addams, Ellen Gates Starr

Hull-House, a national leader in social reform, was a leader in craft activities as well. Addams helped organize the Chicago Arts and Crafts Society, and held regular Friday afternoon programs at the house. The settlement founded the Hull-House Labor Museum, where immigrants practiced Old-World crafts.

Hull-House shops featured pottery, textiles, metalworking, and bookbinding.

SCUOLA D'INDUSTRIE ITALIANE

1905–27
Richmond Hill House, New York, New York
Founders: Gino Speranza, Florence Colgate, Countess Amari

Founded as part of a settlement house, it employed immigrant women to reproduce antique Venetian lace patterns.

Special attention was paid to the conditions under which the women worked.

SOUTH END HOUSE

1901–4
Boston, Massachusetts
Founders: Florence G. Weber, Anne Withington

In association with the Boston Society of Arts and Crafts, Weber and Withington taught immigrant Irishwomen to reproduce Italian lace. In 1904, Weber took over the project and made it into her own shop.

SMALL PRESSES

ABBEY SAN ENCINO

c. 1909–20
Pasadena, California
Founder: Clyde Browne

The Abbey—a mixture of Mission revival and medievalism—was a home and printing shop, with studios for artists and writers. Browne acted as the semiofficial printer for Occidental College, producing volumes in various Morris styles.

ALWIL PRESS

1900–n.d.
Palisades, New York
Founder: Frank B. Rae, Jr.

Rae first worked for the Blue Sky Press and Roycroft Press before founding Alwil. He produced some of the earliest three-color printing in the United States. He printed Ralph Waldo Emerson's *Essay on Nature*.

ARTEMESIA BOOK BINDERY

c. 1900–1930
Los Angeles, California
Founder: Idah Meacham Strobridge

A bookbindery, it published books about the western deserts: *In Miner's Mirage Land* (1904); *The Loom of the Desert* (1907); and *The Land of Purple Shadows* (1909), illustrated by Maynard Dixon.

BLUE SKY PRESS

1899–n.d.
Chicago, Illinois
Founder: Alfred G. Langworthy

Blue Sky showed Arts and Crafts press work at the Art Institute of Chicago Arts and Crafts exhibitions in 1902 and 1906.

THE BOHEMIA GUILD BOOKBINDERY

1902–4
Chicago, Illinois
Founder: Industrial Art League

It printed *Chapters in the History of the Arts and Crafts Movement*, by Oscar Lovell Triggs.

THEODORE L. DE VINNE & COMPANY

1883–c. 1918
New York, New York
Founder: Theodore L. De Vinne

The shop printed high-quality innovative work for many small Arts and Crafts book designers, such as *The Altar Book*, designed by Bertram Goodhue and D. B. Updike. De Vinne printed forty-five volumes for the Grolier Club.

ELSTON PRESS

1900–1904
New York, New York
Founders: Clarke Conwell, Helen Marguerite O'Kane

This small press produced editions with a luxurious format. O'Kane was the designer and Conwell oversaw production. Their books, which emulated the works of William Morris, were included in the 1906 exhibition of the Boston Society of Printers, "The Development of Printing As an Art."

THE GILLIS PRESS

1869–n.d.
New York, New York
Founders: Thomas Gillis, Walter Gillis

The press is noteworthy for its fine printing for the Grolier Club as well as

for various writers on American history and art.

HULL-HOUSE BOOKBINDERY

1899–n.d.
Chicago, Illinois
Founder: Ellen Gates Starr

Starr, who founded Hull-House with her friend Jane Addams, was accomplished in bookbinding. She exhibited at the Art Institute of Chicago Arts and Crafts exhibitions.

MERRYMOUNT PRESS

1893–c. 1930
Boston, Massachusetts
Founder: D. B. Updike

With Bertram Goodhue, Updike produced the foremost book of the American Arts and Crafts movement, *The Altar Book*, for the American Episcopal Church. His typeface was Merrymount. The book was printed by Theodore L. De Vinne.

MONASTERY HILL BINDERY

c. 1917–n.d.
Chicago, Illinois

This bindery produced work for the ceramist Susan Stuart Goodrich Frackelton, and was represented at a number of Art Institute of Chicago Arts and Crafts exhibitions.

THE MONTAGUE PRESS

c. 1907–1930s
Montague, Massachusetts
Founder: Carl Purington Rollins

An admirer of William Morris and the Kelmscott Press, Rollins was originally part of New Clairvaux. In 1918, he was named official printer to Yale University.

MOSHER PRESS

1891–c. 1924
Portland, Maine
Founder: Thomas Bird Mosher

Mosher was dubbed the "passionate pirate" for printing inexpensive but beautifully designed editions of the works of English and Continental writers, among them William Morris and Dante Gabriel Rossetti. For this privilege, he paid few if any royalties.

RICARDO OROZCO

c. 1900–1920
San Francisco, California
Founder: Ricardo Orozco

Orozco issued few books under his own hand and name—only seven by 1920, and some with machine-set text. He used strong red-and-black block designing as well as decorative devices derived from Aztec sources.

PHILOPOLIS PRESS

1906–16
San Francisco, California
Founders: Arthur and Lucia Mathews, John Zeile

Philopolis Press published limited editions of essays and poems on art and California. The magazine *Philopolis* was devoted to the ethical and artistic aspects of rebuilding California after the 1906 earthquake. The Mathewses provided stories and illustrations for the magazine.

POPULAR MECHANICS PRESS

c. 1909–n.d.
Chicago, Illinois

The press developed a series of handbooks on how to make Arts and Crafts furnishings. Henry Haven Windsor's *Mission Furniture: How To Make It* and Fred D. Crawshaw's *Metal Spinning*, both published in 1909, were just two examples.

RIVERSIDE PRESS

1896–present
Cambridge, Massachusetts
Founder: Henry O. Houghton

An offshoot of Houghton, Mifflin and Company, Riverside Press Limited Editions began in 1900. Typefaces designed by Bruce Rogers reflected the periods in which the texts originally were written.

THE ROYCROFT PRESS

1895–1938
East Aurora, New York
Founder: Elbert G. Hubbard

The press, founded to print Hubbard's books and magazines, was instrumental in introducing fine printing and bindings to America's middle class. In 1896, it published Hubbard's *The Song of Songs Which Is Solomon's*, as well as his subsequent writings, including *Contemplations* (1902), *Get Out or Get in Line* (1903), and *Respectability—Its Rise and Remedy* (1905).

THOMAS RUSSELL

c. 1916–20
San Francisco, California
Founder: Thomas Russell

Russell produced three volumes by 1920, including *The Narrative of Edward McGowan* (1917). He printed them at home, controlling all aspects of production with his impeccable editorial scholarship and feeling for detail.

TAYLOR AND TAYLOR

c. 1882–1920
San Francisco, California
Founders: Henry H. Taylor, Edward DeWitt Taylor

The first of San Francisco's artist-printers, they executed commissions for private patrons, the Book Club of California, and San Francisco bookseller-publishers, such as Alexander M. Robertson and Paul Elder. Their designs were classical, with beautiful type and little ornamentation. They produced more than one hundred fifty publications by 1920. They were awarded two silver medals at the first two exhibitions of the American Institute of Graphic Arts, in 1916 and 1920, in New York City.

TOMOYE PRESS

1901–11
San Francisco, California
Founder: John Henry Nash

Nash established the press for Paul Elder and Company, in 1901, in San Francisco.

UNIVERSITY CITY PRESS

1911–n.d.
St. Louis, Missouri
Founder: Edward J. Lewis

This press published *Studio Pottery*, by Frederick H. Rhead, in 1911.

THE VILLAGE PRESS

1903–5
Chicago, Illinois
Founder: Frederic W. Goudy

One of America's most inventive type designers, his work was on view at the Art Institute of Chicago Arts and Crafts Exhibition of 1903.

WAYSIDE PRESS

1895–98
Springfield, Massachusetts
Founder: Will H. Bradley

Bradley was responsible for some of the most striking graphics in the Arts and Crafts tradition. Between 1896 and 1897, he produced seven issues of the magazine *Bradley His Book*, which included contemporary writing and Bradley's graphic designs. In 1898, the press merged with the University Press of Cambridge.

THE ZAHN BINDERY

c. 1904–11
Memphis, Tennessee
Founder: Otto Zahn

The bindery showed Lorentz Schwartz's books at the Art Institute of Chicago Arts and Crafts Exhibition in 1911 and, before that, twenty-five bindings at the Louisiana Purchase International Exposition in 1904.

KARDON
A Centenary Project

1. The second period, 1920–45, is particularly diverse, and research directed at examining the early craft movement is sparse. Therefore, the period will be covered from two vantage points, in two separate exhibitions and publications: "Within Our Shores: Affirming Cultural Identities" will examine the African-American, Native American, and Hispanic contribution; and "Craft in the Machine Age: European and American Modernism" will delve into the influence of European Modernism on this country.

2. Robert Judson Clark, professor, art and archaeology, Princeton University, was unable to participate because of a sudden illness.

3. The three previous exhibitions were: "The Arts and Crafts Movement in America, 1876–1916," 1972, Princeton University Art Museum; "The Art That Is Life," 1987, Museum of Fine Arts, Boston; "American Arts & Crafts: Virtue in Design," 1990, Los Angeles County Museum of Art.

4. Rose Slivka dates the emergence of the American craftsmaker in the late 1930s. See Rose Slivka, "The Art/Craft Connection," in Marcia Manhart and Tom Manhart, *The Eloquent Object* (Tulsa, Oklahoma: Philbrook Museum of Art, 1987), 71.

5. Lee Nordness offered a definition of craft in 1970 that has remained useful. See Lee Nordness, *Objects: USA* (New York: Viking Press, 1970).

6. Beverly Brandt has drawn my attention to the monumental works shown in the Great Exhibition of 1851, in the Crystal Palace in England, as well as Greek "geometric" pots.

7. Cheryl Robertson, "House and Home in the Arts and Crafts Era: Reforms for Simpler Living," in Wendy Kaplan, ed., *"The Art That Is Life": The Arts & Crafts Movement in America, 1875–1920* (Boston: Museum of Fine Arts, 1987), 336–54. Eileen Boris has pointed out that tenement dwellers did not have such a gendered division and that rural homesteads might have had another gender organization, with the barn, for example, as a male space for tools, except for dairying.

8. Leslie Greene Bowman, "Myths and Realities of the American Arts and Crafts Movement," in *American Arts & Crafts: Virtue in Design. A Catalogue of the Palevsky/Evans Collection and Related Works at the Los Angeles County Museum of Art* (Los Angeles: Los Angeles County Museum of Art; Boston: Bulfinch Press/Little, Brown and Company, 1990), 33–42.

BORIS
Crossing Boundaries

1. For the Arts and Crafts movement in the United States in its social context, including the impact of the English example, see Eileen Boris, *Art and Labor: Ruskin, Morris, and the Craftsman Ideal in America* (Philadelphia: Temple University Press, 1986); for a listing of crafts shops and organizations, see Max West, "The Revival of Handicraft in America," U.S. Bureau of Labor Statistics, *Bulletin* 55 (November 1904): 1573–97.

2. For Progressivism, see Robert Wiebe, *The Search for Order, 1877–1920* (New York: Hill and Wang, 1967), who emphasizes the "new middle class," and Nell Irvin Painter, *Standing at Armageddon: The United States, 1877–1919* (New York: W. W. Norton, 1987), who provides us with a sense of the diversity and conflict of the time.

3. For gender and the crafts movement, see Boris, *Art and Labor*, 58–78, 99–138; Cheryl Robertson, "House and Home in the Arts and Crafts Era: Reforms for Simpler Living," in Wendy Kaplan, ed., *"The Art That Is Life": The Arts & Crafts Movement in America, 1875–1920* (Boston: Museum of Fine Arts, 1987), 336–57; for masculine domesticity, Margaret Marsh, "Suburban Men and Masculine Domesticity, 1870–1915," *American Quarterly* 40 (June 1988): 165–86.

4. For one summary of these ideals, see Mary Ryan, *Woman and Womanhood in America* (New York: Franklin Watts, 1982); for manhood, Clyde Griffen, "Reconstructing Masculinity from the Evangelical Revival to the Waning of Progressivism: A Speculative Synthesis," in Mark C. Carnes and Clyde Griffen, eds., *Meanings for Manhood: Constructions of Masculinity in Victorian America* (Chicago: University of Chicago Press, 1990), 183–204.

5. For the home as workplace, see Susan Strasser, *Never Done: A History of American Housework* (New York: Pantheon, 1982); for tenement homework, Cynthia R. Daniels, "Between Home and Factory: Homeworkers and the State," in Eileen Boris and Cynthia R. Daniels, *Homework: Historical and Contemporary Perspectives on Paid Labor at Home* (Urbana: University of Illinois Press, 1989), 13–32; for manhood, Peter Filene, *Him/Her/Self*, 2nd edition (Baltimore: Johns Hopkins University Press, 1986); for intervention, Eileen Boris, "Reconstructing the 'Family': Women, Progressive Reform, and the Problem of Social Control," in Noralee Frankel and Nancy S. Dye, eds., *Gender, Class, Race & Reform in the Progressive Era* (Lexington: University of Kentucky Press, 1991), 73–86.

6. Figures from Sara Evans, *Born for Liberty: A History of Women in America* (New York: Free Press, 1989), 156–57; for black women, Susan Ware, *Modern American Women: A Documentary History* (Chicago: Dorsey Press, 1989), 66; see also, Alice Kessler-Harris, *Out to Work: A History of Wage-Earning Women in America* (New York: Oxford University Press, 1982).

7. Figures cited in Ware, *Modern American Women*, 35–36.

8. Evans, *Born for Liberty*, 127; Nancy S. Dye, "Introduction," in Frankel and Dye, *Gender, Class, Race & Reform*, 1–10; Mrs. John O'Connor, quoted in "Report on the Chicago Society of Arts and Crafts, May 27, 1910," *Handicraft* 3 (August 1910): 184; see also, Eileen Boris, "The Power of Motherhood: Black and White Activist Women Redefine the 'Political,'" *Yale Journal of Law and Feminism* 2 (Fall 1989): 25–49.

9. Mark C. Carnes, "Middle-Class Men and the Solace of Fraternal Ritual," in Carnes and Griffen, eds., *Meanings for Manhood*, 38, 51.

10. For the process of de-skilling, Harry Braverman, *Labor and Monopoly Capitalism: The Degradation of Work in the Twentieth Century* (New York: Monthly Review Press, 1974); for specific crafts, Walter E. Weyl and A. M. Sakolski, "Conditions of Entrance to the Principal Trades," U.S. Bureau of Labor Statistics, *Bulletin* 67 (November 1906), 691–780.

11. Mabel Hurd Willet, "The Employment of Women in the Clothing Trades," *Columbia University Studies in the Social Sciences* 42 (New York: Columbia University Press, 1902); John R. Commons, "Immigration and Its Economic Effects," Part III, *Reports of the Industrial Commission on Immigration*, XV (Washington, D.C.: Government Printing Office, 1901), 316–84; "Men's Ready-Made Clothing," *Report on Condition of Woman and Child Wage-Earners in the United States* 2 (Washington, D.C.: Government Printing Office, 1911), 413–512; see also, David Montgomery, *The Fall of the House of Labor: The workplace, the state, and American labor activism, 1865–1925* (New York: Cambridge University Press, 1987), 116–23.

12. Quoted in Olivier Zunz, *Making America Corporate, 1870–1920* (Chicago: University of Chicago Press, 1990), 12. For the loss of autonomy and growth of white-collar positions, see Zunz, 11–36, 125–48; for the idea of the middle class, Stuart M. Blumin, "The Hypothesis of Middle-Class Formation in Nineteenth-Century America: A Critique and Some Proposals," *American Historical Review* 90 (April 1985), 299–338; Blumin, *The Emergence of the Middle Class: Social Experience in the American City, 1760–1900* (New York: Cambridge University Press, 1989); on the architectural office, Michael Boyle, "Architectural Practice in America, 1865–1955," in Spiro Kostof, ed., *The Architect: Chapters in the History of the Profession* (New York: Oxford University Press, 1977), 309–44.

13. Vida Scudder, *Social Ideals in English Letters* (New York: Chautauquan Press, 1898), 167; on her life, Boris, *Art and Labor*, 183–85.

14. Lummis, quoted in Daniela P. Moneta, ed., *Chas. F. Lummis: The Centennial Exhibition Commemorating His Tramp across the Continent*

(Los Angeles: Southwest Museum, 1985), 49; Oscar Lovell Triggs, *Chapters in the History of the Arts and Crafts Movement* (Chicago: Bohemia Guild of the Industrial Art League, 1902; reprint, New York: Benjamin Blom, 1971), 147–57.

15. Walter Crane, "William Morris," *Scribner's* 22 (July 1897): 99; William Sharp, "William Morris: The Man and the Work," *The Atlantic Monthly* 78 (December 1896): 771–72; Wallace Rice, "The Poetry of William Morris in Relation to His Artistic Life," *The Blue Sky: A Magazine* 5 (April 1902): 29; Horace Traubel, "Collect," *The Conservator* 7 (October 1896): 113.

16. Sharp, "William Morris," 768–72, 775–79; Irene Sargent, "William Morris: A Recent Study by Elizabeth Luther Cary," *The Craftsman* 4, no. 1 (April 1903): 52; Traubel, "Collect," 114; William Clarke, "William Morris," *New England Magazine*, n.s. 16 (April 1897): 745; Crane, "William Morris," 89, 97; "About the World," *Scribner's* 21 (January 1897): 130; "William Morris," *The Conservator* 7 (November 1896): 137; Eltreed Pomery, "A Visit to the Shop of William Morris," *The Craftsman* 1, no. 5 (February 1902): 144; B. O. Flower, "William Morris and Some of His Later Works," *The Arena* 4 [date missing]: 42. For a perceptive study of such associations, T. J. Jackson Lears, *No Place of Grace: Anti-Modernism and the Transformation of American Culture, 1880–1920* (New York: Pantheon, 1981), especially 144–49.

17. On women's culture among reformers, see Kathryn Kish Sklar, "Hull-House in the 1890s: A Community of Women Reformers," *Signs* 10 (Summer 1985): 658–77; for female bonds and the crafts, see below.

18. On these various craft groups, see Boris, *Art and Labor,* especially 48–51, 156–68; aims of the Industrial Art League set forth in Luther Laflin Mills, *1902 Report of the Secretary of the Industrial Art League* (Chicago, n.p.): 4–5; comment on class nature of membership, "Stray Clouds," *The Blue Sky: A Magazine* 5 (April 1902): 72–73.

19. On the craft societies, Boris, *Art and Labor*, 32–52.

20. The subsequent discussion draws heavily on Boris, *Art and Labor*, 99–138. On bookbinding, "Comment," *International Studio* 4 (April 1898): 111–12.

21. Constance Goodard du Bois, "The Indian Woman As a Craftsman," *The Craftsman* 4, no. 4 (July 1903): 91; Gretchen Bayne, "Coverlet Weaving in East Tennessee," *Handicraft* 1 (April 1903): 41–48; for further examples, see Boris, *Art and Labor*, 122–38.

22. Candace Wheeler, *Yesterdays in a Busy Life* (New York and London: Harper & Brothers, 1918); Wheeler, *The Development of Embroidery in America* (New York and London: Harper & Brothers, 1921), 107–21; "The Society of Decorative Art," *Scribner's* 22 (September 1881): 697–712; on the Associated Artists, Wheeler, *Principles of Home Decoration with Practical Examples* (New York: Doubleday, Page & Company, 1903).

23. On Cincinnati women, see Kenneth R. Trapp, "Toward a Correct Taste: Women and the Rise of the Design Reform Movement in Cincinnati, 1874–1880," in Kenneth R. Trapp, ed., *Celebrate Cincinnati Art* (Cincinnati: Cincinnati Art Museum, 1982), 48–70; Margaret Whiting, "Reminiscences" (May 1944), typed photocopy, property of Margery B. Howe, Deerfield, Mass.; Margaret Miller, "The Deerfield Story," *Modern Priscilla* 15 (July 1901): 1–2; on art schools, Isaac Edwards Clarke, *Art and Industry* (Washington, D.C.: Government Printing Office, 1885–92), and U.S. Bureau of Education, *Fine and Manual Arts in the United States: A Statistical Monograph*, Bulletin 6 (1909); on Newcomb, Suzanne Ormond and Mary E. Irvine, *Louisiana's Art Nouveau: The Crafts of the Newcomb Style* (Gretna, La.: Pelican Publishing Company, 1976); "Newcomb Pottery," *New Orleans Times-Picayune* (March 11, 1907): 59–60.

24. For Cincinnati, see also Herbert Peck, *The Book of Rookwood Pottery* (New York: Crown, 1968); on Fry, Fry Collection, Cincinnati Historical Society; on Sheerer, Newcomb Pottery Collection, Howard-Tilton Memorial Library, Tulane University, New Orleans; for Tiffany, Cecilia Waern, "The Industrial Arts of America: The Tiffany Glass and Decorative Co.," *International Studio* 1 (September 1897): 157–58; Rheta Childe Dorr, "Making Glass Mosaics: Women Artisans Who Build Pictures of Tinted Glass," *New York Evening Post* (January 6, 1904): 14.

25. Helen Albee, *Mountain Playmates* (Boston: Houghton Mifflin, 1900), 235–56; Grace L. Slocum, "The Hearthside Loom's Domestic Industry near Providence, R.I.," *House Beautiful* 24 (July 1908): 18–19; on Berea, Katherine Louis Smith, "A Mountain Fireside Industry," *House Beautiful* 11 (May 1902): 406–7; on other mountain industries, Allen H. Eaton, *Handicrafts of the Southern Highlands* (New York: Russell Sage Foundation, 1937; reprint, New York: Dover, 1973); on Tuskegee, communication from Adele Logan Alexander to Eileen Boris, Fall 1986; *The Story of Paul Revere Pottery*, n.d., vertical files, Schlesinger Library, Radcliffe College, Harvard University, Cambridge; Florence G. Weber, "The Lace Makers of Europe," *The Craftsman* 4, no. 6 (September 1903), 487–88; "The Diary of Frances Glessner," in Glessner House Collection, Chicago Architectural Foundation; Barry Shifman, "Janet Payne Bowles: A Biographical Sketch," *Janet Payne Bowles, American Metalsmith and Jeweler* (Indianapolis: Indianapolis Museum of Art, forthcoming 1993), ms. version.

26. For Arts and Crafts and the settlements, Robert A. Woods and Albert J. Kennedy, *The Settlement Horizon: A National Estimate* (New York: Russell Sage Foundation, 1922); Jane Addams, "The Labor Museum at Hull-House," *Commons* 5 (June 30, 1900), in Hull-House Papers, University of Illinois, Chicago; Marion Foster Washburne, "A Labor Museum," *The Craftsman* 6, no. 6 (September 1904): 570–80; Denison House, "Department of Italian Arts and Crafts," *1913 Bulletin*, 30–32; George F. Pozzetta, "Immigrants and Craft Arts: The

Scuola d'Industrie Italiane," in Betty Boyd Caroli et al., eds., *The Italian Immigrant Woman in North America* (Toronto: Multicultural History Society of Ontario, 1978), 138–53.

27. On Starr, see Boris, *Art and Labor*, 180–83; on the trade, Mary Van Kleck, *Women in the Bookbinding Trade* (New York: Russell Sage Foundation, 1913).

28. Ellen Gates Starr, "Bookbinding As an Art and As a Commercial Industry," 7, Starr Papers, Box 8, Sophia Smith Collection, Smith College, Northampton, Mass.; Starr, "The Renaissance of Handicraft," *International Socialist Review* 2 (February 1902): 570–74; Starr, "Art and Labor," *Hull-House Maps and Papers* (New York: T. Y. Crowell, 1895), 165–79.

29. On Deerfield, see "Craft of Colonial Women Revived—A Unique Organization," *New York Evening Post* (August 11, 1897): 5; Florence Griswold, "Home Industries in Old Deerfield," *Independent* 73 (November 7, 1912): 1049–51; Mary Allen, "Deerfield's Progress in Arts and Crafts," paper read at Amherst meeting of National Society of Handicraft, clipping in Deerfield Industries Collection, Historic Deerfield. Much of this analysis is based on this collection and other papers housed there.

30. Christopher Lasch, "Mary Coffin Ware Dennett," in Edward James and Janet W. James, eds., *Notable American Women* (Cambridge: Harvard University Press, 1971), I: 463–65; for Bracken and the league, *1909 Report*, 7, WTUL Papers, Schlesinger Library, Radcliffe College, Harvard University, Cambridge; for more documentation on these points, Boris, *Art and Labor*, passim.

31. Belle Stowe to Clara Newton, September 13, 1886, Clara Newton Papers, Box 1, Cincinnati Historical Society.

32. On dress reform, Sally Buchanan Kinsey, "A More Reasonable Way To Dress," in Kaplan, *"Art That Is Life,"* 358–69; Alice Hubbard, quoted from Kinsey, 364; on Bowles, Sharon Darling, "From 'New Woman' to Metalsmith: A Voyage of Self-Discovery," in Shifman, *Janet Payne Bowles* (forthcoming); for simplified housekeeping, Boris, *Art and Labor*, 77–78; for cooperation, Dolores Hayden, *The Grand Domestic Revolution: A History of Feminist Designs for American Homes, Neighborhoods, and Cities* (Cambridge: MIT Press, 1981).

33. For the most extensive discussion in this vein, Robertson, "House and Home," 336–57; Hubbard quote from Robertson, 344. See also Margaret Marsh, "From Separation to Togetherness: The Social Construction of Domestic Space in American Suburbs, 1840–1915," *Journal of American History* 76 (September 1989): 506–27; Gwendolyn Wright, *Moralism and the Model Home: Domestic Architecture and Cultural Conflict in Chicago, 1873–1913* (Chicago: University of Chicago Press, 1980); see also David P. Handlin, *The American Home: Architecture and Society, 1815–1915* (Boston: Little, Brown and Company, 1979).

34. Robinson, "House and Home," 342–44.

35. Boris, *Art and Labor*, 59, 76.

36. Ibid.

37. Gwendolyn Wright, *Building the Dream: A Social History of Housing in America* (New York: Pantheon, 1982), 158–76; Robert Winter, *The California Bungalow* (Los Angeles: Hennessey and Ingalls, 1980). On Haywood, "Haywood's Battle in Paterson," *Literary Digest* 46 (May 10, 1913): 1043–44.

BRANDT
The Critic and the Evolution of Twentieth-Century American Craft

1. A. Clutton-Brock, *Essays on Art* (New York: Charles Scribner's Sons, 1920), 53.

2. Vernon Lee comments on the equality of the fine and the applied arts in *Laurus Nobilis; or, Chapters on Art and Life* (London: John Lane, The Bodley Head; New York: John Lane Company, 1909), 212.

3. For further information on the Arts and Crafts movement, see Gillian Naylor, *The Arts and Crafts Movement: A Study of Its Sources, Ideals, and Influence on Design Theory* (Cambridge: MIT Press, 1971; reprint, 1980); Eileen Boris, *Art and Labor: Ruskin, Morris, and the Craftsman Ideal in America* (Philadelphia: Temple University Press, 1986); Wendy Kaplan, ed., *"The Art That Is Life": The Arts & Crafts Movement in America, 1875–1920* (Boston: Museum of Fine Arts, 1987); and Gillian Naylor et al., *The Encyclopedia of Arts and Crafts: The International Arts Movement, 1850–1920* (New York: E. P. Dutton; London: Headline Book Publishing, 1989). On the role of critics at international expositions, see Beverly K. Brandt, "'Worthy and Carefully Selected': American Arts and Crafts at the Louisiana Purchase Exposition, 1904," *Journal of the Archives of American Art* 28, no. 1 (January 1988): 2–16.

4. On the involvement of architects in the reform movement, see Beverly K. Brandt, "The Essential Link: Boston Architects and the Society of Arts and Crafts, 1897–1917," *Tiller* 2, no. 1 (September–October 1983): 7–32.

5. Clutton-Brock, *Essays*, 112: In fifteenth-century Italy, "It was the best craftsman who became a painter or sculptor, merely because those were the most difficult crafts. Now it is the gentleman with artistic faculty who becomes a painter; the poor man, however much of that faculty he possesses, remains a workman without any artistic prestige and without any temptation to consider the quality of his work or to take any pleasure in it."

6. Baxter was critic for *The Boston Herald*; Coburn wrote for *The Boston Transcript*, *The Nation*, and *The New York Times Literary Supplement*; Downes wrote for *The Boston Transcript* and *The Atlantic Monthly*, in addition to producing several books on art-historical topics.

7. Charles Fergus Binns, *The Potter's Craft*, 4th edition (1910; reprint, Princeton: D. Van Nostrand Company, 1967), xi.

8. Mrs. Nelson Dawson, *Enamels* (London: Methuen & Co., 1906), 1–2; Clutton-Brock, *Essays*, 51.

9. The term "recipes" appears in Lewis F. Day, *Ornament & Its Application: A Book for Students Treating in a Practical Way of the Relation of Design to Materials, Tools and Methods of Work* (London: B. T. Batsford; New York: Charles Scribner's Sons, 1904), 262. For discussions of theories of "pure Design," see Ernest A. Batchelder, *The Principles of Design* (Chicago: Inland Printer Company, 1904), and Denman W. Ross, *A Theory of Pure Design: Harmony, Balance, Rhythm* (Boston: Houghton Mifflin and Company, 1907; reprint, New York: Peter Smith, 1933), v, 192–94.

10. Day refers to "artistic anarchy" and "accidents" in *The Planning of Ornament* (London: B. T. Batsford, 1887; reprint, New York: Garland Publishing, 1977, as part of the series *The Aesthetic Movement & the Arts and Crafts Movement*, edited by Peter Stansky and Rodney Shewan), 10, 49; Day, *Ornament & Its Application*, 232; A. H. Church refers to "rules of iron" in Batchelder, *Principles of Design*, 126.

11. Batchelder, *Principles of Design*, 21. For further discussions of the issue of style and the reform movement, see Beverly K. Brandt, "'Sobriety and Restraint': The Search for an Arts and Crafts Style in Boston, 1897–1917," *Tiller* 2, no. 5 (Fall 1985): 26–73.

12. Batchelder, *Principles of Design*, 73; Ross, *A Theory of Pure Design*, 7.

13. The dependency of American handicrafts upon European models is discussed in Maude Lawrence and Caroline Sheldon, *The Use of the Plant in Decorative Design* (New York and Chicago: Scott, Foresman and Co., 1912), 5.

14. These recommended reading lists are an invaluable source of information on history, theory, methodology, and criticism as applied to handicrafts. Authors such as Bernard Cuzner, Kate Gordon, Maude Lawrence and Caroline Sheldon, among others, include lists of recommended references within their works. Organizations—the Society of Arts and Crafts, Boston, or the National League of Handicraft Societies—compiled their own reference libraries and published bibliographies in annual reports or magazines such as *Handicraft*. The bibliography of the SACB collection, published in both 1907 and 1916, served as a basis for this research. It is important to note that these bibliographies often listed more foreign publications—especially British ones—than their American counterparts.

15. Lewis F. Day, *Nature in Ornament* (London: B. T. Batsford, 1892), 16; Day, *Ornament & Its Application*, 13, 130; Thorstein Veblen, *The Theory of the Leisure Class* (1899; reprint, New York: Macmillan, 1905).

16. Day, *Ornament & Its Application*, 34–35.

17. The beauty of the vernacular, indicates architecture critic Paul Goldberger, stems from the fact that it is "capable of yielding masterpieces and everyday [works] alike"; Paul Goldberger, *On the Rise: Architecture and Design in a Postmodern Age* (New York: Times Books, 1983), 5.

18. W. Proudfoot Begg, *The Development of Taste and Other Studies in Aesthetics* (Glasgow: James Maclehose and Sons, 1887), 142. Bernard Cuzner, *A Silversmith's Manual, Treating of the Designing and Making of the Simpler Pieces of Domestic Silverware*, 2nd edition (1935; reprint, London: N.A.G. Press, 1949), 186.

19. Clutton-Brock, *Essays*, 53.

20. Binns, *Potter's Craft*, ix; Lewis F. Day, *Instances of Accessory Art* (London: B. T. Batsford, 1880; reprint, New York: Garland Publishing, 1977, as part of the series *The Aesthetic Movement & the Arts and Crafts Movement*, edited by Peter Stansky and Rodney Shewan).

BRAZNELL
Metalsmithing and Jewelrymaking

1. English architect C. R. Ashbee and the Guild and School of Handicraft he founded, in 1888, became the preeminent model for the organization of American metalsmithing shops; see Alan Crawford, *C. R. Ashbee: Architect, Designer & Romantic Socialist* (New Haven: Yale University Press, 1985); W. Scott Braznell, "The Influence of C. R. Ashbee and His Guild of Handicraft on American Arts and Crafts Movement Silver, Other Metalwares, and Jewelry," paper presented at the Winterthur Conference, 1990, in Bert Denker, ed., *The Substance of Style: New Perspectives on the American Arts and Crafts Movement* (Winterthur, Del.: Henry Francis du Pont Winterthur Museum, forthcoming).

2. *Hull-House Bulletin* 2 (June 1897): 4; Sharon S. Darling, *Chicago Metalsmiths* (Chicago: Chicago Historical Society, 1977), 36. Metalwork was being taught by English manual-training instructor George Twose and Frank Hazenplug; other Hull-House metalwork teachers and practitioners were Allesandro G. Colarossi, Isadore V. Friedman, Jessie Luther, Augustus B. Higginson, Ednah S. Girvan (Mrs. Augustus B. Higginson), Frances G. Higginson, Isadore Taylor, and Homer Taylor.

3. George Twose, "The Chicago Arts and Crafts Society's Exhibition," *Brush and Pencil* 2 (May 1898): 76–79; for views of these metalsmiths, see Robert Bruce Kahler, "Art and Life: The Arts and Crafts Movement in Chicago, 1897–1915" (Ph.D. diss., Purdue University, 1966), 124–25.

4. *First Exhibition of the Arts & Crafts*, Copley Hall, Boston, Massachusetts, April 5–16, 1897 (Boston: Thomas P. Smith Printing Company, 1897), 11.

5. *Exhibition of Articles in Gold and Silver*, catalogue (New York: National Arts Club, 1899).

6. Beverly K. Brandt notes that in 1899, the Committee on Workshops and Classes of the Society of Arts and Crafts, Boston, had been disbanded because, according to Herbert L.

Warren, "Voluntary teachers [and] pupils irregular in attendance and tired out after a day's work in the shops made systematic instruction impossible"; see Beverly K. Brandt, "'Mutually Helpful Relations': Architects, Craftsmen, and the Society of Arts and Crafts, Boston, 1897–1917" (Ph.D. diss., Boston University, 1985), 146.

7. Leaflet for "Art Metal" course, annotated 1901, from scrapbook "1878–1903," in office of the curator of decorative arts, Museum of Art, Rhode Island School of Design. I am indebted to Thomas S. Michie for information on the first art-metal and jewelry classes at the school.

8. See "Art School Notes," *Art Interchange* 45 (July 1900): 21. Aranyi left Pratt Institute in 1905 to replace Charles E. Hansen at the Rhode Island School of Design; when Aranyi resigned from the school in late 1906, he was replaced by Joseph H. Harmstone. For Hamann, see his obituary in *The Jewelers' Circular* 95 (November 17, 1927): 63.

9. For Martin, see Dora M. Morrell, "The Arts and Crafts—Beauty in Common Things," *Brush and Pencil* 5 (February 1900): 222–32.

10. Hansen had wide experience here and in Europe, followed by employment at Tiffany & Company and Durand & Company; see leaflet, "Jewelry Design and Die Cutting," annotated 1903, from scrapbook "1878–1903," in office of the curator of decorative arts, Museum of Art, Rhode Island School of Design; *Rhode Island School of Design Year-Book 1902* (Providence: Rhode Island School of Design, 1902), 23. In 1913, the school listed nine day students and seventy-three evening students in its jewelry and silversmithing classes; see *Rhode Island School of Design Bulletin* 1 (January 1913).

11. See Florence N. Levy, ed., "School Reports," *American Art Annual 1903–1904*, vol. 4 (New York: American Art Annual, 1903): 278, 294.

12. Schools to do so included: School of Fine and Applied Arts, James Milliken University, Decatur, Illinois, 1903; Guild of Arts and Crafts, New York, with instruction by Emily Frances Peacock in enameling and (Miss) G. J. Busck in metalwork, 1903; School of the Worcester Art Museum, with classes in metalwork, jewelry, and enameling taught by Edmund B. Rolfe, 1905 (Grove R. Branch taught these classes from 1910); Rochester Mechanics Institute, with metalwork classes taught by Theodore H. Pond with the assistance of Carl H. Johonnot, 1905; Fine Arts Department, Teachers College, Columbia University, with metalwork classes taught by Edward Thatcher, 1906 (in addition, the university had a Department of Industrial Arts, where, in 1910, metalwork was taught by Charles C. Sieffel); Minneapolis Handicraft Guild, with metalwork first taught by H. Stuart Michie, 1906; and the School of the Museum of Fine Arts, Boston, with metalwork taught by George J. Hunt, 1907.

13. In November 1899, *The Art Amateur* began a fourteen-part article entitled "The Arts of Metal," and followed with advice, through 1902, on raising, soldering, repoussé, coloring, and lacquering. From June 1903, Emily Frances Peacock included elementary projects in metal and jewelry in her column, "The Crafts," for *Keramic Studio*, which published others by Laurin H. Martin, Harry S. Whitbeck, Edmund B. Rolfe, and Frank G. Sanford from 1905 to 1908. In the first decade, comparable articles were seen in *Palette and Brush*, *The Craftsman*, *The School Arts Magazine*, *American Homes and Gardens*, and *Handicraft*.

14. Key periodicals include *Art Interchange*, which, at the end of the 1890s and for a few years into the new century, reported on art metal and jewelry seen at early Arts and Crafts exhibitions in Minneapolis, Chicago, and New York. *International Studio* inspired American metalcrafts, with articles illustrating work by Alexander Fisher, C. R. Ashbee, and the Glasgow School of Art; its department "Notes on the Crafts," added to its "American Studio Notes" in 1904, is an important documentary source for art metal and jewelry. See *Brush and Pencil* articles by E. Harvey Middleton, "The Art Industries of America—VII, Enameling on Metal," 16 (September 1905): 66–74; Hugh W. Coleman, "The Art Industries of America—VIII, Ornamental Metal-Work," 16 (October 1905): 98–109, 118–21; Morris Hartmann, "The Art Industries of America—XI, Design and Making of Jewelry," 17 (January 1906): 2–7; Henry P. Tilden, "Martelé, A New Distinctive School," 18 (December 1906): 238–43. *Art and Progress* (later called *The American Magazine of Art*), published by the American Federation of Arts, closely followed Arts and Crafts development. *House Beautiful*, from its beginning in 1896, provided news of Arts and Crafts activities, and in October and November 1906 published Mabel Tuke Priestman's important article "History of the Arts and Crafts Movement in America." *The Craftsman* devoted an early issue to jewelry, enamel, and metal-related crafts (see *The Craftsman* 2, no. 2 [May 1902]), and later, it acquainted readers with René Lalique, Philippe Wolfers, and other vanguard European jewelers, in Irene Sargent, "A Comparison of Critics, Suggested by the Comments of Dr. Pudor," *The Craftsman* 6, no. 2 (May 1904): 135–41. *Arts and Decoration* had regular reports on school activities, framed by advertisements for school programs and special summer classes that included instruction in art metal, silver, and jewelry. Trade journals, especially *The Jewelers' Circular* and *The Keystone*, gave news of exhibitions, schools, graduations, and prizes awarded to students.

15. Others include Frank G. Sanford, "Sheet Metal Work," in *Art Crafts for Beginners* (New York: Century Company, 1904); Fred D. Crawshaw, *Metal Spinning* (Chicago: Popular Mechanics Company, 1909); Edward Thatcher, *Simple Soldering, Both Hard and Soft* (New York: Spon & Chamberlain; London: E. & F. N. Spon, 1910); John D. Adams, *Metalwork and Etching* (Chicago: Popular Mechanics Company, 1911); Thomas F. Googerty, *Hand Forging* (Chicago: Popular Mechanics Company, 1911); William L. Ilgen, *Forge Work* (New York: American Book Company, 1912); Erma Hewitt, *Notes on Jewelry and Metal Work* (Alfred, N.Y.: Sun Publishing Company, n.d.); William H. Varnum, *Industrial Arts Design* (Peoria, Ill.: Manual Art Press, 1916); H. R. Sorensen and S. J. Vaughan, *Handwrought Jewelry* (Milwaukee: Bruce Publishing Company, 1916); Augustus Foster Rose and Antonio Cirino, *Jewelry Making and Design* (Providence: Metal Crafts Publishing Company, 1918).

16. Charles G. Leland, "Handwork in Public Schools," *Century* 24 (June 1882): 890–96; Leland, *Elementary Metal Work: A Practical Manual For Amateurs and for Use in Schools* (London: Whittaker and Company, 1894). Leland's ideas inspired England's Home Arts and Industries Association, founded in 1884, and may have influenced C. R. Ashbee's Guild and School of Handicraft; see Crawford, *Ashbee*, 31, 315.

17. Helen Glen Ward at the Chautauqua Institution, 1903; Edward Thatcher at Byrdcliffe, in Woodstock, New York, 1903; Emily Frances Peacock at the Guild of Arts and Crafts, in New York, 1903.

18. Augustus Foster Rose at Bradley Institute, in Peoria, Illinois, 1906; Augustus Foster Rose and Charles J. Martin at Rhode Island School of Design, 1907; James H. Winn at the Minneapolis Handicraft Guild, 1907; Thatcher Summer School of Metal Work, Woodstock, New York, 1911; Summer Institute of Mechanic Arts, Mount Hermon, California, 1911; Carl F. Hamann's summer school at Lake Ronkonkoma, Long Island, New York, 1911; William H. Varnum at Monhegan Summer School of Metal Work and Jewelry, Monhegan Island, Maine, 1911.

19. One report noted, "Training of crippled soldiers as jewelry workers is one of the most interesting projects being carried on in the Department of Occupational Therapy, Reconstruction Division, Walter Reed General Hospital, Washington, D.C."; see Layton R. Colburn, *The Jewelers' Circular* 78 (April 9, 1919): 49.

20. Among those sharing bench space were Arthur S. Williams, Thorwald C. Christiansen, Margaret Rogers, Mary Peyton Winlock, George J. Hunt, James T. Woolley, David M. Little, and George Christian Gebelein, who remained there to establish his well-known silversmithing shop.

21. For Foster, see Margaretha Gebelein Leighton, et al., *George Christian Gebelein, Boston Silversmith, 1878–1945* (Boston: by author, 1976), 62.

22. For a list of books in the society's library, see *Twenty-Fifth Annual Report of the Society of Arts and Crafts, Boston, 1922* (Boston: Society of Arts and Crafts, 1922), 20–25.

23. Minnette Slayback Carper, "Arts and Crafts Exhibition in St. Louis," *The International Studio* 15 (January 1902): 51–56.

24. F. W. Coburn, "Metal Work at Boston," *The International Studio* 33 (February 1908): 145.

25. Arthur J. Stone, 1913; Josephine Hartwell Shaw and Frank L. Koralewsky, 1914; Margaret Rogers and Frank Gardner Hale, 1915; James T. Woolley, Elizabeth E. Copeland, and husband and wife Eda Lord Dixon and Lawrence B. Dixon, 1916; Herbert Taylor, 1917; Douglas Donaldson and Karl F. Leinonen, 1918; George Christian Gebelein, 1919; and Samuel Yellin, 1920.

26. Hazel H. Adler, "The National Society of Craftsmen," *The International Studio* 60 (February 1917): 121.

27. For a silver chalice set with semiprecious stones, executed by George J. Hunt and designed by Frank E. Cleveland, an associate architect of the Boston firm Cram, Goodhue, and Ferguson, see *Christian Art* 1 (July 1907): 6; for a polo trophy designed by Boston architect C. Howard Walker and executed by Arthur J. Stone in 1912, see Frederick W. Coburn, "Trophies," *Art and Progress* 3 (September 1912): 711–13.

28. See Charles H. Caffin, "American Studio Talk: Applied Art at the Architectural League," *The International Studio* 19 (April 1903): 119–22.

29. "Art Workers Organize," *Keramic Studio* 8 (July 1906): 69, 71.

30. The 1907 exhibition included work from such leading craftsmen as Robert R. Jarvie, Emily Frances Peacock, Leonide Cecilia Lavaron, Madeline Yale Wynne, and Charlotte Howell Busck; Native American jewelry was brought from Laguna, New Mexico, by Josephine Foard, in charge of that work there. See Eva Lovett, "The Exhibition of the National Society of Craftsmen," *The International Studio* 30 (January 1907): 74. Metalwork and jewelry by pupils of Robert Dulk at the New York Evening High School and of Edward Thatcher at Teachers College, Columbia University, were on view from 1909; see J. William Fosdick, "Third Annual Exhibition of the National Society of Craftsmen," *The International Studio* 36 (February 1909): 133.

31. Eileen Boris, *Art and Labor: Ruskin, Morris, and the Craftsman Ideal in America* (Philadelphia: Temple University Press, 1986): 43; also see "Classification of Sales in Treasurer's Report," in annual reports of the society.

32. "Wide Variety in Group of Current Exhibitions: Art at Home and Abroad," *The New York Times Magazine* (April 30, 1916): 14.

33. The Metal Workers Guild was organized at the Society of Arts and Crafts, Boston, in 1907, and was followed by the St. Dunstan's Guild for ecclesiastical arts by 1909, the Jewelers' Guild by 1921, and the Silversmiths' Guild in 1924. See Allen H. Eaton, *Handicrafts of New England* (New York: Harper & Row, 1949), 290; for the Jewelers' Guild, see "The Fine Arts: Exhibition of Jewelry," *Boston Transcript* (October 4, 1921): 13; for the Silversmiths' Guild, see *Twenty-Eighth Annual Report of the Society of Arts and Crafts, Boston, 1924* (Boston: Society of Arts and Crafts, 1925): 21. The Metal Workers Guild of the National Society of Craftsmen was orga-nized by 1910; see J. William Fosdick, "The Fourth Annual Exhibition of the National Society of Craftsmen," *The International Studio* 42 (February 1911): 82.

34. The Chicago exhibitions continued until 1925. The 1902 exhibition was particularly notable for metalwork and jewelry. Following a second Arts and Crafts exhibition at the Detroit Museum of Art, in 1905, these exhibitions were held at the city's Society of Arts and Crafts.

35. The Museum of Fine Arts, Boston, hosted exhibitions of the work of the city's Society of Arts and Crafts in 1911 and again in 1913; also see *Jewelry History* (Newark, N.J.: Newark Museum, 1914). In 1915 and again in 1916, the National Museum, in Washington, D.C., held exhibitions, organized by the American Federation of Arts, entitled "American Industrial Art"; see *Report on the Progress and Condition of the United States National Museum for the Year Ending June 30, 1915* (Washington, D.C.: Smithsonian Institution, United States National Museum, Government Printing Office, 1916), 117–23; "Exhibition of American Industrial Art," *The American Magazine of Art* 7 (July 1916): 381; "Some Notable Works by American Craftsmen," *The American Magazine of Art* 7 (August 1916): 435–42.

36. "American Silver: The Work of Seventeenth and Eighteenth Century Silversmiths," Museum of Fine Arts, Boston, 1906; "Hudson-Fulton Celebration," Metropolitan Museum of Art, New York, 1909; "American Church Silver of the Seventeenth and Eighteenth Centuries, with a Few Pieces of Domestic Plate," Museum of Fine Arts, Boston, 1911; "Silver Used in New York, New Jersey, and the South," Metropolitan Museum of Art, New York, 1911; "Exhibition of Old Silver Owned in Worcester County," Worcester Art Museum, Massachusetts, 1913.

37. J. William Fosdick, "American Handicrafts: The Fourth Annual Exhibition of the National Society of Craftsmen," *Art and Progress* 2 (February 1911): 101; see also *Exhibition of Old and Modern Handicraft* (Baltimore: Handicraft Club of Baltimore, 1913): 50–60, in which the large loan collection of old silver was almost exclusively English and American.

38. See *Rhode Island School of Design Year-Book 1901* (Providence: Rhode Island School of Design, 1901), 52; Samuel Howe, "The Drake Collection of Brass and Copper Vessels," *The Craftsman* 2, no. 2 (May 1902): 73–79.

39. Coburn, "Metal Work at Boston," 145. Gorham veterans included Mary C. Knight, Clemens Friedell, Julius O. Randahl, and James T. Woolley, ex-foreman at Goodnow and Jenks; Tiffany veterans included John P. Petterson and George Christian Gebelein.

40. For the Blanchards, see Leslie Greene Bowman, "Arts and Crafts Silversmiths: Friedell and Blanchard in Southern California," in Edgar W. Morse, ed., *Silver in the Golden State* (Oakland: Oakland Museum of History Department, 1986), 46, 48.

41. For Schon, see Ruth K. Rice, "Carl Schon, Craftsman," *The Art World* 2 (August 1917): 482–83.

42. For Rogers and Richmond, see Claire M. Coburn, "Specimens of Craftsman Jewelry," *Good Housekeeping* 43 (November 1906): 507, 509.

43. The survey was made by a special Committee on Art in the Public Schools, of the American Federation of Arts; see "The Best Art in America," *The American Magazine of Art* 4 (June 1913): 1007–9.

44. Martin Eidelberg, "Tiffany and the Cult of Nature," in Alastair Duncan, Martin Eidelberg, and Neil Harris, *Masterworks of Louis Comfort Tiffany* (New York: Harry N. Abrams, 1989), 82–84; Gardner Teall, "Artistic American Wares at Expositions," *Brush and Pencil* 6 (July 1900): 179–80.

45. For Marshall, see "The Year's Progress among America's Craftsmen," *The Craftsman* 23 (October 1912–March 1913): 583–84; for Stephan, see Wendy Kaplan, ed., *"The Art That Is Life": The Arts and Crafts Movement in America, 1875–1920* (Boston: Museum of Fine Arts, 1987), 158; for Rolfe, see his seven-part article "Enameling on Metal and the Making of Enamels," *Palette and Brush* 2–3 (May–November 1910).

46. Vallory Roudebush, "The Busck Studio," *House Beautiful* 14 (November 1903): 388.

47. Charles H. Barr, "Metal-work and Amateurs," *House Beautiful* 7 (December 1899): 16–24; Frances R. Starrett, "The Arts and Crafts Exhibition in Minneapolis," *House Beautiful* 9 (April 1901): 225, 227. About 1902, Barr moved to Mamaroneck, New York.

48. For Googerty, see his seven-part article "Art-Smithing," *Industrial Arts & Vocational Education* 2–3 (August 1914–February 1915); for Colnik, see Judith Simonsen, "Cyril Colnik," *Lore* 31 [Milwaukee Public Museum quarterly magazine] (Summer 1981): 21–27.

49. One designer commented, "The hand-wrought and special designs are produced at great expense, so that these individual creations and products of thought are not for the general public—their expensiveness enabling but few to buy them"; see Laurence B. Haste, "Silverware from the Designer's Standpoint," *Arts and Decoration* 1 (March 1911): 207.

50. Brandt, "Mutually Helpful Relations," 161–63.

51. George G. Booth silver commissions are in the collections of Cranbrook Academy of Art Museum and the Detroit Institute of Arts; for Julia Marlowe Sothern's patronage of Arthur J. Stone, see Elentia C. Chickering, "Arthur J. Stone, Silversmith," *Antiques* 129 (January 1986): 281.

52. I am indebted to David L. Barquist for bringing to my attention Francis P. Garvan's early patronage of New England studio silversmiths retailed by the Little Gallery, in New York; see papers of Francis P. Garvan, Archives of American Art, Washington, D.C.

I wish to thank Cheryl Robertson for her attentive reading of early versions of this essay and for her insightful comments. Catherine Zusy and Anna Tobin D'Ambrosio kindly shared the fruits of their research with me. —E.S.C.

1. Some of the market-driven publications that view the American Arts and Crafts movement as evidence of American exceptionalism, and that rank the firms according to a technique- or design-based hierarchy, include David M. Cathers, *Furniture of the American Arts and Crafts Movement: Stickley and Roycroft Mission Oak* (New York: New American Library, 1981), and Cathers, *From Architecture to Object: Masterworks of the American Arts & Crafts Movement* (New York: Hirschl & Adler Galleries, 1989). Even revisionist museum publications seem to emphasize the moral aesthetics of various styles, implying that there were heroes and villains in regard to "craftsmanship": Wendy Kaplan, ed., *"The Art That Is Life": The Arts & Crafts Movement in America, 1875–1920* (Boston: Museum of Fine Arts, 1987); Leslie Greene Bowman, *American Arts & Crafts: Virtue in Design* (Los Angeles: Los Angeles County Museum of Art, 1990).

2. David Pye was the first scholar to address the changing meanings of craftsmanship: *The Nature and Art of Workmanship* (London: Cambridge University Press, 1968), esp. 10–12. See also Edward S. Cooke, Jr., "The Study of American Furniture from the Perspective of the Maker," in Gerald W. R. Ward, ed., *Perspectives on American Furniture* (New York: W. W. Norton, 1988), 113–26, and Douglas Harper, *Working Knowledge: Skill and Community in a Small Shop* (Chicago: University of Chicago Press, 1987).

3. Edward S. Cooke, Jr., "The Boston Furniture Industry in 1880," *Old-Time New England* 70 (1980): 82–98; Michael Ettema, "Technological Innovation and Design Economics in Furniture Manufacture," *Winterthur Portfolio* 16, nos. 2–3 (Summer–Autumn 1981): 197–223; and Gregory Weidman, *Furniture in Maryland, 1740–1940* (Baltimore: Maryland Historical Society, 1984).

4. Rosalind Williams, *Dream Worlds: Mass Consumption in Late-Nineteenth-Century France* (Berkeley: University of California Press, 1982), and Grant McCracken, *Culture and Consumption: New Approaches to the Symbolic Character of Consumer Goods and Activities* (Bloomington: Indiana University Press, 1988). "Art furniture" was another segment of the furniture industry in the 1880s, but it only occasionally overlapped with handcrafted at that time: Marilynn Johnson, "Art Furniture: Wedding the Beautiful to the Useful," in *In Pursuit of Beauty: Americans and the Aesthetic Movement* (New York: Metropolitan Museum of Art, 1986): 143–75.

5. See Gustav Stickley, "The Structural Style in Cabinet-Making," *House Beautiful* 15 (December 1903): 19–23.

6. Eileen Boris, *Arts and Labor: Ruskin, Morris, and the Craftsman Ideal in America* (Philadelphia: Temple University Press, 1986).

7. On women carvers in the aesthetic period, see Kenneth R. Trapp, "To Beautify the Useful: Benn Pitman and the Women's Woodcarving Movement in Cincinnati in the Late Nineteenth Century," in Kenneth Ames, ed., *Victorian Furniture* (Philadelphia: Victorian Society in America, 1983). For information on Wynne, see Kaplan, *"Art That Is Life,"* 264–65, and Sharon S. Darling, *Chicago Furniture: Art, Craft & Industry, 1833–1983* (New York and London: W. W. Norton, 1984), 214–31.

8. A recent assessment of Lummis's role is Cheryl Robertson, "Arts & Crafts Domesticity: The Simple Life in the Golden State," in *The Arts and Crafts Movement in the Golden State* (Oakland: Oakland Museum, forthcoming). The disfiguring tool marks are inappropriate to the New Mexican woodworking tradition: Lonn Taylor and Dessa Bokides, *New Mexican Furniture 1600–1940: The Origins, Survival, and Revival of Furniture Making in the Hispanic Southwest* (Santa Fe: Museum of New Mexico Press, 1987).

9. Edward S. Cooke, Jr., in Kaplan, *"Art That Is Life,"* 315.

10. Robert Edwards and Jane Perkins Claney, *The Byrdcliffe Arts and Crafts Colony: Life by Design* (Wilmington: Delaware Art Museum, 1984), and Kaplan, *Art That Is Life*, 313–14.

11. William Smallwood Ayres, ed., *A Poor Sort of Heaven, A Good Sort of Earth: The Rose Valley Arts and Crafts Experiment* (Chadds Ford, Pa.: Brandywine River Museum, 1983), esp. 51–59, and Ayres, "The Constructional Theory of Furniture Making: More Honored in the Breach Than in the Observance," *Tiller* 1, no. 1 (September–October 1982): 21–30.

12. Timothy J. Andersen, Eudorah M. Moore, and Robert W. Winter, eds., *California Design 1910* (Pasadena: California Design Publications, 1974; reprint, Salt Lake City: Peregrine Smith, 1980), 63, and Kaplan, *Art That Is Life*, 321.

13. *The Craftsman* frequently published plans and directions, including cutting lists of stock. H. H. Windsor published a broad selection of designs in *Mission Furniture: How To Make It*, 3 vols. (Chicago: Popular Mechanics Press, 1909).

14. Ayres, "Constructional Theory of Furniture Making," 21–30.

15. Quotation from *Fashionable Furniture* (catalogue of Nelson-Matter Furniture Company, Grand Rapids, Michigan, 1904). See also *The Upholstery Dealer and Decorative Furnisher* 5 (January 1904): 43.

16. Pye presents a pertinent discussion about the quality of regulated workmanship, the inappropriate use of intentional roughness, and the historical role of free workmanship in inexpensive work.

17. *The Grand Rapids Furniture Record* 7, no. 5 (October 1903): 515.

18. Temple Scott, "Mission Furniture," *The International Studio* 12 (February 1901).

19. Anna T. D'Ambrosio, "'The Distinction of Being Different': Joseph P. McHugh and the American Arts and Crafts Movement," paper presented at the Winterthur Conference, 1990, and Kaplan, *"Art That Is Life,"* 185.

20. The best sources on Stickley's furniture include Coy Ludwig, *The Arts and Crafts Movement in New York State, 1890s–1920s* (Hamilton, N.Y.: Gallery Association of New York State, 1983), 62–67; Catherine Zusy's entries in Kaplan, *"Art That Is Life,"* 243–46; and Bowman, *American Arts & Crafts,* 70–87.

21. Don Marek, *Arts and Crafts Furniture Design: The Grand Rapids Contribution, 1895–1915* (Grand Rapids, Mich.: Grand Rapids Art Museum, 1987), 50–55; Kaplan, *"Art That Is Life,"* 247; and Bowman, *American Arts & Crafts,* 68–69.

22. Marek, *Arts and Crafts Furniture Design,* 37–49; Kaplan, *"Art That Is Life,"* 165–68; and Bowman, *American Arts & Crafts,* 52–54. The connection between the rustic and the Arts and Crafts movement is discussed by Craig Gilborn in *Adirondack Furniture and the Rustic Tradition* (New York: Harry N. Abrams, 1987), esp. 44–47 and 240–51.

23. Andersen et al., *California Design,* 88–95, and Kaplan, *"Art That Is Life",* 191–93.

24. Randell L. Makinson, *Greene and Greene: Furniture and Related Designs* (Santa Barbara: Peregrine Smith, 1979); Edward S. Cooke, Jr.'s entries in Kaplan, *"Art That Is Life,"* 401–6; Bowman, *American Arts & Crafts,* 46–51; and Edward S. Cooke, Jr., "Scandinavian Modern Furniture in the Arts and Crafts Period: The Collaboration of the Greenes and the Halls," *American Furniture* 1 (forthcoming).

25. Ludwig, *Arts and Crafts Movement,* 87–88; Kaplan, *"Art That Is Life,"* 237–41; and Bowman, *American Arts & Crafts,* 58–63.

26. Gilborn, *Adirondack Furniture,* 325–26, plates 17–19 and 33–35.

27. Elmer Gray, "The Architect and the Arts and Crafts," *Architectural Record* 21 (June 1907): 132–33.

28. On Elmslie, see Darling, *Chicago Furniture,* 253–56, and Kaplan, *"Art That Is Life,"* 201–5. Wright's quotation appeared in Darling, 260–61. Elmslie and Wright repeatedly emphasized the geometric relationships underlying all structures.

29. Among the better publications on Wright's early furniture are David A. Hanks, *The Decorative Designs of Frank Lloyd Wright* (New York: E. P. Dutton, 1979); Cheryl Robertson and Terrence Marvel, *The Domestic Scene (1897–1927): George M. Niedecken, Interior Architect* (Milwaukee: Milwaukee Art Museum, 1981); Darling, *Chicago Furniture,* 256–66; Edward S. Cooke, Jr., entries in Kaplan, *"Art That Is Life,"* 391–95; and Bowman, *American Arts & Crafts,* 92–95.

30. Maher as quoted in Edward S. Cooke, Jr., entries on Maher in Kaplan, *"Art That Is Life,"* 396–400. In 1913, George Elmslie and his partner, William Purcell, made a similar argument for the development of an overall design scheme from geometrically derived abstractions of nature: "After the motif is established the development of it is an orderly procession from start to finish, it is all intensely organic, proceeding from main motif to minor motifs, interblending, inter-relating and to the last terminal, all of a piece. It is the play work in the architect's day, his hour of refinement." See "The Statics and Dynamics of Architecture," *The Western Architect* 19 (January 1913).

31. *The Grand Rapids Furniture Record* 19 (September 1909): 534–35, and *Limbert's Arts and Crafts Furniture* (1905 catalogue; reprint, Watkins Glen, N.Y.: American Life Foundation, 1982).

32. For a historiographic review of the literature on craftsmen from this period, see Edward S. Cooke, Jr., "The Study of American Furniture from the Perspective of the Maker," in Ward, *Perspectives on American Furniture*, 113–26. The 1981 quotation is from *American Crafts 1981* (Manchester, N.H.: League of New Hampshire Craftsmen, 1981), 2.

33. On the need for better design education, see "The Artist-Designer," *The Furniture Manufacturer and Artisan* 70 (April 1915): 187–88, and A. W. Williams, "A Defense of Quantity Production," *The Furniture Manufacturer and Artisan* 77 (July 1918): 41–42. The increased importance of school-trained designers is also discussed by Robert Edwards, "The Art of Work," in Kaplan, *"Art That Is Life,"* 221–36, but the lag in school-trained craftspeople is pointed out by Edward S. Cooke, Jr., in *New American Furniture: The Second Generation of Studio Furnituremakers* (Boston: Museum of Fine Arts, 1989), 10–31.

34. Among the important early treatises on pure design are Denman W. Ross, *A Theory of Pure Design: Harmony, Balance, Rhythm* (Boston: Houghton Mifflin and Company, 1907), and Ernest A. Batchelder, *Design in Theory and Practice* (New York: Macmillan Company, 1910).

35. Among the recent exhibition catalogues that assume that architect-designed furniture is implicitly the best or most important, and that Frank Lloyd Wright ushered in the architect's interest in furniture, are Emilio Ambasz et al., *Furniture by Architects: Contemporary Chairs, Tables and Lamps* (Boston: Hayden Gallery, Massachusetts Institute of Technology, 1981), and *Shape and Environment: Furniture by American Architects* (Stamford, Conn.: Whitney Museum of American Art, Fairfield County, 1982).

LEVIN
Ceramics: Seeking a Personal Style

1. Charles F. Binns, "The Use of American Wares by American Decorators," *Keramic Studio* 1, no. 4 (August 1899): 81.

2. Paul Evans, *Art Pottery of the United States* (New York: Charles Scribner's Sons, 1974), 173.

3. Ibid., 251.

4. John N. Norwood, quoting Marshall Fry, in *1900–1950, Ceramics at Alfred University* (Alfred, N.Y.: Alfred University Press, 1950). This pamphlet is from the archives of the Scholes Library, Alfred University.

5. Susan R. Strong, "The Searching Flame," *American Ceramics* 1, no. 3 (1982): 47.

6. [Mary] Louise McLaughlin, "Losanti Ware," *Keramic Studio* 3, no. 8 (December 1901): 178.

7. Irene Sargent, "Some Potters and Their Products," *The Craftsman* 4, no. 5 (July 1903): 334.

8. For a discussion of structural naturalism as the American variant of Art Nouveau, see Kristen Keen, *American Art Pottery 1875–1930* (Wilmington: Delaware Art Museum, 1978).

9. Charles F. Binns, "Clay in the Studio," *Keramic Studio* 4, no. 12 (April 1903): 269.

10. Adelaide Alsop Robineau, frame 653, roll 76, Archives of American Art, Smithsonian Institution, Washington, D.C., from an article in *The International Studio* (September 1905).

11. *The Art Academy of the People's University* (St. Louis: People's University Press, 1910).

12. For an in-depth history of Newcomb Pottery, see Jessie Poesch, *Newcomb Pottery: An Enterprise for Southern Women, 1895–1940* (Exton, Pa.: Schiffer Publishing, 1984).

13. Charles F. Binns, "Pottery in America," *The American Magazine of Art* 7, no. 4 (February 1916): 135.

14. Claire Fox, "Henry Chapman Mercer: Tilemaker, Collector, Builder Extraordinary," *Antiques* 104, no. 4 (October 1973): 678.

15. Kenneth R. Trapp, *Toward the Modern Style: Rookwood Pottery. The Later Years: 1915–1950* (New York: Jordan-Volpe Gallery, 1983).

16. Susan R. Strong, "The Publications by the Artists and Their Effects on the Ceramics Movement," *NCECA Journal* 6 (1985): 66.

17. Charles F. Binns, "Pottery Making," *The American Magazine of Art* 10, no. 1 (November 1918): 22.

18. Adelaide Alsop Robineau, frame 1101, roll 854, Archives of American Art, Smithsonian Institution, Washington, D.C.

PAPANICOLAOU
Colored Light: Glass 1900–1920

1. John La Farge, "Windows, III," in Russell Sturgis, ed., *A Dictionary of Architecture and Building* (New York: Macmillan and Company, 1902), col. 1080. The passage is quoted in Henry A. La Farge, "Painting with Colored Light:- The Stained Glass of John La Farge," in Henry Adams et al., *John La Farge*, exhibition catalogue, Carnegie Museum of Art, Pittsburgh, and National Museum of American Art, Washington, D.C. (New York: Abbeville Press, 1987), 220.

2. Jane Hayward, "Painted Windows," *Bulletin of the Metropolitan Museum of Art* 30 (December 1971–January 1972): 98–101, and Catherine Brisac, *A Thousand Years of Stained Glass* (New York: Doubleday, 1986), are among many works that discuss light symbolism in the context of medieval glass. Brisac is particularly valuable as she was an authority on nineteenth-century glass in Europe.

3. Robert Sowers, *Stained Glass: An Architectural Art* (New York: Universe Books, 1965), discusses the properties of glass and light from the point of view of a glass artist.

4. La Farge relates that even as early as his first trip to France he was analyzing medieval windows according to the color theories of Chevreul; see Royal Cortissoz, *John La Farge, A Memoir and a Study* (New York: Da Capo, 1971), 87–88, and Kathleen A. Foster, "John La Farge and the American Watercolor Movement: Art for the Decorative Age," in Adams et al., *John La Farge*, 150 (see note 1). La Farge used color complementaries as part of the symbolism of his great Resurrection window in Methuen, Massachusetts; see La Farge, "Painting with Colored Light," fig. 158.

5. Alice Cooney Frelinghuysen, "A New Renaissance: Stained Glass in the Aesthetic Period," in *In Pursuit of Beauty, Americans and the Aesthetic Movement* (New York: Metropolitan Museum of Art, 1986), 188, ill. and fig. 6.5, p. 176, and La Farge, "Painting with Colored Light," 197–98, fig. 145.

6. Hugh F. McKean, *The "Lost" Treasures of Louis Comfort Tiffany* (New York: Doubleday, 1980), 4, 51, figs. 42, 43, and Alastair Duncan, "Stained Glass: Secular Windows and Ecclesiastical Settings," in Duncan, Martin Eidelberg, and Neil Harris, *Masterworks of Louis Comfort Tiffany* (New York: Harry N. Abrams, 1989), 126.

7. Will H. Low, "Old Glass in New Windows," *Scribner's* 4 (1888): 675–86.

8. H. Weber Wilson, *Great Glass in American Architecture, Decorative Windows and Doors before 1920* (New York: E. P. Dutton, 1986).

9. Thomas P. F. Hoving, "Stained Glass Windows," introduction to Hayward, "Painted Windows," 97.

10. James L. Sturm, *Stained Glass from Medieval Times to the Present, Treasures To Be Seen in New York* (New York: E. P. Dutton, 1982), 47–59. The history of the Lamb studio has not yet been written. It developed a distinctive variation on the opalescent style that relied much more on enamels, and seems also to have had connections with artists of the La Farge circle. This represents one of the great unsolved problems of the opalescent school; see Arlene Pancza-Graham, "Leon Dabo and the Rose of St. John the Baptist," *Stained Glass* 78 (Spring 1983): 31–34.

11. This divergence was noticed by their contemporaries; see Diane Chalmers Johnson, *American Art Nouveau* (New York: Harry N. Abrams, 1979), 74–75.

12. Told to the author by John Nussbaum, a glass painter who had worked with Guthrie in the 1960s.

13. In addition to the essay by Frelinghuysen (see note 5), see Kenneth M. Wilson, *New England Glass and Glassmaking* (New York: Thomas Y. Crowell Company, 1972), which provides a thorough picture of the northeast art-glass manufacturers—the New England Glass Company, the Boston and Sandwich Company, and the Mount Washington Glass Company. Albert Christian Revi, *Nineteenth Century Glass: Its Genesis and Development*, rev. ed. (New York: Nelson, 1967) and Revi, *American Art Nouveau Glass* (Camden, N.J.: Nelson, 1968), discuss the Tiffany furnaces in historical context. Adeline Pepper, *The Glass Gaffers of New Jersey* (New York: Charles Scribner's Sons, 1971), is invaluable for treating the glass house from the opposite perspective, that of the shop workers, who frequently migrated from one glass house to another and whose role in the dissemination of style has not been appreciated by scholars working from the artist-designer perspective.

14. Revi, *Nineteenth Century Glass*, 114, 140–47, 149, 178, includes references to Nash. Robert Koch, *Louis C. Tiffany's Glass, Bronzes, Lamps: A Complete Collector's Guide* (New York: Crown, 1971), 40, 52, 62–75, includes a priceless interview with a former Tiffany gaffer that vividly describes the furnaces from the vantage point of one of the shop workers.

15. Paul V. Gardner, *The Glass of Frederick Carder* (New York: Crown, 1971).

16. Koch, *Tiffany's Glass, Bronzes, Lamps*, 52, 63, 67–68, and Wilson, *New England Glass*, 283, 368, fig. 357.

17. Pepper, *Glass Gaffers*, 278–80, 283–85, figs. 209–17, plates 1–3, 18, 19.

18. Otto Heinigke, "Random Thoughts of a Glassman," *The Craftsman* 3, no. 3 (December 1902), reprinted in *Stained Glass* 30 (Winter 1935–36): 75–90, and Harry Eldredge Goodhue, "Stained Glass in Private Houses," *Architectural Record* 18 (November 1905), 347–54. Lange's glass can be seen in Randell L. Makinson, *Greene & Greene: Architecture As a Fine Art* (Salt Lake City: Peregrine Smith, 1977), 166, ill. 165, and in Steven Adams, *The Arts and Crafts Movement* (Secaucus, N.J.: Chartwell, 1987), 90–91.

19. Sturm, *Stained Glass*, 76–77, discusses the Prairie School as a precursor to the Modernist glass of the Art Deco period and beyond, illustrating the Wright and Elmslie windows in New York and a panel by Giannini and Hilgart, a studio that executed windows for Wright. David A. Hanks, *The Decorative Designs of Frank Lloyd Wright* (New York: E. P. Dutton, 1979), discusses Wright's designs and the studios

Wright employed. For Elmslie's 1911 panel from the Cross House, in the Metropolitan Museum of Art, see Robert Judson Clark, ed., *The Arts and Crafts Movement in America, 1876–1916* (Princeton, N.J.: Princeton University Press, 1972), 63, no. 77, and for the 1913 panel from the Purcell House, in the Minneapolis Institute of Arts, see Wendy Kaplan, ed., *"The Art That Is Life": The Arts and Crafts Movement in America, 1875–1920* (Boston: Museum of Fine Arts, 1987), 205.

20. The favored studios are illustrated in George Herbertson Charles, "Stained and Painted Glass," in Ralph Adams Cram, *American Churches* (New York: The American Architect, 1915), 67–83. Charles Connick, *Adventures in Light and Color* (New York: Random House, 1937), gives a highly personal account of the glass world in these years. For a survey of the Neo-Gothic, see Sturm, *Stained Glass*, 60–75. Articles on individual artists include Peter Cormack, "Christopher Whall: Founder of the English Glass Renaissance," *Stained Glass* 76, no. 4 (Winter 1981–82): 318–22; Linda M. Papanicolaou, "J. Gordon Guthrie," *Stained Glass* 77, no. 4 (Winter 1982–83): 356–59; Richard L. Hoover, "*The World's* Liberty," *Stained Glass* 81 (Summer 1986): 90–93, which is an article on Heinigke; and Noreen O'Gara, "Charles J. Connick," *Stained Glass* 82 (Spring 1987).

21. Robert Koch, *Louis C. Tiffany, Rebel in Glass* (New York: Crown, 1964), 83, and Duncan, "Stained Glass," 136–38.

22. Duncan, "Stained Glass," plates 103, 104, and ill. p. 183.

THURMAN
Textiles: As Documented by The Craftsman

1. "Embroidery Lessons with Colored Studies" (New London, Conn.: The Brainerd & Armstrong Company, 1905).

2. Dianne Ayres, "A Primer on Arts and Crafts Textiles," *Arts and Crafts Quarterly Magazine* (April 1991): 4–9.

3. Valley Supply Company, St. Louis, Missouri, 1911–12 sales catalogue.

4. Ayres, "Primer," 4–9.

5. Isabelle Anscombe and Charlotte Gere, *Arts & Crafts in Britain and America* (New York: Rizzoli International Publications, 1978), 19.

6. Gustav Stickley, *The Craftsman* 1, no. 1 (October 1901): 1.

7. Gustav Stickley, *The Craftsman's Story*, sales catalogue (Eastwood, N.Y.: Craftsman Workshops, 1905), 22–23.

8. *The Craftsman* 4, no. 6 (September 1903).

9. *The Craftsman* 5, no. 3 (December 1903).

10. *The Craftsman* 8, no. 4 (July 1905): 25.

11. *Craftsman Fabrics and Needlework from the Craftsman Workshops*, with new introduction by

Richard M. Rasnick (1905; reprint, Madison, Wis.: Razmataz Press, 1989).

12. *The Craftsman* 6, no. 2 (May 1904).

13. *The Craftsman* 8, no. 5 (August 1905): 704–5.

14. *The Craftsman* 4, no. 5 (August 1903): 387.

15. *The Craftsman* 6, no. 6 (September 1904).

16. *The Craftsman* 20, no. 6 (September 1911): 26a.

17. Wendy Kaplan, ed., *"The Art That Is Life": The Arts & Crafts Movement in America, 1875–1920* (Boston: Museum of Fine Arts, 1987), 316.

18. *The Craftsman* 13, no. 1 (October 1907).

19. John B. Moore, *The Catalogues of Fine Navajo Blankets, Rugs, Ceremonial Baskets, Silverware, Jewelry & Curios* (Cottonwood Press, Navajo Indian Reservation, New Mexico: Crystal Trading Post, 1903–11; reprint, Albuquerque, N.M.: Avanyu Publishing, 1987).

20. Lester L. Williams, *C. N. Cotton and His Navajo Blankets: A Biography of C. N. Cotton, Gallup, New Mexico Indian Trader, and reprintings of three mail order catalogs of Navajo blankets and rugs originally printed between 1896 and 1919* (Albuquerque, N.M.: Avanyu Publishing, 1989).

21. *The "Pendleton" Line—General Catalogue Showing Colored Engravings* (Pendleton, Oregon: Pendleton Woolen Mills, about 1915; reprint, Albuquerque, N.M.: Avanyu Publishing, 1987).

22. *The Craftsman* 5, no. 1 (October 1903): 94.

23. Ibid., 95.

24. Ibid., 94.

25. Ibid., 95–99.

26. *The Craftsman* 19, no. 5 (February 1911): 34a.

27. Charles Francis Saunders, *House and Garden* (October 1910): 221–22.

28. *The Craftsman* 25, no. 4 (January 1914): 9a.

29. *House and Garden* (October 1917): 28–29; *The Craftsman* 11, no. 6 (March 1907): 784–90.

30. Charles E. Pellew, *The Craftsman* 16, no. 2 (May 1909): 232–35.

31. Kaplan, *"Art That Is Life,"* 320–21.

32. *The Craftsman* 13, no. 3 (December 1907): 353.

33. See Exhibitions listing in Resource section of this book.

34. See Exhibitions listing in Resource section of this book.

35. *The Craftsman* 5, no. 2 (November 1903): 184.

36. Gillian Moss, "Deerfield Blue and White—An Arts and Crafts Society," *American Art and Antiques* 2, no. 5 (October 1979): 72.

37. *The Craftsman* 5, no. 3 (December 1903): 286–89.

38. Ibid.

39. *The Craftsman* 13, no. 6 (March 1908): 712.

40. Ibid., 712, 714.

41. *House and Garden* (August 1910): 86.

42. Ibid., 87, 123.

43. One portiere is in The Art Institute of Chicago, accession no. 1971.680; the other is in the St. Louis Art Museum.

44. *Architectural Record* 15, no. 4 (April 1904): 377–78.

45. Frank Lloyd Wright Fellowship Lecture, Taliesin West, Arizona (August 22, 1954), 7–9.

46. Ernst Wasmuth, *Ausgefuehrte Bauten und Entwuerfe von Frank Lloyd Wright* (1910; reprint, Palos Park, Ill.: Prairie School Press, 1975), plate XXXIB.

47. Ibid., plate LVI.

48. Bruce Brooks Pfeiffer, *Frank Lloyd Wright Preliminary Studies: 1899–1916*, vol. 9 (Tokyo: A.D.A. Edita Tokyo Company, 1985), 144.

49. Suzanne Ormond and Mary E. Irvine, *Louisiana's Art Nouveau: The Crafts of the Newcomb Style* (Gretna, La.: Pelican Publishing Company, 1976), 7.

50. Ibid., 81.

51. Telephone interview between Mickey Wright, research assistant, department of textiles, The Art Institute of Chicago, and Gary Barker, head of Student Craft Industries, Berea College, April 21, 1992.

52. Caryl Coleman, *The Craftsman* 2, no. 4 (July 1902): 189–94.

53. Ibid.

54. Oscar Lovell Triggs, *The Craftsman* 3, no. 1 (October 1902): 25.

55. Oscar Lovell Triggs, *The Craftsman* 3, no. 4 (January 1903): 218–19.

56. Ibid., 222.

57. Ibid., 221. Subsequent issues carried articles on the formation of schools of various kinds—among them, two in New York City: Greenwich House Handicraft School, in Greenwich Village, and the New York School of Applied Design for Women; see *The Craftsman* 13, no. 6 (March 1908), and *The Craftsman* 18, no. 3 (June 1910).

KORNWOLF
The Arts and Crafts in American Houses and Gardens

1. These magazines were published as follows: *House Beautiful* (Chicago, 1896–present); *House and Garden* (Philadelphia, 1901–present); *Indoors and Out* (Boston, 1905–7); *The Craftsman* (New York, 1901–16); *The Ladies' Home Journal* (Philadelphia, especially the years 1900–1907); *Handicraft* (Boston Society of Arts and Crafts, 1910–12); *Country Life in America* (New York, 1901–17). Many were inspired by the English magazines *The Studio* (London, 1893–present) and *Country Life* (London, 1898–present).

2. When Lutyens's penchant for witty monumentality began to surface, Jekyll reminded him that "my house is to be built for me to live in and to love; it is not to be built as an exposition of architectonic inutility"; see Gertrude Jekyll, *Home and Garden* (London: Longmans, 1900).

3. Christopher Hussey, *The Life of Sir Edwin Lutyens* (London: Country Life, 1950), 28–35.

4. William Morris, quoted from "The Beauty of Life," in *The Collected Works of William Morris*, May Morris, ed., vol. 22 (London: Longmans Green, 1910–15), 70–71.

5. For the Country Life movement, see William L. Bowers, *The Country Life Movement in America, 1900–1920* (Port Washington, N.Y.: Kennikat Press, 1974).

6. These issues are treated in James D. Kornwolf, *M. H. Baillie-Scott and the Arts and Crafts Movement* (Baltimore and London: Johns Hopkins Press, 1972), and in Kornwolf essay, in Doreen Bolger Burke et al., *In Pursuit of Beauty: Americans and the Aesthetic Movement* (New York: Metropolitan Museum of Art and Rizzoli International Publications, 1986), 341–83.

7. Scudder, quoted from Eileen Boris, "Dreams of Brotherhood and Beauty: The Social Ideas of the Arts and Crafts Movement," in Wendy Kaplan, ed., *"The Art That Is Life": The Arts & Crafts Movement in America, 1875–1920* (Boston: Museum of Fine Arts, 1987), 214. For the Sargent-Stickley collaboration, see John Crosby Freeman, *The Forgotten Rebel: Gustav Stickley and His Craftsman Mission Furniture* (Watkins Glen, N.Y.: Century House, 1966), 15.

8. See Edward Bok, *The Americanization of Edward Bok: The Autobiography of a Dutch Boy Fifty Years After* (New York: Charles Scribner's Sons, 1920; reprint, New York: Pocket Books, 1965), 171, 179. The emphasis upon simplicity was a reaction to the "complexity" of the Victorian era, and became a catchword in the period; see Charles Keeler, *The Simple Home* (San Francisco: Paul Elder, 1904; Santa Barbara, and Salt Lake City: Peregrine Smith, 1979).

9. See Gustav Stickley, *The Best of Craftsman Homes* (1909, 1912; reprint, Santa Barbara: Peregrine Smith, 1979), 7; see also Mary Ann Smith, *Gustav Stickley, The Craftsman* (Syracuse, N.Y.: Syracuse University Press, 1983).

10. Wright, quoted from *The Future of Architecture* (New York: Horizon Press, 1955).

11. Wright, quoted from "The Art and Craft of the Machine," reprinted in Edgar Kaufman, Jr., and Ben Raeburn, eds., *Frank Lloyd Wright: Writings and Buildings* (Cleveland: World Publishing Company, 1960): 55–73.

12. According to Walter L. Creese, the term *garden city* was an American idea; see Creese, *The Search for Environment: The Garden City, Before and After* (New Haven and London: Yale University Press, 1966): 144–52. Creese states that, for Morris, the town was "to be impregnated with the beauty of the country, and the country with the intelligence and vivid life of the town." Everything was to be "clean, orderly, and tidy," houses were to be "surrounded by acres and acres of garden," while the town was to become "a garden with beautiful houses in it." The term gained international prominence with the appearance of Ebenezer Howard's *Garden Cities of Tomorrow* (London: Sonnenschein and Company, 1901; Cambridge, Mass.: MIT Press, 1965).

13. See Oscar Lovell Triggs, *Chapters in the History of the Arts and Crafts Movement* (Chicago: Bohemia Guild of the Industrial Art League, 1902; reprint, New York: Benjamin Blom, 1971).

14. Priestman published in *House Beautiful* and the *International Studio* between 1900 and 1910, and she wrote *Art and Economy in Home Decoration* (New York: John Lane Company, 1910).

15. See Leonard K. Eaton, *Two Chicago Architects and Their Clients: Frank Lloyd Wright and Howard Van Doren Shaw* (Cambridge, Mass., and London: MIT Press, 1969).

16. Scudder, quoted from Boris, "Dreams of Brotherhood and Beauty," 208.

17. See Wilhelm Miller, *The Prairie Spirit in Landscape Gardening* (Urbana, Ill.: University of Illinois, 1915).

18. Wright, quoted from *The Future of Architecture*, 130, 240.

19. See Creese, *The Search for Environment*, 266–7.

20. For Bradley, see Robert Koch, "Will Bradley," *Art in America* (Fall 1962): 78–83. Ellis's premature death, in 1904, cut short his promising role in the movement. Ellis wrote two articles in *The Craftsman*: "A Note of Color," *The Craftsman* 5, no. 2 (November 1903): 152–63; "Craftsman House," *The Craftsman* 4, no. 4 (July 1903): 274–76. See Roger Kennedy, "Long, Dark Corridors: Harvey Ellis," *The Prairie School Review* 5, nos. 1 and 2 (1968): 16–17; Jean R. France et al., *A Rediscovery—Harvey Ellis: Artist, Architect* (Rochester, N.Y.: Memorial Art Gallery, University of Rochester, 1972).

21. For Eyre, see Edward Teitelman and Betsy Fahlman, "Wilson Eyre and the Colonial Revival in Philadelphia," in Alan Axelrod, ed., *The Colonial Revival in America* (New York: W. W. Norton, 1985), 71–90.

22. With its owner, Price designed the Martin McLanahan House, in Rose Valley, in 1906. Its bold chimneys, casement bay windows, broad arched loggia supporting a balcony, and broad dormer windows, also admitting to balconies, affirm a design wholly consonant with Eyre's style at the time.

23. For Mellor and Meigs, see *A Monograph of the Work of Mellor, Meigs, and Howe* (New York: Architectural Book Publishing Company, 1923).

24. The history of the Garden City movement in American town planning has yet to be written, but the Russell Sage Foundation played a major role. It was created by Mrs. Russell Sage in 1907, with a ten million dollar endowment for the purpose of social betterment. Its thrust, owing much to Ruskin and Morris, was for

more careful land use and for improved housing for lower-income groups. This was the intention behind its creation of Forest Hills, Long Island, in 1909, followed in 1910 by the unfulfilled plotting of nearby Garden City. After World War I, the foundation continued to work for city and regional planning, employing Raymond Unwin between 1922 and 1931 to develop a regional plan for New York City. For Forest Hills, see articles in the Sage Foundation book *Forest Hills Gardens* (New York: Russell Sage Foundation, Homes Company, c. 1911), and Susan Holbrook Perdue, "Forest Hills Gardens, Architecture and Landscape Planning in a Model Garden Suburb, 1908–1915" (M.A. thesis, University of Virginia, 1985).

25. For Hilton Village, the earliest of dozens of federally supported communities, see Ruth Hanners Chambers, *Hilton Village: The Nation's First Government-Built Planned Community* (Newport News, Va.: Woman's Club of Hilton Village, 1967); see also Henry Vincent Hubbard and Theodora Kimball, *An Introduction to the Study of Landscape Design* (New York: Macmillan Company, 1917). As noted, Gustav Stickley was one of the first to popularize garden cities in the United States; see his "Rapid Growth of the Garden City Movement, Which Promises To Re-Organize Social Conditions All over the World," *The Craftsman* 17, no. 3 (December 1909): 296–310.

26. For the Arts and Crafts in the Midwest, see H. Allen Brooks, *Frank Lloyd Wright and the Prairie School Tradition* (New York: George Braziller, 1984), and *The Prairie School: Frank Lloyd Wright and His Midwest Contemporaries* (Toronto: University of Toronto Press, 1972). *The Prairie School Review*, a periodical published in Park Forest, Illinois, between 1964 and 1977, contains many useful articles on the architecture of this period in the Midwest. *The Ladies' Home Journal* carried "A Home in a Prairie Town" (February 1901): 17, and "A Small House with 'Lots of Room' in It" (July 1901): 15. For an extensive bibliography on Wright, see Robert Sweeney, *Frank Lloyd Wright: An Annotated Bibliography* (Los Angeles: Hennessey & Ingalls, 1978).

27. For Jensen, one of the country's equivalents to Gertrude Jekyll, see Leonard K. Eaton, *Landscape Artist in America, The Life and Work of Jens Jensen* (Chicago: University of Chicago Press, 1964).

28. There is no book-length study of Spencer, who published seven illustrated articles on small farmhouses in *The Ladies' Home Journal* in that period. The Magnus House was illustrated in *Indoors and Out* (July 1906): 194–95. For Griffin, see James Birrell, *Walter Burley Griffin* (Brisbane, Australia: University of Queensland Press, 1964). For Mahony, see David Van Zanten, "The Early Work of Marion Mahony," *The Prairie School Review* 3, no. 2 (1966): 5–24.

29. *Rockledge* is no longer extant. For Maher, see William Rudd, "George W. Maher: Architect of the Prairie School," *The Prairie School Review* 1, no. 1 (1964): 5.

30. The Coxhead House, 2421 Green Street, San Francisco, designed about 1895, is a remarkable transplant of an English town house to the Pacific coast. Crammed on a lot barely twenty-feet wide, Coxhead devised an ingenious plan that obviates crowdedness as much as is possible. The narrow lot engendered a number of brilliant design decisions.

31. For the Greenes, see Randell L. Makinson, *Greene & Greene—Architecture As a Fine Art* (Santa Barbara: Peregrine Smith, 1977), and his *Greene & Greene: Furniture and Related Designs* (Salt Lake City: Peregrine Smith, 1979); see also Timothy J. Andersen, Eudorah M. Moore, and Robert W. Winter, eds., *California Design 1910* (Pasadena: California Design Publications, 1974).

32. Gill, quoted from Stephen W. Jacobs, "California Contemporaries of Frank Lloyd Wright, 1885–1915," in Millard Meiss, ed., *Problems of the 19th and 20th Centuries: Studies in Western Art*, vol. 4 (Princeton: Princeton University Press, 1963), 50.

33. There is still no book-length study of Gill; for his work and that of other California architects, see Esther McCoy, *Five California Architects* (New York: Reinhold, 1960); Bruce Kammerling, "Irving Gill: The Artist As Architect," *Journal of San Diego History* (Spring 1979); and David Gebhard's essay on Gill in *California Design 1910* (see note 31).

34. Irving Gill, "The Home of the Future," *The Craftsman* 30 (May 1916): 140–51.

THOMAS
William Price's Arts and Crafts Colony

1. Thorstein Veblen, *The Theory of the Leisure Class* (New York: Macmillan Company, 1899; reprint, New York: New American Library, 1953). Chapters headed "Conspicuous Consumption" and "Pecuniary Canons of Taste" establish the framework for Veblen's biting assessment of the United States at the turn of the century. That he was a member of the same age cohort that rejected opulence is presumably not a coincidence.

2. Lincoln Steffens, *The Shame of the Cities* (Chicago: McClure, Phillips & Company, 1904), in surveying America's great cities, found them ruled by political machines and far distant from the revolutionary values of the eighteenth century.

3. The spread of the Arts and Crafts from its English sources to America has been documented in, for example, Lionel Lambourne, *Utopian Craftsmen: The Arts and Crafts Movement from the Cotswolds to Chicago* (Salt Lake City: Peregrine Smith, 1980). Ashbee has received a splendid biography, Alan Crawford, *C. R. Ashbee: Architect, Designer & Romantic Socialist* (New Haven: Yale University Press, 1985).

4. The effects of republican values on American architectural production is discussed in Andrew Jackson Downing, *The Architecture of Country Houses* (New York: D. Appleton and Company, 1851), particularly in the chapter "The Villa."

5. American millennial and social experimentation is surveyed in Dolores Hayden, *Seven American Utopias* (Cambridge: MIT Press, 1976). See, particularly, the introduction; however, because of its stated focus, it does not treat the secular turn-of-the-century examples. Similarly, the Arts and Crafts focus of this piece limits a discussion of other communities.

6. Rose Valley has been discussed in four principal modern sources: Peter Ham et al., eds., *A History of Rose Valley* (Rose Valley, Pa.: Borough of Rose Valley, 1973); George E. Thomas, "William L. Price: Builder of Men and of Buildings" (Ph.D. diss., University of Pennsylvania, 1975); George E. Thomas, "Rose Valley Community," in Darell Sewell, ed., *Philadelphia: Three Centuries of American Art* (Philadelphia: Philadelphia Museum of Art, 1976), 465–67; and William Smallwood Ayres, ed., *A Poor Sort of Heaven, A Good Sort of Earth: The Rose Valley Arts and Crafts Experiment* (Chadds Ford, Pa.: Brandywine River Museum, 1983).

7. William L. Price, "Is Rose Valley Worth While?" *The Artsman* 1, no. 1 (October 1903): 6.

8. William L. Price, "Some Humors of False Construction," *The Artsman* 1, no. 9 (June 1904): 321.

9. For a brief biography of Traubel, see *The Artsman*, with introduction by Gertrude Traubel and Joseph Niver, Sr. (1903–7, *The Art That Is Life*; reprint, Millwood, N.Y.: Kraus Reprint Company, 1979), iii–viii.

10. The seal is discussed in [M.] Hawley McLanahan, "Rose Valley in Particular," *The Artsman* 1, no. 1 (October 1903): 13–14.

11. William L. Price, "Architecture and Rathskellers," *Architectural Review* 11, no. 2 (November 1904): 234.

12. Price, "Some Humors of False Construction," 327.

13. William L. Price, "Do We Attack the Machine?" *The Artsman* 1, no. 5 (February 1904): 171.

14. Price, "Is Rose Valley Worth While?" 10–11.

15. William L. Price, "Choosing Simple Materials for the Home," in Charles Osbourne, ed., *Country Houses and Gardens of Moderate Cost* (Philadelphia: John C. Winston Company, 1907), 33.

16. Ibid.

17. William L. Price, unpublished typescript in possession of author, c. 1904.

18. Price and [M. Hawley] McLanahan, "Group of Houses in Rose Valley, Pa.," *The Brickbuilder* 20, no. 9 (September 1911): 185.

19. C. R. Ashbee, unpublished memoirs, Victoria and Albert Museum, London, notebook 3, November 1908, 41–42.

20. William L. Price, "The House of the Democrat," in Gustav Stickley, *More Craftsman Homes* (New York: Craftsman Publishing Company, 1912), 7–9. This marks Price's connection with an important figure in the Arts and Crafts world.

Selected Bibliography

This listing is confined to the most important or current surveys, the leading monographs, and the most useful writings of the period. It does not attempt to provide comprehensive information on individual artists or institutions.

Readers are referred to the extensive bibliographies provided in Leslie Bowman Greene, *American Arts & Crafts: Virtue in Design. A Catalogue of the Pavlevsky/Evans Collection and Related Works at the Los Angeles County Museum of Art*, and Robert Judson Clark, ed., *The Arts and Crafts Movement in America, 1876–1916*. Representative journals of the period are *The Craftsman, Handicraft, House Beautiful, The International Studio, Keramic Studio, The Ladies' Home Journal, The Potter*, and *Wood Craft*. In addition, there is the recent *Tiller*.

Adams, Henry, et al. *John La Farge* (exh. cat.). New York: Abbeville Press, 1987.

Adler, Hazel H. *The New Interior*. New York: Century Company, 1916.

Andersen, Timothy J., Eudorah M. Moore, and Robert W. Winter, eds. *California Design, 1910*. Pasadena: California Design Publications, 1974. Reprint. Salt Lake City, Utah: Peregrine Smith, 1980.

Anscombe, Isabelle. *Arts & Crafts Style*. Oxford: Phaidon, 1991.

———. *A Woman's Touch*. New York: Viking Press, 1984.

Anscombe, Isabelle, and Charlotte Gere. *Arts & Crafts in Britain and America*. New York: Rizzoli International Publications, 1978.

The Architecture of Purcell and Elmslie. Introduction by David Gebhard. Reprint of sections from *Western Architect*, January 1913, January 1915, and July 1915. Park Forest, Ill.: Prairie School Press, 1965.

Arts and Crafts in Detroit, 1906–1976. The Movement, The Society, The School (exh. cat.). Detroit: Detroit Institute of Arts, 1976.

Ayres, William Smallwood, ed. *A Poor Sort of Heaven, A Good Sort of Earth: The Rose Valley Arts and Crafts Experiment*. Chadds Ford, Pa.: Brandywine River Museum, 1983.

Balch, David Arnold. *Elbert Hubbard: Genius of Roycroft*. New York: F. A. Stokes Company, 1940.

Bascom, John. *Aesthetics. The Science of Beauty*. New York: G. P. Putnam's Sons, 1886.

Batchelder, Ernest A. *Design in Theory and Practice*. New York: Macmillan Company, 1910.

———. *The Principles of Design*. Chicago: Inland Printer Company, 1904.

Begg, W. Proudfoot. *The Development of Taste and Other Studies in Aesthetics*. Glasgow: James Maclehose and Sons, 1887.

Binns, Charles Fergus. *The Potter's Craft*. 4th ed. 1910. Reprint. Princeton: D. Van Nostrand Company, 1967.

Binstead, Herbert E. *The Furniture Styles*. Chicago: Trade Periodical Company, 1909.

Blasberg, Robert W. *The Fulper Art Pottery: An Aesthetic Appreciation, 1909–1929*. New York: Jordan-Volpe Gallery, 1979.

———. *Grueby* (exh. cat.). Syracuse, N.Y.: Everson Museum of Art, 1981.

Bok, Edward. *The Americanization of Edward Bok: The Autobiography of a Dutch Boy Fifty Years After*. New York: Charles Scribner's Sons, 1920. Reprint. New York: Pocket Books, 1965.

Boris, Eileen. *Art and Labor: Ruskin, Morris, and the Craftsman Ideal in America*. Philadelphia: Temple University Press, 1986.

Bowers, William L. *The Country Life Movement in America, 1900–1920*. Port Washington, N.Y.: Kennikat Press, 1974.

Bowman, Leslie Greene. *American Arts & Crafts: Virtue in Design. A Catalogue of the Palevsky/Evans Collection and Related Works at the Los Angeles County Museum of Art*. Los Angeles: Los Angeles County Museum of Art; Boston: Bulfinch Press/Little, Brown and Company, 1990.

Bragdon, Claude. "Harvey Ellis: A Portrait Sketch." *Architectural Review* 15 (December 1908).

Brandt, Frederick R. *Late Nineteenth and Early Twentieth Century Decorative Arts*. Richmond: Virginia Museum of Fine Arts, 1985.

Brennan, Shawn. *Reflections: Arts & Crafts Metalwork in England and the United States* (exh. cat.). New York: Kurland-Zabar, 1990.

Brooks, H. Allen. *The Prairie School: Frank Lloyd Wright and His Midwest Contemporaries*. Toronto: University of Toronto Press, 1972.

Burke, Doreen Bolger, et al. *In Pursuit of Beauty: Americans and the Aesthetic Movement*. New York: Metropolitan Museum of Art/Rizzoli International Publications, 1986.

Callen, Anthea. *Women Artists of the Arts and Crafts Movement*. New York: Pantheon, 1979.

Calloway, Stephen. *Twentieth-Century Decoration: 1900–1980*. New York: Rizzoli International Publications, 1988.

Carpenter, Charles H., Jr. "The Silver of Louis Comfort Tiffany." *Antiques* 117, no. 2 (February 1980).

Caruthers, J. Wade. "Elbert Hubbard: A Case of Reinterpretation." *Connecticut Review* 1 (October 1967).

Cathers, David M. *From Architecture to Object: Masterworks of the American Arts & Crafts Movement* (exh. cat.). New York: Hirschl & Adler Galleries, 1989.

———. *Furniture of the American Arts and Crafts Movement: Stickley and Roycroft Mission Oak*. New York: New American Library, 1981.

———. *Genius in the Shadows: The Furniture Designs of Harvey Ellis* (exh. cat.). New York: Jordan-Volpe Gallery, 1981.

———. *Stickley Craftsman Furniture Catalogs*. New York: Dover Publications, 1979.

Caye, Roger. "Paul Revere, Silversmith, and Modern Emulators: The Handwrought Silverwork of Robert Jarvie, Craftsman." *Arts and Decoration* 4 (August 1914).

Champney, Freeman. *Art and Glory: The Story of Elbert Hubbard*. New York: Crown, 1968.

Chicago Arts and Crafts Society. *A Catalogue of the Second Exhibition of the Chicago Arts and Crafts Society*. Chicago: R. R. Donnelley & Sons, 1899.

Clark, Garth. *American Ceramics, 1876 to the Present*. New York: Abbeville Press, 1987.

———. *The Biloxi Art Pottery of George Ohr* (exh. cat.). Jackson: Mississippi State Historical Museum, 1978.

Clark, Garth, Robert A. Ellison, Jr., and Eugene Hecht. *The Mad Potter of Biloxi: The Art and Life of George E. Ohr*. New York: Abbeville Press, 1989.

Clark, Garth, and Margie Hughto. *A Century of Ceramics in the United States, 1878–1978*. New York: E. P. Dutton/Everson Museum of Art, 1979.

Clark, Robert Judson, ed. *The Arts and Crafts Movement in America, 1876–1916* (exh. cat.). Princeton: Princeton University Press, 1972.

Clutton-Brock, A. *Essays on Art*. New York: Charles Scribner's Sons, 1920.

Conforti, Michael P. "Orientalism on the Upper Mississippi: The Work of John S. Bradstreet." *The Minneapolis Institute of Arts Bulletin* 65 (1981–82).

Cooper-Hewitt Museum. *American Art Pottery*. New York: Cooper-Hewitt Museum/University of Washington Press, 1987.

Coulter, Mary J. "History of the Art Crafts Movement in America." *California's Magazine* 2 (1916).

Craftsman Fabrics and Needlework from the Craftsman Workshops. 1905. Reprint. Introduction by Richard M. Rasnick. Madison, Wis.: Razmataz Press, 1989.

Crane, Walter. *The Bases of Design*. London: George Bell and Sons, 1898. Reprint, as part of series *The Aesthetic Movement & the Arts and Crafts Movement*. Edited by Peter Stansky and Rodney Shewan. New York and London: Garland Publishing, 1977.

Creese, Walter L. *The Search for Environment; The Garden City, Before and After*. New Haven, Conn., and London: Yale University Press, 1966.

Cuzner, Bernard. *A Silversmith's Manual, Treating of the Designing and Making of the Simpler Pieces of Domestic Silverware*. 2nd ed. London: N.A.G. Press, 1949.

Darling, Sharon S. *Chicago Ceramics and Glass*. Chicago: Chicago Historical Society, 1979.

————. *Chicago Furniture: Art, Craft & Industry, 1833–1983*. New York and London: W. W. Norton, 1984.

————. *Chicago Metalsmiths*. Chicago: Chicago Historical Society, 1977.

————, ed. *Teco: Art Pottery of the Prairie School* (exh. cat.). Erie, Pa.: Erie Art Museum, 1986.

Dawson, Mrs. Nelson. *Enamels*. London: Methuen & Company, 1906.

Day, Lewis F. *Enameling; A Comparative Account of the Development and Practice of the Art*. London: B. T. Batsford, 1907.

————. *Instances of Accessory Art*. London: B. T. Batsford, 1880. Reprint, as part of series *The Aesthetic Movement & the Arts and Crafts Movement*. Edited by Peter Stansky and Rodney Shewan. New York and London: Garland Publishing, 1977.

————. *Nature in Ornament*. London: B. T. Batsford, 1892. Reprint, as part of series *The Aesthetic Movement & the Arts and Crafts Movement*. Edited by Peter Stansky and Rodney Shewan. New York and London: Garland Publishing, 1977.

————. *Ornament & Its Application: A Book for Students Treating in a Practical Way of the Relation of Design to Materials, Tools and Methods of Works*. London: B. T. Batsford; New York: Charles Scribner's Sons, 1904. Reprint. Detroit: Gale Research Company, 1970.

————. *The Planning of Ornament*. London: B. T. Batsford, 1887. Reprint, as part of series *The Aesthetic Movement & the Arts and Crafts Movement*. Edited by Peter Stansky and Rodney Shewan. New York and London: Garland Publishing, 1977.

Day, Lewis F., and Mary Buckle. *Art in Needlework: A Book about Embroidery*. London: B. T. Batsford, 1900. Reprint, as part of series *The Aesthetic Movement & the Arts and Crafts Movement*. Edited by Peter Stansky and Rodney Shewan. New York and London: Garland Publishing, 1977.

DeGarmo, Charles. *Aesthetic Education*. Syracuse, N.Y.: C. W. Bardeen, 1913.

de Wolfe, Elsie. *The House in Good Taste*. New York: Century Company, 1913.

Dietz, Ulysses G. *The Newark Museum Collection of American Art Pottery*. Newark, N.J.: Newark Museum, 1984.

Dirlam, H. Kenneth, and Ernest E. Simmons. *Sinners, This Is East Aurora: The Story of Elbert Hubbard and the Roycroft Shops*. New York: Vantage Press, 1964.

Doat, Taxile. *Grand Feu Ceramics: A Practical Treatise on the Making of Fine Porcelain and Grès*. Syracuse, N.Y.: Keramic Studio Publishing Company, 1905.

Doros, Paul E. *The Tiffany Collection of the Chrysler Museum at Norfolk*. Norfolk, Va.: Chrysler Museum, 1979.

Duncan, Alastair, Martin Eidelberg, and Neil Harris. *Masterworks of Louis Comfort Tiffany*. New York: Harry N. Abrams, Inc., 1989.

Dunn, Roger T. *On the Threshold of Modern Design: The Arts and Crafts Movement in America* (exh. cat.). Framingham, Mass.: Danforth Museum of Art, 1984.

Eaton, Allen H. *Handicrafts of New England*. New York: Harper and Brothers, 1949.

————. *Handicrafts of the Southern Highlands*. New York: Russell Sage Foundation, 1937. Reprint. New York: Dover Publications, 1973.

Eaton, Leonard K. *Landscape Architect in America: The Life and Work of Jens Jensen*. Chicago: University of Chicago Press, 1964.

————. *Two Chicago Architects and Their Clients: Frank Lloyd Wright and Howard Van Doren Shaw*. Cambridge, Mass., and London: MIT Press, 1969.

Edwards, Robert, and Jane Perkins Claney. *The Byrdcliffe Arts and Crafts Colony: Life by Design* (exh. cat.). Wilmington: Delaware Art Museum, 1984.

Eidelberg, Martin, ed. *From Our Native Clay: Art Pottery from the Collections of the American Ceramic Arts Society* (exh. cat.). New York: American Ceramic Arts Society / Turn of the Century Editions, 1987.

Evans, Paul. *Art Pottery of the United States*. New York: Charles Scribner's Sons, 1974. 2nd ed. New York: Feingold and Lewis, 1987.

Fidler, Patricia J. *Art with a Mission: Objects of the Arts and Crafts Movement* (exh. cat.). Lawrence, Kans.: Spencer Museum of Art/University of Kansas, 1991.

Fox, Claire. "Henry Chapman Mercer: Tilemaker, Collector, Builder Extraordinary." *Antiques* 104, no. 4 (October 1973).

France, Jean R., et al. *A Rediscovery—Harvey Ellis: Artist, Architect* (exh. cat.). Rochester, N.Y.: Memorial Art Gallery, University of Rochester, 1972.

Freeman, John Crosby. *The Forgotten Rebel: Gustav Stickley and His Craftsman Mission Furniture*. Watkins Glen, N.Y.: Century House, 1966.

Frelinghuysen, Alice Cooney. *American Porcelain: 1770–1920* (exh. cat.). New York: The Metropolitan Museum of Art, 1989.

Gardner, Paul V. *The Glass of Frederick Carder*. New York: Crown, 1971.

Gilborn, Craig. *Adirondack Furniture and the Rustic Tradition*. New York: Harry N. Abrams, Inc., 1987.

Gordon, Kate. *Esthetics*. New York: Henry Holt and Company, 1909.

Graef, Paul. *Neubauten in Nordamerika*. Berlin: M. Spielmeyer, 1905.

Gray, Stephen, ed. *A Catalog of the Roycrofters*. New York: Turn of the Century Editions, 1989.

Gray, Stephen, and Robert Edwards, eds. *Collected Works of Gustav Stickley*. New York: Turn of the Century Editions, 1981.

Gray, Stephen, and Kenneth R. Trapp, eds. *Arts and Crafts Furniture: Shop of the Crafters at Cincinnati*. New York: Turn of the Century Editions, 1983.

Greene and Greene Interiors '83: The Duncan-Irwin House (exh. cat.). Pasadena: Friends of the Gamble House/University of Southern California, 1983.

Hamilton, Charles F., Kitty Turgeon, and Robert Rust. *History and Renaissance of the Roycroft Movement*. Buffalo, N.Y.: Buffalo and Erie County Historical Society, 1984.

Handlin, David P. *The American Home: Architecture and Society, 1815–1915*. Boston: Little, Brown and Company, 1979.

Hanks, David A. *The Decorative Designs of Frank Lloyd Wright*. New York: E. P. Dutton, 1979.

Hanks, David A., with Jennifer Toher. "Tradition and Reform." In *High Styles: Twentieth-Century American Design* (exh. cat.). New York: Whitney Museum of American Art, 1985.

Harper, Douglas. *Working Knowledge: Skill and Community in a Small Shop*. Chicago: University of Chicago Press, 1987.

Harris, George. *The Theory of the Arts; or, Art in Relation to Nature, Civilization, and Man*. London: Trubner and Company, 1869.

Harrison, Constance Cary. *Woman's Handiwork in Modern Homes*. New York: Charles Scribner's Sons, 1882.

Hazlitt, William. *Criticisms on Art*. London: C. Templeman, 1844.

Henzke, Lucile. *American Art Pottery*. Camden, N.J.: Thomas Nelson, 1970.

———. *Art Pottery of America*. Exton, Pa.: Schiffer Publishing, 1982.

Heskett, John. *Industrial Design*. New York and Toronto: Oxford University Press, 1980.

Holden, Florence P. *Audiences: A Few Suggestions to Those Who Look and Listen*. Chicago: A. C. McClurg and Company, 1896.

Hooper, Luther. *Hand-Loom Weaving Plain & Ornamental*. From *The Artistic Crafts Series of Technical Handbooks*. Edited by William R. Lethaby. New York: Macmillan Company; London: J. Hogg, 1910.

Hubbard, Elbert, ed. *The Book of the Roycrofters*. East Aurora, N.Y.: The Roycrofters, 1907.

Hubbard, Henry Vincent, and Theodora Kimball. *An Introduction to the Study of Landscape Design*. New York: Macmillan Company, 1917.

Hunter, Dard, II. *The Life Work of Dard Hunter: A Progressive Illustrated Assemblage of His Works As Artist, Craftsman, Author, Papermaker, and Printer*. Vol. 1. Chillicothe, Ohio: Mountain House Press, 1981.

James, George Wharton. *Indian Basketry*. 2nd ed., rev. and enl. New York: Henry Malkan, 1902.

Jones, Harvey L. *Mathews: Masterpieces of the California Decorative Style* (exh. cat.). Oakland: Oakland Museum, 1972.

Jordy, William H. *American Buildings and Their Architects*. Vol. 3, *Progressive and Academic Ideals at the Turn of the Twentieth Century*. New York: Doubleday, 1972.

Kaplan, Wendy, ed. *"The Art That Is Life": The Arts & Crafts Movement in America, 1875–1920*. Boston: Museum of Fine Arts, 1987.

Keeler, Charles. *The Simple Home*. San Francisco: Paul Elder, 1904. Reprint. Santa Barbara, and Salt Lake City: Peregrine Smith, 1979.

Keen, Kristen. *American Art Pottery 1875–1930*. Wilmington: Delaware Art Museum, 1978.

Koch, Robert. "Elbert Hubbard's Roycrofters As Artist-Craftsmen." *Winterthur Portfolio* 3 (1967).

———. *Louis Comfort Tiffany, 1848–1933* (exh. cat.). New York: Museum of Contemporary Crafts of the American Craftsmen's Council, 1958.

———. *Louis C. Tiffany, Rebel in Glass*. New York: Crown, 1964.

Kornwolf, James D. *M. H. Baillie-Scott and the Arts and Crafts Movement*. Baltimore and London: Johns Hopkins Press, 1972.

Lambourne, Lionel. *Utopian Craftsmen: The Arts and Crafts Movement from the Cotswolds to Chicago*. Salt Lake City: Peregrine Smith, 1980.

Lamoureux, Dorothy. *The Arts and Crafts Studio of Dirk van Erp* (exh. cat.). San Francisco: San Francisco Craft and Folk Art Museum, 1989.

Lee, Vernon [Violet Paget]. *Laurus Nobilis; or, Chapters on Art and Life*. London: John Lane, The Bodley Head; New York: John Lane Company, 1909.

Levin, Elaine. *The History of American Ceramics*. New York: Harry N. Abrams, Inc., 1988.

Lewis, John N. C. *The Twentieth Century Book*. New York: Reinhold, 1967.

Limbert's Holland Dutch Arts and Crafts Furniture, Charles P. Limbert Company Cabinetmakers. Reprint. New York: Turn of the Century Editions, 1981.

Little, Nina Fletcher. *Little by Little: Six Decades of Collecting American Decorative Arts*. New York: E. P. Dutton, 1984.

Ludwig, Coy. *The Arts and Crafts Movement in New York State, 1890–1920s*. Hamilton, N.Y.: Gallery Association of New York State, 1983.

Lynes, Russell. *The Tastemakers: The Shaping of American Popular Taste*. New York: Harper, 1954. Reprint. New York: Dover Publications, 1980.

Macomber, H. Percy. "The Future of the Handicrafts." *The American Magazine of Art* 9 (March 1918).

Maher, George W. "An Architecture of Ideas." *Arts and Decoration* 1 (June 1911).

Makinson, Randell L. *Greene & Greene: Architecture As a Fine Art*. Salt Lake City: Peregrine Smith, 1977.

———. *Greene & Greene: Furniture and Related Designs*. Santa Barbara: Peregrine Smith, 1979.

Marek, Don. *Arts and Crafts Furniture Design: The Grand Rapids Contribution, 1895–1915*. Grand Rapids, Mich.: Grand Rapids Art Museum, 1987.

Mayhew, Edgar de Noailles, and Minor Myers, Jr. *A Documentary History of American Interiors: From the Colonial Era to 1915*. New York: Charles Scribner's Sons, 1980.

McCoy, Esther. *Five California Architects*. New York: Reinhold, 1960.

McCracken, Grant. *Culture and Consumption: New Approaches to the Symbolic Character of Consumer Goods and Activities*. Bloomington: Indiana University Press, 1988.

McKean, Hugh F. *The "Lost" Treasures of Louis Comfort Tiffany*. New York: Doubleday, 1980.

McLean, Ruari. *Modern Book Design from William Morris to the Present Day*. London: Faber and Faber, 1958.

Merrill, Nancy O. *A Concise History of Glass Represented in the Chrysler Museum Glass Collection*. Norfolk, Va.: The Chrysler Museum, 1989.

Miller, Wilhelm. *The Prairie Spirit in Landscape Gardening*. Urbana, Ill.: University of Illinois, 1915.

Mr. S. G. Burt's Record Book of Ware at Art Museum: 2,292 Pieces of Early Rookwood Pottery in the Cincinnati Art Museum in 1916. Cincinnati: Cincinnati Historical Society, 1978.

Moore, John B. *The Catalogues of Fine Navajo Blankets, Rugs, Ceremonial Baskets, Silverware, Jewelry & Curios*. Cottonwood Pass, Navajo Indian Reservation, New Mexico: Crystal Trading Post, 1903–11. Reprint. Albuquerque: Avanyu Publishing, 1987.

Morris, William. *The Collected Works of William Morris*. 24 vols. Edited by May Morris. London: Longmans Green, 1910–15.

Naylor, Gillian. *The Arts and Crafts Movement: A Study of Its Sources, Ideals, and Influence on Design Theory*. Cambridge: MIT Press, 1971.

Naylor, Gillian, et al. *The Encyclopedia of Arts and Crafts: The International Arts Movement, 1850–1920*. New York: E. P. Dutton; London: Headline Book Publishing, 1989.

Norwood, John N. *1900–1950, Ceramics at Alfred University*. Alfred, N.Y.: Alfred University Press, 1950.

Ormond, Suzanne, and Mary E. Irvine. *Louisiana's Art Nouveau: The Crafts of the Newcomb Style*. Gretna, La.: Pelican Publishing Company, 1976.

Pear, Lillian Myers. *The Pewabic Pottery: A History of Its Products and Its People*. Des Moines, Iowa: Wallace Homestead Book Company, 1976.

Peck, Herbert. *The Book of Rookwood Pottery*. New York: Crown, 1968.

Pepper, Adeline. *The Glass Gaffers of New Jersey*. New York: Charles Scribner's Sons, 1971.

Perdue, Susan Holbrook. "Forest Hills Gardens, Architecture and Landscape Planning in a Model Garden Suburb, 1908–1915." Master's thesis, University of Virginia, 1986.

Perry, Barbara. *Fragile Blossoms, Enduring Earth: The Japanese Influence on American Ceramics* (exh. cat.). Syracuse, N.Y.: Everson Museum of Art, 1989.

Poesch, Jessie. *Newcomb Pottery: An Enterprise for Southern Women, 1895–1940*. Exton, Pa.: Schiffer Publishing, 1984.

Pye, David. *The Nature and Art of Workmanship*. London: Cambridge University Press, 1968.

Reed, Cleota. *Henry Chapman Mercer and the Moravian Pottery and Tile Works*. Philadelphia: University of Pennsylvania Press, 1987.

Riley, Noel. *Tile Art: A History of Decorative Ceramic Tiles*. Secaucus, N.J.: Chartwell Books, 1987.

Robertson, Cheryl, and Terrence Marvel. *The Domestic Scene (1897–1927): George M. Niedecken, Interior Architect*. Milwaukee: Milwaukee Art Museum, 1981.

Rohlfs, Charles. "My Adventures in Wood-Carving." *Arts Journal* (October 1925).

Ross, Denman W. *A Theory of Pure Design: Harmony, Balance, Rhythm*. Boston: Houghton Mifflin and Company, 1907. Reprint. New York: Peter Smith, 1933.

The Roycrofters. *Roycroft Furniture* (sales cat.). 1906. Reprint. New York: Turn of the Century Editions, 1981.

Ruskin, John. *The Works of John Ruskin*. 39 vols. Edited by E. T. Cook and A. Wedderburn. London: George Allen, 1903–12.

Sanders, Barry, ed. *The Craftsman: An Anthology*. Salt Lake City: Peregrine Smith, 1978.

Schoeser, Mary. *Fabrics and Wallpapers: Twentieth-Century Design*. New York: E. P. Dutton, 1986.

Smith, Mary Ann. *Gustav Stickley, The Craftsman*. Syracuse, N.Y.: Syracuse University Press, 1983.

Stein, Roger B. *John Ruskin and Aesthetic Thought in America, 1840–1900*. Cambridge: Harvard University Press, 1967.

Stickley, Gustav. *The Best of Craftsman Homes*. 1909, 1912. Reprint. Santa Barbara, Calif.: Peregrine Smith, 1979.

———. *Craftsman Homes: Architecture and Furnishings of the American Arts and Crafts Movement*. 1909. Reprint. New York: Dover Publications, 1979.

Strong, Susan R. *History of American Ceramics: An Annotated Bibliography*. Metuchen, N.J., and London: Scarecrow Press, 1983.

Sturgis, Russell. *The Artist's Way of Working in the Various Handicrafts and Arts of Design*. New York: Dodd, Mead and Company, 1910.

Swanson, Margaret, and Ann Macbeth. *Educational Needlecraft*. New York: Longmans, Green, and Company, 1911.

Sweeney, Robert. *Frank Lloyd Wright: An Annotated Bibliography*. Los Angeles: Hennessey & Ingalls, 1978.

Taylor, Lonn, and Dessa Bokides. *New Mexican Furniture 1600–1940: The Origins, Survival, and Revival of Furniture Making in the Hispanic Southwest*. Sante Fe: Museum of New Mexico Press, 1987.

Throop, Lucy Abbot. *Furnishing the Home of Good Taste*. New York: McBride, Nast & Company, 1912.

Trapp, Kenneth R. *Toward the Modern Style: Rookwood Pottery. The Later Years: 1915–1950* (exh. cat.). New York: Jordan-Volpe Gallery, 1983.

Trapp, Kenneth R., et al. *The Arts and Crafts Movement in California: Living the Good Life*. New York: Abbeville Press, 1993.

Triggs, Oscar Lovell. *Chapters in the History of the Arts and Crafts Movement*. Chicago: Bohemia Guild of the Industrial Art League, 1902. Reprint. New York: Benjamin Blom, 1971.

Tucci, Douglass Shand. *Ralph Adams Cram, American Medievalist* (exh. cat.). Boston: Boston Public Library, 1975.

Ulchla, Karen Evans, ed. *The Society of Arts and Crafts, Boston: Exhibition Record, 1897–1927*. Boston: Boston Public Library, 1981.

Volpe, Tod M., and Beth Cathers. *Treasures of the American Arts and Crafts Movement: 1890–1920*. London: Thames and Hudson; New York: Harry N. Abrams, Inc., 1988.

Ward, Gerald W. R., ed. *Perspectives on American Furniture*. New York: W. W. Norton, 1988.

Webb, Judson T. *Pottery Making. An Illustrated Text Book on Art Pottery Making for Teachers and Artists*. Chicago: Lewis Institute, 1914.

Weidman, Gregory. *Furniture in Maryland, 1740–1940*. Baltimore: Maryland Historical Society, 1984.

Weidner, Ruth Irwin. *American Ceramics before 1939: A Bibliography*. Westport, Conn.: Greenwood Press, 1982.

Weiss, Peg, ed. *Adelaide Alsop Robineau: Glory in Porcelain*. Syracuse, N.Y.: Syracuse University Press/Everson Museum of Art, 1981.

West, Max. "The Revival of Handicraft in America." U.S. Bureau of Labor Statistics, *Bulletin* 55 (November 1904).

Wharton, Edith, and Ogden Codman, Jr. *The Decoration of Houses*. New York: Charles Scribner's Sons, 1909.

Wheeler, Candace. *The Development of Embroidery in America*. New York and London: Harper & Brothers, 1921.

———. *Principles of Home Decoration with Practical Examples*. New York: Doubleday, Page & Company, 1903.

———. *Yesterdays in a Busy Life*. New York and London: Harper & Brothers, 1918.

White, Mary. *More Baskets and How To Make Them*. New York: Doubleday, Page & Company, 1902. Reprint. Detroit: Gale Research Company, 1972.

Wigley, Thomas B. *The Art of the Goldsmith and Jeweler: A Treatise on the Manipulation of Gold in the Various Processes of Goldsmith's Work, and the Manufacture of Personal Ornaments, Etc.* London: Charles Griffin and Company, 1898.

Williams, Lester L. *C. N. Cotton and His Navajo Blankets: A Biography of C. N. Cotton, Gallup, New Mexico, Indian Trader, and reprintings of three mail order catalogs of Navajo blankets and rugs originally printed between 1896 and 1919*. Albuquerque: Avanyu Publishing, 1989.

Windsor, H. H. *Mission Furniture: How To Make It*. 3 vols. Chicago: Popular Mechanics Press, 1909.

Wright, Frank Lloyd. *The Art and Craft of the Machine*. Chicago: National League of Industrial Art, 1902.

CHECKLIST OF THE CATALOGUE

Note: The checklist entries are in alphabetical order, organized by medium. For all dimensions, height precedes width precedes depth.

BOOKS

Alice Hubbard. *Woman's Work.*
East Aurora, New York: The
Roycroft Press, 1908.
Designed by Dard Hunter,
typography by Charles Rosen
Collection Wolfsonian
Foundation, Miami

Walt Mason. *Uncle Walt: The Poet
Philosopher.* Chicago: George
Matthew Adams, 1910.
Designed by Will Bradley
Collection Wolfsonian
Foundation, Miami

Gustav Stickley, ed. *The
Craftsman.* v. 23, nos. 4–6. New
York: United Crafts, 1913.
Collection Winterthur Library,
Printed Books and Periodicals

Elihu Vedder. *The Digressions of
V.* Boston: Houghton, Mifflin
and Company, 1910.
Collection Wolfsonian
Foundation, Miami

CERAMICS

Lenore Asbury
Vase. 1917
Designed for Rookwood Pottery
Stoneware, 21¹/₂ × 7 × 7″
Collection Cooper-Hewitt
Museum, National Museum of
Design, Smithsonian Institution,
New York. Gift of Marcia and
William Goodman

Arthur E. Baggs
Vase. c. 1907–9
Designed for Marblehead Pottery
Ceramic, 11⁷/₈ × 5¹/₂ × 5¹/₂″
Private collection

Charles Fergus Binns
Vase. 1905
Stoneware, 7⁵/₈ × 4⁷/₈ × 4⁷/₈″
Collection Museum of Ceramic
Art at Alfred, Alfred University,
Alfred, New York

Charles Fergus Binns
Vase. 1909
Stoneware, 8³/₈ × 4⁷/₈ × 4⁷/₈″
Collection Museum of Ceramic
Art at Alfred, Alfred University,
Alfred, New York

Charles Fergus Binns
Vase. 1916
Stoneware, 10⁵/₈ × 5³/₄ × 5³/₄″
Collection Museum of Ceramic
Art at Alfred, Alfred University,
Alfred, New York

Theophilus A. Brouwer, Jr.
Vase. c. 1894–1911
Designed for Middle Lane
Pottery
Ceramic, 11¹/₂ × 7¹/₁₆ × 7¹/₁₆″
Private collection

Byrdcliffe Pottery
Bowl. 1917–18
Glazed earthenware,
2³/₄ × 5⁵/₈ × 5⁵/₈″
Collection The Newark Museum,
New Jersey

Matthew A. Daly
Vase. 1892
Produced at Rookwood Pottery
Ceramic, 24 × 8¹/₂ × 8¹/₂″
Private collection

Taxile Doat
Vase. 1913
Produced at University City
Pottery
Porcelain, 10¹/₄ × 8 × 8″
Private collection

Esther Huger Elliot and Joseph
Fortune Meyer
Humidor. c. 1904
Produced at Newcomb Pottery
Ceramic, 7¹/₂ × 7 × 7″
Collection Dr. Thomas C. Folk

Fulper Pottery
Vase. 1914
Glazed stoneware,
12¹/₈ × 10 × 10″
Collection The Newark Museum,
New Jersey

Grueby Faience Company
Vase. c. 1905–10
Matte-glazed earthenware,
10¹/₂ × 5⁷/₈ × 5⁷/₈″

Collection The Newark Museum,
New Jersey

Grueby Faience Company
Vase. c. 1905–12
Ceramic, 10¹/₄ × 9 × 9″
Private collection

Dard Hunter
Dinnerware Service. c. 1907–26
Ceramic, serving platter:
10¹/₄ × 10¹/₄″; pitcher:
5¹/₄ × 5³/₄ × 5³/₄″; footed dish:
3³/₈ × 9 × 9″
Designed for the Roycroft Inn,
Produced at Buffalo Pottery
Company
Private collection

Charles Dean Hyten
Mission Ware Vase. c. 1910–20
Produced at Niloak Pottery
Marbled earthenware,
8³/₈ × 5 × 5″
Collection The Newark Museum,
New Jersey. Louis Bamberger
Bequest Fund

John Kunsman
Teapot, Lid, and Stand. 1909
Designed for Fulper Pottery
Stoneware, 9 × 10 × 7″
Collection Dr. Thomas C. Folk

Maria de Hoa LeBlanc and
Joseph Fortune Meyer
Vase. c. 1910
Produced at Newcomb Pottery
Earthenware, 6¹/₂ × 5¹/₂ × 5¹/₂″
Collection The Newark Museum,
New Jersey

William A. Long
Olla. 1906–11
Produced at Clifton Art Pottery
Unglazed red earthenware,
8¹/₄ × 14 × 14″
Collection The Newark Museum,
New Jersey. Frank Conlin, Jr.,
Memorial Fund

Mary Louise McLaughlin
Vase. c. 1898–1906
Ceramic, 6 × 4⁵/₈ × 4⁵/₈″
Private collection

Henry Chapman Mercer
Inkwell. c. 1910

Produced at Moravian Pottery
and Tile Works
Ceramic, 5¹/₂ × 5¹/₂ × 5¹/₂″
Collection Dr. Thomas C. Folk

Henry Chapman Mercer
Tile (Byzantine Four Flowers). c.
1910
Produced at Moravian Pottery
and Tile Works
Red earthenware, 7¹/₈ × 5⁷/₈″
Collection The Newark Museum,
New Jersey. Gift of Moravian
Pottery and Tile Works

Henry Chapman Mercer
Tile (Fluminus Impetus . . .).
c. 1910
Produced at Moravian Pottery
and Tile Works
Red earthenware, 7 × 5³/₄″
Collection The Newark Museum,
New Jersey. Gift of Moravian
Pottery and Tile Works

Henry Chapman Mercer
Tile (Persian Antelope). c. 1910
Produced at Moravian Pottery
and Tile Works
Earthenware, 7 × 5³/₄″
Collection The Newark Museum,
New Jersey. Gift of Moravian
Pottery and Tile Works

William B. Mundie
Vase. c. 1906
Designed for Teco Pottery/Gates
Potteries
Ceramic, 13 × 10 × 10″
Collection Stephen Gray

Maria Longworth Nichols
(Storer)
Vase. 1879–80
Produced at Rookwood Pottery
Stoneware, 10¹/₂ × 8⁵/₁₆ × 8⁵/₁₆″
Collection Cooper-Hewitt
Museum, National Museum of
Design, Smithsonian Institution,
New York. Gift of Marcia and
William Goodman

Maria Longworth Nichols
(Storer)
Low Vase. 1882
Produced at Rookwood Pottery
Ceramic, 6⁷/₈ × 9 × 9″
Collection Dr. Thomas C. Folk

Maria Longworth Nichols
(Storer)
Vase. 1895
Produced at Rookwood Pottery
Ceramic, $8^{1}/_{2} \times 3^{5}/_{8} \times 3^{5}/_{8}''$
Private collection

George E. Ohr
Bowl with Handle and Spout.
c. 1898–1909
Earthenware, $4 \times 7^{5}/_{8} \times 4^{5}/_{8}''$
Collection Cooper-Hewitt
Museum, National Museum of
Design, Smithsonian Institution,
New York. Gift of Marcia and
William Goodman

George E. Ohr
Vase. c. 1898–1909
Ceramic, $7^{1}/_{8} \times 5^{1}/_{8} \times 5^{1}/_{8}''$
Private collection

George E. Ohr
Vase. c. 1898–1909
Ceramic, $9^{1}/_{2} \times 7^{1}/_{4} \times 7^{1}/_{4}''$
Private collection

George E. Ohr
Teapot and Coffeepot. c. 1900
Earthenware, $7^{5}/_{16} \times 10^{5}/_{16} \times 7''$
Collection National Museum of
American History, Smithsonian
Institution, Washington, D.C.

Elizabeth Overbeck and Hannah
Overbeck
Vase. c. 1910–31
Ceramic, $14^{1}/_{2} \times 10 \times 10''$
Collection Stephen Gray

Mary Chase Perry (Stratton)
Tile Frieze. c. 1906
Designed for Pewabic Pottery
Ceramic, $16 \times 38^{1}/_{2}''$
Collection Pewabic Pottery

Mary Chase Perry (Stratton)
Monumental Vase. c. 1906–10
Designed for Pewabic Pottery
Ceramic, $28^{3}/_{4} \times 15^{3}/_{4} \times 15^{3}/_{4}''$
Collection Pewabic Pottery

Mary Chase Perry (Stratton)
Vase. c. 1912–20
Designed for Pewabic Pottery
Ceramic, $15 \times 9 \times 9''$
Collection Pewabic Pottery

Mary Chase Perry (Stratton)
Vase. c. 1915–25
Designed for Pewabic Pottery
Ceramic, $18 \times 13^{1}/_{4} \times 13^{1}/_{4}''$
Collection Pewabic Pottery

Frederick Hurten Rhead
Vase. c. 1914–17
Designed for Rhead Pottery
Ceramic, $4 \times 3^{1}/_{2} \times 3^{1}/_{2}''$
Private collection

Cadmon Robertson
Vase. 1910
Designed for Hampshire Pottery
White earthenware, $11^{3}/_{4} \times 5 \times 5''$
Collection The Newark Museum,
New Jersey

Hugh Robertson
Vase. 1884–90
Produced at Chelsea Keramic Art
Works
Ceramic, $7^{1}/_{2} \times 2 \times 2''$
Collection The Brooklyn
Museum. Gift of Mrs. Charles
Messer Stow (53.257.1)

Hugh Robertson
Vase. 1885–88
Produced at Chelsea Keramic Art
Works
Ceramic, $7^{1}/_{8} \times 2 \times 2''$
Collection The Brooklyn
Museum. Gift of Arthur W.
Clement (43.128.154)

Hugh Robertson
Vase. c. 1885–88
Produced at Chelsea Keramic Art
Works
Ceramic, $8 \times 4^{3}/_{8} \times 4^{3}/_{8}''$
Private collection

Hugh Robertson
Vase. c. 1885–89
Produced at Chelsea Keramic Art
Works
Stoneware, $7^{1}/_{4} \times 4 \times 4''$
Collection Cooper-Hewitt
Museum, National Museum of
Design, Smithsonian Institution,
New York. Gift of Marcia and
William Goodman

Adelaide Alsop Robineau
Monogram Vase. 1905
Porcelain, $12^{1}/_{4} \times 5 \times 5''$
Collection Everson Museum of
Art, Syracuse, New York

Adelaide Alsop Robineau
Lantern. 1908
Porcelain, $8 \times 6 \times 6''$
Collection Everson Museum of
Art, Syracuse, New York

Adelaide Alsop Robineau
Vase. 1910
Porcelain, $11^{1}/_{2} \times 2^{3}/_{4} \times 2^{3}/_{4}''$
Collection Everson Museum of
Art, Syracuse, New York

Saturday Evening Girls' Club
Bowl (with Rabbits). c. 1910
Produced at Paul Revere Pottery
Earthenware, $2^{1}/_{4} \times 5^{1}/_{2} \times 5^{1}/_{2}''$
Collection The Newark Museum,
New Jersey

Kataro Shirayamadani
Vase. 1898
Produced at Rookwood Pottery
Earthenware with electro-
deposited copper,
$12^{5}/_{16} \times 4^{1}/_{4} \times 4^{1}/_{4}''$
Collection Cooper-Hewitt
Museum, National Museum of
Design, Smithsonian Institution,
New York. Gift of Marcia and
William Goodman

Kataro Shirayamadani
Vase. 1909
Produced at Rookwood Pottery

Earthenware, $13 \times 7 \times 7''$
Collection Dr. Thomas C. Folk

Jacques Sicard
Vase (with Beetles). 1904
Produced at Weller Pottery
Ceramic, $11^{1}/_{2} \times 5^{1}/_{2} \times 5^{1}/_{2}''$
Private collection

Louis Comfort Tiffany
Water Lilies with Frogs. c. 1904
Designed for Tiffany Studios
Ceramic, $6^{3}/_{8} \times 7^{1}/_{2} \times 7^{1}/_{2}''$
Collection Dr. Thomas C. Folk

Louis Comfort Tiffany
Vase (Fiddleheads). 1905–14
Designed for Tiffany Studios
Glazed earthenware, $9^{1}/_{4} \times 5 \times 5''$
Collection The Newark Museum,
New Jersey. Wallace M. Scudder
Bequest Fund

Anna Marie Valentien
Vase. 1901
Produced at Rookwood Pottery
Ceramic, $14^{7}/_{8} \times 6^{1}/_{2} \times 6^{1}/_{2}''$
Private collection

Artus Van Briggle
Vase (Irises). 1903
Glazed earthenware,
$11^{5}/_{16} \times 4 \times 4''$
Collection The Newark Museum,
New Jersey. Estate of John
Cotton Dana

Charles Volkmar
Vase. c. 1910
Glazed earthenware,
$6^{1}/_{8} \times 5^{1}/_{4} \times 5^{1}/_{4}''$
Collection The Newark Museum,
New Jersey

Grace Young
Vase. 1899
Produced at Rookwood Pottery
Ceramic, $15^{1}/_{2} \times 6 \times 6''$
Collection The Brooklyn
Museum. Gift of Mr. and Mrs.
Jay Lewis. (84.176.4)

GLASS

Martin Bache
Vase. c. 1890
Designed for Quezal Art Glass
and Decorating Company
Glass, $7^{1}/_{2} \times 3^{3}/_{4} \times 3^{3}/_{4}''$
Collection The Brooklyn
Museum. Gift of Mrs. Alfred
Zoebisch (59.143.16)

Frederick Carder
Vase (Gold Aurene). c. 1904–33
Designed for Steuben Glass
Works
Glass, $7 \times 4 \times 4''$
Collection Stephen Milne

Frederick Carder
*Vase (Gold-Decorated Aurene with
Millefiori Flowers).* 1905
Designed for Steuben Glass
Works
Glass, $11 \times 8^{1}/_{2} \times 8^{1}/_{2}''$
Collection Stephen Milne

Frederick Carder
Vase (Blue Aurene). c. 1905–33
Designed for Steuben Glass Works
Glass, $8^{1}/_{4} \times 8^{1}/_{4} \times 8^{1}/_{4}''$
Collection Stephen Milne

Frederick Carder
Cintra Bowl. c. 1916–17
Designed for Steuben Glass Works
Glass, $8^{3}/_{4} \times 10 \times 10''$
Collection Stephen Milne

Dard Hunter
Flower Motif Window. c. 1907
Designed for the Roycroft Inn
Stained glass, lead, wood,
$33^{1}/_{2} \times 28^{1}/_{8} \times 1^{3}/_{4}''$
Private collection

John La Farge
*Joshua Commanding the Sun to
Stand Still.* 1909
Fused cloisonne stained glass,
$18 \times 14''$
Collection Mary and Oliver
Hamill

John La Farge
Samoan Girl Dancing the Siva.
1909
Fused cloisonne stained glass,
$18 \times 14''$
Collection Mary and Oliver
Hamill

Louis Comfort Tiffany
Vase. 1886–1900
Designed for Tiffany Glass
Company
Glass, $13^{3}/_{4} \times 3 \times 3''$
Collection The Brooklyn
Museum. Gift of Charles W.
Gould (14.739.12)

Louis Comfort Tiffany
Vase (Peacock Feather). c. 1892–
1902
Designed for Tiffany Glass and
Decorating Company
Favrile glass, $10^{3}/_{4} \times 6 \times 6''$
Collection The Metropolitan
Museum of Art, New York

Louis Comfort Tiffany
Vase (Lava). c. 1893–1925
Designed for Tiffany Furnaces
Favrile glass, $5^{1}/_{16} \times 3 \times 3''$
Collection The Metropolitan
Museum of Art, New York

Louis Comfort Tiffany
Vase (Irregular). c. 1896–1900
Designed for Tiffany Glass and
Decorating Company
Glass, $6^{1}/_{2} \times 5^{1}/_{4} \times 5^{1}/_{4}''$
Collection The Brooklyn
Museum. Gift of Charles W.
Gould (14.739.18)

Louis Comfort Tiffany
Vase (Pinched). 1896–1919
Designed for Tiffany Furnaces
Glass, $8 \times 5 \times 5''$
Collection The Brooklyn
Museum. Bequest of Laura L.
Barnes (67.120.114)

Louis Comfort Tiffany
Egyptian Onion Flower-Form Vase. c. 1900
Designed for Tiffany Glass and Decorating Company
Glass, $21^3/_4 \times 5^1/_2 \times 5^1/_2$"
Private collection

Louis Comfort Tiffany
Vase (Peacock). c. 1900
Designed for Tiffany Glass and Decorating Company
Glass, $13^1/_2 \times 4 \times 4$"
Collection The Brooklyn Museum. Gift of Charles W. Gould (14.739.8)

Louis Comfort Tiffany
Vase (Pinched Green). c. 1900
Designed for Tiffany Glass and Decorating Company
Glass, $10 \times 3^1/_4 \times 3^1/_4$"
Collection The Brooklyn Museum. Gift of Mrs. Anthony Tamburro, in memory of her father, Rene de Quelin (64.246.7)

Louis Comfort Tiffany
Vase (Pressed & Cased). c. 1900
Designed for Tiffany Glass and Decorating Company
Glass, $8^5/_8 \times 2^1/_2 \times 2^1/_2$"
Collection The Brooklyn Museum. Gift of Mrs. Anthony Tamburro, in memory of her father, Rene de Quelin (62.262.8)

Louis Comfort Tiffany
Vase (Trumpet). c. 1900
Designed for Tiffany Glass and Decorating Company
Glass, $18^1/_4 \times 5^1/_4 \times 5^1/_4$"
Collection The Brooklyn Museum. Gift of Mary Berman in memory of Mr. and Mrs. Harry Berman (59.78.1)

Louis Comfort Tiffany
Purple Winged Dragonfly Shade and Bronze Table Lamp. 1900–1910
Tiffany Studios
Design attributed to Clara Driscoll
Leaded glass, patinated bronze, and metal filigree, $22 \times 16 \times 16$"
Courtesy The Neustadt Museum of Tiffany Art, New York

Louis Comfort Tiffany
Vase (Opaque & Iridescent). 1900–1910
Designed for Tiffany Furnaces
Favrile glass, $11 \times 5 \times 5$"
Collection The Brooklyn Museum. Gift of Charles W. Gould (14.739.16)

Louis Comfort Tiffany
Vase (Paperweight). 1901–5
Designed for Tiffany Glass and Decorating Company
Glass, $7^1/_2 \times 10 \times 10$"
Collection The Brooklyn Museum. Gift of Charles W. Gould (14.739.14)

Louis Comfort Tiffany
Window (Landscape Scene with Iris and Flowering Magnolia). c. 1905
Designed for Tiffany Studios
Stained glass, $60^1/_4 \times 42$"
Collection The Metropolitan Museum of Art, New York

Louis Comfort Tiffany
Window (Parrots and Magnolias). c. 1910–20
Designed for Tiffany Studios
Leaded Favrile glass, $26 \times 17^3/_4$"
Collection The Metropolitan Museum of Art, New York

Louis Comfort Tiffany
Vase (Opaque). 1913–20
Designed for Tiffany Furnaces
Glass, $9^5/_8 \times 5 \times 5$"
Collection The Brooklyn Museum. Gift of Charles W. Gould (14.739.15)

Louis Comfort Tiffany
Vase (Lava). 1915
Designed for Tiffany Furnaces
Favrile glass, $37^7/_8 \times 3^3/_8 \times 3^3/_8$"
Collection The Metropolitan Museum of Art, New York

Louis Comfort Tiffany
Vase (Lava). 1915
Designed for Tiffany Furnaces
Favrile glass, $5^3/_{16} \times 3 \times 3$"
Collection The Metropolitan Museum of Art, New York

Louis Comfort Tiffany
Vase. c. 1917
Designed for Tiffany Furnaces
Favrile glass, $12^5/_{16} \times 4^{11}/_{16} \times 4^{11}/_{16}$"
Collection The Metropolitan Museum of Art, New York

METALS

Art Crafts Shop, Buffalo
Jewelry Box. c. 1905
Copper, enamel, $3^3/_4 \times 7^3/_4 \times 5$"
Collection John Markus

Art Crafts Shop, Buffalo
Candlesticks. c. 1910
Copper, enamel, $26^3/_4 \times 9^7/_8 \times 8^5/_8$" each
Collection Elaine Dillof

Jane Carson Barron and Frances Barnum Smith
Cross. c. 1904
Silver, amethyst, enamel, $16 \times 3^1/_2 \times 2^1/_2$"
Courtesy ARK Antiques, New Haven, Connecticut

George Porter Blanchard
Bowl. c. 1904
Sterling silver, $3^1/_4 \times 10^1/_8 \times 10^1/_8$"
Private collection. Courtesy ARK Antiques, New Haven, Connecticut

Elizabeth Eaton Burton
Book Cover. c. 1905
Suede, copper, $10 \times 7^1/_2$"
Private collection. Courtesy David Rago

Elizabeth Eaton Burton
Lamp. c. 1905
Copper, abalone shells, $32^1/_2 \times 24^3/_4 \times 24^3/_4$"
Collection Tazio Nuvolari

Carence Crafters
Plant Holder. c. 1910
Copper, silver wash, $10^7/_8 \times 5^1/_2 \times 2^1/_8$"
Collection Ira Simon

Elizabeth E. Copeland
Box. c. 1914
Silver, enamel, $2^1/_2 \times 3^1/_8 \times 3^1/_8$"
Collection The Brooklyn Museum (96.1)

Elverhoj Colony
Necklace. c. 1900–1920
Gold, pearl, tourmaline, length: 14"
Collection Joyce Jonas

Forest Craft Guild
Desk Set. c. 1910
Copper, obsidian glass, letter rack: $4^1/_2 \times 6 \times 2$"; pen tray: $11 \times 3^5/_{16}$"
Collection Don Marek

Clemens Friedell
Vase. 1915
Silver, $17^1/_4 \times 6 \times 6$"
Private collection

Gorham Manufacturing Company
Martelé Vase. 1898
Silver, gold wash, $15 \times 7 \times 7$"
Courtesy Historical Design Collection, Inc., New York

Frank Gardner Hale
Necklace. c. 1918
Gold, blister pearl, peridot, pink tourmaline, length: 17"
Collection Marilee Boyd Meyer

Frank Gardner Hale
Brooch. c. 1920
Gold, zircons, diamonds, Montana sapphires, tourmalines, peridot, $2^1/_2 \times 1^1/_2$"
Private collection

Robert R. Jarvie
Tray. c. 1906
Copper, $5^5/_8 \times 11^1/_8 \times 11^1/_8$"
Collection Ira Simon

Robert R. Jarvie
Candlesticks. c. 1910
Bronze, average height: 14"; average base: 7"
Collection Ira Simon

Robert R. Jarvie
Hot Beverage Service. c. 1915
Sterling silver, coffeepot: $7^3/_4 \times 7^1/_2 \times 3^1/_4$"; creamer: $5 \times 6 \times 2^3/_4$"; tray: $21 \times 15^3/_4$"
Collection Museum of Fine Arts, Boston. Gift of a friend of the Department of American Decorative Arts and Sculpture, John H. and Ernestine A. Payne Fund, and Curator's Fund

Kalo Shop
Necklace. c. 1905
Gold, semiprecious stones, length: 16"
Private collection

Kalo Shop
Candelabrum. c. 1910
Silver, $28^1/_2 \times 19^1/_2 \times 6^1/_4$"
Private collection

Karl E. Kipp
Planter. 1905
Copper, $3^1/_4 \times 5^3/_4 \times 5^3/_4$"
Collection Marilee Boyd Meyer

Karl E. Kipp
Cufflinks. c. 1910
Sterling silver, box: $3 \times 2^1/_2 \times 1^1/_2$"
Collection Bill Drucker

Mary Catherine Knight
Bowl. c. 1903
Silver, enamel, $1^{15}/_{16} \times 4^1/_4 \times 4^1/_4$"
Collection The Cleveland Museum of Art. John L. Severance Fund

Karl F. Leinonen
Bowl and Spoon. c. 1900–1920
Hand-raised sterling silver, bowl: $1^3/_4 \times 5^7/_8 \times 5^7/_8$"; spoon length: $6^1/_4$"
Private collection

Attributed to Eva Macomber
Box. c. 1907
Produced by Society of Arts and Crafts, Boston
Copper, enamel, $4^1/_2 \times 6^3/_8 \times 6^3/_8$"
Collection Museum of Fine Arts, Boston. Gift of Lois and Stephen Kunian

George Washington Maher
Coffee and Tea Service. 1912
Designed for Rockledge
Silver, tray: $24^1/_2 \times 20$"; coffeepot: $9^1/_2 \times 8^1/_2 \times 8^1/_2$"; creamer: $5 \times 5^1/_4 \times 5^1/_4$"
Private collection

George Washington Maher
Urn. 1912
Designed for *Rockledge*
Bronze, copper, $30^1/_2 \times 12^1/_2 \times 12^1/_2$"
Collection Norwest Corporation, Minneapolis

Forest Emerson Mann
Necklace. c. 1906
Silver filigree, amazonstones, California pearls, chain: $14^1/_2$"; pendant: $2^7/_8 \times 2$"
Collection Don Marek

Paul Manship
Candelabra. 1916
Bronze, $58^1/_2 \times 12^1/_2 \times 12^1/_2''$
each
Collection Cranbrook Academy
of Art Museum, Bloomfield Hills,
Michigan. Gift of George and
Ellen Booth

Marcus & Company
Humidor. c. 1915–20
Copper, silver, arrowheads,
$8 \times 6^1/_4 \times 6^1/_4''$
Collection Norwest Corporation,
Minneapolis

Attributed to Frank J. Marshall
Box. c. 1910
Produced by Society of Arts and
Crafts, Boston
Copper, enamel,
$1^1/_2 \times 4^1/_2 \times 4^1/_2''$
Collection Museum of Fine Arts,
Boston. Gift of Lois and Stephen
Kunian

Edward Everett Oakes
Necklace. c. 1920
Aquamarine, pearl, gold, chain:
$15^3/_4''$; pendant: $1^1/_2 \times 1/_4''$
Collection Marilee Boyd Meyer

Theodore Hanford Pond
Vase. c. 1910
Copper, $17^1/_2 \times 4^1/_4 \times 4^1/_4''$
Collection Norwest Corporation,
Minneapolis

Katherine Pratt
Creamer, Sugar Bowl, and Tray. c.
1900–1920
Hand-raised sterling silver, tray:
$8^1/_4 \times 5''$; creamer: $5^1/_8 \times 4^3/_4 \times 4''$
Private collection

Jessie M. Preston
Jewelry Box. c. 1904–7
Bronze, $17/_8 \times 4^1/_4 \times 2^1/_2''$
Private collection. Courtesy ARK
Antiques, New Haven,
Connecticut

Jessie M. Preston
Candlesticks. c. 1915
Bronze, $12^3/_4 \times 7^3/_4 \times 7^3/_4''$ each
Collection Elaine Dillof

Julius Olaf Randahl
Pitcher. 1915
Silver, $87/_8 \times 8^1/_8 \times 47/_8''$
Collection The Art Institute of
Chicago. Twenty-fifth
Anniversary Gift of Mr. and
Mrs. Louis Marks, Gift of Mr.
and Mrs. Lawrence S. Dreiman

Margaret Rogers
Necklace and Earrings. c. 1920
Gold, cornelian, necklace: $17^1/_2''$;
earrings: $1/_2 \times 1/_2''$
Collection Marilee Boyd Meyer

Louis Rorimer
Coffee and Tea Service. c. 1910
Designed for the Rokesley Shop
Silver, moonstones, ebony,
coffeepot: $11^1/_8 \times 9^3/_4 \times 5''$;

teapot: $7^1/_8 \times 107/_8 \times 5''$; sugar
bowl: $3^3/_4 \times 8^{13}/_{16} \times 3''$
Collection The Cleveland
Museum of Art. Gift in memory
of Louis Rorimer, from his
daughter, Louise Rorimer
Dushkin, and his granddaughter,
Edie Soeiro

Roycroft Shops
Vase. c. 1910
Copper, silver,
$66^3/_4 \times 3^1/_2 \times 2^1/_2''$
Collection Kurland-Zabar

Josephine Hartwell Shaw
Pendant Necklace. c. 1900–1920
Gold, jelly-opal, length: 16"
Collection Joyce Jonas

Shreve and Company
Punch Bowl. c. 1910–1920
Silver, $10^1/_8 \times 13^1/_2 \times 13^1/_2''$
Collection Milwaukee Art
Museum. On loan from Warren
Gilson

Gustav Stickley
Tray. c. 1905
Copper, $15 \times 15''$
Private collection

Arthur J. Stone
Tea Service. 1907
Sterling silver, ivory, gold wash,
kettle: $9^1/_4 \times 10^1/_8 \times 7^1/_8''$; teapot:
$5^1/_4 \times 11^5/_8 \times 5^{15}/_{16}''$; creamer:
$4 \times 6 \times 4''$
Collection Museum of Fine Arts,
Boston. Gift of a Friend of the
Department of American
Decorative Arts and Sculpture,
John H. and Ernestine A. Payne
Fund, and Curator's Fund

Louis Comfort Tiffany
Necklace. c. 1918
Black opal, 18k gold, sapphires,
green garnets, chain: $14^1/_2''$;
pendant: $1^1/_2 \times 2^1/_2''$
Collection Ira Simon

Tiffany & Company
*Tea and Coffee Service "Special
Hand Work."* c. 1915
Sterling silver, kettle on stand
with lamp: $17^7/_8 \times 9 \times 4''$;
coffeepot: $9 \times 8^1/_2 \times 4''$; creamer:
$37/_8 \times 5 \times 3^1/_2''$
Collection Museum of the City of
New York. Gift of Ms. Claire
Lewis

Dirk Van Erp
Vase. c. 1911
Hammered copper, $24 \times 10 \times 10''$
Collection Susan Fetterolf and
Jeffrey Gorrin

Dirk Van Erp
Table Lamp. c. 1912
Copper, mica, $20 \times 18 \times 18''$
Collection Norwest Corporation,
Minneapolis

Mildred Watkins
Pendant and Chain. c. 1904–14

Silver, enamel, pendant:
$1^3/_4 \times 1^1/_2''$
Collection The Art Institute of
Chicago. Dr. Julian Archie
Endowment; Neighbors of
Kenilworth, Edgar J. Schoen, and
Village Associates of the Women's
Board of the Art Institute of
Chicago Funds

Mildred Watkins
Teapot. c. 1913
Sterling silver,
$11^1/_2 \times 93/_{16} \times 4^3/_8''$
Collection Yale University Art
Gallery, New Haven. Gift of
ARK Antiques

James H. Winn
Lavaliere. 1895–1917
Silver, gold, turquoise, length:
$16^1/_4''$
Collection The Art Institute of
Chicago. Restricted gift of
Warren L. Batts, Mrs. Jacob H.
Biscof, Mrs. Arthur S. Bowes,
and the Art Rental and Sales
Gallery

Madeline Yale Wynne
Belt Buckle. c. 1900
Copper, $2^3/_8 \times 9^1/_2''$
Collection Pocumtuck Valley
Memorial Association, Memorial
Hall Museum, Deerfield,
Massachusetts

Samuel Yellin
Gothic Chest. 1918
Wrought iron, $34^1/_2 \times 18^1/_2 \times 11''$
Collection Yellin Metalworkers,
Philadelphia

Marie Zimmermann
Candelabra. c. 1920
Bronze, crystal,
$28^1/_8 \times 307/_8 \times 85/_8''$
Collection Mitchell Wolfson, Jr.
Courtesy Wolfsonian Foundation,
Miami

TEXTILES

Anonymous
"Collars and Cuffs" Sack Kit.
c. 1910
Linen, $14 \times 12''$
Collection John Bryan

Anonymous
Workbag. c. 1910
Linen, $22^1/_8 \times 14''$
Collection John Bryan

Mrs. Carrie E. Clapp
Basket. c. 1905
Palm leaves, $4^1/_4 \times 8 \times 8''$
Collection Pocumtuck Valley
Memorial Association, Memorial
Hall Museum, Deerfield,
Massachusetts

Deerfield Society of Blue and
White Needlework
Wall Hanging. c. 1910
Linen, $37 \times 36^1/_2''$

Collection Pocumtuck Valley
Memorial Association, Memorial
Hall Museum, Deerfield,
Massachusetts

Nonoluck Silk Company
*Partially-worked Panel Intended as
a Pillow.* c. 1910–15
Stenciled linen embroidered with
cotton, $23^3/_4 \times 24^1/_8''$
Collection The Art Institute of
Chicago

Richardson Silk Company
Pillow Sham, Design No. 525.
c. 1910
Linen embroidered with silk,
$23^1/_2 \times 16^1/_2''$
Collection The Art Institute of
Chicago

Richardson Silk Company
*Partially-worked Panel Intended as
a Pillow, Design No. 2951.*
c. 1910–15
Stenciled cotton embroidered
with silk, $16^3/_4 \times 21^1/_8''$
Collection The Art Institute of
Chicago

Roycroft Shops
Doily. c. 1910
Leather, $17^1/_2 \times 17^1/_2''$
Collection Raymond Groll

Anna Frances Simpson
Table Runner. c. 1909–29
Produced at Newcomb College
Linen, silk, $5'3^1/_2'' \times 16''$
Collection Museum of Art,
Rhode Island School of Design,
Providence. Gift of Mrs. Eliot A.
Carver

Gustav Stickley
Carpet. c. 1905
Cotton, wool, soft wood paper
fibers, $6'103/_4'' \times 3'107/_8''$
Collection The Art Institute of
Chicago

Gustav Stickley
Table Runner. c. 1905
Linen, $90 \times 15''$
Collection John Bryan

Gustav Stickley
Table Runner with Napkins.
c. 1905
Linen, runner: $71^1/_4 \times 15^1/_4''$
Collection John Bryan

Gustav Stickley
Bedspread. c. 1912
Linen, $9'6'' \times 6'10''$
Collection John Bryan

H. E. Varren Company
*Panel Intended as a Pillow, Design
No. 215.* c. 1910
Stenciled, painted cotton,
$227/_8 \times 17^1/_2''$
Collection The Art Institute of
Chicago

Margaret Whiting
Door Curtain (detail). 1899

Linen, 8'3" × 6'4"
Collection Pocumtuck Valley
Memorial Association, Memorial
Hall Museum, Deerfield,
Massachusetts. Gift of Gertrude
Cochrane Smith

Madeline Yale Wynne
Witch Basket. c. 1901–10
Raffia, 7⁷/8 × 6¹/8 × 6¹/8"
Collection Pocumtuck Valley
Memorial Association, Memorial
Hall Museum, Deerfield,
Massachusetts

WOOD

John S. Bradstreet
Center Table. c. 1904
Designed for William Prindle
House
Cypress with *jin-di-sugi* finish,
27¹/4 × 30 × 30"
Collection Tazio Nuvolari

John S. Bradstreet
Flip-top Card Table. c. 1904
Designed for William Prindle
House
Cypress with *jin-di-sugi* finish,
30¹/4 × 35¹/2 × 19³/4"
Collection The Minneapolis
Institute of Arts. Gift of
Wheaton Wood

Harvey Ellis
Fall-front Desk. c. 1903–4
Designed for Craftsman
Workshops
Quartersawed white oak, pewter,
copper, exotic wood inlays,
46¹/2 × 42 × 11¹/2"
Collection Virginia Museum of
Fine Arts. Gift of Sydney and
Frances Lewis

Harvey Ellis
Side Chair. c. 1903–4
Designed for United Crafts
Stained curled maple, pewter,
wood inlays, 40¹/2 × 16¹/2 × 15¹/2"
Collection The Newark Museum,
New Jersey. Sophronia Anderson
Bequest fund

George Grant Elmslie
Box Chair. 1912
Designed for Babson House
Oak, 37 × 25 × 23¹/8"
Collection Dr. David Gebhard

Charles Sumner Greene and
Henry Mather Greene
Chiffonier. c. 1909
Designed for Gamble House
master bedroom
Black walnut, ebony, lignum
vitae, semiprecious stone inlay,
62 × 37¹/2 × 21"
Collection Gamble House

Frank Jeck
Infant's Crib. 1922

Hand-carved cherry, velvet
hangings, 64¹/2 × 44¹/4 × 24¹/4"
Collection Glencairn Museum,
Bryn Athyn, Pennsylvania

Charles P. Limbert
Square Center Table. 1904
Stained oak,
30¹/2 × 33¹/2 × 33¹/2"
Courtesy Struve Gallery, Chicago

Charles P. Limbert
Bench #243. 1905
Oak, 24 × 30 × 18"
Collection Victorian Chicago
Arts and Crafts Antique Gallery

Charles P. Limbert
Wastebasket. c. 1908
Quartersawed oak,
17³/4 × 11 × 11"
Collection David Rago

George Washington Maher
Standing Clock. 1912
Designed for *Rockledge*
Oak, copper, silk, brass,
80 × 31¹/2 × 15¹/8"
Collection Tazio Nuvolari

George Washington Maher
Armchair. c. 1914
Designed for *Rockledge*
Oak with studded, padded
leather upholstery,
59¹/4 × 33 × 26³/8"
Collection The Metropolitan
Museum of Art, New York.
Purchase Theodore R. Gamble,
Jr. Gift in honor of his mother,
Mrs. Theodore Robert Gamble

Lucia Kleinhaus Mathews
"Young Girl in White." c. 1900–
1915
Oil on wood panel; carved,
painted wood frame,
22¹/16 × 20¹/4 × 2¹/8"
Collection The Oakland
Museum. Gift of Harald Wagner

Lucia Kleinhaus Mathews
Clock. c. 1906–15
Painted, gilded wood; metal,
glass, 14³/4 × 6 × 4"
Collection The Oakland
Museum. Gift of the Concours
d'Antiques, The Art Guild

Lucia Kleinhaus Mathews
Figural Box. 1916
Painted wood, 4¹/4 × 13¹/8 × 8³/8"
Collection Donald Magner

George M. Niedecken
Dainty (Curio) Cabinet. 1907
Curly birch, metal-capped feet,
plate glass, 53 × 37 × 17"
Collection David and Jean
Sullivan. Courtesy Milwaukee Art
Museum

George M. Niedecken
Upholstered Armchair. 1907

Walnut, walnut veneer, velour
upholstery, 46¹/2 × 25¹/4 × 25³/4"
Collection Nicole Teweles

William L. Price
Music Stand. c. 1901–6
Carved, stained oak,
43¹/2 × 20 × 16"
Collection Mr. and Mrs. Hyman
Myers

Charles Rohlfs
Rocking Chair. c. 1900
Carved quartersawed oak,
leather, 31 × 24 × 34"
Collection Susan Fetterolf and
Jeffrey Gorrin

Charles Rohlfs
Candelabra. 1900–1902
Wood, copper, lapis shells,
17¹/4 × 18¹/4 × 8³/8"
Collection Donald Magner

Charles Rohlfs
Plant Stand. 1901
Fumed quartersawed oak,
hammered copper, brass bucket,
48 × 18 × 18"
Collection Beth Cathers

Charles Rohlfs
Fall-front Desk. 1902
Carved quartersawed oak,
54¹/8 × 14 × 35¹/4"
Collection Tazio Nuvolari

William Roth
Umbrella Stand. 1910
Designed for Roycroft Shops
Quartersawed oak, hammered
copper, 30 × 13¹/2 × 13¹/2"
Private collection

Roycroft Shops
Magazine Stand. c. 1906–12
Oak, 63¹/4 × 21³/4 × 17³/4"
Collection Tazio Nuvolari

Roycroft Shops
Funereal Box. c. 1910
Mahogany, copper,
8¹/4 × 14¹/4 × 12¹/8"
Collection Tazio Nuvolari

Roycroft Shops
Wastepaper Basket. c. 1910
Mahogany, copper, 13 × 11 × 11"
Collection Tazio Nuvolari

Roycroft Shops
Wastepaper Basket. c. 1910
From the home of Ralph Waldo
Emerson
Maple, 13 × 12¹/4 × 12¹/4"
Collection Tazio Nuvolari

Roycroft Shops
*Picture Frame with Drawings
Attributed to Karl Kipp.*
c. 1910–12
Stained oak, Roycroft paper
matte, graphite on paper,

20³/4 × 24³/4"
Private collection

Roycroft Shops
Child's Chest. 1912
Designed for Elbert Hubbard's
granddaughter Lynette
Quartersawed oak, copper,
mirror, 33³/4 × 25³/4 × 11"
Private collection

Roycroft Shops
*Picture Frame with Portrait of
Elbert Hubbard.* c. 1912
Stained oak, gelatin silver print,
glass, 26 × 23³/8 × 3/4"
Private collection

Gustav Stickley
Settle. 1901–2
Oak, 40¹/4 × 60 × 27"
Collection Barbara Taff and Alan
Sachs

Gustav Stickley
Corner Cupboard. c. 1902
Designed for the Stickley home
Oak, wrought iron,
72 × 42 × 29¹/2"
Collection Mrs. Barbara Fuldner

Gustav Stickley
Three-panel Screen. c. 1904
Oak, 59¹/4 × 75¹/2"
Collection Beth Cathers

Gustav Stickley
Sideboard. c. 1905–10
Oak, copper, 47¹/2 × 56 × 21³/4"
Collection Yale University Art
Gallery. Gift of Dr. and Mrs.
Matthew Newman

Gustav Stickley
Round Table. c. 1907–8
Quartersawed oak,
30 × 35¹/2 × 35¹/2"
Collection Sydney and Frances
Lewis. Courtesy Virginia
Museum of Fine Arts

Ernest Stowe
Desk. c. 1900–1911
Varnished pine, white birchbark,
yellow birch, cedar,
54¹/2 × 43⁵/8 × 25"
Collection Adirondack Museum,
Blue Mountain Lake, New York.
Warren W. Kay Collection

Frank Lloyd Wright
Armchair. 1904
Wood, 32 × 23 × 23"
Collection Albright-Knox Art
Gallery, Buffalo. Gift of Darwin
R. Martin, 1968

Frank Lloyd Wright
Table. 1904
Wood, 27 × 27 × 26¹/4"
Collection Albright-Knox Art
Gallery, Buffalo. Gift of Darwin
R. Martin, 1968

References to illustrations are in *italics*. Footnote citations are indicated by the letter *n* directly following a page number.

A

Abbey San Encino press, Pasadena, California, 275
Abnakee Rug Industry, Pequahet, New Hampshire, 39, 269
Acadian community, Louisiana Gulf coast, 253
Adams, Emile C., 274
Addams, Jane, 275
Adirondack Furniture and the Rustic Tradition (Gilborn), 282n22
Aesthetic movement, 65–72
Agua Caliente society, Warner's Ranch, California, 256
Alaska-Yukon-Pacific Exposition (1909), Seattle, Washington, 254
Albee, Helen R., 39, 269
Alberhill Coal and Clay Company, Riverside, California, 261
Alberhill Pottery, Riverside, California, 261; *Vase* (Robertson), *78*
Aldrich, Mary L., 274
Alfred University, Alfred, New York, New York School of Clayworking and Ceramics, 24, 77, 79–80, 271
Alhambra Ceramic Works, Chicago, 263
Allen, Charles Dexter, 257
Allen, Mary and Frances, 41–42
Allen-Higgins Company, Worcester, Massachusetts, 271
Alton Manufacturing Company, Sandwich, Massachusetts, 94
Alwil Press, Palisades, New York, 275
Amari, Countess, 40–41, 275
Amateur Work (periodical), 259
American Arts and Crafts movement, 26, 28, 29–31, 44, 46, 61, 64–65, 68–72, 76, 77, 83, 87–88, 95, 99, 101, 111–124, 282n22
American Ceramic Society, Columbus, Ohio, 79, 256
The American Chap-book (periodical), 259
American Craft Museum, New York, 22–28, 99; A Centenary Project, 22–28, 29–31, 277n1; Foundation of the American Craft Movement, 1900–1918, symposium (1990), 23; Ideal Home: 1900–1920 exhibition (1993), 23–24, 26–28; Twentieth-Century American Craft: A Neglected History symposium (1990), 22
American Encaustic Tiling Company, Zanesville, Ohio, 261
The American Magazine of Art (periodical), 259, 280n14
American Terra Cotta and Ceramic Company, Crystal Lake, Illinois, 261

American Women's League, St. Louis, 82, 256
The Anatomy of Pattern (Day), 52
Anderson, A. H., 62, 253
Anonymous: *"Collars and Cuffs" Sack Kit, 215; Workbag, 215*
Apollo Silver Company, New York, 267
Apollo Studios, New York, 267
Aranyi, Joseph, 55, 280n8
Architectural League of New York, 58, 106
Architectural Record (periodical), 259
Architecture, 111–35; *"A Home in a Prairie Town"* (Wright), *119; Alice Barber Stephens House* (Price and McLanahan), *132, 133; Alterations to Rose Valley Guest House* (Price and McLanahan), *131; Casas Grandes Project* (Gill), *124; Dining Room* (Stickley), *113; Dodge House North Elevation* (Gill), *123; Drawing of Station Square* (Atterbury, Olmsted et al), *116; Gamble House Dining Room* (Greene and Greene), *122; General Plan of Hilton Village* (Hubbard and Joannes), *117; Hilton Village Street Fronts and House Rows* (Hubbard and Joannes), *118; Inglenook, Schoen House* (Price and McLanahan), *127; Library of "A Bradley House"* (Bradley), *112; McLanahan House* (Price and McLanahan), *134; Rockledge* (Maher), *121; Rose Valley Improvement Co. House* (Price and McLanahan), *135; Trier Center Neighborhood Site Plan* (Griffin), *120*
The Architecture of Country Houses (Downing), 125, 286n4
Arden community, Arden, Delaware, 127, 253
Arequipa Pottery, Fairfax, California, 86, 261
Armstrong, David Maitland, 93, 99, 237
Arroyo Guild of Craftsmen, Pasadena, California, 256
Art Academy of Cincinnati, 274
The Art Amateur (periodical), 280n13
Art and Progress (periodical), 259, 280n14
Art Association of Indianapolis, 273
Art Craft Institute, Chicago, 272
Art Crafts Shop, Buffalo, New York, 62, 267; *Candlesticks, 184; Jewelry Box, 185*
Artemesia Book Bindery, Los Angeles, 275
Art Institute of Chicago, 56, 59, 83; Antiquarian Society, 256; Arts and Crafts Exhibition (1897–1921), 58, 59, 89, 254, 281n34; School of the, Department of Decorative Design, 272; *The Sketch Book,* 261
Art Interchange.(periodical), 280n14
Artists' Biographies, 237–52
Art Metal Company, Los Angeles, 267

Art Metalwork with Inexpensive Equipment (Payne), 56
Art Nouveau style, 81, 84, 87, 89
Arts and Crafts Exhibition (1903), Syracuse, New York, 254
Arts and Decoration (periodical), 280n14
Artschwager, Richard, 29
The Artsman: The Art That Is Life (periodical), 117, 259–60; Poster, *37*
Art Students' League, New York, 272
Art Students' League of Buffalo, Buffalo Chapter American Institute of Architects, Buffalo Society of Artists, Buffalo, New York, The Joint Annual Exhibition (1900), 254
Asbury, Lenore, 237; *Vase, 167*
Ashbee, C. R., 55, 60, 61, 101, 111, 125, 134, 279n1, 280n16
Associated Artists: *Harper's New Monthly Magazine,* 38, 39
Atascadero Community, Atascadero, California, 253
Atlan Ceramic Art Club, Chicago, 256
Atterbury, Grosvenor, 117; *Drawing of Station Square, 116*
At the Sign of the Live Oak, Oakland, California, 256
Avery Coonley House, Riverside, Illinois, 109, 115
Avon Faience Company, Tiltonville, Ohio, 266
Ayers, John W., 74, 269–70
John W. Ayers Company, Chicago, 74, 269–70

B

Babbitt, Mrs. J. H., 256
Henry B. Babson House, Riverside, Illinois: *Carpet* (Elmslie), 108, *109*
Bache, Martin, 95, 237, 266–67; *Vase, 170*
Bachelder, Oscar Louis, 264
Baggs, Arthur Eugene, 85–86, 237, 263; *Vase, 138*
Baillie-Scott, M. H., 69, 111, 114, 116; *Houses and Gardens,* 123
Baker, Gary E., 23
Barnet Pottery, Chicago, 261
Barr, Charles H., 62
Barron, Jane Carson, 60, 62, 237; *Cross, 10*
The Bases of Design (Crane), 49, *51*
Basket Fraternity, Pasadena, California, 256
Batchelder, Ernest Allen, 88, 237, 261; *The Principles of Design,* 48, *48, 49, 50*
Batchelder Tile Company, Pasadena, California, 88, 261
Bauhaus movement, 91, 124, 130
Beaux-Arts Village, Puget Sound, Washington, 126, 253
Begg, W. Proudfoot, 50
Bellis, John O., 267

John O. Bellis silversmith, San Francisco, 267
Berea College, Berea, Kentucky, 39–40, 106, 109–10
Berea Fireside Industries, Berea, Kentucky, 109–10
Biedenweg, William E., 266
Bigelow, Kennard & Co., 48, 49
Biloxi Art Pottery, Biloxi, Mississippi, 77, 261
Biltmore Industries, Asheville, North Carolina, 272
Bing, Samuel, 101
Binns, Charles Fergus, 77, 79–80, 82, 84, 85, 87, 90, 237, 271; *The Potter's Craft,* 47; *Vases, 8, 139*
M. H. Birge & Sons Company: *Interior No. 14,* 44
Blakeslee, Mary, 60, 268
Blanchard, George Porter, 60; *Bowl, 205*
Blanchard, Ida, 60
Blanchard, Porter George, 60, 237
Blanchard, Richard, 60
Blashfield, E. H., 93
Blue Sky Press, Chicago, 275
F. C. Bogk House, Milwaukee, Wisconsin, 109
Bohemia Guild, Chicago, 256
Bohemia Guild Bookbindery, Chicago, 275
Bok, Edward William, 113, 127, 237, 260, 285n8
The Book of the Roycrofters (Roycroft Press), 104
Books, 136–37. See also Small Presses; *The Craftsman* (Stickley), 137; *The Digressions of V* (Vedder), 137; *The Poet Philosopher* (Mason), 136; *To-Morrow: A Monthly Hand-Book of the Changing Order* (Bracken), 36; *Woman's Work* (Hubbard), 136
Boris, Eileen, 23, 32–45
Bowles, Janet Payne, 38, 40, 43, 62, 238
Bowman, Leslie Greene, 23
Boyes, Dr. Charles W., 257
Bracken, Julia, 42
Bradley, Will H., 116, 238, 276; *Library of "A Bradley House," 112; Uncle Walt* (Mason), 136
Bradley Polytechnic Institute, Peoria, Illinois, 272
Bradstreet, John Scott, 108, 238; *Center Table, 220; Curtain Panels, 108, 108; Flip-top Card Table, 221*
Bragdon, Charles F., 259
Bragdon, William V., 90, 262; *Mission Design Tile, 90*
Bragdon and Thomas tilemakers, Berkeley, California, 90, 262
Brainerd and Armstrong Company, 100
Branch, Grove R., 280n12
Brandt, Beverly K., 46–54
Brauckman, Cornelius, 85, 263
Braznell, W. Scott, 23, 55–63
Bresler, Frank H., 270
F. H. Bresler Company, Milwaukee, 74, 270

Brigham, Louise, 238
Brigham, Walter Cole, 238
Britton, Percy, 266–67
Brouwer, Theophilus Anthony, Jr., 77, 79, 238, 264; *Vase, 140*
Brouwer Pottery, Westhampton, New York, 77, 264
Brown, Bolton Coit, 67, 253
Brown, Dr. Philip King, 86, 261
Brown, Edith, 40, 87, 259, 264–65
Brown, Edmund Llewellyn, 270
Browne, Clyde, 275
Brush and Pencil (periodical), 47, 260, 280n14
Bryn Athyn community, Bryn Athyn, Pennsylvania, 66–67, 253
Buck, Lawrence, 257
Buffalo China, Buffalo, New York, 262
Buffalo Pottery, Buffalo, New York, 262
Bulletin of Arts and Crafts (periodical), 260
The Bungalow Magazine (periodical), 33, 260
Burnap, James, 263
Burroughs, John, 132
Burton, Elizabeth Eaton, 62, 238; *Book Cover, 187; Lamp, 185*
Burton, Scott, 29
Busck, Charlotte, 105
Busck, G.J., 280n12
Busck Studio, New York, 62
Bush-Brown, Lydia, 105, 238
Buston, Mary A., 259
Bustroem, Verena, 259
Byrdcliffe Colony, Woodstock, New York, 67, 127, 253
Byrdcliffe Pottery, Woodstock, New York, 262; *Bowl, 142*

C

Cahuilla Basketmakers, Southern-central California, 256–57
California College of Arts and Crafts, Oakland, 68, 110, 272
California Exhibition of Applied Arts (1916), Los Angeles, 254–55
California Faience, Berkeley, 90, 262; *Mission Design Tile* (Bragdon), 90
California Guild of Arts and Crafts, Berkeley, School of the, 110, 272
California School of Arts and Crafts, Berkeley, 272
California School of Design, San Francisco, 272
California School of Fine Arts, San Francisco, 272
Calumet Copper Mine Women, Calumet, Michigan, 257
Cambridge Art Pottery, Cambridge, Ohio, 262
Carder, Frederick, 94–95, 238, 267; *Cintra Bowl, 2; Vase (Blue Aurene), 169; Vase (Gold Aurene), 169; Vase (Gold-Decorated Aurene with Millefiori Flowers), 168*
Carence Crafters, Chicago, 267; *Plant Holder, 187*
Carey, Arthur A., 62, 262, 268
Carlson Currier Company, 100
Carnes, Mark C., 34
Carter, Sybil, 272
Sybil Carter Lace Association, White Earth, Minnesota, 272
Casas Grandes project, Hollywood Hills, California, 124
Casey, Charles L., 262
Cathedral of St. John the Divine, New York, 97–99

Caulkins, Horace James, 81, 84, 88, 238–39, 265
Cellini, Benvenuto, 47
Cellini Shop, Evanston, Illinois, 267
Central Art Association, Chicago, 257
Ceramic Art Company, 79
Ceramics, 77–91, 138–67, 261–66; *Beaver Tile* (Grueby), *88; Bowl* (Byrdcliffe Pottery), *142; Bowl with Handle and Spout* (Ohr), *156; Bowl (with Rabbits)* (Saturday Evening Girls' Club), *150; Byzantine Four Flowers Tile* (Mercer), *145; Dinnerware Service* (Hunter), *153; Fiddleheads Vase* (Tiffany), *147; Fluminus Impetus Tile* (Mercer), *144; Humidor* (Elliot and Meyer), *98; Inkwell* (Mercer), *150; Irises Vase* (Van Briggle), *149; Jar* (Pewabic Pottery), *84; Lantern* (Robineau), *165; Lidded Teapot* (Ohr), *78; Low Vase* (Nichols), *154; Mission Design Tile* (Bragdon), *90; Mission Ware Vase* (Hyten), *153; Monogram Vase* (Robineau), *164; Monumental Vase* (Perry), *158; Olla* (Long), *152; Persian Antelope Tile* (Mercer), *145; Teapot, Lid and Stand* (Kunsman), *152; Teapot and Coffeepot* (Ohr), *157; Tile Frieze* (Perry), *151; Vase* (Asbury), *167; Vase* (Baggs), *138; Vase* (Brouwer), *140; Vase* (Daly), *141; Vase* (Doat), *142; Vase* (Fulper Pottery), *6; Vase* (Hurten), *161; Vase* (LeBlanc and Meyer), *151; Vase* (McLaughlin), *145; Vase* (Mundie), *9; Vase* (Ohr), *157; Vase* (Robertson), *78, 160; Vase* (Robineau), *164; Vases* (Binns), *8, 139; Vases* (Grueby Faience), *148; Vase* (Shirayamadani), *143; Vases* (Nichols), *154, 155; Vases* (Overbeck Pottery), *86, 160; Vases* (Perry), *158, 159; Vases* (Robertson), *162, 163; Vases* (Shirayamadani), *143, 166; Vase* (Valentien), *149; Vase* (Volkmar), *138; Vase (with Beetles)* (Sicard), *166; Vase* (Young), *140; Water Lilies with Frogs* (Tiffany), *146; William Jervis Pottery Shops* (Rose Valley), *130*
Chalk and Chisel Club, Minneapolis, 105
Chautauqua Institution, Lake Chautauqua, New York, 272
Chautauqua Sunday School Assembly, Lake Chautauqua, New York, 272
Chelsea Keramic Art Works, Chelsea, Massachusetts, 77–78; *Vase* (Robertson), *162, 163*
Cheney, Frank, Ralph, Rush, and Ward, 269
Cheney Brothers textiles, Manchester, Connecticut, 269
Cherry, Kathryn E., 82, 272
Chetimachez Indian community, Avery's Island, Louisiana, 253
Chicago Arts and Crafts Society, 55, 59, 66, 105, 106, 111, 254
Chicago Ceramic Association, 257
Chicago Terra Cotta Company employees, 264
Chicago World's Columbian Exposition (1893), 99
Cincinnati Museum Association, 274
Cincinnati Pottery Club, 39, 80, 83, 257
Clapp, Carrie E., 239; *Basket, 217*
Cleveland Museum of Art, Exhibition of Work by Artists & Craftsmen of the Western Reserve (1919–present), 106, 255

Cleveland Pottery and Tile Company, 262
Cleveland School of Art, 60
Clewell, Charles W., 267
Clewell Metal Art, Canton, Ohio, 267
Cliff Dwellers Club of Chicago, *43*, 257
Clifton Art Pottery, Newark, New Jersey, 85, 262; *Olla* (Long), *152*
Clifton Porcelain Tile Company, Newark, New Jersey, 262
Clingman, George, 69
Clutton-Brock, A., 48, 54, 279n5
Cobden-Sanderson, T. J., 41
Coburn, Frederick W., 47, 58, 60, 239
Codman, William C., 55
Cole, Henry, 46
Coleman, Caryl, 110
Colgate, Florence, 275
Colnik, Cyril, 62
Colonna, Edward, 60
Columbia University, New York: Department of Industrial Arts, 280n12; Teachers College, Department of Fine Arts, 272, 280n12
Communities, 27–28, 36–37, 66–68, 85–87, 125, 253–54
Conklin, Ida Pell, 62
Connick, Charles J., 239; *Holy Grail Window, 98*
Conti, Timothy A., 70
Conwell, Clarke, 275
Cook, Charles Howell, 262
Cooke, Edward S., Jr., 24, 64–76
Cook Pottery, Trenton, New Jersey, 262
Cooper-Hewitt Museum, New York, 105
Cooper Union for the Advancement of Science and Art, New York, 272
Copeland, Elizabeth E., 57, 62, 239; *Box, 187*
Copper Shop, Oakland, California, 267
Copper Work (Rose), 56
Cotton, C. N., 104
Country Life in America (periodical), 111
Country Life movement, 112
Cowan, R. Guy, 91, 262
Cowan Pottery Studio, Cleveland, 91, 262
Cox, Kenyon, 93
Cox, Paul, 83–84
Coxhead, Ernest, 121, 239, 286n30
Craft: aesthetic quality of, 25, 29, 46, 48, 65–72, 75–76, 114–15, 282n1; architecture and, 72, 74–75, 76, 105, 107–9, 111–24; as art, 29–31, 35, 282n4; conventionalization of, 49–50, 106; critical reception of, 29, 31, 46–54, 69, 110; as differentiated from folk art, 25–26, 29; distribution and marketing of, 30, 31, 58–59, 67, 70, 75, 129–30, 281n49; division of labor and, 29, 35–36, 63, 65, 68, 110, 114, 125, 126, 282n13; domestic environment of, 26–28, 43–45, 64–76, 100–110, 113; education and ideology in, 30, 31, 49, 55–58, 64–76, 113–14, 279n14; entrepreneurism in, 31, 36, 68–69, 90–91; fit for its purpose, 25, 29, 50, 72–75, 132, 279n17; gender issues in, 31, 32–45, 65–66, 79, 80–82, 105, 112–13, 277n7; history of, 22–23, 30–31; innovation in, 25–26, 29, 48, 92–93, 94, 99; as material culture, 29–30, 125–35, 286n1; materials of, 24, 29, 114–15, 132; scale of, 25, 30; as social reform and social critique, 31, 32–45, 85–87, 106,

114, 125–35, 286n2; tactile quality of, 25, 30, 66; technique of, 24–25, 29; toward a definition of, 24–26, 64–65, 282n2
Crafters society, Chicago, 257
Craftsman Farm, Morris Plains, New Jersey, 126
Craftsman Homebuilders Club, 103
The Craftsman (periodical), 40, 42, 44, 47, 70, 101–10, 111–12, 113, 116, 117, 124, 134–35, 137, 260, 280n14, 282n13, 286n25
Craftsman's Guild, Chicago, 257
Craftsman Workshops, Eastwood, New York, 62, 101–7, 110, 126, 271; *Fall-front Desk* (Ellis), *222*
Cram, Ralph Adams, 96–99, 239, 260
Crane, Walter, 36; *The Bases of Design, 49, 51*
Craven Art Pottery, East Liverpool, Ohio, 262
Creese, Walter L.: *The Search for Environment: The Garden City, Before and After, 285n12*
Cross, Charles, 262
Cross, Nellie Agnes, 262
Cross, Richard, Jr., 262
Crossware Pottery, Chicago, 262
Crowninshield, Frederic, 239
Culbertson, J. D., 266
Cusick, Albert L., 262
Cuzner, Bernard, 50–51

D

Dahlquist, Edward and Elizabeth Burnap, 265
Daly, Matthew A., 239; *Vase, 141*
D'Ascenzo, Nicola: *Tabard Inn Food Co. Window, 95*
Davidson, Mabel, 262
Davis, Katharine, 269
Davis, Lila Whitcomb, 62
Day, Lewis Foreman, 54, 239; *The Anatomy of Pattern, 52; Nature in Ornament, 49; Ornament & Its Application, 49–50*
Dayton Society of Arts and Crafts, 257
Dedham Pottery, Dedham, Massachusetts, 79, 262
Deerfield Society of Blue and White Needlework, Deerfield, Massachusetts, 41–42, 66, 106, 257; *Wall Hanging, 215*
Deerfield Society of Village Industries, Deerfield, Massachusetts, 257
DeMoll, Carl, 130
Denison House, Boston, 40
Dennett, Mary Ware, 42, 239, 268
Detroit Museum of Art, 59, 106, 281n34; George Leland Hunter Loan Exhibition of Tapestries (1919), 255
Detroit Society of Arts and Crafts, 57
De Vinne, Theodore L., 275
Theodore L. De Vinne & Company, New York, 275
Dixon, Harry Saint John, 68, 239–40
Dixon, Lawrence B. and Eda Lord, 62
Doat, Taxile, 82–83, 240; *Grand Feu Ceramics, 81–82, 85; Vase, 142*
Dodge House, Los Angeles, California: *North Elevation* (Gill), *123, 123*
Donaldson, Douglas, 57, 61, 62, 240, 254–55
Donnelley, Richard Robert, 273
R. R. Donnelley and Sons, Chicago, 273

Douglas, Miss O. S., 259
Dow, Arthur Wesley, 240
Downes, William Howe, 47, 240
Downing, Andrew Jackson: *The Architecture of Country Houses, 125,* 286n4
Drake, Alexander W., 59
Driscoll, Clara, 240
Duffner and Kimberly, glassmakers: *The Lawyers' Club Window, 94*
Dumont, John F., 259
Dunbar, Jessie Ames, 62
Durand Art Glass Company, Vineland, New Jersey, 95
Durant Kilns, Bedford Village, New York, 262

E

Eberhardt, Hugo, 266
Hugo Eberhardt and Company, Chicago, 266
Eberts, W. E., 262
Edson, Millicent Strange, 62
Eidelberg, Martin, 23
Elliot, Esther Huger, 240; *Humidor, 150*
Ellis, Harvey, 69–70, 115, 116, 240, 259, 285n20; *Fall-front Desk, 222; Side Chair, 231*
Elmslie, George Grant, 72, 95–96, 108, 240, 282n28, 283n30; *Box Chair, 12; Carpet, 109; Side Chair, 73*
Elston Press, New York, 275
Elverhoj Colony, Milton-on-the-Hudson, New York, 62, 253; *Necklace, 212*
Emerson, Ralph Waldo, 125, 128; *Wastepaper Basket* (Roycroft Shops) of, *230*
English Arts and Crafts movement, 23, 25, 26, 29, 30, 32, 46, 55, 99, 111–12
Evans, Sara, 34
Exhibition of Art Craftsmanship (1903), Rochester, 254
Exhibitions, 23–24, 58–59, 64, 106, 136–235, 254–56, 277n3
Eyre, Wilson, 240; *House and Garden, 116–17*

F

Fabray, Thillman, 259
Fellowship Farms, Westwood, Massachusetts, 126, 253
Fels, Joseph, 127, 253
Field, Marshall, 268
Fine Arts Journal (periodical), 260
Fink, Allen, 262
Finn, Clara C., 269
Fisher, W. G., 264
Flanagan, Joseph E., 266
Flanagan and Biedenweg Company, Chicago, 266
Florentine Pottery, Chillecothe, Ohio, 262
Fogliati, A., 240
Forest Craft Guild, Grand Rapids, Michigan, 62, 257; *Desk Set, 188*
Forester, Leonard, 262
Forest Hills Gardens, Long Island, New York, 117, 285–86n24; *Drawing of Station Square* (Atterbury, Olmsted et al), *116*
Forve, Pettebone Company, Los Angeles, 268
Foster, Seth, 269
Foster, Sybil, 57

Four Winds Summer School, Syracuse, New York, 272
The Fra: For Philistines and Roycrofters (periodical), 260
Frackelton, Susan Stuart Goodrich, 84, 258, 262
Frackelton China and Decorating Works, Milwaukee, 262
Franzheim, Charles W., 266
Freeman, Sarah J., 257
Friedell, Clemens, 60, 241; *Vase, 189*
Frost Art Metal Shops, Dayton, Ohio, 62
Fry, Laura, 39, 79
Fry, Marshall T., 259
Fulper, Abra(ha)m, 262–63
Fulper Pottery Company, Flemington, New Jersey, 87, 262–63; *Teapot, Lid and Stand* (Kunsman), *152; Vase, 6*
Furniture, 64–76, 282n4. *See also* Wood; *Armchair* (Maher), *225; Armchair* (Wright), *13; Bench #243* (Limbert), *224; Box Chair* (Elmslie), *12; Center Table* (Bradstreet), *220; Chair* (Old Hickory), *70; Chest* (Rose Valley Shops), *129; Chiffonier* (Greene and Greene), *223; Child's Chest* (Roycroft Shops), *230; Corner Cupboard* (Stickley), *231; Dainty (Curio) Cabinet* (Niedecken), *222; Desk* (Stowe), *235; Fall-front Desk* (Ellis), *222; Fall-front Desk* (Rohlfs), *227; Flip-top Card Table* (Bradstreet); *221; Hall Chair* (Stickley Brothers), *69; Infant's Crib* (Jeck), *226; Magazine Stand* (Roycroft Shops), *230; Music Stand* (Price), *227; Pair of Side Chairs* (Price), *67; Plant Stand* (Rohlfs), *226; Rocking Chair* (Maher), *74; Rocking Chair* (Rohlfs), *224; Rose Valley Furniture Shops, 126; Round Table* (Stickley), *232; Settle* (Stickley), *233; Sideboard* (Rose Valley Shops), *129; Sideboard* (Stickley), *234; Sideboard* (Stowe), *71; Side Chair* (Ellis), *231; Side Chair* (Elmslie), *73; Side Chair* (McHugh), *68; Square Center Table* (Limbert), *224; Table* (Wright), *232; Tall Slat-back Chair* (Wright), *73, 74; Umbrella Stand* (Roth), *227; Upholstered Armchair* (Niedecken) *222*
Furniture Shop, San Francisco, 70, 270

G

Gamble House, Pasadena, California, 122–23; *Chiffonier* (Greene and Greene), *71, 108, 223; Dining Room* (Greene and Greene), *122*
Gannett, William, *House Beautiful,* 118
Garden Cities of Tomorrow (Howard), 285n12
Garden City, Letchworth, England, 112, 115, 117, 285n12
Garden City movement, 285n12, 285–86n24, 286n25
Garland, Hamlin, 43, 257
Gates, William Day, 261
Gates Potteries, Crystal Lake, Illinois, 261
Gaw, Elizabeth Eleanor D'Arcy, 241, 267
Gebelein, George Christian, 57, 60, 62–63, 241
George, Henry, 114, 127
Gerlach, Ernest, 267

German Settlement Society, Hermann, Missouri, 253
Germer, George Ernest, 63, 241
Giannini, Orlando, 266
Giannini and Hilgart glassmakers, Chicago, 266
Gilborn, Craig: *Adirondack Furniture and the Rustic Tradition,* 282n22
Gilchrist, Edmund, 117
Gill, Irving John, 114, 115, 122, 123–24, 241; *Casas Grandes Project, 124; Dodge House North Elevation, 123*
Gillis, Thomas, 275
Gillis, Walter, 275
Gillis Press, New York, 275
Girvan, Ednah S. (Mrs. Augustus B. Higginson), 61
Glass, 92–99, 168–83, 266–67; *Blue Aurene Vase* (Carder), *169; Cintra Bowl* (Carder), *2; Egyptian Onion Flower-Form Vase* (Tiffany), *176; Flower Motif Window* (Hunter), *181; Gold Aurene Vase* (Carder), *169; Gold-Decorated Aurene Vase* (Carder), *168; Holy Grail Window* (Connick), *98; Irregular Vase* (Tiffany), *174; Joshua Commanding the Sun to Stand Still* (La Farge), *179; Landscape Scene Window* (Tiffany), *180; Lava Vases* (Tiffany), *182, 183; The Lawyers' Club Window* (Duffner and Kimberly), *94; Liberal Arts Window, The figure of Astronomy* (Willet and Willet), *24; Liberal Arts Window* (Willet and Willet), *97; Opaque & Iridescent Vase* (Tiffany), *14; Opaque Vase* (Tiffany), *170; Paperweight Vase* (Tiffany), *15; Peacock Feather Vase* (Tiffany), *172; Peacock Vase* (Tiffany), *173; Pinched Green Vase* (Tiffany), *172; Pinched Vase* (Tiffany), *175; Plymouth Church of the Pilgrims Window* (Heinigke), *95; Pressed & Cased Vase* (Tiffany), *173; Purple Winged Dragonfly Shade and Bronze Table Lamp* (Tiffany), *181; Samoan Girl Dancing the Siva* (La Farge), *178; Tabard Inn Food Co. Window* (D'Ascenzo), *95; Te Deum Window* (Young), *96; Test Panel with Evangelist Symbol* (Heinigke), *93; Trumpet Vase* (Tiffany), *171; Vase* (Bache), *170; Vase* (Tiffany), *177; Window* (Tiffany), *1*
Glessner, Frances McBeth (Mrs. John J.), 26, 40, 57
Goetz, Bernard, 264
Goetz, Isidore, 264
Goetz, Louis, 264
Gohlke, William S., 70
Goldberger, Paul: *On the Rise: Architecture and Design in a Postmodern Age,* 279n17
Good Housekeeping (periodical), 260
Goodhue, Bertram Grosvenor, 241, 260
Goodhue, Harry Eldredge, 95
Googerty, Thomas F., 62
Gorham, Jabez, 268
Gorham Manufacturing Company, Providence, 55, 60, 268; *Martelé Vase, 189; Views, Exterior and Interior of the Gorham Manufacturing Company Silversmiths, 56*
Goudy, Bertha, 257
Goudy, Frederic W., 257, 276
Grace United Methodist Church Quilting Club, Austin, Texas, 257
The Grammar of Ornament (Jones), 50
Grand Feu Ceramics (Doat), 81–82, 85

Grand Feu Pottery, Los Angeles, 85, 263
Grand Rapids Arts and Crafts School of Design, Grand Rapids, Michigan, 273
Grand Rapids Arts and Crafts Shop, Grand Rapids, Michigan, 268
Grand Rapids Furniture Exposition Association, Grand Rapids, Michigan, Grand Rapids Furniture Market (1878–c. 1950), 69, 255
Graves, William H., 263
Gray, Elmer, 72
Great Exhibition (1851), London, England, 46, 277n6
Greene, Charles Sumner, 241
Greene, Henry Mather, 241
Greene and Greene, architects, 26, 70–71, 95, 108, 113, 115, 122–23, 127; *Chiffonier, 71, 223; Gamble House Dining Room, 122*
Greenwich House Handicraft School, New York, 83, 274, 285n57
Grierson, Clare L., 257
Griffin, Walter Burley, 114, 241; *Trier Center Neighborhood Site Plan, 119–121, 120*
Gropius, Walter, 124
Grosvenor, Fredrika, 269
Grosvenor Studio, Los Angeles, 269
Grueby, William Henry, 87, 88, 241–42, 263; *Beaver Tile, 88; Bigelow, Kennard & Co., 48*
Grueby Faience and Tile Company, Boston, 263
Grueby Faience Company, Boston, 49, 88, 263; *Vases, 148*
Guerrier, Edith, 40, 259, 264–65
Guild and School of Handicraft, London, England, 55, 60
Guild of Allied Arts, Buffalo, New York, 257
Guild of Arts and Crafts, New York, 280n12
Guild of Arts and Crafts, San Francisco, 257
Guild of Book Workers, New York, 257
Guild of Handicraft Industries, New York, 257–58
Guilds and Societies, 24, 57–59, 105–6, 256–59, 281n33
Guthrie, J. Gordon, 93–94, 284n12; *The Lawyers' Club Window, 94*
Gyllenberg, Frans J. R., 242

H

Haga, Kristopher, 60, 269
Halcyon Art Pottery, Halcyon, California, 86–87, 263
Hale, Frank Gardner, 61, 62, 242; *Brooch, 11; Necklace, 213*
Hall, Dr. Herbert J., 85, 263
Hall, John, 70–71, 270
Hall, Peter, 70–71, 270
Peter Hall Manufacturing Company, Pasadena, California, 70–71, 270
Hamann, Carl F., 55
Hampshire Pottery, Keene, New Hampshire, 263; *Vase* (Robertson), *160*
Hancock, W. S., 262
Handicraft Guild of Indiana, 258
Handicraft (periodical), 47, 260
Handicraft Shop, Boston, 60, 62, 268
Handicraft Shop for Italian Needlecrafts, Philadelphia, 269
Handley, E. H., 270
Haney, James P., 259
Hansen, Charles E., 55–56, 280n10

Hardenberg, Elizabeth R., 259, 262
Harper, William Rainey, 272
Harper's New Monthly Magazine, 39
Jean B. Hassewer Company, 72
Hawkes, Samuel, 267
Hawkes, Thomas G., 267
Hawkes, Townsend, 267
Haywood, Big Bill, 44
Hazen, Grace, 57, 58, 61
Hazenplug, Frank, 279n2
Heinigke, Otto, 95, 97, 242; *Plymouth Church of the Pilgrims Window, 95; Test Panel with Evangelist Symbol, 93*
Heintz, Edwin A., 267
Heintz, Otto L., 267
Heintz Art Metal Shop, Buffalo, New York, 62, 267
Helicon Hall, 43
M. Heminway & Sons Silk Company, 100
Henry Street Settlement, New York, 83, 274
John Herron Art Institute of Indianapolis: Annual Exhibition of Works by Indiana Artists (1908–n.d.), 255; Art School of the, 273
Heywood, Henry, 271
Heywood Brothers and Company, Chicago, 271
Hickox, Elizabeth Conrad, 242
Higgins, Loulie, 269
Loulie Higgins textiles, Columbus, Georgia, 269
Hilgart, Fritz, 266
Hill, Walter B., 262
Hillside Club, Berkeley, California, 258
Hilton Village, Newport News, Virginia, 115, 117; *General Plan of Hilton Village* (Hubbard and Joannes), *117; Hilton Village Street Fronts and House Rows* (Hubbard and Joannes), *118*
Hoffman, Julia, 273
Holtzer, J. A., 93
Home and Garden (Jekyll), 285n2
Horti, Paul, 242
Houghton, Henry O., 276
House and Garden (periodical), 44, 105, 111, 116–17
House Beautiful (periodical), 47, 111, 118, 260, 280n14
Houses and Gardens (Baillie-Scott), 123
Hoving, Thomas, 93
Howard, Ebenezer: *Garden Cities of Tomorrow*, 285n12
Hubbard, Alice G., 242; *Woman's Work*, 43–44, *136*
Hubbard, Elbert G., 104, 126, 242, 254, 260, 261, 268, 270, 276; *Child's Chest* (Roycroft Shops), *230*
Hubbard, Henry Vincent, 114, 117, 242, 260; *General Plan of Hilton Village, 117; Hilton Village Street Fronts and House Rows, 118*
Hudson Bay Fur Company, Seattle, 105
Hull-House, Chicago, 40, 55, 83, 111, 113, 275, 279n2; Bookbindery, *41*, 275; Labor Museum, 40; Textile Room, *41*
Humboldt State Normal School, Arcata, California, 273
Humboldt State University, Arcata, California, 273
Hunt, George J., 60, 280n12
Hunt, William Morris, 273
Hunter, Dard, 242–243; *Dinnerware Service, 153; Flower Motif Window, 181; Woman's Work* (Hubbard), *136*
Hyten, Charles Dean, 243, 264; *Mission Ware Vase, 153*

I

The Ideal House, 44
Independent magazine, 35
Indian Splint Manufacturing Company, Geneva, New York, 270
Indoors and Out (periodical), 111
Industrial Art League, Chicago, 36–37, 42, 105, 256, 258, 270, 275
Industrial Revolution, 29
In Pursuit of Beauty: Americans and the Aesthetic Movement (Johnson), 282n4
International Exhibition of Modern Decorative Arts (1902), Turin, Italy, 72, 83
International Studio (periodical), 47, 57–58, 69, 260, 280n14
International style, 124
International Workers of the World, 44
Iowa State University, Ames, Iowa, Ceramics Engineering Program, 273
Ipson, Louis, 264
Irelan, Linna, 77

J

Jackson, Frank G.: *Theory and Practice of Design, An Advanced Textbook on Decorative Art, 52, 53*
Jacobus, Pauline Bogart, 265
James, George Wharton, 243, 256
Jarvie, Robert Riddle, 60, 62, 243, 268; *Candlesticks, 194; Hot Beverage Service, 204; Tray, 195*
Jarvie Shop, Chicago, 60, 268
Jeck, Frank, 66–67, 243; *Infant's Crib, 226*
Jekyll, Gertrude, 111, 285n2; *Home and Garden*, 285n2
Jensen, Jens, 115, 118, 119, 243
Jervis, William P., 263; *William Jervis Pottery Shops, 130, 130*
Jervis Pottery, Oyster Bay, New York, 263
The Jewelers' Circular (periodical), 56, 57, 280n14
Jewelers' Guild, 281n33
Jewelry, 55–63, 207–13. See also Metals; *Belt Buckle* (Wynne), *193; Brooch* (Hale), *11; Cross* (Barron and Smith), *10; Cufflinks* (Kipp), *207; Lavaliere* (Winn), *207; Necklace and Earrings* (Rogers), *208; Necklace* (Elverhoj Colony), *212; Necklace* (Hale), *213; Necklace* (Kalo Shop), *211; Necklace* (Mann), *208; Necklace* (Oakes), *210; Necklace* (Tiffany), *210; Pendant and Chain* (Watkins), *207; Pendant Necklace* (Shaw), *209*
Joannes, Francis Y., 115, 117; *General Plan of Hilton Village, 117; Hilton Village Street Fronts and House Rows, 115, 118*
John, Johan Michael, 270
John Furniture, New Braunfels, Texas, 270
Johnson, Marilynn: *In Pursuit of Beauty: Americans and the Aesthetic Movement*, 282n4
Johnson, Thomas, 266–267
Johonnot, Carl H., 280n12
Jones, Owen: *The Grammar of Ornament, 50*

K

Kahn, Isaac, 266
Kalo Shop, Chicago, 60, 268; *Candelabrum, 191; Necklace, 211*
Kardon, Janet, 22–28
Kay, Charles de, 258
Keeler, Charles and Louise, 256
Kelly, Herbert, 62
Kelmscott Press, Hammersmith, England, 104
Kendrick, George P., 55, 263
Keramic Studio (periodical), 47, 81, 83, 85, 91, 260, 280n13
The Keystone (periodical), 280n14
King, E. L., 75, 121
Kipp, Karl E., 62, 243, 269; *Cufflinks, 207; Planter, 197*
Klapp, Elinor E. (Mrs. William H.), 61
Knight, Mary Catherine, 60, 243, 268; *Bowl, 197*
The Knight Errant (periodical), 260
Koehler, Florence D., 61, 243
Koralewsky, Frank L., 62, 243
Kornwolf, James D., 111–24
Krasser, Frederick, 62
Kunsman, John, 243; *Teapot, Lid and Stand, 152*

L

Ladies' Home Journal (periodical), 47, 111, 112, 113, 118, 119, 260
La Farge, John, 92–99, 243–44, 273, 283n4; *Joshua Commanding the Sun to Stand Still, 179; Samoan Girl Dancing the Siva, 178*
Lakeside Press, Chicago, 273
Lamb, Charles Rollinson, 93, 258
Lamb, Frederick Stymetz, 93, 244
J. & R. Lamb Studios, New York, 93, 271, 283n10
Landscape Architecture (periodical), 111, 260
Lane, Mrs. David, 258
Lange, Emil, 95, 267
Langworthy, Alfred G., 275
Lathrop, Francis, 93
Lau, Willy H., 271
W. H. Lau and Company, Chicago, 271
Lauber, Joseph, 99, 271
Lavaron, Leonide Cecilia, 62
LeBlanc, Maria de Hoa, 244; *Vase, 151*
Lebolt, J. Myer, 268
Lebolt and Company, Chicago, 268
Le Boutillier, Addison, 88; *Bigelow, Kennard & Co., 48*
Le Dernier Cri (periodical), 260
Lee, Mother Ann, 101, 254
Leinonen, Karl F., 244; *Bowl and Spoon, 204*
Leland, Charles G., 56, 280n16
Lenox, Incorporated, Trenton, New Jersey, 79, 263
Lenox, Walter Scott, 263
Leonard, Anna B., 259, 260
Lessell, John, 263
Lessell Art Ware, Parkersburg, West Virginia, 263
Francis E. Lester Company, Mesilla Park, New Mexico, 104
Levin, Elaine, 77–91
Lewis, Edward J., 82–83, 253, 256, 274, 276
Lewis Courts, Sierra Madre, California, 123–24
Lewisohn, Alice, 274
Lewisohn, Irene, 274
Limbert, Charles P., 70, 75, 244, 270; *Bench #243, 224; Square Center Table, 224; Wastebasket, 224*
Charles P. Limbert and Company,

Grand Rapids, Michigan, 70, 75, 270
Linden, Frank L., 266
Linden Company, Chicago, 266
Linden Glass Company, Chicago, 266
Linderoth Ceramic Company, Chicago, 263
Linderoth, Sven, 263
Littlefield, Rev. George Emery, 253
Lockport Village Cooperative, Lockport, Illinois, 258
Long, William A., 85, 262; *Olla, 152*
Longwood Art Industrial and Stock Company, Longwood, Illinois, 253
Loos, Adolf, 124
Los Angeles County Museum of Art, American Arts & Crafts: Virtue in Design exhibition (1990), 277n3
Los Angeles County Museum of History, Science, and Art, Exhibit of Decorative Landscapes and Textiles (1919), 255
Los Angeles Pressed Brick company, 263
Los Angeles Society of Arts and Crafts, 59, 258
Louisiana Purchase International Exposition (1904), St. Louis, 58, 59, 72, 82, 255
Low, John Gardner, 88, 263
Low, Will Hicok, 93, 244
J. and J. G. Low Art Tile Works, Chelsea, Massachusetts, 88, 263
Low Tile Company, Chelsea, Massachusetts, 263
Lummis, Charles Fletcher, 36, 66, 244, 282n8
Luther, Mabel Wilcox, 62
Lutyens, Edwin, 111, 285n2

M

Mackintosh, Charles Rennie, 132
Macomber, Eva, 244; *Box, 196*
Magnus House, Winnetka, Illinois, 119, 121
Maher, George Washington, 74–75, 107–8, 109, 244; *Armchair, 225; Coffee and Tea Service, 205; Portiere, 107; Rocking Chair, 74; Rockledge, 121, 121; Standing Clock, 225; Urn, 192*
Mahony, Marion, 119–21, 244
Mann, Forest Emerson, 244, 257, 260, 273; *Necklace, 208*
Manship, Paul, 244–45; *Candelabra, 190*
Manual Arts High School of Los Angeles, 273
Manufacturing Jewelry and Designers advisory committee, Providence, 55
Marblehead Pottery, Marblehead, Massachusetts, 85–86, 87, 263; *Vase* (Baggs), *138*
Marcus, William, 268
Marcus & Company, New York, 268; *Humidor, 188*
Markham, Herman C., 263
Markham, Kenneth S., 263
Markham Pottery, Ann Arbor, Michigan, 263
Mark Hopkins Institute of Art, San Francisco, 272
Marsh, Margaret, 32
Marshall, Frank J., 62, 245; *Box, 196*
Marshall Field and Company Craft Shop and Craftsman Showroom, Chicago, 268
Martin, Laurin H., 55, 57, 62

Maryland Institute, 61
Mason, Maude, 259
Mason, Walt, 245; *The Poet Philosopher,* 136
Massachusetts Institute of Technology, Cambridge, Massachusetts, 122
Massachusetts Normal School of Art, 38
Masters in Art Series, 49
Mathews, Arthur Frank, 70, 245, 270, 276
Mathews, Gertrude Singleton, 265
Mathews, Lucia Kleinhans (Kleinhaus), 70, 245, 270, 276; *Clock, 228; Figural Box, 228; "Young Girl in White,"* 228
Matthews, Alonzo R., 270
Matthews, Eschines P., 270
Matthews Brothers Furniture Company, Milwaukee, 74, 270
Maybeck, Bernard Ralph, 121–22, 245
May Show (1919–present), Cleveland, 255
McCoy, James W., 264
J. W. McCoy Pottery, Roseville, Ohio, 264
McCutcheon's fabrics, New York, 106
McHugh, Joseph P., 69, 245, 270; *Side Chair, 68*
Joseph P. McHugh and Company, New York, 270
McLanahan, M. Hawley, 128. *See also* Price and McLanahan, architects
McLaughlin, Mary Louise, 39, 79, 80–81, 83, 245, 257; *Vase, 145*
McMaster, Hope, 269
Meigs, Arthur Ingersoll, 117, 245
Mellor, Walter, 117, 245
Mercer, Henry Chapman, 88, 132, 245–46, 264; *Inkwell, 144; Tile (Byzantine Four Flowers), 145; Tile (Fluminus Impetus . . .), 144; Tile (Persian Antelope), 145*
Merrimac Pottery, Newburyport, Massachusetts, 264
Merrymount Press, Boston, 275
Metal Office Furniture Company, Grand Rapids, Michigan, 268
Metals, 55–63, 184–213, 267–69; *Book Cover* (Burton), *187; Bowl and Spoon* (Leinonen), *204; Bowl* (Blanchard), *205; Bowl* (Knight), *197; Box* (Copeland), *187; Box* (Macomber), *196; Box* (Marshall), *196; Candelabra* (Manship), *190; Candelabra* (Zimmermann), *199; Candelabrum* (Kalo Shop), *191; Candlesticks* (Art Crafts Shop), *184; Candlesticks* (Jarvie), *194; Candlesticks* (Preston), *194; Coffee and Tea Service* (Maher), *205; Coffee and Tea Service* (Rorimer), *203; Creamer, Sugar Bowl, and Tray* (Pratt), *203; Desk Set* (Forest Craft Guild), *188; Gothic Chest* (Yellin), *198; Hot Beverage Service* (Jarvie), *204; Humidor* (Marcus & Company), *188; Jewelry Box* (Art Crafts Shop), *185; Jewelry Box* (Preston), *193; Lamp* (Burton), *185; Martelé Vase* (Gorham Manufacturing), *189; Pitcher* (Randahl), *200; Planter* (Kipp), *197; Plant Holder* (Carence Crafters), *187; Punch Bowl* (Shreve and Company), *201; Table Lamp* (Van Erp), *184; Tea and Coffee Service* (Tiffany & Company), *202; Teapot* (Watkins), *206; Tea Service* (Stone), *200; Tray* (Jarvie), *195; Tray* (Stickley), *195; Urn* (Maher),

192; Vase (Friedell), *189; Vase* (Pond), *193; Vase* (Roycroft Shops), *186; Vase* (Van Erp), *194*
Metal Workers Guild, 281n33
Metcalf, Helen, 274
Metropolitan Museum of Art, New York, 59, 105; The Hudson-Fulton Celebration (1909), 255
Meyer, Frederick Henry, 110, 246, 272
Meyer, Joseph Fortune, 83, 246; *Humidor, 150; Vase, 151*
Meyer, W. T., 56
Michie, H. Stuart, 280n12
Michigan Chair Company, Grand Rapids, 270
Middle Ages, 36, 66–67, 92, 97, 99
Middle Lane Pottery, East Hampton, New York, 77, 264; *Vase* (Brouwer), *140*
Mies van der Rohe, Ludwig, 123
Miller, Ellen, 38, 106, 246, 257
Miller, James A., 268
Miller, Lewis, 272
Miller, Wilhelm: *The Prairie Spirit in Landscape Gardening,* 114, 115
James A. Miller and Brother metalworkers, Chicago, 268
Millet, F. D., 93
Millet, Louis J., 65, 107–8, 272; *Portiere, 107*
James Milliken University, Decatur, Illinois, School of Fine and Applied Arts, 280n12
Mills, Helen Keeling, 63
Milroy, Elizabeth, 23
Minneapolis Arts and Crafts Society, 105
Minneapolis College of Art and Design, 273
Minneapolis Handicraft Guild, 59, 105, 258, 273, 280n12
Minneapolis School of Art, Department of Handicraft, 273
Minneapolis Society of Fine Arts, 273
Minnesota State Art Society, Minneapolis, Annual Exhibition (1903–1907), 255
Mission Furniture: How To Make It (Windsor), 282n13
Mission Inn, Riverside, California, 253
Modernism, 50, 91, 134, 284n19
Monastery Hill Bindery, Chicago, 275
Montague Press, Montague, Massachusetts, 275
Montclair Art Museum, Montclair, New Jersey, State-wide Crafts Exhibition (1906), 255
Moore, John B., 104
Moravian Pottery and Tile Works, Doylestown, Pennsylvania, 88, 264; *Byzantine Four Flowers* (Mercer), *145; Fluminus Impetus Tile* (Mercer), *144; Inkwell* (Mercer), *144; Persian Antelope Tile* (Mercer), *145*
More Craftsman Homes (Stickley), 286n20
Morin, G. E., 264
G. E. Morin Studio, Los Angeles, 264
Morris, William, 25, 32, 36, 46, 104, 111–12, 113–14, 115, 125–26, 127; *News from Nowhere, 131*
Morris House, Haverford, Pennsylvania, 117
Morris Society, Chicago, 37, 105, 258
Morse, T. Vernette, 257
Morton, Johannes, 253
Mosher, Thomas Bird, 276
Mosher Press, Portland, Maine, 276

Motif-rhythm theory, 74–75, 109, 114, 115
Moulton, Richard Green, 258
Mower, Mary, 257
Mundie, William Bryce, 246; *Vase, 9*
Munstead Wood, Surrey, England, 111
Museum of Fine Arts, Boston, 59; "The Art That Is Life" exhibition (1987), 277n3; School of the, 40, 57, 273, 280n12

N

Nacke, Karl G., 56
Nash, Arthur J., 94, 95, 246
Nash, C. E., 270
Nash, J. D., 270
Nash, John Henry, 276
Carl Enos Nash Company, Los Angeles, 270
National Academy of Design, New York, 38, 273
National Arts Club, New York, 55, 57, 58–59, 258
National League of Handicraft Societies, Boston, 105, 258
National League of Mineral Painters, 84, 258
National Museum, Washington, D.C., 59, 281n34
National Society of Craftsmen, New York, 59, 258, 281n30; *Bulletin of Arts and Crafts,* 260
National Terra Cotta Society, Chicago, Clay Products Show (1912), 255
The Nature and Art of Workmanship (Pye), 282n2
Nature in Ornament (Day), 49
Navajo School of Indian Basketry, Los Angeles, 273
Neo-Gothic style, 96–99
Nerthart, Henry J., 267
Newark Museum, Newark, New Jersey, 59
New Clairvaux community, Montague, Massachusetts, 36, 253–54
Newcomb, Josephine Louise LeMonnier, 109, 274
Newcomb Guild, New Orleans, 39
Newcomb Pottery, New Orleans, 38–39, 83–84; *Humidor* (Elliot and Meyer), *150; Vase* (LeBlanc and Meyer), *151*
News from Nowhere (Morris), 131
New Ulm Lacemakers, New Ulm, Minnesota, 258
New York Evening School, 59
New York School of Applied Design for Women, 273, 285n57
New York Society of Decorative Art, 38, 105, 258
New York Society of Keramic Art, 259
Nichols (Storer), Maria Longworth, 39, 79, 83, 246, 265; *Low Vase, 154; Vases, 154, 155*
Nickerson, Thomas S., 87, 264
Niedecken, George Mann, 246, 271; *Dainty (Curio) Cabinet, 222; Upholstered Armchair, 222*
Niedecken-Walbridge Company, Milwaukee, 74, 271
Nielson, Christian, 264
Nielson Pottery, Zanesville, Ohio, 264
Niloak Pottery, Benton, Arkansas, 264; *Mission Ware Vase* (Hyten), *153*
Nonoluck Silk Company: *Partially-worked Panel Intended as a Pillow,* 214

Nordhoff, Emily Hunter, 41
Normal College Arts and Crafts Club, New York, 259
Norse Pottery, Edgerton, Wisconsin, 264
Northwestern Terra Cotta Company, Chicago, 264
Norton, Charles Eliot, 65, 259
Novick, Falick, 60
Nutting, Wallace, 246–47

O

Oakes, Edward Everett, 61, 247; *Necklace, 210*
Oakwood Pottery, Dayton, Ohio, 264
Ohio State University, Columbus, Ceramics Engineering Program, 273
Ohr, George Edgar, 77, 79, 87, 247, 261; *Bowl with Handle and Spout, 156; Lidded Teapot, 78; Teapot and Coffeepot, 156; Vase, 157*
O'Kane, Helen Marguerite, 275
Old Hickory Chair Company, Martinsville, Indiana, 70, 72, 270; *Chair, 70*
Olmsted, Frederick Law, Jr., 114, 117, 247; *Drawing of Station Square, 116*
Olmsted, Frederick Law, Sr., 247
Omar Khayyam Pottery, Candler, North Carolina, 264
Onken, Oscar, 270–71
On the Rise: Architecture and Design in a Postmodern Age (Goldberger), 279n17
Opalescent Glass movement, 92–99, 284n13
Oregon School of Arts and Crafts, Portland, 273
Ornament & Its Application (Day), 49–50
Orozco, Ricardo, 276
Orton, Edward, Jr., 256
Otis Art Institute, Los Angeles, 61, 273
Overbeck, Mary Frances, Margaret, Hannah, and Elizabeth, 85, 264
Overbeck Pottery, Cambridge City, Indiana, 85, 264; *Vases, 86, 160*
Owens, J. B., 264
J. B. Owens Pottery Company, Roseville, Ohio, 264

P

Pacific Embroidery Company, San Francisco, 100
Palette and Brush (periodical), 260–61
Palmer, Lillian MacNeill, 268
Palmer Copper Shop, San Francisco, 268
Panama-California Exposition (1915–16), San Diego, 255
Panama-Pacific International Exposition (1915), San Francisco, 62, 68, 89, 255
Pan-American Exposition (1901), Buffalo, New York, 59, 69, 72, 81, 255
Papanicolaou, Linda M., 92–99
Paris Exposition (1900), 62, 81
Parker, Barry, 112, 115, 117
Parmelee, C. W., 274
James A. Patten House: *Portiere* (Maher and Millet), *107*
Patterson, John, 264

John Patterson and Sons Pottery Company, Wellsville, Ohio, 264
Patterson Brothers Company, Wellsville, Ohio, 264
Pauline Pottery, Chicago, 265
Paul Revere Pottery, Boston, 40, 87, 264–65; *Bowl (with Rabbits)* (Saturday Evening Girls' Club), *150*
Payne, Arthur F.: *Art Metalwork with Inexpensive Equipment,* 56
Peacock, Emily Frances, 280n12; *Keramic Studio,* 280n12
Pellew, Charles E., 105
Pendleton Woolen Mills, Pendleton, Oregon, 104
Penman, Edith, 259, 262
Pennsylvania Museum School of Industrial Art, Philadelphia, 56, 68, 273
People's Industrial College, Saugatuck, Michigan, 273–74
People's University, 82–83
Periodicals, 47, 56, 111, 259–261, 280n14, 285n1
Perreault, John, 29–31
Perry (Stratton), Mary Chase, 81, 83, 84–85, 87, 88, 91, 247, 265; *Monumental Vase, 158; Tile Frieze, 151; Vases, 158, 159*
Peters, John D., 265
Peters and Reed Pottery, Zanesville, Ohio, 265
Petterson, John Pontus, 60, 247
Pewabic Pottery, Detroit, 81, 83, 84–85, 88, 265; *Jar, 84; Monumental Vase* (Perry), *158; Tile Frieze* (Perry), *151; Vase* (Perry), *158, 159*
Philadelphia Centennial International Exposition (1876), 77–79, 88
Philadelphia College of Art, 273
Philadelphia Colleges of the Arts, 273
Philadelphia Museum of Art, An Exhibition of Tiles (1915), 255
Philips, Mrs. L. Vance, 259
The Philistine (periodical), 261
Philopolis Press, San Francisco, 276
Pickard, Wilder A., 265
Pickard China Studio, Chicago, 265
Pike, William J., 266
Pike Stained Glass Studios, Rochester, New York, 266
Pitcairn, Raymond, 66–67
Pitman, Benn, 65
Poillon, Mrs. Cornelius, 265
Poillon, Mrs. Howard A., 265
Poillon Pottery, Woodbridge, New Jersey, 265
Pond, Ellen J., 273
Pond, Theodore Hanford, 61, 247, 274, 280n12; *Vase, 193*
Popular Mechanics (periodical), 261
Popular Mechanics Press, Chicago, 276
Porcelain League of Cincinnati, 257
Potter, Horace E., 60, 62, 247
The Potter (periodical), 91, 261
The Potter's Craft (Binns), 47
Potter Studio, Cleveland, 60, 268
Pottery and Glass (periodical), 261
Prairie School movement, 72–75, 95–96, 114–15, 134, 284n19
The Prairie Spirit in Landscape Gardening (Miller), 114, 115
Pratt, Katherine, 57, 247; *Creamer, Sugar Bowl, and Tray, 203*
Pratt Institute, Brooklyn, New York, 55, 57, 59, 83
Pressey, Rev. Edward Pearson, 253–54
Preston, Emily, 257
Preston, Jessie M., 62, 247–48; *Candlesticks, 194; Jewelry Box, 193*

Price, William L., 67–68, 117, 125–35, 127, 248, 253, 254, 286n20. *See also* Price and McLanahan, architects; *The Artsman,* 117; *The Artsman* poster, *37; Music Stand, 227; Pair of Side Chairs, 67*
Price and McLanahan, architects: *Alice Barber Stephens House, 132, 133; Alterations to Rose Valley Guest House, 131; Inglenook, Schoen House, 127; McLanahan House, 134, 285n22; Rose Valley Improvement Co. House, 135*
priestman, Mabel Tuke, 114
Princeton University Art Museum, Princeton, New Jersey, Arts and Crafts Movement in America, 1876–1916, exhibition (1972), 64, 277n3
The Principles of Design (Batchelder), 48, 49, 50
Principles of Home Decoration with Practical Examples (Wheeler), 105
William Prindle House, Duluth, Minnesota: *Center Table* (Bradstreet), *220; Curtain Panels* (Bradstreet), *108, 108; Flip-top Card Table* (Bradstreet), *221*
Production Centers, 261–71
Progressive Era, 32
Providence Handicraft Club, 39, 259
Purcell, William, 283n30
Purdue University, 39
Pye, David: *The Nature and Art of Workmanship,* 282n2, 282n16

Q

Quezal Art Glass and Decorating Company, Brooklyn, New York, 94, 95, 266–67; *Vase* (Bache), *170*
Quisiana Workshop, La Porte, Indiana, 270

R

Rae, Frank B., Jr., 275
Randahl, Julius Olaf, 60, 248; *Pitcher, 200*
Randall, Theodore, 256
Redlands Pottery, Redlands, California, 265
Reed, Adam, 265
Revelation Kilns, Detroit, 81, 265
Rhead, Frederick Hurten, 82, 83, 86, 90, 91, 248, 261, 265; *Vase, 161*
Rhead Pottery, Santa Barbara, California, 265; *Vase* (Rhead), *161*
Rhode Island School of Design, Providence, 38, 55–56, 59, 274, 280n10
Ricardo Orozco press, San Francisco, 276
Rice, Mrs. Clarence C. (Jean), 262
Richardson, Henry Hobson, 126, 248
Richardson Silk Company, 100; *Partially-worked Panel Intended as a Pillow, 219; Pillow Sham, 219*
Richmond, Florence A., 61
Richmond Hill House, New York, 40–41, 275
Riverside Press, Cambridge, Massachusetts, 276
Roberts, Will, 130
Robertson, Alexander W., 77, 79, 86–87, 248, 263, 265; *Vase, 78*
Robertson, Cadmon, 248; *Vase, 160*
Robertson, Cheryl, 44
Robertson, Hugh Cornwall, 77–79, 248, 262; *Vases, 162, 163*

Robineau, Adelaide Alsop, 81, 82–83, 84–85, 87, 89, 248, 259, 260–61, 265, 272; *The Apotheosis of the Toiler, 83; Lantern, 165; Lantern Vase, 82; Monogram Vase, 164; Poppy Vase, 83; Vase, 164; Viking Ship Vase, 82*
Robineau, Samuel, 82–83; *Keramic Studio,* 81–82, 91
Robineau Pottery, Syracuse, New York, 82, 265
Roblin Art Pottery, San Francisco, 77, 265
Rochester Arts and Crafts Society, 259
Rochester Athenaeum and Mechanics Institute, 274, 280n12
Rochester Institute of Technology, 274
Rockledge, Homer, Minnesota, 121, 121; *Armchair* (Maher), *225; Coffee and Tea Service* (Maher), *205; Rocking Chair* (Maher), *74; Standing Clock* (Maher), *225; Urn* (Maher), *192*
Rogers, Margaret, 61, 248; *Necklace and Earrings, 208*
Rogers House, Spring Lake, New Jersey, 116
Rohlfs, Charles, 72, 248–49, 270; *Candelabra, 226; Fall-front Desk, 227; Plant Stand, 226; Rocking Chair, 224*
Charles Rohlfs Workshop, Buffalo, New York, 72, 270
Rokesley Shop, Cleveland, 268; *Coffee and Tea Service* (Rorimer), *203*
Rolfe, Edmund B., 62, 280n12
Rollins, Carl Purington, 275
Rookwood Pottery, Cincinnati, 39, 83, 84, 87, 89, 265; *Low Vase* (Nichols), *154; Vase* (Asbury), *167; Vase* (Daly), *141; Vase* (Nichols), *154, 155; Vase* (Shirayamadani), *143, 166; Vase* (Valentien), *149; Vase* (Young), *140*
Rorimer, Louis, 249; *Coffee and Tea Service, 203*
Rose, Augustus F.: *Copper Work,* 56
Rose Valley Association, Moylan, Pennsylvania, 36, 67–68, 117, 125–35, 254; *Chest, 129; Furniture Shops, 126; Sideboard, 129*
Rose Valley Improvement Company, Moylan, Pennsylvania, 134, 135
Roseville Pottery Company, Roseville, Ohio, 265
Ross, Denman Waldo, 48–49, 67, 249
Roth, William, 249; *Umbrella Stand, 227*
Royal Society Package Goods, 100
Roycroft community, East Aurora, New York, 27, 62, 104, 126, 254; Copper Shop, 268; Furniture Shop, 270; Leather Shop, 271
Roycroft Inn, East Aurora, New York: *Dinnerware Service* (Hunter), *153; Flower Motif Window* (Hunter), *181*
Roycroft Press, East Aurora, New York, 260, 261, 276; *The Book of the Roycrofters,* 104
Roycroft Shops, East Aurora, New York: *Child's Chest, 230; Doily, 217; Funereal Box, 229; Magazine Stand, 230; Mahogany Wastepaper Basket, 230; Maple Wastepaper Basket, 230; Picture Frame with Drawings Attributed to Karl Kipp, 229; Picture Frame with Portrait of Elbert Hubbard, 229; Umbrella Stand* (Roth), *227; Vase, 186*
Ruskin, John, 25, 32, 46, 65, 106, 114, 125

Russell, Thomas, 276
Thomas Russell press, San Francisco, 276
Russell Sage Foundation, 285–286n24
Rustic Hickory Furniture Company, La Porte, Indiana, 270
Rutgers University, New Brunswick, New Jersey, New Jersey School of Clayworking and Ceramics, 274

S

Sackett, Clara B., 257
Sage, Mrs. Russell, 97, 285–286n24
Samson, Thorwald P. A., 264
San Francisco Art Association, 272
San Francisco Institute of Art, California School of Design of the, 272
Sargent, Irene, 47, 65, 113
Saturday Evening Girls' Club, Boston, 87, 259; *Bowl (with Rabbits), 150*
Saunders, Charles Francis, 105
Schon, Carl, 61
School Crafts Club, New York, 259
Schools, 24, 55–57, 109–10, 271–274, 280n12, 285n57
Schreiber, George L., 253
Scribner's (periodical), 36
Scudder, Vida Dutton, 35, 113, 114
Scuola d'Industrie Italiane, New York, 40–41, 275
The Search for Environment: The Garden City, Before and After (Creese), 285n12
Settlement Houses, 24, 34, 40–41, 274–75
Settlement Society of Philadelphia, 253
Shaker communities, 101, 254
The Shame of the Cities (Steffens), 286n2
Shaw, Josephine Hartwell, 61, 249; *Pendant Necklace, 209*
Shawsheen Pottery, Billerica, Massachusetts, 265
Sheerer, Mary G., 39, 83
Sheldon, Nellie, 265
Nellie Sheldon pottery, Los Angeles, 265
Sherman, Julia Munson, 62
Shirayamadani, Kataro, 249; *Vases, 143, 166*
Shop of the Crafters, Cincinnati, 270–71
Shreve, George R., 269
Shreve and Company, San Francisco, 61, 269; *Punch Bowl, 201*
Sicard, Jacques, 87, 249; *Vase (with Beetles), 166*
Sieffel, Charles C., 280n12
Silversmiths' Guild, 281n33
Simpson, Anna Frances, 249; *Table Runner, 5*
Sinclair, Upton, 43
The Sketch Book (periodical), 261
Small Presses, 275–76
Smedley, Ruth, 60, 268
Smith, D. Robertson, 70
Smith, Frances Barnum, 60, 249; *Cross, 10*
Smith, Mrs. Gertrude Roberts, 109
Societies. *See* Guilds and Societies
Society of Arts and Crafts, Boston, 37, 48, 55, 57–58, 59, 67, 105, 259, 279n14, 279–80n6; exhibitions (1897–present), 255–56, 281n35; *Handicraft,* 260
Society of Arts and Crafts, Grand Rapids, Michigan, 105

Society of Printers for the Study and Advancement of the Art of Printing, Boston, Development of Printing as an Art exhibition (1906), 256
Solon, Albert L., 86
South End House, Boston, 275
South Park Association, Chicago, 37
Spencer, Robert, 119
Speranza, Gino, 275
Spierling, Ernest J., 266
St. Dunstan's Guild for Ecclesiastical Arts, 281n33
St. Louis World's Fair (1904), 58, 59, 72, 82, 255
Stangl Pottery, Flemington, New Jersey, 262–63
Starr, Ellen Gates, 41, 42, 275
Stearns, George, 269
Stearns and Foster Company, Cincinnati, 269
Stearns Technical Textiles Company, Cleveland, 269
Steelcase metalworkers, Grand Rapids, Michigan, 268
Steele, Zulma, 67
Steffens, Lincoln: *The Shame of the Cities,* 286n2
Stephan, Wilhelmina P., 60, 62
Stephens, Alice Barber: *Alice Barber Stephens House* (Price and McLanahan), *132, 133; Rose Valley String Quartet at Music Stand, 128*
Stephens, Charles, 132–33
Stephens, Frank, 253
Steuben Division of Corning Glass Works, Corning, New York, 95, 267
Steuben Glass Works, Corning, New York, 94–95, 267; *Blue Aurene Vase* (Carder), *169; Gold Aurene Vase* (Carder), *169; Gold-Decorated Aurene Vase* (Carder), *168*
Steward, Florence Pratt, 256
Stickley, Albert, 70, 249–50, 271
Stickley, Charles, 249–50
Stickley, Gustav, 27, 62, 69–70, 101–7, 110, 126, 249, 271. *See also The Craftsman; Bedspread, 218; Carpet, 216; Corner Cupboard, 231; Dining Room, 113; More Craftsman Homes,* 286n20; *Round Table, 232; Settle, 233; Sideboard, 234; Table Runner, 218; Table Runner with Napkins, 218; Three-panel Screen, 234; Tray, 195*
Stickley, John George, 249–50, 271
Stickley, Leopold, 249–50, 271
Stickley Brothers Company, Grand Rapids, Michigan, 70, 271; *Hall Chair, 69*
L. and J. G. Stickley furniture-makers, Fayetteville, New York, 67, 271
Stone, Arthur J., 59–60, 250; *Tea Service, 200*
Stone, Wilbur Macy, 257
Storrow, Mrs. James, 87, 259, 264–65
Stourbridge Glass Company, Corona, New York, 94, 267
Stowe, Ernest, 72, 250; *Desk, 235; Sideboard, 71*
Stowell, M. Louise, 259
Strobridge, Idah Meacham, 275
Student Craft Industries, Berea, Kentucky, 109–10
The Studio (periodical), 112, 116, 118
Sturdy, Harry, 267
Sturdy-Lange Studios, Los Angeles, 267
Sullivan, Louis Henry, 122, 124, 250
Sunland Community, Sunland, California, 254
Sutton, M. A., 262
Swarthmore College, Swarthmore, Pennsylvania, 127

T

Taft, James Scholly, 263
Taft, Lorado, 257
Talbot, Mrs. Arnold, 39, 259
Taylor, Edward DeWitt, 276
Taylor, Henry H., 276
Taylor and Taylor press, San Francisco, 276
Teal, Arthur E., 70
Temple Art Glass Company, Chicago, 267
Texas Women's Association fair (c. 1915), Houston, 256
Textiles, 100–110, 214–19, 269; *Basket* (Clapp), *217; Bedspread* (Stickley), *218; Carpet* (Elmslie), *109; Carpet* (Stickley), *216; "Collars and Cuffs" Sack Kit* (Anonymous), *215; Curtain Panels* (Bradstreet), *108, 108; Doily* (Roycroft Shops), *217; Door Curtain* (Whiting), *214; Handbag* (H. E. Varren), *102; Panel Intended as a Pillow Design No. 215* (H. E. Varren Company), *216; Partially-worked Panel Intended as a Pillow* (Nonoluck Silk Company), *214; Partially-worked Panel Intended as a Pillow* (Richardson Silk), *219; Pillow Sham* (Richardson Silk), *219; Portiere* (Maher and Millet), *107; Table Runner* (Simpson), *5; Table Runner* (Stickley), *218; Table Runner with Napkins* (Stickley), *218; Wall Hanging* (Deerfield Society), *215; Witch Basket* (Wynne), *217; Workbag* (Anonymous), *215; A Zuni Blanket Weaver at her Loom, 38*
Thatcher, Edward, 280n12
Theory and Practice of Design, An Advanced Textbook on Decorative Art (Jackson), *52, 53*
The Theory of the Leisure Class (Veblen), 125
Thomas, Chauncey R., 90, 262
Thomas, George E., 125–35
Thread and Thrum Workshop, Hyannis, Massachusetts, 269
Thresher, Brainerd Bliss, 60, 61, 250
Throop Polytechnic Institute, Pasadena, California, 274
Thurman, Christa C. Mayer, 23, 100–110
Tiffany, Charles Lewis, 269
Tiffany, Louis Comfort, 26, 38, 39, 61–62, 87, 92–99, 250, 258, 265, 267; *Egyptian Onion Flower-Form Vase, 176; Necklace, 210; Purple Winged Dragonfly Shade and Bronze Table Lamp, 181; Vase (Fiddleheads), 147; Vase (Irregular), 174; Vase (Opaque), 170; Vase (Opaque & Iridescent), 14; Vase (Paperweight), 15; Vase (Peacock), 173; Vase (Peacock Feather), 172; Vase (Pinched), 175; Vase (Pinched Green), 172; Vase (Pressed & Cased), 173; Vases, 171, 177; Vases (Lava), 182, 183; Vase (Trumpet), 171; Water Lilies with Frogs, 146; Window (Landscape Scene with Iris and Flowering Magnolia), 180; Window (Parrots and Magnolias), 1*
Tiffany & Company, New York, 269; *Tea and Coffee Service "Special Hand Work," 61, 61, 202*
Tiffany Furnaces, Corona, New York, 267, 284n14; *Lava Vase* (Tiffany), *182, 183; Opaque Vase* (Tiffany), *170; Pinched Vase* (Tiffany), *175; Vase* (Tiffany), *171*
Tiffany Glass and Decorating Company, Corona, New York, 267;

Egyptian Onion Flower-Form Vase (Tiffany), *176; Irregular Vase* (Tiffany), *174; Peacock Feather Vase* (Tiffany), *172; Peacock Vase* (Tiffany), *173; Pinched Green Vase* (Tiffany), *172; Pressed & Cased Vase* (Tiffany), *173; Trumpet Vase* (Tiffany), *171*
Tiffany Glass Company, Corona, New York, 267; *Vase* (Tiffany), *177*
Tiffany Pottery, Corona, New York, 265
Tiffany Studios, Corona, New York, 93–94, 95, 99, 267; *Fiddleheads Vase* (Tiffany), *147; Landscape Scene Window* (Tiffany), *180; Purple Winged Dragonfly Shade and Bronze Table Lamp* (Tiffany), *181; Water Lilies with Frogs* (Tiffany), *146*
Tile Shop, Berkeley, California, 262
Tillinghast, Mary Elizabeth, 93, 99, 250
Tobey, Charles, 271
Tobey and Christianson Cabinet Company, Chicago, 271
Tobey Furniture Company, Chicago, 69, 271
Todd, Emery W., 60, 250
To-Morrow: A Monthly Hand-Book of the Changing Order (Bracken), 36
Tomoye Press, San Francisco, 276
Tookay Shop, East Aurora, New York, 269
Trapp, Kenneth R., 23
Trask, Spencer, 258
Traubel, Horace: *The Artsman, 36,* 128
Trentvale Pottery, East Liverpool, Ohio, 266
Tre'o Shop, Evanston, Illinois, 269
Trier Center Neighborhood, Winnetka, Illinois, 119–21, *120*
Triggs, Oscar Lovell, 36, 65, 110, 114, 250, 258, 273–74
Trippett, Wesley H., 265
Trocholli, Giovanni, 67
Troy School of Arts and Crafts, Troy, New York, 274
Tschirner, Fred, 262
Tulane University, New Orleans, Sophie Newcomb Memorial College for Women, 24, 38–39, 83–84, 109, 274
Twose, George, 279n2
Twyman, Joseph, 258
Twyman, William, 105

U

Union Glass Company, Somerville, Massachusetts, 94
United Crafts, Eastwood, New York, 69–70, 271; *Side Chair* (Ellis), *231*
Unity Temple, Oak Park, Illinois, 115
University City Pottery, St. Louis, 82–83, 274; *Vase* (Doat), *142*
University City Press, St. Louis, 276
University of Cincinnati School of Design, 274
University of Illinois, Champaign-Urbana, Ceramics Engineering Program, 274
University of North Dakota, Grand Forks, Ceramics Department, 274
University of the Arts, Philadelphia, 273
University of Washington, Seattle, Design Department, 274
Unwin, Raymond, 112, 115, 117
Updike, D. B., 275

Upjohn, Charles Babcock, 266
C. B. Upjohn Pottery, Zanesville, Ohio, 266

V

Valentien, Albert, 266
Valentien, Anna Marie Bookprinter, 250–51, 266; *Vase, 149*
Valentien Pottery, San Diego, 266
Valley Supply Company, 100
Van Briggle, Anne Gregory, 84
Van Briggle, Artus, 83, 84, 87, 251, 266; *Vase (Irises), 149*
Van Briggle Pottery Company, Colorado Springs, Colorado, 83, 84, 266
Vance, Eleanor P., 272
Vance, J. Nelson, 266
Vance Faience Company, Tiltonville, Ohio, 266
Van Dorn, James H., 269
Van Dorn Ironworks, Cleveland, 269
Van Erp, Dirk, 62, 251, 267; *Table Lamp, 184; Vase, 194*
Dirk Van Erp Studios, San Francisco, 267
van Rensselaer, Mariana Griswold, 47
H. E. Varren Company, 100, 269; *Handbag, 102; Panel Intended as a Pillow Design No. 215, 216*
Vaughan, Lester, 62
Veblen, Thorstein: *The Theory of the Leisure Class,* 125, 286n1
Vedder, Elihu, 93, 251; *The Digressions of V, 137*
Vesey, Belle Barnet, 261
Village Press, Chicago, 276
Vincent, John H., 272
Vinson, Carolyn Hadlow, 60, 268
Volkmar, Charles, 81, 83, 251, 259, 262, 266; *Vase, 138*
Volkmar, Leon, 83, 266
Volkmar Kilns, Metuchen, New Jersey, 266
Volund Shop, Park Ridge, Illinois, 60, 269
Voysey, C.F.A., 69, 101, 111, 114, 118

W

Wagner, A. M., 266
A. M. Wagner Studio, Los Angeles, 266
Walker, Charles Howard, 251
Walker, Edna, 67
Walrath, Frederick E., 266
Walrath Pottery, Rochester, New York, 266
Walter Reed Hospital, Washington, D.C., Department of Occupational Therapy, 56, 280n19
Warren, Herbert Langford, 251, 258
Washington University, St. Louis, 122
Watkins, Mildred G., 57, 60, 62, 251; *Pendant and Chain, 207; Teapot, 206*
Watson, Dawson, 67
Wayside Press, Springfield, Massachusetts, 276
Weber, Florence G., 40, 275
Wednesday Club, St. Louis, 58
Wege, Peter, Sr., 268
Weidebine, William, 266–67
Weir, Caroline Alden, 257
Weller, Samuel A., 266
Weller Pottery, Zanesville, Ohio, 87, 266; *Vase with Beetles* (Sicard), *166*
Welles, Clara Barck, 38, 60, 268
Westbrook, Mrs. George R., 259

Wheatley, T. J., 266
Wheatley Pottery Company, Cincinnati, 266
Wheeler, Candace Thurber, 38, 39, 251, 258; *Principles of Home Decoration with Practical Examples,* 105
Wheeling Potteries Company, Tiltonville, Ohio, 266
Wheelock, Marjory, 68
White, Hervey, 67, 253
Whitehead, Ralph Radcliffe, 67, 127, 251–52, 253, 266
White Pines Pottery, Woodstock, New York, 266
Whiting, Frederic Allen, 252, 268
Whiting, Margaret, 38, 106, 252, 257; *Door Curtain, 214*
Whitman, Walt, 125, 128
Wilde, Fred H., 86
Willet, William and Ann Lee, 97, 252; *Liberal Arts Window, 24,* 97
Wilson, Frederick, 252
Windsor, H. H.: *Mission Furniture: How To Make It,* 282n13

Winn, James H., 61–62, 252; *Lavaliere, 207*
Winslow, William Herman, 269
Winslow Brothers Company, Chicago, 269
Wisconsin Designer-Craftsmen, Milwaukee, 259
Withington, Anne, 275
Woman's Home Companion (periodical), 47
Women's Educational Industrial Union of Boston, 57
Wood, 220–35, 269–71; *Candelabra* (Rohlfs), *226; Clock* (Mathews), *228; Figural Box* (Mathews), *228; Funereal Box* (Roycroft Shops), *229; Mahogany Wastepaper Basket* (Roycroft Shops), *230; Maple Wastepaper Basket* (Roycroft Shops), *230; Picture Frame with Drawings* (Roycroft Shops), *229; Picture Frame with Portrait* (Roycroft Shops), *229; Standing Clock* (Maher), *225; Three-panel Screen* (Stickley), *234; Waste-*

basket (Limbert), *224; "Young Girl in White"* (Mathews), *228*
Wood, Grant, 60, 269
Woodworth, Margery, 269
Woolley, James T., 60
Worcester Art Museum, Worcester, Massachusetts, School of the, 280n12
Worst, Edward F., 258
Wright, Frank Lloyd, 72–74, 89, 95–96, 108–9, 111, 113–14, 115, 118–19, 129–30, 252, 282n28; *"A Home in a Prairie Town,"* 118, *119; Armchair, 13; Table, 232; Tall Slat-back Chair, 73,* 74
Wynne, Madeline Yale, 55, 57, 61, 65–66, 252; *Belt Buckle, 193; Witch Basket, 217*

Y

Yale, Charlotte L., 272

Yale, Julian, 55
Ye Handicrafters society, Brooklyn, New York, 259
Yellin, Samuel, 62, 252; *Gothic Chest, 198*
Young, George F., 265
Young, Grace, 252; *Vase, 140*
Young, Henry Wynd: *Te Deum Window, 96*

Z

Zahn, Otto, 276
Zahn Bindery, Memphis, Tennessee, 276
Zanesville Tile Company, Zanesville, Ohio, 264
Zeile, John, 276
Zimmermann, Marie, 62, 252; *Candelabra, 199*
Zorach, Marguerite Thompson, 105, 252

PHOTOGRAPH CREDITS

Adirondack Museum: 70, 71, 235; Albright-Knox Art Gallery: 13, 232 below; Architectural Drawing Collection, University Art Museum, University of California at Santa Barbara: 124; The Art Institute of Chicago: 58, 89, 102, 107, 108, 109, 120, 200 below, 207 above, 214 below, 216, 219; Avery Architectural Library, Columbia University: 24, 95 left; Morley Baer: 78 above, 90; Beverly Brandt: 48, 49, 50, 51, 52, 53; The Brooklyn Museum, Patricia Layman Bazelon: 2, 14, 15, 140 left, 163 left, 163 above middle, 170, 171 left, 172 right, 173, 174, 175, 177, 187 below right; Cathy Carver: 5; Chicago Historical Society: 26, 36, 43; James Chotas: 88, 95 right; The Cleveland Museum of Art: 197 below, 203 above; Sheldan Comfert Collins: 61, 138 right, 140 right, 142 above, 144 above, 145 below, 146, 148 left, 149 right, 150 below, 152 below, 153 below, 154 below, 155, 157, 161, 162, 166 right, 181 left, 202, 220, 224 below right, 225 right, 226 above, 226 below right, 227 above left, 227 right, 228

below, 229 all, 230 all, 234 above; Cooper-Hewitt Museum, National Museum of Design, Smithsonian Institution: 143, 154 above, 156 above, 163 right, 167; Detroit Institute of Arts: 84; Steven Dwine: 96; Rich Echelmeyer: 67, 226 below left; Robert L. Edwards: 37; P. Richard Eells: 222 below; M. Lee Fatherlee: 228 above right and left; Courtney Frisse: 164, 165; Richard Harris: 227 below left; Robert Hashimoto: 207 below left; Thomas Heinz: 119; Eva Heyd: 2, 9, 10, 11, 141, 160 right, 166 left, 168, 169, 176, 184 above, 185 above, 187 above right, 189, 191, 193 below, 194 above right and left, 195 below, 203 below, 204 above, 205, 207 below right, 208 above, 209, 210 above, 211, 212, 213, 215 above right and left, 217 below right, 218 all, 224 above left; The Huntington Library: 112; Jane Addams Memorial Collection, Special Collections, the University Library, the University of Illinois at Chicago: 41 above left; Jerry Kobylecky: 231 right; Balthazar

Korab: 190; Kurland-Zabar: 186; Efraim Lev-Er: 201, 222 above right; Library of Congress: 33, 39, 40, 42, 44; Harley Little: 233; Los Angeles County Museum of Art: 69; David Lubbers: 224 below left; Dennis Mc-Waters: 232 above; Amanda S. Merullo: 193 above, 214 above, 215 below, 217 above right, 217 left; The Metropolitan Museum of Art, New York: 1, 93, 171 right, 172 left, 180, 182, 183, 225 left; Marilee Boyd Meyer: 197 above; The Minneapolis Institute of Arts: 221; Museum of Fine Arts, Boston: 68, 73, 74, 196, 200 above, 204 below; Brian Oglesbee: 8, 139; Peter Olson: 198; National Museum of American History, the Smithsonian Institution: 156 below; The Neustadt Museum of Tiffany Art, New York: 181 above; New York Public Library: 54, 56 below; Newport News City Planning Department: 117, 118; Norwest Corporation: 184 below, 188 above, 192, 193 right; Scott Nyde: 78 below; Linda Papanicolaou: 94, 97; K. R. Postle: 86; Marvin Rand: 12, 122, 123,

223; Rockefeller Archives Center: 116; Clive Russ: 178, 179; Scholes Library Archives, Alfred University: 80; John W. H. Simpson: 98; Sophia Smith Collection, Smith College: 41 below right; Struve Gallery: 224 above right; Tim Thayer: 151 above, 158, 159; George E. Thomas: 126, 127, 128, 129, 130, 131, 132, 133, 134, 135; Michael Tropea: 187 left, 194 below, 195 above, 210 below; Don Van Essen: 188 below, 208 below; Virginia Museum of Fine Arts: 222 above left; Adam Clark Vroman: 38; Sarah Wells: 6, 138 left, 142 below, 144 below, 145 above right and left, 147, 148 right, 149 left, 150 above, 151 below, 152 above, 153 above, 160 left, 231 left; Winona County Historical Society: 121; Henry Francis du Pont Winterthur Museum, Decorative Arts Photographic Collection: 56 above, 113, 137 right; The Wolfsonian Foundation: 136, 137 left, 199; Yale University Art Gallery: 206, 234 below.